T0283242

AGENT ZO

Also by Clare Mulley

The Woman Who Saved the Children: A Biography of Eglantyne Jebb:
Founder of Save the Children

The Spy Who Loved: The Secrets and Lives of Christine Granville,
Britain's First Female Special Agent of the Second World War

The Women Who Flew for Hitler: The True Story of Hitler's Valkyries

The Library Book: A History of the Gibson Library and its Collection

AGENT ZO

THE UNTOLD STORY OF A FEARLESS
WORLD WAR II RESISTANCE FIGHTER

CLARE MULLEY

PEGASUS BOOKS
NEW YORK LONDON

AGENT ZO

Pegasus Books, Ltd.
148 West 37th Street, 13th Floor
New York, NY 10018

ISBN: 978-1-63936-762-7

10 9 8 7 6 5 4 3 2

Printed in the United States of America
Distributed by Simon & Schuster
www.pegasusbooks.com

To Ian, who sculpts lives from clay,
then spends his evenings reading draft chapters

'Where the devil doesn't dare to go, there he sends a woman.'

Polish proverb

'No one has ever yet doubted the courage and resource of the Polish soldier.'

Major General Sir Colin Gubbins, 1963[1]

'Men keep talking about their own participation. And yet this complete passing over in silence of [women's] work, stalled with sentimental or praising cliché . . . is tantamount to falsifying the history.'

Elżbieta Zawacka, 'Zo', 1961[2]

'I am what is called a feminist . . . You have to fight for women's rights.'

Elżbieta Zawacka, 'Zo', 1989[3]

CONTENTS

PART FOUR

To assist the reader, whenever an unfamiliar Polish or German word is first mentioned, it will be in italics, with a translation or explanation given; thereafter it will be in roman. Loanwords and more commonly anglicised words will appear in roman from the first instance. Place names are given as they were at the time and within their contemporary borders, but with a footnote giving their modern equivalent and location when first mentioned. Individuals are introduced with their full name, then consistently referred to by either one of their given names or their nom-de-guerre, largely as Zo would have known them at the time.

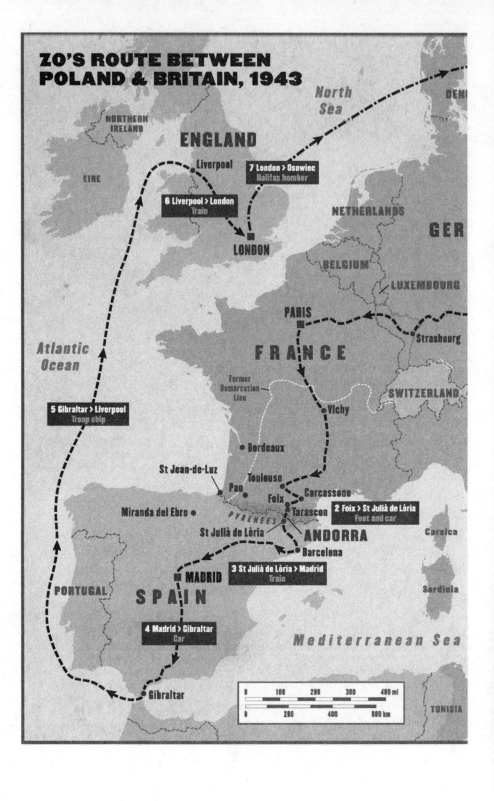

ZO'S ROUTE BETWEEN POLAND & BRITAIN, 1943

North Sea

NORTHERN IRELAND

ENGLAND

EIRE

Liverpool

7 London > Osowiec
Halifax bomber

6 Liverpool > London
Train

LONDON

NETHERLANDS

GER

BELGIUM

LUXEMBOURG

Atlantic Ocean

PARIS

FRANCE

Strasbourg

SWITZERLAND

5 Gibraltar > Liverpool
Troop ship

Former Demarcation Line

Vichy

Bordeaux

St Jean-de-Luz

Toulouse

Pau

Foix

Carcassone

Miranda del Ebro

PYRENEES

Tarascon

2 Foix > St Julià de Lòria
Foot and car

Corsica

St Julià de Lòria

ANDORRA

Barcelona

3 St Julià de Lòria > Madrid
Train

MADRID

Sardinia

PORTUGAL

S P A I N

4 Madrid > Gibraltar
Car

Mediterranean Sea

Gibraltar

| 0 | 100 | 200 | 300 | 400 mi |

| 0 | 200 | 400 | 600 km |

TUNISIA

DEN

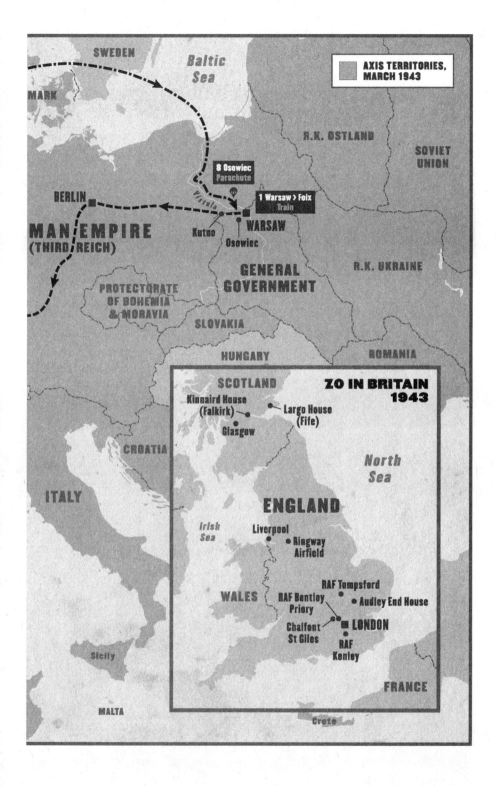

PREFACE

Sitting on the edge of the circular hole cut in the floor of the mighty four-engine British Halifax bomber, her legs dangling down as though she were a child perched on an adult's chair, Elżbieta Zawacka – nom-de-guerre 'Zo' – considered her likely fate.

A few weeks earlier she had scraped through parachute training at an airfield outside Manchester; her aching ankles were still tightly bandaged after a series of hard landings. Night drops were the hardest to master as distances were deceptive in the dark, and telegraph wires or even trees were often impossible to see until too late. Now, Zo risked a vertiginous glance down through the open hatch where her legs were taking the full force of the wind that also whipped around the hold space. Absolute darkness. It was almost two in the morning and, although there was a full moon, scudding clouds obscured the light. But if she couldn't see the depth below, Zo could feel it: hundreds of feet of emptiness. Gripping the reassuringly solid lip of the hatch, she felt the chill from the cold metal run up her arms.

Even if she survived the drop, Zo knew that the Gestapo were hunting for her in the towns and cities of occupied Poland below. Her younger sister, clever, sweet-natured Klara, had been arrested over a year earlier, and had not been seen since. Their brother Egon and cousin Leonard had both been transported to Auschwitz. Zo had no idea where her parents were but knew that, if the Gestapo had traced them, they would probably have faced brutal interrogation before imprisonment or execution. Yet having started the war digging anti-tank ditches and making petrol bombs to throw at enemy forces in the face of the Soviet advance, she was not about to give up on her hard-won mission because of Nazi German terror.

Somewhere beneath her, Zo knew, a large and defiant resistance movement was waiting for her return. Her dearest friend, courageous Marianna Zawodzińska, was probably also awake, coughing into the night as she worked out ciphers in her chilly Warsaw attic room. Zofia Franio, a qualified doctor, sometimes tended to Marianna, when not busy with the all-female demolition units that were making such an impact across the country. Waiting most avidly, however, was Emilia Malessa, head of the foreign communications team with the Polish resistance 'Home Army'. As effortlessly elegant as she was ruthlessly efficient, Emilia had at first intimidated Zo, but years of shared clandestine endeavour had brought them close. Now Zo was bringing back new orders from the Polish prime minister and commander-in-chief of the armed forces, exiled in London, that would have a profound impact on all their lives.

⚓

Polish women were among the first to take up arms during the Second World War. While women in Britain volunteered on the home front, as land girls, office clerks, drivers and factory workers, releasing men for military service overseas, in Poland the 'home front' was, immediately, the frontline. Thousands of women rushed to the defence of their country, their homes and families, in response to the twin invasions from Nazi Germany and the Soviet Union in September 1939. Many, like Zo, had years of military training. Others were defiant teenagers, young mothers, doctors, teachers and farm workers, even grandmothers who felt unable to witness the brutality of the latest occupation of their homeland without taking action.

Around 40,000 women would eventually be sworn in as members of the Polish Home Army, making it the largest resistance force in occupied Europe. Initially, they served in liaison, as messengers and couriers, as paramedics and in logistics; the day-to-day functioning of the early underground resistance would have been impossible without them. Soon it was hard to find any unit that did not include women. Whether gathering intelligence; publishing and circulating clandestine newsletters; smuggling weapons, information and money across borders; laying landmines or undertaking assassinations, women eventually made up one tenth of the Home Army.

The women's motivations, their training, false papers and weapons were largely the same as those of their male counterparts, and the risk they faced was just as fundamental. But female and male experience never entirely overlapped. Mainly volunteers, rather than conscripts, the women had no military status or rank, could not officially join armed units, and found themselves 'perceived as simple, ordinary,

modest, properly unnoticed', Zo noted.[4] Where the chauvinistic occupying forces were concerned, this myopia was an advantage that the
women were quick to exploit. The lack of official recognition from
their own authorities, however, held the women back. Zo, a born soldier, would have none of that. While serving your country, 'you have
to fight,' she argued passionately, 'for women's rights.'[5]

⚓

Zo's Halifax banked sharply as it dropped altitude and air speed.
Hours earlier, the Special Duties Squadron pilot had taken off from
Bedfordshire and brought them over the North Sea, heading out to
avoid German airspace. Over Denmark, they had been briefly caught
in anti-aircraft artillery fire. With the extra fuel tanks for the return
journey stored fore and aft, the Halifax was effectively a flying gasoline bomb. Zo had heard the repeated crack of the shelling over the
roar of the engines and felt some of the fire hit the steel of the aircraft's
wings, but there had been no significant damage. Turning to evade
more flak, they had headed on to Sweden and then, over the Baltic,
turned again to catch sight of the River Vistula, a ribbon of reflected
light leading them inland to the drop zone, a forest glade some twenty
miles from Warsaw.

'Ladies first,' Zo's fellow jumpers had said, courteous but curious
about their comrade-in-arms.* Impatient to be back, and determined
not to betray her nerves, Zo had not demurred. She had not even
smiled at the men, although she felt a deep bond with them. Naturally
serious, she simply nodded. Yet after over four hours spent huddled in
the freezing fuselage, stiff and weighed down by her drop-suit overalls, heavy kit and the parachute strapped to her back, when it was
time to go she had needed a hand to haul her up from her sitting
position. Using the ropes and cables fixed inside the body of the aircraft, she had slowly edged forwards, carefully weighing each step as
she clambered around the packages destined for the resistance below.
The larger containers, metal barrels packed with guns, ammunition,
explosives, medicine and radio sets, were waiting to follow from the
bomb bay.

* Most accounts say Zo dropped first, but some place her as the second of the three
to jump.

The two pistols Zo was so pleased with, a knife, flask, compass and a small tin with two cyanide pills were strapped into her drop-suit pockets, along with a spade with which to bury her suit and chute on landing. The suit belt was filled with dollars and reichsmarks. Underneath, she wore a heavy overcoat – not new, but thick and warm. It was already late September and the Polish nights were cold. Beneath this she had buttoned a woollen cardigan over a simple, navy-blue silk dress. There were cheap stockings stuffed into her coat pocket; she did not want to snag them on her bandages. Such dressings were not unusual, but this was the only time that a member of the Polish special force paratroopers, the *Cichociemni* or 'Silent Unseen', would parachute into occupied Europe wearing a dress, because Zo was the only female member of this elite force.* In Polish, this made her the only *Cichociemna*.

Through the hatch, Zo could suddenly see the light of torches laid out in an arrow on the ground below to mark the drop zone and show wind direction. She shivered. Moments later she was shaking with the cold and her own fear, and adrenaline. Once again she was struck by the apparent madness of plunging from relative safety into the abyss. Then she breathed in something of the Polish fields below; the smell of fallen leaves, earthy and damp, of cut potatoes and the dry stalks of grain already harvested. She smiled. The red light beside the hatch switched to green, the dispatcher shouted, 'Go!' and, automatically straightening her legs, Zo plunged into the night.

For a breathless second she fell like the condemned; abruptly, straight down and with no thought of landing. The sudden acceleration was shocking. Her whole body tensed, a defensive action that seemed to make her smaller, meaner – like a nut, tight and hard, falling from a tree. Like a bomb, released from a British bomb bay, pulled by her own weight, down towards Poland, in a condensed roar of sound, the wind now coming not from ahead, but from beneath her.

Seconds later, a violent jolt shot Zo's thoughts back to the present. Her static line, the umbilical cord attaching the cover of her parachute pack to the aircraft hold, had reached full length and yanked out her chute. Relief flooded through her as she heard the silk unfolding and her mad rush earthwards suddenly halted, as though she had been

---

* The literal translation of Cichociemni is quiet and shadowy or dark, but Silent Unseen is the usual term.

caught on a celestial peg. The Halifax's engines were already just a distant hum, and she could feel herself swaying gently in her harness. She savoured the moment. How miraculous to be at once still slowly falling through the Polish night, and yet also suspended. Only once would she later confess, to a fellow resistance soldier before an enemy engagement, that despite her previous three years of active service behind enemy lines, 'probably for the first time in her life, she had been afraid' when she had to drop from the Halifax.[6] Usually, she preferred to recall that, 'Nothing fell, you lay in the air', and, 'It is wonderful, to fly.'[7]

Knowing that she probably only had seconds before impact, Zo then set to work manipulating the cords of her chute so that she would face forwards, and trying to turn, as she had been taught, so that her side would hit the ground first and she would not break her legs on landing. Then, with shocking speed, the ground seemed to rise up to meet her.

Part One

1

Born to Fight
(March 1909–September 1939)

'A woman, whose name has not been determined, was literally slashed in half' ran the story in the *Warsaw National Journal*. 'In a dining car, a male passenger was run clean through by metal fittings . . .'[1]

It was just after midday when the express steam train from Katowice raced towards Pruszków on its way to Warsaw, at over fifty miles an hour. Eyewitnesses to the disaster spoke of the train's locomotive suddenly leaping off the rails at full speed, then hurtling over the sleepers for a further hundred yards, its carriages flying behind. Panic erupted on board, as train conductors shouted to the passengers to hold fast to the rings on the compartment walls. A moment later, the airborne locomotive caught the high tension, electric-traction powerlines beside the tracks, turned about and crashed down again, only to be smashed into by its own tender, still half full of water for the route ahead. Steam and smoke gushed from the engine's boiler as the locomotive landed on its side, carriages piling up behind. Screams could be heard through the appalling din of collision, as 'the violently stopped cars smashed into each other, and the weaker ones succumbed to the overwhelming force and were turned into splinters'.[2]

The bodies of the train diver and his assistant were later found under the twisted remains of the locomotive. Six people had lost their lives: four men, a child and a woman in quasi-military clothes, who was about forty years old, travelling alone with no luggage or papers to identify her. A further three passengers would later die from their injuries. Most had been in the wooden, second and third-class carriages, destroyed when hit by the sturdier, steel-framed international sleeping-car.

When the last passengers trapped in the sleeper had been finally cut free with acetylene torches, the Warsaw papers patriotically claimed that 'the strong steel construction of the Polish cars limited the dimensions of the disaster'.[3] That and the speedy response of the paramedics were perhaps the only chinks of light in the catastrophe. Emotions were running high not only because of the fatalities but also as, in the summer of 1939, Poland was on the brink of war. It was soon reported that the train disaster was the result of a bomb or other act of sabotage by German or Soviet agents. Further down the press pages, a national search was launched for the unidentified female passenger who had suffered such catastrophic injuries.

ℬ

Elżbieta Zawacka was in Silesia, almost two hundred miles from Pruszków, on the day of the crash. Blonde and blue-eyed, young-looking for her age and rather short, she had the kind of open, honest face that people invariably describe as earnest in a man, and innocent in a woman. Yet as a female mathematics graduate, unmarried at thirty and choosing to live alone, she was already raising eyebrows.

Elżbieta was a senior instructor with the Polish 'Women's Military Training' organisation, the PWK as it was known from its Polish acronym.* Instead of learning to type, sew or cook, or reading fashion magazines and heading out to dance and flirt in Warsaw's famous *boîtes*, or nightclubs, Elżbieta preferred to spend her spare hours putting cadets through their paces in the muddy Polish countryside. She had spent the morning of the rail disaster at a training camp, which was pitched in a beautiful bend of a tributary of the River Oder that flows from the mountains of the Silesian Beskids into what was then Czechoslovakia. The female cadets had already raised the tents and built the wooden cabins that would serve as the mess and medical huts. Elżbieta was there to inspect the work and oversee military exercises and sporting events. It being mild, after the flag-raising that evening, a Polish white eagle was to be created from a mountain of pinecones, followed by a patriotic lecture, songs and laughter around a campfire.

Elżbieta was never happier than when at one of these camps, sharing her twin enthusiasms for her nation and for women's service. She had joined the PWK ten years earlier, as a university student. Their camps provided opportunities for wild swimming, hiking and competitive sports, often frowned upon for women, as well as training in horseriding, driving and, most wonderful of all to her mind, firearms.

* *Przysposobienie Wojskowe Kobiet* (PWK).

The organisation also instilled a sense of greater purpose in its cadets: the powerful knowledge that they could make a significant contribution to the national defence in times of need. It was here that Elżbieta found her tribe – young women who shared not only her love of the outdoors, but also her sense of patriotic duty. Joining the PWK, she laughed, was 'the most important event of my life'.[4]

⚓

Elżbieta had grown up as the seventh of eight children, learning to fight for attention from an early age. Her father, Władysław Zawacki, knew how that felt. A proud man, he could trace his family back to the seventeenth century. When his mother died young, however, he had been enrolled in the Prussian Army after just two years of schooling. For the rest of his life, he would spend a part of every evening trying to better himself with a copy of *Meyer's Great Encyclopedia*, bought with his savings as a young non-commissioned officer. Later, he would instil the importance of education in his own children. Elżbieta's mother had lost both her parents when young. Perhaps that and their work ethic was what drew the couple together, even though they 'differed from each other like night and day', as Elżbieta put it. Vivacious Marianna had grown up working on her father's farm. Like Władysław, she had had little formal education, but she was smart, hard-working and 'eternally active and energetic'.[5]

After their wedding, Władysław exchanged his greatcoat and boots for a less romantic uniform as a clerk in the Gdańsk shipyards. He still proudly waxed his handsome moustache, but as Marianna washed his shirts and starched his collars, she couldn't help thinking how tedious their life was. The air tasted different in the city, she tried to explain, and 'the earth did not smell like bread'.[6] Selling up, they moved, with two children in tow, to a suburb of the ancient city of Toruń, which straddles the River Vistula one hundred miles south. Here, the increasingly 'pedantic and solid' Władysław found congenial work as a court clerk, while Marianna could enjoy walking in the countryside.[7] It was here, too, that six more children arrived. Elżbieta was born on a crisp March morning in 1909. She had powerful lungs and a sturdy constitution, and – officially – she was German.

Toruń had been established by the Teutonic Knights in the 1200s and had flourished as a Hanseatic League town. A crenellated brick barbican protected the city, but for centuries Polish- and German-speakers had lived side by side within its walls. Toruń had both Catholic and Protestant churches, and the architecture, merchant guilds and even the local folktales, such as that of a plague of fat frogs being piped away from the town, all borrowed from Germanic tradition. It was not always a peaceful coexistence, but the city largely prospered. Then, in the late eighteenth century, Poland was partitioned between its three powerful neighbours, the Austrian, German-Prussian, and Russian empires. Prussian troops took Toruń in 1793, only to be defeated by successive French and Russian forces. As each invader reinforced the forts and added to the city's defences with moats and palisades, the local economy became dependent on the military purse, eventually creating a garrison town.

By the time Elżbieta arrived in the crowded Zawacki house on picturesque Elm Street, Toruń was once again in Prussian-annexed territory. Despite their Polish roots, people in the community were forbidden to speak their own language. Since Władysław worked in a German law court, inspectors would regularly visit the family to check on everything – from the language of their prayer book to the chatter of the children. Evidence of Polish culture, regarded as seditious, would have cost him his job, and possibly his liberty.

Like thousands of women across former Polish territory, however, Marianna secretly continued to observe national traditions. She wore colourful dresses echoing folk designs; she sang her children to sleep with Polish lullabies; and when they woke, she taught them to pray the Catholic way. All the Zawacki children grew up speaking German. They were sent to German schools and surrounded by German culture, but they all knew that they were Polish. Learning to lead a double life, with secret layers of identity, concealment came to them naturally.

Marianna was a strong woman, with deeply held values, who raised her children with tough love while her husband worked long hours. She was also a romantic. In her rare moments of leisure, she loved to read the chivalrous tales of knights and maidens that inspired her choice of children's names. Her eldest, born in Gdańsk, was called Maria after her mother and the Virgin: a universally acceptable name. A dutiful child, Maria would help raise her younger siblings. Then came Janek, the first-born son and favourite, or so his siblings thought. Janek was such a traditionally Polish name, however, that when the family moved to Toruń, he had to be called by the more German 'Hans'.

Two years later, Alfons arrived, known as Ali by all who loved him. Eryk, who followed, was the only child to die in infancy. Over the next couple years first Egon was born, and given the Germanic middle name Konstanty, and then the romantically monikered Adelajda Łucja. Named after an impressive German empress, Adelajda was promptly and permanently known simply as 'Dela'. Little Elżbieta, called by the German diminutive of 'Liza' – her first alias – seemed to be the fat little full stop at the end of the family line. It was a position in which she thrived, the apple of her indulgent but often absent father's eye.

Elżbieta's earliest memories were of a large garden with a stream and 'a scent of grass and mystery'.[8] 'We were dirty,' she admitted proudly, and by evening, 'barely standing, because we had so many important things to do all day'.[9] Egon, fair as wheat and just three years her senior, was the first person she idolised, although he didn't take much notice. Their father considered him a rogue, but Elżbieta would willingly collect worms, make slingshots, or climb the trees searching for birds' nests to impress him. When their impatient mother eventually herded her brood inside for supper, it was always Elżbieta who found it the hardest to leave the garden, and then she only came reluctantly, traipsing behind Egon. On moonlit nights, she could often be found outside again, fast asleep.

It was a dark day for Elżbieta when Egon followed his older siblings to school. Still high-spirited, he would break his arm three times during gymnastics, until it was permanently twisted. Elżbieta longed to follow him. Her mother turned a blind eye when she saw her bending over Egon's schoolbooks instead of helping with the chores. She and Władysław were unusual in being as ambitious for their daughters as they were for their sons, but schooling was expensive, and the times increasingly uncertain.

By 1913, Toruń had a gasworks and electric trams, but also a military airfield and a garrison with 30,000 soldiers marching over its cobbled streets. When Janek, Ali and Egon were not in school, they liked to wear military-style outfits, complete with caps and braid, albeit with short trousers. It irritated Elżbieta that she was given a white pinafore. When war came the following summer, Poles were conscripted into the armies of each of the three powers that had partitioned their homeland – soon finding themselves fighting each other. Yet the prospect of these mighty empires being weakened also renewed hopes for Polish independence.

The Zawacki family was luckier than many during what was then known as the Great War. Although he was mobilised, Władysław's poor health meant he remained in Toruń, and his sons were too young to serve. In 1915, Marianna, now forty-one, gave birth to their last child, a daughter named Klara. Dela, who was 'a very beautiful girl', cooed over the new baby, but six-year-old Elżbieta could not see the appeal.[10] She had finally started at a German school for girls and her only interest lay in proving herself to her brothers. But with another mouth to feed, it was increasingly difficult to keep the family afloat.

Selling their house with the garden, the family moved into rented rooms. Marianna took in sewing and slowly sold off their possessions. 'She was the engine of the house,' Elżbieta recalled, keeping her children fed and disciplined.[11] In the evenings, she also told them tales of historic Polish uprisings, the last, in 1863, still vivid in the memories of their older neighbours. They listened even more avidly to stories of their grandfather evading German conscription in the 1870s, and their grandmother defiantly pouring kerosene on her cabbage patch to deny food to marauding soldiers.

All the family were thrilled when, in an attempt to attract more troops for the fight against Russia, in November 1916, Austria and Germany declared they would recognise Polish independence. As Minister for War for the prospective Polish nation, Józef Piłsudski led his Polish Legions alongside Austria-Hungary. Once certain that Germany and Austria would be defeated, however, he refused to make his men swear loyalty to these powers. The Legions were disbanded and Piłsudski imprisoned in Magdeburg, making him a focal point for resurgent Polish nationalism.

Elżbieta was secretly, ardently, a Polish patriot, but thoughts of food consumed her even more than dreams of freedom. By the end of 1917, the children were permanently hungry. Sometimes, if Elżbieta were lucky, the local baker's wife would give her a small bread roll. Although it was invariably 'completely black', she would wolf it down while still in the street.[12] That winter, Janek was sent home from school, coughing and gasping for breath. Marianna sold her last earrings to buy butter and milk, but was not able to save her eldest son. He died in January 1918, not yet eighteen. Muted by grief, Marianna stopped wearing her colourful skirts.

Within a few months, the German authorities brought forward the school leaving exams to secure another cohort of young soldiers. Ali, a year younger than Janek, was an excellent student, but angry and rebellious. Shouting 'Long live Spartacus!' in support of the German Marxist revolutionary movement, he hoped to be expelled or arrested. Instead, he was irritated to find himself ignored and then conscripted. Elżbieta, still only nine, watched as her mother stood on the table to reach the gas lamp outlet and suffocate the lice in Ali's clothes before he left. Posted deep inside Germany, rather than to the front, Ali joined the military insurrection later known as the Greater Poland Uprising – becoming the second hero of Elżbieta's young life.

Released from detention after the armistice, on 14 November 1918 Piłsudski became Chief of State of all Polish territories. Under the terms of the Treaty of Versailles, signed the following June, Toruń was among the lands incorporated into this reborn Polish Republic. German soldiers, some with flat caps, others still in steel helmets with a spike on top, marched towards the railway station as the astounded citizens watched on. Later, the Poles processed through the same streets, then crowded into the churches to sing hymns of thanksgiving. Polish borders were still disputed. The war with Soviet Russia would continue until 1920 and Toruń's walls were plastered with posters calling for men to volunteer. But, after 123 years of annexation, Poland was back on the map of Europe.

⚓

Elżbieta did not know whether her father's cheeks were ruddier from the cold, or from his evident emotion. It was a brisk, misty morning in January 1920, and her small hand was held tightly in his as he pulled her through the crowds. Like everyone else, they were heading to the ceremonial gate erected on the edge of Toruń, which had been decorated with symbols of the local guilds. The atmosphere was festive but the conversation hushed as, for the first time, Elżbieta heard the stirring melody of the Polish national anthem, 'Dąbrowski's Mazurka', being played openly on the street. Then General Haller, the Polish commander of the Pomeranian front, led his distinctive, blue-uniformed troops through the arch and into the city. What impressed Elżbieta most was not the horses, nor the military display, but the sight of the grown men around her in their stiff shirt fronts – 'those Germanised officials' as she remembered her father's friends, with tears coursing down their cheeks.[13] Even her father could not contain himself. Elżbieta watched and listened, just as she had listened to her mother's patriotic stories, and quietly absorbed it all.

Polish independence would bring many changes but was not a panacea. Not long after Haller's parade, Elżbieta's eldest sister, Maria, contracted pneumonia. Dutiful Maria had helped support her family through the war but, long undernourished, she was not strong enough to survive the bitter winter months that followed. Elżbieta carried a pot of soup to the hospital, but Maria died a few days later. She was buried next to her brother. Somehow, she had never seemed to belong to the exciting post-war future and, of all the siblings, Elżbieta found that it was her face that 'blurred the fastest'.[14]

Elżbieta was keen to harness her ambitions to those of her reborn nation, but being Polish was not as easy as expected. When Poles moved in to replace the departing Germans, she was shocked to find herself the subject of their contempt: jeered at for being German herself because she could not speak her native tongue. Never shy of confrontation, she gave as good as she got, but she also learnt that there were other ways to fight for what was hers. Language classes were eventually rewarded with a place at a Polish school. Clever and diligent, she shone in all her lessons, especially in mathematics – her brothers' favourite class.

Back home after his brief mobilisation, Ali had wanted to study mathematics in Gdańsk but his parents could not afford the fees. Instead, he entered cadet school, eventually joining an infantry regiment in Lwów. Tall and broad-shouldered, he made a striking officer, his fine figure accentuated by his uniform. 'Women clung to him,' Elżbieta couldn't help noticing.[15] Within a few years, Ali had married a general's daughter, Zofia Popławska, who Elżbieta both adored and resented for capturing her brother's heart. Dressed in fashionably floaty pale cotton, cream stockings and pumps, and with a matching cloche hat framing her short, dark curls, Zofia looked like an elegant butterfly beside her great branch of a man, who stood a good ten inches taller than her. She loved to slip her arm in his when they walked out, if anything making Ali stand taller. Without meaning to diminish her, he in turn affectionately abbreviated Zofia's name to its first syllable: 'Zo'.

By the time Egon finished school, his parents had saved enough to send him to the new university in Poznań. Dela was just as bright, often beating her brothers at chess, but chose to find work locally, handing her wages to her parents. With just two years between them, she and Elżbieta helped their mother to home-school little Klara. No one worried about Klara. Elżbieta felt that her younger sister had 'a special kind of cleverness', *schlagfertig* in German, a kind of quick-wittedness that seemed to protect her from the world.[16] Two years after Dela left school, Elżbieta was working towards her own leaver's exams, determined to exceed her brothers' achievements. Marianna sold their pillows to a feather shop to raise the required fee, and Elżbieta passed with flying colours.

If the first passion of Elżbieta's life, all the more fervent because forbidden, was for Poland, the second was for mathematics. Although women accounted for a quarter of Polish university students between the wars, one of the highest proportions in Europe, studying further mathematics was still an unusual female choice. Poland's annexations had meant that, for generations, female activism had focused on preserving Polish culture, language and history, so when women's higher education was promoted in 1918, it was largely in the humanities. Keen to support her fledgling nation, Elżbieta felt she could add more through mathematics. Like Egon before her, she enrolled in Poznań University, earning her way through private tutoring.

Elżbieta's student ID from 1927 shows a clear-eyed, sincere young woman with a determined gaze. Dressed in a simple plaid shirt, she has no form of decoration, no pretensions in her fresh face or neatly parted hair, and no smile; but nor is there any false modesty. A few weeks later, her hair had been cut into a bob, as practical as it was fashionable. Much as she admired Ali's wife, Zofia, Elżbieta had neither the money nor the desire for tailored pleats or fur collars. Her own clothes were largely simple, her room likewise ascetic; a metal-framed bed with thin mattress, a wooden chair and desk, and her coat on a hook on the wall. Inside her head, however, everything was new and rich and exciting.

Mathematics occupied Elżbieta for the best part of the next four years, but she also debated literature, law, philosophy and politics, and joined class outings to the local Jewish cemetery and other historic sites.* Women had been enfranchised when Poland regained independence, and progressive laws, such as the decriminalisation of homosexuality, were still proudly being passed. By her second year, however,

---

* Led by Elżbieta's tutor Professor Zdzisław Krygowski.

conversations were turning to the threat of war. One of her tutors, the brilliant mathematician Marian Rejewski, was already secretly working in cryptology for the Polish Cipher Bureau. Short-sighted, with perfectly round glasses, the mole-like Rejewski did not appear impressive, but within a few years he and his team were pioneering the decryption of German Enigma ciphers.[*]

Elżbieta's chosen thesis, on 'Differential Equations of the Periods of Elliptic Integrals', did not appear to have a military application. Wondering how to best support her nation, she attended a session with the university's new Women's Military Training association. At first sceptical, by the end of the hour she was an enthusiastic convert, declaring that the PWK concept of trained and armed women engaging in military defence had set her 'on fire'.[17]

Exceptional women had long played an active role in Poland's armed struggles. In 1812, Joanna Żubr had become the first woman awarded the Virtuti Militari, the nation's highest award for valour, and Emilia Plater, who had dressed as a man to raise a small unit for the 1831 uprising, received the rank of captain. These women were marginal historical figures in Elżbieta's day, inspiring others through various soft-focus portraits as wasp-waisted romantic heroines as much as soldiers in the field. Such women were not satisfied to dwell on the turned page, however, but continued to stride through more recent military engagements. Among those who now inspired Elżbieta was Maria Wittek, who had secured a place at the NCO school of a clandestine military formation in 1917. Joining the ranks of the Women's Volunteer Legion, an emergency auxiliary unit of the Polish Army, she had taken part in the defence of Lwów in 1920. The Silver Cross of the Virtuti Militari that she received would be the first of many honours, but she was demobilised when the legion was disbanded in 1922.

Reluctant to let her experience go to waste, in 1928 Wittek became the founding commander of a new women's military training organisation: the PWK.[†] Officially, their role was administrative, kitchen-based

* Rejewski led a team of mathematicians, including Jerzy Różycki and Henryk Zygalski (whose seminars Elżbieta also attended). Their pioneering Enigma work was later developed with French and British mathematicians, including Alan Turing.
† Another PWK founder, Wanda Gertz, had cut off her hair and wore male uniform to enlist in 1915. Later serving with the Women's Volunteer Legion, she also received the Virtuti Militari.

or required sewing machines, but Wittek was determined there should also be army training, including in the use of firearms. Her aim was to prepare women so that in future their military service might be strategic rather than spontaneous, but it proved a challenge to enlist sufficient volunteers. Notions of acceptable womanhood were changing but war was still largely considered to be a man's business. Female military training was frowned upon. 'Women's society as a whole was passive', Elżbieta wrote in frustration, signing up to change things.[18]

Elżbieta first pitched a heavy canvas PWK tent in the hot summer of 1931. She had paid a hefty thirty zlotys to join the month-long camp. It was a considerable sum, but she was investing both in the PWK mission and also, as she put it, in 'searching for my place, my identity'.[19] When she found herself among several thousand cadets at beautiful Garczyn, forty miles from the Baltic coast, Elżbieta finally stopped trying to emulate her elder brothers. Here, she learnt that she could love mathematics and the military for their own sake, and in her own right, as a woman and a soldier. The first PWK cadets to arrive had prepared a lakeside clearing. Elżbieta was delighted to find it was 'a total wilderness': all huge skies, dark woods, deep lakes and hard work.[20] Once the tents and a few wooden huts were up, and a fir tree, felled and stripped, had been erected as the flagpole, the women ran down to the lake to bathe. Elżbieta experienced an almost religious exultation at such moments, laughing among female friends after a day of shared endeavour.

Although the PWK valued initiative, there was a clear military command structure, strict discipline and considerable ritual. Mornings started with a reveille so punctual that Elżbieta could set her watch by it, yet she was often late to parade. She tore her shirt and lost her blue beret and khaki garrison cap. 'Zawacka does not take proper care of her uniform!' she heard herself reprimanded archly by Zofia Grzegorzewska, who was a few years older and several ranks her senior.[21] When she laughed during parade, the same Russian-accented voice snapped, 'Zawacka does not know how to stand to attention!'[22] Elżbieta meant no disrespect, but she was naturally rebellious. Like most of the women, she was used to fighting for attention but had no experience of military authority.

One Sunday afternoon, Elżbieta requested permission to get away 'from the hubbub' of the camp with a couple of friends.[23] Not knowing that Zofia had had to fight for permission on their behalf, the girls enjoyed some carefree hours swimming in the lake, before sitting in their towels, their backs against the larch trees, discussing books and birdsong. The light was fading and the mosquitoes out in force by the time they headed back. Inevitably they got lost and, while pushing their canoe through thick reeds, Elżbieta slid in the silt, got a soaking and lost a shoe. It was with much suppressed hilarity that they finally rushed towards the glade, only to find, 'leaning forwards, through the forest', the camp commander, Maria Wittek herself, searching for them in the gloaming.[24] When Elżbieta nervously reported this incident, she was treated to Zofia's 'booming laughter' and the frostiness between them melted.[25]

Zofia was an unpaid but enthusiastic PWK instructor. With her short dark bob, even shorter temper and her long tickings-off, Elżbieta had cast her 'as a Bolshevik'.[26] Now, getting to know her, she laughingly conceded that although Zofia had clearly once lived in Russian-annexed territory, the PWK had 'tempered her a bit'.[27] Usually found with a sketchbook in hand, Zofia was well loved for her jokey cartoons of the cadets towing mattresses behind bicycles, practising archery with predictable results, and huddling under blankets around a smoking campfire. Elżbieta thought her very talented. Together, they made an illustrated songbook that Maria Wittek presented to Aleksandra Piłsudska, the wife of the Polish leader.

Zofia also helped to run courses in medicine and map-reading, archery and anti-aircraft defence. Elżbieta much preferred these to the cookery classes or telegraphy training, although she grudgingly accepted that this was work which 'women do much better than men'.[28] Photographs show her grinning among a row of cadets with rifles, and learning to shoot while lying on her belly in a ditch. Soon she would be confidently riding a horse, driving a truck that could serve as an ambulance, and practising emergency medicine for battle wounds and gas and chemical attacks.

As the days grew into weeks, instead of irritating her, the discipline, drills and flag-raising began to reinforce Elżbieta's sense of belonging to a national movement of real value. What had started as an adventure was being burnished into serious service. At the end of her first summer, she signed up as an instructor. 'We knew that war was coming,' she said, and, 'we had to prepare women as a part of the regular army.'[29]

Once she had graduated from university, Elżbieta started teaching at a boarding school where she also established a PWK troop. As there were still few organised sports for girls, her weekend field games, such as 'capturing' the local railway station, took her students by storm.[30] Soon she was running several more PWK units, and signing up hundreds of girls for the summer and winter camps deep in the Polish countryside. Most were held at Garczyn, in the Polish lake district or in Spała where wild stags still roamed the forests. Others were in the wilderness of Koszewniki, now in Belarus, and at Istebna on the tree-lined banks of the River Olza in Silesia, where in winter the PWK cadets flew down the slopes on home-made skis. Wherever she went, Elżbieta knew she would find a dozen or more instructors and several hundred cadets. It quickly became a community with deep bonds. 'We loved each other,' Elżbieta felt, 'because we believed in the same idea.'[31]

When they were not at the same camp, Zofia would write to Elżbieta every day, affectionately calling her 'Ela', while Elżbieta wrote to her as 'Zo' in return. When they met again, Zofia would give her albums full of drawings. One teasingly showed a cadet paddling a canoe between the bulrushes on a moonlit lake. The two women were now so close that they felt they 'could not live without each other'.[32] It was 'not any lesbian love', Elżbieta later chose to assert, but 'a great spiritual friendship'.[33]

In the summer of 1934, a third PWK instructor began to share the women's intimacy. Dark-eyed Marianna Zawodzińska was beautiful, but her 'serious and rather restrained manner' kept her out of the limelight at PWK camps full of louder women.[34] Like Elżbieta, she was in her mid-twenties, worked as a teacher, and she had the same strong sense of duty. There the similarities ended. Elżbieta inspired her cadets through force of character. She was a well-armoured galleon in full sail, carrying everyone along with her. Marianna was more sensitive. She connected with her cadets not through camp songs or comic sketches, but by making herself available for the serious study of literature. The loyalty she inspired among her girls bordered on ardour. 'We could feel her warmth and radiance,' one teenager gushed. She was 'full of the personal charm that it is difficult to put into words, as with a landscape or a melody'.[35]

Elżbieta and Zofia were both drawn to Marianna. Elżbieta shared her love of poetry and novels – from *Gone with the Wind* to the Polish classic *Pan Tadeusz*. 'It sounds so funny, pretentious,' Elżbieta confessed, but the long discussions generated by the three women's reading, often late into the night, inspired them to create a secret 'spiritual co-operative'.[36] Together, the young idealists swore a solemn pledge that each held as sacred: 'a commitment that our whole lives were to serve Poland'.[37]

As well as her teaching and PWK commitments, Elżbieta now started studying for a masters. Exhausted by her punishing schedule, she began to reproach herself for, as she put it, not being able to 'keep three cows by the tail'.[38] In the summer of 1935, she cycled straight from a PWK camp to her finals. Having almost fallen asleep on her bike, that moonlit night she climbed out of bed to walk into the camp clearing. But Elżbieta was no longer at the camp. She was on the third floor of her student block in Poznań. She woke to the terrifying sight of the street far below as friends pulled her back from the open window. Falling now began to hold a unique terror for her, but she obtained her MA in mathematics.

The Zawacka siblings were now widely dispersed. Ali and his wife, the first 'Zofia' whom Elżbieta had loved, were living near Lwów. Dela was with their parents in Toruń, and Egon was travelling. Even the youngest, clever Klara, had now packed her books and best pleated skirts to study law in Poznań. Klara had hoped to find work in Toruń but became a legal advisor in the eastern territories that bordered Soviet Russia. There she fell deeply in love but, even after her engagement, Elżbieta could somehow never find the time to meet her sister's fiancé. The family were only brought together again by bad news.

In the freezing January of 1936, Ali was summoned for officer training in Warsaw. A passionate skier, he raced down the slopes to the station and took his seat on the draughty train in clothes still wet with sweat. His damp linen shirt chilled on his skin. By the time he reached the capital, he was shaking uncontrollably. When he was diagnosed with severe pneumonia, the garrison medics explained that childhood malnutrition had severely weakened his lungs. It was an indication of the seriousness of his condition that a cable was dispatched to his wife, Zofia, that same evening. By the time Zofia arrived at his bedside, Ali was in a coma, his organs failing. Distraught, she wordlessly gathered up her young husband's effects and walked from the ward. Moments later a gunshot resonated from the bathroom. Zofia had taken her life with Ali's service pistol. He died soon after, without regaining consciousness.

Marianna Zawacka did not have the strength to bury another of her children, so Klara stayed with her while the others met in Warsaw. Władysław and Egon followed Ali's hearse. Elżbieta chose to walk behind Zofia's, honouring the woman who could not bear to live without the man they had both loved. As her death was a suicide, the priest refused to conduct a service for Zofia. She was not even to be laid to rest in consecrated ground but, as Elżbieta watched, Ali and Zofia were quietly 'buried together, one on top of the other, in a narrow grave'.[39]

Elżbieta and Klara spent the next week with their parents. One afternoon they were stopped by a Romani woman, keen to tell their fortunes for some coins. Neither sister believed in such prophecies but 'for a laugh' Elżbieta held out her hand.[40] After tracing the creases and noting the calluses, the woman told her, 'You will live for a long time: eighty-five years.[41] Elżbieta snorted, but she was secretly pleased. She filed the fortune in her mind, turning it over until it became as worn as the coin that had paid for it. Was it eighty years, or eight-five? Later, she could not be sure, but she held on to the prediction and found herself emboldened by it.

Elżbieta qualified as a senior PWK instructor in 1937 and was appointed commander of the Silesian region, overseeing nineteen districts. She found it 'hard service', with new branches 'springing up like mushrooms after rain'.[42] The Universal Military Obligation Act, passed the next spring, rewarded the PWK's long struggle by finally permitting women to be called up as auxiliaries. 'War hangs in the air,' Elżbieta told her team.[43] Many of the women started taking clerical work with the air force and navy. Some served in communications, and others in anti-aircraft detachments and as pilots. PWK recruitment boomed. Soon there were 47,000 members and 1,500 instructors. 'We were young and hungry for action,' Elżbieta said proudly. 'We didn't consider ourselves inferior to men, and we wanted to prove it. We wanted to serve Poland.[44]

In the summer of 1939, Elżbieta and Zofia ran an instructor course near Katowice. When Zofia was called to Warsaw, she and Elżbieta grabbed a last chat at their favourite spot, a natural spring near the camp clearing. 'I am completely content,' Zofia told Elżbieta, who smiled across at her, sharing the 'deep feeling of happiness'.[45] The spring water burbled, an occasional thrumming betrayed a woodpecker high up in the trees and, further off, the women could hear the hum and laughter of camp life. At seven the next morning, Elżbieta drove Zofia to the station, waving her off in her second-class carriage on the express.

That afternoon a message arrived at the camp, belatedly warning Zofia to delay her journey. There had been a catastrophe at Pruszków, a train 'blown off the rails'.[46] The next day's papers brought more news of the disaster, and the search for the identity of a female casualty. Elżbieta immediately set off to find Zofia. When she had no joy, she offered to help identify the body. Zofia 'was not crushed', Elżbieta later recalled. 'Only her face was bruised from the impact.[47] Thrown from her seat, her body had smashed into a metal luggage rack, killing her instantly.

It was Elżbieta who accompanied Zofia's body back to her home town to be buried. Hundreds of PWK instructors turned out for the funeral. Elżbieta helped to shoulder the coffin, seemingly too light for the weight of her bereavement. When she later spoke about these days, she said only that 'it was a great loss for the organisation, and an unspeakable one for me'.[48] To her closest friends she agonised that she had put Zofia 'on that train . . . into that unfortunate carriage'.[49] Marianna comforted her, silently sharing the depth of her grief.

Over the next few days, there was fervent speculation about what had caused the derailing. A fire in Warsaw's main station had led to the rerouting of all long-distance trains. When the express had been diverted to Pruszków, travelling at over twice the recommended speed, disaster became inevitable. The focus of the investigation then shifted to Warsaw. The capital's main station was a prestigious new building in the modernist style. The international hub of the Second Polish Republic, it was also a potential target for her enemies. Soon there were rumours of sabotage. Eventually it was determined that the Warsaw fire had been inadvertently caused by careless electricity contractors. Such a meaningless reason for Zofia's death could not find traction in Elżbieta's mind. She had lost too many of those she loved to pneumonia or to despair; deaths that were ultimately rooted in the First World War. To the end of her life, she would resolutely lay the blame for Zofia's death at the door of Nazi Germany. 'She died in a train crash near Pruszków', she wrote, 'as a result of German sabotage action against the main railway station in Warsaw.'[50] Or she would say, 'there was a secret attack . . . on the railway, a German diversion before the war.'[51] For Elżbieta, anything less was unacceptable, and often, after recounting Zofia's death, her next sentence would begin, 'Then the war came.'[52]

2

On the Frontline
(September–October 1939)

Elżbieta was shaken awake by the force of an explosion. As she pushed aside her covers, she could feel the low rolling shudder of a series of further detonations resonating through the walls of her dorm room and the metal frame of her cot. It was five in the morning on 1 September 1939, and the sky was brighter than it should have been for just a few minutes after dawn. At first she thought that the Polish Air Force might be undertaking exercises from nearby Katowice airport. Hastily pulling on her PWK uniform, she splashed some water on her face and headed downstairs to the telephone. For the last two days she had been based in the Silesian headquarters of the Polish Red Cross, where she had been ordered to report a week earlier. In the hall she discovered that the telephone line was down. No one stumbling around the draughty building had received any notice of exercises. Seconds later, a blazing shower of incendiaries made it clear that the airport was under attack.

Confirmation came over the radio later that morning. Nazi German land and air forces had crossed the Polish border a little before five and were pushing into Silesia. 'As of now, we are all soldiers,' the broadcast ended, causing Elżbieta a wry smile.[1] In the PWK she held the rank of commander, but as the organisation did not have legal military status, officially its members were civilians without rank, pay, rations or other recognition. Although she received no direct orders that morning, Elżbieta already had an emergency plan for the dozen female instructors under her command. Directing her team into action she knew, deep inside, that whatever her official status, from that moment onwards, 'I was a soldier.'[2]

⚓

When Poland's former leader, Marshal Piłsudski, had died four years earlier, in 1935, he seemed to have left his reborn nation relatively secure on the international stage. Having signed non-aggression pacts with both the Soviet Union and Nazi Germany, Stalin and Hitler were among the world leaders who sent condolences at the news of his death. Hitler had even ordered a Holy Mass for Piłsudski to be held in Berlin.

The PWK had also paid tribute to the Marshal, with banners and speeches as his funeral train travelled from Warsaw to Kraków, the route lit by bonfires as rural people paid their respects. Maria Wittek had then continued the PWK's military training. Hitler's aggressive territorial expansion over the next few years had betrayed his intentions and it seemed best to prepare. When, in March 1939, the German leader flouted both the spirit and letter of the Munich Agreement, Britain guaranteed Poland's sovereignty in the desperate hope of containment. France followed suit. It had little effect.

The following month had been one of 'feverish' activity for the PWK.[3] Now aged thirty, Elżbieta had been working with dozens of women's groups across Silesia to raise money and generate recruits for the national defence. Women from the riflewomen's association, rowing clubs and even craft circles were also being trained in emergency medicine, self-defence, social work and the sewing of gas masks. Elżbieta later estimated that a million women attended 'social emergency' lectures, and 'often men listened too'.[4] Although many of these women 'didn't want to fight . . . didn't care about the rifle', she realised they all wanted to play their part.[5]

A British Staff delegation had arrived in Warsaw in May, after the War Office 'stressed the importance of inspiring confidence among Poles'.[6] Among them was Colin Gubbins, a wiry Scots Highlander seemingly as undistinguished as his toothbrush moustache – 'then almost a part of the Royal Artillery officer's uniform'.[7] Behind his traditional façade, however, Gubbins's original mind and daring spirit would take him on to head the British Special Operations Executive, or SOE. Unfortunately, that spring the delegation's main achievement was to inflate Polish expectations of British assistance.

By then, Elżbieta was already busy inspecting the Silesian social-work camps scattered along the German and Czechoslovak borders. PWK fieldwork had ended as usual that July, as thousands of cadets arrived to pitch their tents at summer training camps. While Elżbieta was giving rousing talks about national defence, Hitler was in his

Alpine residence instructing his senior military commanders that 'the destruction of Poland has priority'.[8] Nothing was to stand in the way of this operation, not even the regime's long-standing enmity with the Soviet Union. On 23 August, Joachim von Ribbentrop, the tight-lipped Nazi minister of foreign affairs, had flown to Moscow. Having been welcomed at the airport with swastika banners hastily requisitioned from a Soviet film studio, where they had been serving as props in an anti-Nazi propaganda film, he was driven to the Kremlin.[9] There Ribbentrop met his Soviet counterpart, the deceptively gentle-looking Vyacheslav Molotov. As well as signing a mutual non-aggression pact, the men also agreed a Secret Protocol, quietly outlining how Poland was to be carved up between their acquisitive nations.

In the words of future British prime minister Winston Churchill, the Nazi–Soviet Pact hit the world 'like an explosion'.[10] More detonations quickly followed. Throughout that summer, the SS and Abwehr organised a series of targeted, false-flag operations on Polish soil, designed to supply 'evidence' of anti-German sentiment. A war memorial was destroyed in Cieszyn; a German bookshop blown up in Poznań; in Nowy Sącz a railway bridge was detonated; and a bomb left in Tarnow station killed twenty-four. The German papers then ran stories about 'Polish terror'.[11] It was little wonder Elżbieta was convinced Germany was behind the Pruszków train disaster.

Elżbieta was one of several hundred female instructors who had stood in line before the first PWK conscription commission in mid-August. As hostilities grew, the government had started to consider giving the organisation a formal auxiliary role. 'Finally, women could be soldiers', Elżbieta wrote, prematurely as it happened. 'The joy was enormous.'[12] Dr Zofia Franio, one of the PWK elders, conducted the medical inspections for the conscription board, her prematurely grey hair pinned back into a bun. 'At first glance she had a stern and haughty face', the recruits felt, never daring to argue with her, but 'on closer acquaintance it became apparent that she was a woman of great and good heart'.[13] Zofia was not one to talk about herself, but the few details she occasionally let slip from her remarkable past had already given her legendary status among the instructors.

Born in 1899, Zofia had been a medical student in Petrograd when the battlecruiser *Aurora*, moored in the city for repairs, fired the first shot of the October Revolution.* Fleeing west, she reached Warsaw in 1918 and served as a medic at various field hospitals. Later, she became a founding member of the PWK and commander of the university unit. She also ran a thriving medical practice and, a deeply compassionate woman, a free clinic for the poorer residents of the capital. Signing off Elżbieta as fit for military service, she held her eye for a moment then gave her a quick hug. Two days later the PWK had been mobilised.

Elżbieta had ordered the immediate closure of the summer camps and recalled all PWK instructors from leave. In what she described as 'the feverish atmosphere' of the last days of that oppressively hot August, she had set up service points with chocolate, tea, water and cigarettes at railway stations and on the major roads, ready to support the future army on the move.[14]

The 'thunderclap announcement of general mobilisation', as she put it, came on 30 August, less than two days before German tanks, trucks and infantry crossed the border.[15] Luftwaffe bombing had been designed to ease the passage of the invading army by taking out strategic targets such as the main Polish airbases, while protecting key bridges across the Vistula. The strikes were of limited success. Part of the Polish Air Force was destroyed on the ground, but most of it had already been relocated to smaller, less obvious airfields. From these, the Poles managed to inflict significant damage on the Luftwaffe, but ultimately the odds against them would prove overwhelming.

Woken by the Katowice bombardment, Elżbieta sent out several PWK officers to assess the local situation. Some were immediately caught up in the first wave of civilians rushing from the front. Extending the aid stations for soldiers, Elżbieta added childcare points and other support. With typical toughness, she also tried, she wrote, 'to counteract panic with our calmness' and 'to shame those in despair'.[16]

Other PWK women were still reporting for duty. Among them was Teresa Delekta, Elżbieta's deputy, who arrived carrying samples of the new gas mask she had been hoping to promote. Elżbieta was even more delighted when some 'fiery Silesian women', workers from the local coalmines, turned up demanding weapons and grenades so they could join the national defence.[17] 'The mood was very militant',

* Petrograd became known as Leningrad between 1924 and 1991. It is now the city of St Petersburg. The October Revolution was a key moment in the wider Russian Revolution of 1917–23.

Elżbieta noted, and when the munitions were not forthcoming, the women threatened to rough up the PWK team.[18] Elżbieta intervened, detailing them to support local anti-aircraft defences. 'Outraged, threatening, they left', she recorded, adding with satisfaction that 'the mood was still wonderful. The traditions of the Silesian uprisings were revived.'[19]

That night, the troops from the local garrison started pulling out of Katowice. Despite pockets of stubborn resistance, the Wehrmacht had the dual advantages of the flat terrain of the Central European Plain, and the driest summer on record – perfect conditions for tanks and motorised infantry. 'Hitler's Nazi hordes trampled through fields of corn,' one veteran later recalled, 'crushing beneath their tanks the large glossy ears awaiting harvesting.'[20] As the defenders prayed for rain to clog up the roads, the first enemy units reached the outskirts of Katowice and turned their guns on the army headquarters.

At midday, a Polish Army major notified Elżbieta that the Germans were expected to enter the city within twenty-four hours. He had reserved a seat for her in his vehicle and ordered the PWK to disperse. Elżbieta refused to leave without her team of instructors. She sent Teresa Delekta to the nearest army unit to secure a travel order and transport for them all, but the military had already left the city.

It was almost dark before Elżbieta managed to requisition a municipal bus to take her and her team to the regional command centre in Lublin. The women climbed on board, still in uniform and carrying rucksacks full of maps, provisions and three PWK banners. The spare seats were taken by some Girl Scout instructors. Elżbieta did a final check, and one Scoutmaster jumped off as they were about to leave, electing to scatter shards of glass and nails on the road behind them. 'The next day,' Elżbieta recorded, 'the Germans entered and began their bloody liquidation of the resistance organised by the Silesian insurgents.'[21]

The women only stopped when they were 150 miles northeast of Katowice, pulling up for a few hours' sleep. In the morning, Elżbieta let the Scout leaders drive the bus to Kraków, leaving her PWK contingent to hitchhike on towards Lublin. A requisitioned rubbish truck took them some of the way, followed by a risky ride in a lorry carrying barrels of petrol: a tempting target for the enemy aircraft they began to see overhead.

Surprised by the Polish defence, the Luftwaffe was increasing its bombing raids. That afternoon the roads were repeatedly strafed by Stuka dive-bombers whose machine guns pumped at the earth below like sewing-machine needles hemming the fields. As they attacked, Elżbieta and her team would run for cover, jumping into roadside ditches, their sweaty rucksacks thumping against their backs. Once, sheltering in woodland, they met the remnants of a Polish artillery battery, lost in unfamiliar territory. Elżbieta handed over her maps, receiving a pistol in exchange – although without ammunition it was just another weight in her bag. Later, she gave it to some soldiers on the road.

When they finally arrived at the nearest bridge across the Vistula, Elżbieta discovered that it had been blown up to frustrate the German advance. Tired and hungry, several of the team became mutinous. Elżbieta held firm. They would continue, on foot if necessary, to the next bridge at Sandomierz. She also refused permission for the women to exchange their uniforms for civilian clothes, even when they were overtaken on the road by the first enemy motorbikes and later a solitary German tank. On the fifth day of their journey, the women met a Polish military convoy bringing supplies to units already on the far side of the Vistula. By chance, the captain recognised Elżbieta as Ali's sister, and offered them a lift.

'It was hell' at Sandomierz, Elżbieta later reported. 'A crowd of thousands of carts, and squealing, biting horses' joined 'a sea of desperate people who were no longer allowed on the bridge, as it had already been mined'.[22] Being still in uniform, the women were the last group permitted across before the bridge was blown. The explosion was terrific, and terrible: Polish infrastructure destroyed by Polish mines. Looking back, Elżbieta saw the shattered spans were now rubble in the river, and rearing horses were adding to the chaos among the stranded crowds.

Boarding a freight train on the eastern side of the river, the women shared the last of their supplies with a group of Polish pilots. After running out of fuel, the airmen had been forced to set fire to their machines to prevent them from falling into enemy hands. But not before they had shot down one of the enemy, they proudly told Elżbieta. When a Luftwaffe aircraft circled above the train, she watched sympathetically as they reached for their rifles and fired a few more bitter shots.

The women finally reached Lublin on the morning of 8 September. The city had suffered heavy bombing the night before and Elżbieta had to pick her way between craters and the slumping remnants of buildings. Some embers were still glowing in the early morning light. Spotting an atlas among the debris of a bookshop, Elżbieta carefully clambered over to retrieve a map of Poland. A policeman pushed her roughly away, reproaching her for stealing. When she argued back, she was lucky not to be arrested. The war was still too new, too incredible, for many to have adjusted, even as the new reality lay spread out before them, charred and smoking.

When she eventually reported for duty, Elżbieta was ordered on to Lwów, the cosmopolitan university city a further 140 miles southeast.* Initially considered too deep behind Polish lines to need defending, the pace of the German invasion had given Lwów strategic importance, protecting the route to Romania through which Polish forces might retreat to regroup overseas. It now had to be defended at all costs. Although she was exhausted, Elżbieta's spirits rose – for once duty and opportunity seemed to go hand in hand. Klara lived not far from Lwów. Having passed her command to Teresa Delekta, telling her to follow with the others when they could, she squeezed into a truck heading east.

The garrison commander in Lwów, Władysław Langner, was an experienced soldier and deeply principled man. He had served under Piłsudski during the First World War, and again in the Polish–Bolshevik conflict. Now he had just three infantry platoons and one motorised brigade with which to defend Lwów, so he was quick to accept Maria Wittek's offer of her women's battalion, recruited from the PWK. When Elżbieta arrived at Wittek's door at one o'clock the next morning, she was immediately signed up.

Langner had already organised a series of defensive positions, exploiting the city's natural high ground, and created barricades and anti-tank ditches on the main approach roads. The women were organising field kitchens, and propaganda to counteract defeatism as the city struggled to cope with the numbers of displaced people arriving from the west. Lwów would soon double its population, supplies were low and the makeshift hospitals were already struggling.

To Elżbieta's relief, she was appointed to command the women's anti-aircraft defence unit. As she was heading off, a sudden blast of air

---

* 'Lwów', once German Lemberg, is now the Ukrainian city of Lviv, once more under Russian attack at the time of writing.

sent her flying across the road. Debris whistled past but, apart from her ringing ears, she found she was unhurt. Shakily getting to her feet, she watched as the building opposite started to collapse, slowly at first but picking up speed as it slid miserably to its knees. Choking clouds of dirt billowed up, slowly clearing to reveal dust-covered bodies on the street. Enemy troops had not yet arrived but the bombing of Lwów had started and Elżbieta realised that the front already ran through everyone's lives, whether soldier or civilian, man, woman or child.

Over the next few days, Elżbieta largely dedicated herself to the anti-aircraft teams, securing supply lines, arranging shifts and running rapid training in fire defence. She also helped to dig anti-tank ditches and construct barricades. In quieter moments, while feeling irrationally guilty for not being able to reach Klara, she organised the sewing of bandages. At some point, Dr Zofia Franio arrived, along with several of her PWK team. One had been killed during an air raid near Lublin, and Teresa Delekta had received a neck injury from flying shrapnel, serious though not fatal. Less than two weeks since the invasion, the war was already personal.

When German ground forces reached within seventy kilometres, Maria Wittek prioritised the manufacture of petrol bombs – one of the few handmade weapons that could have impact against enemy tanks. Another determined PWK instructor, Wacława Zastocka, universally known as Wacka, took off her trademark tie, rolled up her shirt sleeves and set up round-the-clock production in a sports hall. Soon Elżbieta joined her, filling wine bottles with gasoline, then adding rags to serve as wicks. When Lwów's powerplant was hit, they brought in a roaring generator to keep the lights on. The noise and stench were almost unbearable and, as the front approached and they found themselves working 'under heavy artillery fire', the women knew that a single spark might be enough to ignite the fumes, killing them all.[23]

Elżbieta also took her turn delivering the home-made supplies to the city's defensive positions. Driving through Lwów between air raids with a truck full of petrol bombs was not for the faint-hearted. 'You will live for a long time: eighty-five years', she remembered, and her luck held.[24]

One day, a convoy of forty trucks, cars and buses passed through, carrying Poland's gold reserves and national treasures to Romania. Later, Elżbieta's former mathematics tutor, Marian Rejewski, and his team of pioneering Enigma codebreakers crossed the border in a single battered truck. Then, on 13 September, the British Military Mission arrived. 'As I drove into the main square, I saw women, children and old men pulling up the paving stones ... and building barricades with their bare hands against the brutal invader,' Colin Gubbins later recalled.[25] 'Britain would fight on until Poland was once more free,' he vowed.[26]*

German guns were pounding the outskirts of Lwów by the time General Langner received military reinforcements. Among them was Colonel Maczek, who noted that Lwów was 'dark, dirty ... illuminated only by occasional dying fires from the raids'.[27] His forces were soon helping to repel the first Germans: two motorised infantry divisions and a battery of 150mm guns. Afterwards, one of the Polish defenders cautiously went to look at the German casualties. 'Why are you doing this?' he asked the dead men pitifully. 'Why are you invading our country?'[28]

When Lwów was almost surrounded and their supply lines cut, Langner ordered military provisions to be shared with the civilian population. The strategic importance of food supply was not lost on Elżbieta, but she was still hoping for more active engagement at the barricades. Her courage astounded the men. After centuries of partitions and annexations, the motto of the Polish Armed Forces fighting alongside various allies was 'For Your Freedom and Ours'. For a few weeks in Lwów, there was another example of shared military endeavour: men and women serving with a common purpose.

On 17 September, General Langner received what Elżbieta called the 'incredible news' of a Soviet invasion from the east.[29] Instead of a declaration of war, Stalin had simply announced that the Polish state had 'ceased to exist', thereby voiding all previous treaties. The Soviets, he claimed, were coming to protect the local Ukrainian and Belarusian populations.[30] Unaware of the secret Ribbentrop–Molotov pact to divide Poland between Germany and the Soviet Union, that afternoon the Polish supreme command telephoned Langner to confirm that 'we are not at war with the Bolsheviks'.[31] Meanwhile, Langner's units were slowly 'bleeding away', as he put it, under Nazi German attack. [32]

Two days later, Langner was handed the first German demand,

* Gubbins received the Polish Cross of Valour for his work with the British Military Mission in 1939. This was one of the first Polish awards to British personnel during the war, being made official in spring 1940.

dropped by aircraft, for his surrender. 'I have no intention of capitulating', he wrote baldly.[33] He knew that Soviet tanks and infantry were already approaching down the now sodden country roads from the east, and on 20 September he received a Soviet offer to 'agree on a joint action'.[34] Yet rumours were also arriving of Polish detachments being disarmed and detained by Red Army units. With no more reinforcements, and his food and ammunition reserves running low, Langner knew he would eventually have to surrender. The only question was, to whom.

The first Soviet motor corps arrived that afternoon: two brigades of tanks, followed by an infantry division and cavalry corps. A few hours later, Elżbieta joined the Polish officers' last briefing, which took place in one of Lwów's cinemas. Their three military options were to surrender and become German prisoners of war; to be detained by the Soviets; or to retreat across the border into Romania. Knowing that neither the Germans nor the Soviets were likely to accept Polish women as POWs because officially they were still civilians, Elżbieta thought that either side would probably just shoot them. But the women had another option. Unlike men of service age, they could disappear among the civilians in Lwów. It was hard to 'throw away the uniform', as Elżbieta put it, but ultimately the entire women's battalion took the same decision.[35] Her participation in the September campaign over, Elżbieta was given a room by a dentist.

Langner's surrender terms – freedom of movement for his men, protection of civilians and respect for private property – were accepted without discussion. Although outnumbered and under-equipped, his defence of Lwów had lasted an impressive ten days. Furthermore, he was surrendering not to the official enemy but, as he noted with some pride, 'to the Soviet Army, with which we did not fight, and with which we were ordered not to fight'.[36]

The Soviets, who had never recognised the Geneva Convention, immediately broke the surrender terms. 'With a treachery rarely equalled in history,' Colin Gubbins fumed, 'the Polish liaison parties were first welcomed with warmth, and then arrested and transported, never to be heard of since.'[37] Among them was Klara's fiancé. Told to report for transportation home, he found his weapons confiscated and himself among thousands sent east to various 'distribution camps'.

'We constantly hear suicide shots,' Elżbieta noted grimly, as some despairing Polish officers took their own lives rather than surrender their weapons.[38] Others managed to slip away in civilian clothes, tramping through forests and swimming icy rivers to reach either Romania or what was now German-occupied Poland to the west. If their hands were calloused, they might even survive if picked up by Red Army soldiers. Men with good watches or books in their pockets stood less chance. Nevertheless, Langner himself eventually managed to reach Romania, and then France.

Elżbieta was shocked at how shabby the Russian soldiers looked. Watching some of the 'clunky Soviet tanks' pull up, she was fascinated that one was filled with 'dirty, unwashed' female soldiers.[39] Although their war was only a few days old, these women wore ill-fitting uniforms under 'horrible, filthy greatcoats', and had to shoulder their few rifles with dirty lengths of string.[40] The Red Army had clearly allocated them the oldest, most moribund equipment. Yet the men did not look much better in their shoddy uniforms and dirty boots. Some were even barefoot. 'It was such a wretched army!' Elżbieta thought contemptuously, 'Such a lousy army from the Soviet Union.'[41]

Lwów changed rapidly under Soviet occupation. Machine-gun wagons and artillery hauled by stunted ponies rattled down the streets, while Russian soldiers looted the shops and houses for any food, bedding, valuables or bicycles. Yet within days, welcome signs in Russian started to appear and, Elżbieta noticed scornfully, every day 'more and more of the girls and women of Lwów paraded in red berets, scarves and blouses'.[42] Posters of Stalin, Lenin, Marx and Engels were soon pasted onto walls, and loudspeakers wired up in the streets broadcast 'propaganda about the benefits of communism and socialist justice'.[43] Elżbieta, meanwhile, had to queue for food throughout the night.

In late September, the German–Soviet Treaty of Friendship was signed, publicly dividing Poland between the two powers. In Soviet-held territory, Polish laws were renounced, the land was collectivised, businesses nationalised, places of worship and education closed, and political parties outlawed. The luckier of those women deemed not to have 'productive' skills were directed to 'sewing factories'. Others were given hard manual labour.

A month later, elections were arranged for a local deputy to the Soviet Union. Refusing to vote for any Russian representative on Polish soil, Elżbieta decided to cross into Nazi-occupied Poland before the new wartime border closed completely. She was not the only woman from the battalion determined to return home. Dr Zofia Franio and

Wacka Zastocka were also planning to head west, but when Wacka contracted typhoid Zofia insisted on staying to nurse her. For them, the risky journey would have to wait.

Elżbieta decided to take her chances with another friend, Nina Kowalska. Whichever route they took, they would have to cross the River San. This tributary of the Vistula had served as the defensive line just a few weeks earlier, and now formed the demarcation between the Soviet and German zones. The best way, Elżbieta decided, was to bribe a smuggler to take them across by boat after dark. When a Russian patrol turned up, however, the boatman scarpered with their money. Left penniless, the women considered swimming the river, but it was now October, the water was breathtakingly cold, and Nina was still feverish from her own earlier bout of typhoid.

Their last option was bluff. Walking straight up to the German checkpoint on the only bridge, Elżbieta pulled her scarf away from her blonde hair, tilted up her face and fixed her clear blue eyes on the guards, before addressing them in their own language. She had elderly parents in German Silesia, she said. She wanted to return home. Her accent was perfect and her eyes shone with sincerity. Incredibly, the guards let both women across.

Once in the German zone, Elżbieta and Nina met several other friends heading west. Pooling their resources, and with Elżbieta doing the talking when required, they clambered onto a freight train to Kraków. As she travelled, Elżbieta took in the devastation left by the Blitzkrieg. Most of the railway stations had suffered bomb damage, as had all of the towns further west. Hitching onwards, she saw teams of forced labourers clearing the main roads of burnt-out vehicles, and using rubble to fill in bomb craters and ditches. It was at least easy enough to get a ride in a cart, as the roads were clogged with returning civilians. Every hour or so, this pathetic traffic would get pushed to the verges as German army trucks ploughed past, transporting soldiers and supplies.

Elżbieta reached Toruń in late October. If she closed her eyes, her home town sounded much as it had in her childhood, with German spoken in the street and the echoing sound of boots on cobbles. But now there were also blood-red flags hanging from the requisitioned buildings. New emotions were also on show: great cheer among the German officers, who considered themselves back on home ground; and the more familiar grief, fear and simmering anger among the locals.

The first German soldiers had arrived in the city within a week of the invasion. There had been skirmishes. A few defenders were killed on the approach roads, and in the city centre some potshots from windows had been met by machine-gun fire. But Toruń had been taken quickly. Now part of the territory annexed directly into the Third Reich, the city was under military control.

Over five days in October, 1,500 citizens had been detained in the local fort. They were still in custody when Elżbieta arrived, although six hundred would later be shot in the nearby Barbarka forest. To Elżbieta's relief, her parents and her sister Dela were all still living in their pre-war apartment. Protected by her father's service record, and perhaps also the undesirability of their small home, the family were considered 'safe' and told to join the regional register of *Volksdeutsche* – ethnic Germans.

Of the rest of Zo's family, Egon's crooked arm, permanently damaged by repeated childhood breaks, meant that he had never been drafted. Evacuated east, the last his parents had heard was that he had been detained by Russian troops. There had been no word from Klara, but their cousin, Leonard Zawacki, was in Toruń. Having served in the defence of Warsaw, Leonard had been captured but managed to escape custody in the chaos when his transport train stopped at the destroyed rail-bridge over the Vistula.

Leonard was hoping to return to a quiet civilian life in his home town, a few miles further north. Elżbieta was travelling in the opposite direction. After just one day in Toruń, she headed back south to seek out the resistance in Warsaw and continue the fight. 'I was a soldier after all', she wrote, 'and the war was not over.'[44]

3

Resistance
(November 1939–July 1940)

Elżbieta had thrived in uniform but, in the cold, damp November of 1939, as temperatures dropped below zero, she was serving her country in a plain skirt, long-sleeved cotton blouse and tightly knitted cardigan. Standing inside a stranger's apartment, next to the traditional tiled stove – sadly unheated despite the chill – she recited her resistance oath of allegiance. For a fleeting moment her warm breath hung in the air in front of her, the only tangible record of her pledge. Then it was gone. Within half an hour Elżbieta would also disappear, melting away into the capital of what was now Nazi-occupied Poland, to start her service in a new kind of clandestine war.

Elżbieta had sworn her allegiance to the Polish Victory Service, one of several resistance organisations that developed in response to the annexation and occupation of Polish territory. It was intolerable to her that her country should be broken up again, just twenty years since regaining independence. She had been a child when her father had taken her by the hand in Toruń to hear the Polish national anthem played in public. Now she felt a personal responsibility to defend her country, and she was not alone. Over time, the Polish Victory Service would evolve into the legendary Home Army, the first national resistance movement in occupied Europe. With eventually over 400,000 men and 40,000 women in its ranks, it was also the largest resistance organisation of the Second World War.[*]

The 'Home Army' name was chosen to distinguish the Polish resistance both as an army under military leadership, and from the existing Polish Armed Forces that had evaded capture to regroup overseas.

---

[*] On 13 November 1939, the Polish Victory Service (*Służba Zwycięstwu Polski*, SZP) became the Union of Armed Struggle (*Związek Walki Zbrojnej*, ZWZ). The ZWZ was renamed the Home Army (*Armia Krajowa*, AK) on 14 February 1942. For simplicity, I refer only to the Home Army.

'I commanded two armies', General Władysław Sikorski, the Polish prime minister and commander-in-chief, made clear. One was largely in France, the other, in Poland, was 'secret, underground'.[1]

The choice of name also lent the resistance an appropriately homely resonance. The domestic and the military had been blurred as soon as Nazi Germany had invaded, targeting civilians as well as serving soldiers. Despite defeat, Poland never capitulated and in the war of resistance that followed, apartment blocks and farmhouses became the new front line. Military intelligence was annotated in cookery books, messages were hidden inside baskets of vegetables and children's dolls, and women like Elżbieta swore their allegiance while standing next to kitchen stoves.

Elżbieta felt that her circuitous journey from Lwów to Toruń, evading checks, moving between groups of civilians, and acclimatising to swastika flags, had been 'a kind of courier training'.[2] While she had been wearing out her shoe leather, Nazi Germany and the Soviet Union had divided Poland into three zones. The west, including Toruń, was annexed directly into the Third Reich. Lwów was in Soviet-annexed territory to the east. The German-occupied zone in between, encompassing Warsaw, became known as the 'General Government'. Borders were quickly organised, and anyone crossing without the right papers faced arrest.

On leaving Toruń, Elżbieta had headed first to Poznań. She had not been surprised to find the ancient buildings of her old university city already draped in Nazi red, white and black, but was disgusted to find a swastika flag hanging limply from the window of her old bedroom. That night she had angrily caught a goods train to Warsaw. On arrival, there were none of the usual newsvendors and drinks sellers on the concourse calling out 'beer, lemonade, chocolate'. Instead, paving slabs had been uprooted and a mass grave dug for unknown soldiers. It was still covered in candles when Elżbieta skirted past.

Several hundred tonnes of explosives had been dropped on the Polish capital. The hospital, where a company of a hundred women had served as nurses, was derelict, and many of the city's elegant boulevards, churches and galleries had been destroyed. Those that remained were shell-scarred, and part of the Royal Castle had collapsed. Even the once immaculate lawns of the city's parks had been scarred by anti-aircraft gun emplacements and were now scabbed with dark mounds – evidence of further hurried graves. Across the city, the stench of decay hinted at other bodies still beneath the rubble.

'Nobody spoke loudly, nobody laughed,' Elżbieta noticed as she headed to the apartment of her dearest friend, Marianna Zawodzińska. 'You couldn't hear any children.'[3] People were scared. Before the invasion, Hitler had ordered that as well as the country's Jewish population, 'whatever we find in the shape of an upper class in Poland will be liquidated'. Government officials, military reservists and other members of the Polish intelligentsia were already being arrested.[*] As a teacher on a modest income, Marianna was not on the Gestapo lists, but she was already conspiring against them. Overjoyed to find Elżbieta on her doorstep, she quickly ushered her inside.

The outbreak of war had found Marianna in Warsaw with her two younger sisters, Celina and Stefa. Marianna's first action had been to destroy the Warsaw PWK's documents. It was a sad bonfire. Among the records were personal letters and photographs, reduced to ash for fear they might incriminate someone. All the sisters had then served in the city's defence, the younger ones as medical orderlies running supplies between chemists and hospitals. After the occupation, they had quickly joined the resistance.

Elżbieta had sat up straight when she discovered that her friend 'was already a soldier of the underground'.[4] Marianna was a courier, relaying messages between Warsaw and Kraków. She had proudly showed Elżbieta the 'broken slippers' in which she hid clandestine papers.[5] Efficient communication was a prerequisite for all other resistance activities, and 80 per cent of Polish liaison officers, messengers and couriers were women. Elżbieta had been all admiration. Her delight had turned to horror, however, when she learnt that while travelling for hours on unheated trains, Marianna had started coughing up blood. Even at the PWK, her friend had always seemed 'delicate' and this 'physical fragility', so out of sync with Marianna's bold spirit, evoked 'a special kind of emotion' in Elżbieta.[6] She was 'like a bird thrown from its nest', she reflected romantically, wounded even before being caught up in the storms of war.[7]

It was the following day, 2 November 1939, when Marianna had taken Elżbieta to an apartment whose door was opened by a woman so inconspicuous that Elżbieta had almost waited for someone else to appear before she stepped inside. Little was said as the three of them

---

[*] By 1944, 10,000 members of the Warsaw intelligentsia alone had been murdered.

walked into the cold kitchen but, when asked, Elżbieta quickly gave
'Zelma' as her chosen nom-de-guerre. Then she had raised her hand
and repeated the resistance oath.

Once sworn in, Elżbieta proposed organising her PWK friends and
teaching contacts across Silesia into a resistance circuit. The network
was to be named 'Coal', after the Silesian mines, and Elżbieta set off
for Katowice the next day. It was exactly two months since she had
left the city on the requisitioned municipal bus. Now officially part
of the Greater German Reich, Katowice was not only decked out in
swastika flags; its street names had been translated into German, with
Nazi generals stepping in for Polish heroes where required. Seeing that
there were too many Germans in the town altogether, Elżbieta packed
her few possessions into a basket and caught the tram to a nearby
industrial centre where the PWK had once had a base.*

Almost everything Elżbieta needed could be traded, so she paid her
way by giving the German language lessons that were suddenly invaluable. She also quickly undertook her first small act of defiance – which
was also an act of love. The morning after she arrived, she hid Zofia
Grzegorzewska's joyous PWK sketchbooks, along with hundreds of
their letters, in a disused mineshaft. Then she set about more practical
resistance work.

Elżbieta knew that her most precious resource was the PWK community, but creating a clandestine network of activists proved harder
than expected. The women who had returned from mobilisation had
buried their uniforms and were keeping a low profile to avoid the regular round-ups for enforced work details. For a frustrating few days
Elżbieta got nowhere. Once she had traced one instructor, however,
she discovered 'a kind of natural underground network based on trust,
as it was in the PWK'.[8] The way she saw it, 'the Nazi invasion caused
patriotism to go underground' and, if anything, its roots grew deeper
as a result.[9]

Soon several women had joined the Coal network with what,
Elżbieta felt sure, was 'great joy and relief'.[10] For her, leading a resistance circuit in the middle of Nazi-annexed territory was 'a beautiful
job. It gave me joy.'[11] For many families, survival was already an
all-consuming effort, but Elżbieta was far from alone in finding both
pride and purpose in resistance. Some women were hiding wounded

* This was Sosnowiec.

servicemen. Others were running relief efforts, or secretly storing dried foods and medicines to support an uprising the following spring – when the Allied offensive was expected.

At the end of November, Elżbieta traced her former deputy, Teresa Delekta, to a monastery just north of Kraków. Wrapping herself up against the Polish winter, she hitched twenty-five miles, mainly in horse carts, before walking the last six to the monastery. Although concerned about Teresa, there was no pretence that she had arrived for anything other than recruitment. 'Zawacka came . . .' her friend reported cheerfully, 'to let me know that she had started organising the underground.'[12] Elżbieta swore her in there and then, and Teresa secretly added the resistance oath to her twice daily prayers. Soon they had recruited another old friend, a mining engineer able to supply explosives. Within a month, fifty trusted women had been sworn into the Coal network.

One of their first endeavours was to organise the distribution of the local resistance press. After the Germans had confiscated all household radios, a local group had hidden a few sets and started producing a digest of foreign radio reports. Elżbieta arranged for three courageous sisters to smuggle copies to various cafés, bakeries and pharmacies. 'Women were most frequently used' for this kind of work, one male resister offered blithely, 'because men were apt to become dissatisfied and insist on playing more important roles.'[13] Nevertheless, the women were risking their lives to keep the wider resistance and local community informed.

Soon, the network was asked to collect data about German arrests, and the names of Poles who had registered themselves on the Volksdeutsche 'ethnic German' list – and were therefore considered to be untrustworthy, 'bakery-fresh Germans'.[14] Once a week, Elżbieta would type up the lists 'borrowed' from a Nazi office by their Polish translator. She had reservations about the value of this work. In German-annexed territory, securing a precious brown Volksdeutsche identity card was a basic living requirement. Not to do so risked being deported and could be a life-threatening act of defiance – one that was often misplaced. Having signed up as Volksdeutsche, Elżbieta's German-speaking parents could not only stay in their home but were also better placed to hide someone from the network occasionally.

Elżbieta's own priority was military reconnaissance. Soon she had an intelligence officer in every town across Silesia, each producing weekly reports on enemy troop numbers, deployment and morale. The information was gathered by women working in post offices and telephone exchanges who eavesdropped on conversations, read telegrams and intercepted letters. Translators, typists and office cleaners memorised maps and paperwork. Those who took in washing noted the numbers and type of uniforms passing through, bakery workers recorded changing garrison orders, and barmaids risked local opprobrium to chat with the enemy and report back military gossip. Most valuable of all were the women whose houses or places of work overlooked police stations, military installations, regional roads or railway tracks, enabling them to count the number and direction of troop trains and general military freight.

None of this intelligence held value, however, unless Elżbieta could get it to Warsaw. Her Coal network was structured in cells, each working in isolation to minimise risk. 'Letterboxes', where messages and reports could safely be left for her, were organised in busy pharmacies, laundrettes and bakeries. Each woman had her favourite way of concealing papers. One hid them in the whalebone of her corset, another inside the cover of a prayer book. Elżbieta liked to use a small mirror and wooden clothes brush, both with removable backs. Hiding the military within the domestic like this, never failed to make her smile. Every week, she checked the reports, cross-referencing them, before writing a digest. Then, memorising all she could and hiding the rest, she made the increasingly dangerous journey to Warsaw.

It was December when Elżbieta first returned to the capital. As the Third Reich undertook the 'Germanisation' of the territory it had annexed, thousands of Poles who were Jewish or who would not sign the Volksdeutsche list, or who were otherwise deemed undesirable, were being forcibly deported. Such large-scale human movement provided the perfect cover for Elżbieta. Trains were crammed with shocked and desperate people, many carrying a strange assortment of personal possessions. The German soldiers charged with managing the railways largely concerned themselves with confiscating 'illegal' foodstuffs, but, as her train approached the border, Elżbieta saw wooden observation towers with visible machine guns, and a series of defensive trenches and barbed wire entanglements. Her heart was racing as she went through the checks but her papers, soft and warm in her hand, were given only a cursory glance.

Outside the central station, Warsaw's electric trams were running again, the first carriages now reserved for Germans. There were fewer horse carts, but Warsaw had a new form of transport. *Rikshas* were tricycle-taxis with a low bench slung between the two front wheels. Elżbieta took one look, and started walking. Forced labour crews, largely Jewish, had cleared much of the rubble, and shops and cafés were open again but many displayed 'Only for Germans' signs, and she passed Polish beggars on every street.

Maria Wittek added Elżbieta's report to those being microfilmed and smuggled to the Polish government, now in Angers, in France. There, intelligence officials would assemble a national picture, enabling them to both direct resistance strategy, and plan for their armed forces overseas. Forty-five thousand Polish troops had now regrouped in France, as well as several thousand pilots, including a few women. The Poles also shared their intelligence with their allies, all keen to know how the Nazis were organising inside occupied territory, as well as troop movements and the creation of any fuel or ammunition dumps that might provide an indication of Hitler's intentions.

Wittek's dark hair was now streaked with grey. Her piercing stare, which had silently controlled a generation of PWK cadets, had calcified into a furrowed brow and her cheekbones had hollowed from lovely to austere. She was now reporting directly to General Stefan Rowecki, the former commander of the Warsaw Armoured-Motorised Brigade. Known by his nom-de-guerre of 'Grot', meaning 'Spearhead', Rowecki would lead the way in uniting Poland's early resistance efforts, creating the Home Army as a single national body from the many, politically diverse organisations that had developed independently. All patriotic Poles were needed, he made clear, be they Catholic or Jewish, male or female. Wittek's new 'Women's Auxiliary Service' was already providing couriers, messengers and ammunition carriers, signallers and cipher clerks, and intelligence and counter-intelligence officers such as Elżbieta.

Over the course of the war, these women would become invaluable in part simply because so many men were killed, arrested or escaped overseas, but also because they shared a crucial quality that distinguished them from their male counterparts. During the Great War, the Dutch dancer Margaretha Zelle, better known as Mata Hari, had lodged the idea of *femme fatale* spies in some romantic minds. Although women serving in the resistance deployed whatever skills and resources they had, their distinguishing superpower was not, in fact, irresistible sexual allure, but simply their ability to be consistently overlooked and underestimated.

Inside Nazi Germany, women were famously expected to focus their attention on the Church, the kitchen and their children, with their labour in fields and factories an unspoken but obvious extra. It was perhaps unsurprising, therefore, that the German occupational forces were initially blind to the possibility that more than a few 'exceptionally deranged' women were playing an active role in the danger and daily grind of organised resistance.

The largely male Polish underground leadership, including Rowecki, knew that their sisters had been raised in a spirit of patriotism, but even they were amazed by the level and range of women's active engagement. Within liaison alone, it was remarkable what could be hidden in the clogs and baskets of country girls clumping through the fields, and how willing elderly ladies were to transport resistance newspapers, rolls of film and weapons through occupied city streets. 'Liaison women', one male resistance officer wrote, 'were a vital link in our operations and in many ways more exposed than those they helped.' Yet 'they neither held high rank nor received any great honours for their heroism.'[15] Quite simply, 'there would have been no Home Army without women' was the blunt way Elżbieta put it.[16]

Yet Polish women were never entirely exempt from enemy attention and when German soldiers started to realise what the laughing girls in cafés and pregnant ladies to whom they sometimes offered their seat on a tram were really up to, their response was invariably brutal. Back during the September 1939 invasion, an impetuous 24-year-old had taken a machine gun to the roof of Warsaw's central post office and started firing, but it was only in October, when she ripped down a Nazi-propaganda poster, that she was caught.* Within two days she had been sentenced to death for the new crime of 'sabotage; that is, tearing down posters'.[17] Accepting gloves and biscuits from her father, but refusing a blindfold, before she was shot she reportedly called out, 'Poland is not yet lost!' It was the first official execution in Warsaw during the war.

The Nazi authorities hoped that their brutal act of retaliation would provide a powerful example to Warsaw's population, male and female

---

* Elżbieta Zahorska, the daughter of a well-known poet.

alike. It did. Rowecki posthumously awarded the young woman the Cross of Valour, and the resistance created a new branch of operations called 'Minor Sabotage' in her honour, to encourage even the smallest acts of defiance. Posters were soon being regularly defaced, and walls painted everywhere with symbols of resistance.* Elżbieta's team painted the carriages of forced labour trains with the turtle sign, reminding those being transported to work slowly and, if possible, to sabotage the German war effort.

Before she returned to Silesia, Maria Wittek appointed Elżbieta as one of her personal liaison officers, giving her specific instructions on the intelligence she required – enemy unit numbers and plans of barracks and airfields, as well as details of the mining industry and factory production, and a clear picture of local morale. In mid-December, when snow was thick on the ground, Wittek also sent Elżbieta a visitor.

Henryk Kowalówka, known as 'Topol' or 'Poplar-tree', the Home Army's district commander, was as tall, straight and rough round the edges as his nom-de-guerre implied. He liked to make Elżbieta laugh ('a little', she qualified) 'with his bearish manner', and he appreciated her evident organisational skills and strong sense of security.[18] Having been arrested some weeks earlier, Topol was well known to the Gestapo. He had reportedly escaped barefoot, after his boots had been confiscated. Now he needed Elżbieta to locate the other Polish officers hiding across her region. As a result, over the next few weeks the Coal network helped to fill the Home Army's ranks with men, while the women remained as auxiliaries.

Elżbieta was back in Warsaw in the first week of 1940. With temperatures plummeting to minus 30°C, and few able to afford fuel, most meetings now took place in the city's cafés over steaming cups of tea and black bread sandwiches smeared with beetroot marmalade, cheese, herring or sardines. While careful not to return to the same place too often, her favourite haunt was the 'Pastry' in the Old Town, where everyone from head cook to lowest bottle-washer was a signed-up member of the resistance. Not only did Elżbieta meet many PWK friends there, she also loved the poppyseed cake. She had been

---

* The famous 'Fighting Poland' *kotwica* (anchor) symbol would be designed in 1942 by Anna Smoleńska, an art history student, 'to show the enemy that despite everything, our spirit is unbroken'. She perished in Auschwitz the following year.

drawn to the sweet yeast buns known as *babka* and traditional *pączki* doughnuts ever since she was a hungry child, and she saw no harm in serving herself an occasional treat while also serving her country.

One afternoon, Elżbieta was delighted to see Wacka at the Pastry. A few weeks after Dr Zofia Franio had nursed her through typhoid in Lwów, Wacka had been arrested while trying to cross the so-called 'Boundary of Peace' between Soviet-annexed territory and the General Government.[19] When a Moscow prosecutor came to inspect the prison where she was being held, Wacka had started 'lamenting and begging for mercy'.[20] These were 'apparently the right tactics', she later reported, as she was released on condition that she leave the border zone within two hours.[21] She had not waited that long. A few days later Maria Wittek had sworn her into the resistance in Warsaw.

Dr Zofia Franio had reached the capital separately, immediately starting work at a clinic for the poor. Once also sworn into the resistance, she requested permission to join 'the direct fight against the occupiers'.[22] Her plan was to organise former PWK instructors into five-woman sabotage units. Groups of women, she rightly argued, were less suspicious than those of able-bodied men. Such a radical proposal required high-level approval, but the needs of war prevailed. Zofia recruited four friends and hosted their first training session in her apartment that February.

'I have no misgivings about Polish women's courage and patriotism', Zofia's sabotage instructor wrote. 'But in my opinion . . . blowing up railway tracks and bridges was beyond their powers.'[23] An expert in the destruction of train tracks, he had introduced himself to Zofia with the fitting nom-de-guerre of 'Rail'. But while she was quietly impressed by his credentials, he saw only 'a charming lady' with greying hair and a surprisingly 'youthful figure in a sports outfit'.[24] If Zofia's gender caused Rail concern, however, her 'careful and wise gaze' stopped him from voicing it.[25] Three hours later he was a convert to the idea of female sappers. 'How wrong I was,' he admitted.[26] Zofia not only had military experience and medical knowledge, but also 'the kind of strength that won people's respect and trust'.[27]

Over the next few months, Zofia's team learnt how to prepare a range of explosive devices, and stored several tonnes of material in the attic of a bombed-out house. Explosives and fuses were transported hidden under apples in large farm bags. 'With this "merchandise" we would walk past the barracks where the Wehrmacht was quartered', one of the team wrote proudly.[28] Finally, the women learnt how to lay their mines.

Although too busy with intelligence work to join a sabotage team, Elżbieta was a frequent guest at Zofia's that spring, often sleeping in an armchair when she could not find a bed elsewhere. Marianna would also sometimes walk over, passing the dull days between courier jobs by 'devouring books' in the company of friends.[29] The flat was one of the few places where the women felt safe. In those rooms, Elżbieta felt warmed not only by blankets and coffee, but also by the 'deep friendship' she witnessed between Zofia and her flatmate, Maria Szczurowska.[30] When Maria Wittek joined them, Elżbieta would listen to the conversation of her elders, and could not help feeling 'so small, so little active in my own Silesia, in the face of the great affairs of Warsaw'.[31] She was determined to do more.

One evening, Zofia Franio saw blood in Marianna's handkerchief. Diagnosing a pulmonary haemorrhage, almost certainly a sign of tuberculosis, she dismissed her from her courier duties and referred her to a sanatorium outside the city. Elżbieta visited whenever she could, bringing apples, pickles, biscuits and books. As the weather improved, they went for short walks in the fields, but mostly they sat on Marianna's bed, discussing the war, when the Allies might act, and the best contribution each woman might make. Now that Zofia Grzegorzewska was dead, Marianna said solemnly, it was left to the two of them to honour their youthful pledge to save Poland. Resistance work was not enough, she argued. They needed to be politically active. 'She always had leftist convictions,' Elżbieta sighed.[32] Her own more pragmatic view was to focus on winning the war.

Elżbieta was now smuggling messages and reports between cities several times a week. She deliberately took circuitous train routes to evade the most thorough checks and avoid appearing too often at the same stations. Sometimes she had to wait for hours as troop trains and forced labour transports took priority on the tracks. In the evenings, stuck alone on platforms or in waiting rooms, she sang patriotic songs under her breath. One morning, she was astounded to see a Polish officer with a German orderly behind, carrying his case. So sure was she of her compatriot's treachery that she sang the refrain from a resistance song from the window of her coach as it pulled past. Seeing the man's back stiffen, she cursed her foolishness, but still her luck held.

German security tightened that spring as the occupying forces strained to keep their grip on a country now blooming with resistance graffiti. Many people were taking extraordinary risks to prepare for the Allied offensive that they expected any day. In Warsaw, one courageous woman disguised a rifle as a sapling, hidden among sprouting twigs wrapped in brown paper.* Annoyed at the space she was taking on their tram, a joker beside her commented that she might as well be carrying a gun. Discovery would have meant execution but it seemed so unlikely that she braved it out. Later, the same woman evaded a street round-up by hiding on the coupling between two tram carriages.

Ever more women *were* disappearing into Gestapo cells, however. Within a year of the invasion, 'the average life of a liaison woman did not exceed a few months', one courier reported, and every Pole shuddered when they heard diesel trucks hurtling down the streets.[33] 'The sound of grinding brakes is often the forerunner of tragedy for those within earshot', a diplomat at the American Embassy wrote, and those left to continue the work were 'always in danger'.[34]

Elżbieta was now travelling on 'borrowed fingers' – identity papers that relied on fingerprints rather than photographs. Increasingly, she also seemed to be on borrowed time. It was Topol who asked her to smuggle not only reports, but also a large amount of cash across the General Government border. With the help of railway staff, male resistance couriers could wear borrowed uniforms and carry a staff key to open locked doors. Military night trains sometimes even 'felt safer than the streets of Warsaw', one such courier wrote, as few border guards wanted to disturb carriages full of their own sleeping soldiers.[35] Elżbieta's travel was of necessity more complex. Taking a train to the last station before the frontier, she asked a local friend to carry the money over the 'green border' – using little-known forest paths. She herself would cross by train, 'more or less clean' as she put it, before collecting the cash on the far side.[36]

When Elżbieta talked about her 'friends' in the resistance, many were indeed devoted to her – but some would later qualify this description. Most of the women 'were ready to support her in conspiracy operations', one later wrote, but others 'were forced by the heroine to

---

* Name unknown, but a friend of Teresa 'Grazyna' Kleniewska-Karska. See Marek Stella-Sawicki (ed.) *First to Fight, Poland's Contribution to the Allied Victory in World War Two* (2009), p.223.

participate in that risky work'.[37] It was not that Elżbieta used threats or blackmail to get people to do her bidding, but rather that her total immersion in the resistance meant she found it hard to imagine that others might have different priorities. 'Hatred of the Germans, a desire to fight them, and most of all nostalgia for the loss of the independent Polish state', one courier wrote, 'did not leave much room in the souls of ordinary people for anything else.'[38] Elżbieta was one of these 'ordinary' people, and her plans were usually communicated as a fait accompli that few could resist, even if it meant risking their lives. 'A friend' in Elżbieta's eyes, her colleague clarified, might be better described as 'a woman useful in [her] ventures'.[39]

On this occasion, Elżbieta's 'friend' agreed to take the reports but not the money, which was bulky and harder to hide. As a result, Elżbieta was still carrying the cash when she caught her train. Half an hour later, as they approached the frontier, the passengers were informed they were to be subject to personal searches. Feeling her skin redden, Elżbieta made her way to the toilet cubicle at the end of her coach. Once locked in, she tied the banknotes firmly into a wedge, leaving the end of the string trailing as she pushed the lot deep into a cavity behind the air vents.

She was still flushed and her shirt was damp with sweat when she hurried back to her seat. Perhaps it was this that caught the guard's attention, or maybe she was just unlucky. Either way, she was among those ordered off the train for further checks. Standing towards the back of the selected group, Elżbieta watched as a battered inkpad was pulled from a desk drawer and each person was fingerprinted to check against their papers. When her turn came, she was, she said, 'sweating like a mouse'.[40] Moving her finger, she smudged her prints. With the German passengers impatient to depart, Elżbieta was released with the others. With hindsight, she chose to report that 'it wasn't dangerous'.[41]

When she tried to return to her carriage, however, Elżbieta found that it had now been reserved for Germans. As her 'borrowed fingers' were for a Pole, it was impossible for her to retrieve the money. 'I did not do well,' she conceded glumly.[42] Memorising the coach number, she sent one of her former students, a young woman called Irena Klasa, to retrieve the money when the train reached Częstochowa.[43] Irena did very well. Having boarded the right carriage and found the string in the toilet vent, she was horrified to discover the wedge of notes jammed tight, swollen from the damp. When the bundle finally emerged, many of the notes were badly torn. 'She was so cheeky,' Elżbieta later laughed.[44] Taking the ripped notes to a German bank, Irena claimed that her dog had savaged them. The clerk exchanged the money. 'These were all minor adventures,' Elżbieta concluded, although impressed by Irena's creativity, she promoted her to serve as her own liaison officer.[45] From then on, whenever Elżbieta had parcels too large to be easily hidden, she walked the forest paths herself.

That spring, Elżbieta received a guarded letter from her mother. Reading between the lines there was wonderful news: Klara and Egon had both been in touch. Egon was teaching German in a small town near Toruń, where his language skills, fair looks and crooked arm led many to assume he was a Volksdeutsche deemed unfit for military service. Their cousin Leonard had also reached his home town, although only to be taken hostage there by an ethnic-German 'self-protection league'. Local Germans had set up such groups at the start of the war, fearing Polish aggression. Ten of the hostages in Leonard's group were shot in the town square in a reprisal action, but three weeks later he and the others were simply deported into the General Government.

Klara had stayed in Soviet-annexed territory in the east, waiting for her fiancé to return after his demobilisation. It was some months before she accepted that he was not coming and, with a heavy heart, had made her way alone across the two borders that now separated her from Toruń. She arrived exhausted, depressed, filthy and, above all, angry. Her mother bustled around her, fed her, loved her and grew ever more anxious. Klara was not prepared to tolerate the Germanisation of her home town, the detention of civilians or the deportations for forced labour.* To her mother's horror, her 'unbridled language' drew growing attention to the family.[46] Whenever there was a knock at their door, she would bundle Klara into a cupboard before opening up.

Elżbieta hurried home. At first, she and Klara held each other close. Then they sat at arm's length on the old family couch, assessing the changes they saw in each other. Elżbieta had become the soldier she had long aspired to be, but Klara had lost her fiancé and with him all her imagined future. Elżbieta had rarely seen anger of such power and purpose as in her younger sister that day. This was something to be

---

* Several hundred Toruń citizens, arrested in March 1940, were shot that August. Among them was Jadwiga Kowalska, a PWK member who had survived for six months on the 'delicious' marmalade, poppyseed cake and cocoa sent by her family.

harnessed. Without hesitation, she swore Klara into the resistance.

Elżbieta found a room for her sister with Nina Kowalska, the friend with whom she had fled Lwów the year before. Fluent in German, Klara quickly found office work where she might pick up useful information, and also started serving as a messenger. Klara was small fry, not in much more danger than most Polish civilians, but no one was ever safe. In May 1940, Teresa Delekta narrowly avoided arrest by checking herself into a hospital as an epilepsy patient. The next month, twenty-nine locals were detained and executed by firing squad. After a few weeks, Teresa returned to work.

Elżbieta was travelling on the papers of a wealthy Silesian woman who worked in banking when an officious Gestapo man decided he did not like her identity documents. Pushed into a border-control hut, she saw the door shake its frame as it was locked from the other side. Elżbieta was carrying the latest intelligence reports hidden inside a clothes brush. She did not know much about her assumed identity, and knew even less about banking. 'Dear God!' she thought, her adrenaline pumping. 'What can I do, what can I do?'[47]

The hut's only window was firmly jammed shut. Grabbing a metal ruler from the desk, she forced it open, squeezed through and ran into the forest beyond. Determined to put some distance between herself and the border, she blindly charged on, praying there were no dogs on her heels. An hour later she met a forester's wife, by chance a PWK veteran, who offered her help. This time it was all Elżbieta could do not to burst into tears. It 'was the first really serious mortal danger' she had faced, she later confessed. 'They would have shot me straight away . . . there was no question of looking for evidence and so on, just smack and it would be over.'[48]

After so many months of risking her life, and the lives of others, to report on the appalling situation inside her homeland, Elżbieta could not understand why there had been so little response from the Western Allies. Despite having declared war on Nazi Germany, the British referred to this period as the 'Bore War' – a pun on the previous Boer War – or as the *Sitzkrieg*, meaning 'Sitting War', suggesting participants were putting their feet up after the German Blitzkrieg. Eventually the American term, the 'Phoney War', became widely accepted. In France, they called it the 'funny' or 'strange' war, the *Drôle de Guerre*. In Poland, by contrast, the period since September 1939 had simply been the start of brutal, total war.

On 10 May 1940, Hitler's forces invaded Holland, Belgium and France. Polish servicemen were now fighting on French soil and in the skies above, alongside their allies in the Battle of France. General Sikorski, the Polish prime minister and commander-in-chief, had already flown to London to liaise with Churchill. Communications between him and the Home Army were now further hampered as the rest of the Polish cabinet joined the mass exodus from France and fled across the Channel. The whole government was eventually squashed into the Polish Embassy in London, at 47 Portland Place, where two armchairs and a table formed the domain of the Ministry of Foreign Affairs, and a couple of more delicate seats served the Ministry for Information. Sikorski had already reserved his own office by fixing his calling card on the door, outside of which the three young daughters of the ambassador could often be heard sliding down the staircase handrail.

Elżbieta was anxiously following the news through the BBC. She spent much of May in Warsaw, now in a linen dress, the wooden soles of her shoes clacking along the streets as she moved between various apartments, giving and receiving information. At end of the month, she visited Marianna again. Her illness having ruled out further courier work, Marianna showed Elżbieta her impressive new skills at coding messages for radio transmission. When the work was done, they shared some 'wonderfully sunny days on the beach', Elżbieta later told a friend, referring to the broad, sandy bank of the River Świder where it joins the Vistula.[49] A thousand miles away, on the broader beaches of Dunkirk, almost 200,000 men from the British Expeditionary Force, 140,000 French and Belgian troops and, along the western seaboard of France, another 30,000 Poles, were at that moment being evacuated under enemy fire. France had been defeated and the Allied forces driven from the continent.

Until the fall of France, Elżbieta's reports had been crunched by Home Army intelligence officers in Warsaw, with the crucial details transmitted to Angers by radio and the rest hidden in the bags of brave couriers travelling in relay to France through Romania, Hungary, Yugoslavia and Italy. Orders and information on the wider war were sent back by return. In the words of one intelligence officer, 'the ability to communicate with the government-in-exile was of prime importance to the leaders of the underground'.[50] Without it, the resistance would have been fighting blind, responding to enemy provocation rather than enacting a co-ordinated strategy of attack. The fall of France brought this communication to an abrupt end.

Elżbieta and Marianna now stayed up late, discussing how the war might yet be won. Britain was relying on the Royal Navy to blockade, the RAF to bomb, and the people of occupied Europe to sabotage and undermine the enemy. It was not at all clear how long they might hold out. There was no more talk of a Polish national uprising to support an Allied offensive and, Elżbieta noticed, 'the more uncertain and opportunistic' members of the local resistance, as she judged them, had simply stopped showing up.

'And then, when no one in Poland expected it, Winston Churchill's voice rang out', one Home Army officer later wrote. 'A strong voice full of energy, determination and faith in victory . . .'[51] Britain would fight on. Unbeknownst to Elżbieta, among other initiatives Churchill had approved the creation of a secret organisation known as the Special Operations Executive, or SOE, to arm, train and help coordinate the resistance in occupied countries. General Sikorski had likewise ordered the formation of a Polish special forces parachute unit from the cream of the veterans now in Britain who had already seen action in Poland and France. Known as the Cichociemni, or the 'Silent Unseen' in English, this elite force would be funded and trained in Britain, where SOE regarded them as their P (for Polish) Section. For now, however, these plans were unknown outside London. In Poland, Elżbieta could only be sure of one thing: she too would keep up the fight. As resistance communications had been severed between Poland and France, she would offer to create new routes. If necessary, she decided, she would use her language skills to take the fight into Nazi Germany itself.

4

Navigating Nazi Germany
(July 1940–April 1942)

Elżbieta had been German before. When she was born, in 1909, her ancient home town of Toruń had been annexed into the German Empire. German was her first language. It was her only language until Poland regained independence after the First World War. Not only did she still speak German with no trace of a Polish accent, she sometimes thought in German, and her written Polish occasionally borrowed German grammar structure. German idioms, customs and traditions came as second nature to her. As a child she had even been known as 'Liza', the German diminutive of her name, all while knowing that deep inside she was truly Polish. As a result, Elżbieta had developed the most important qualities of what, in the shadowy world of the resistance, was known as a perfect legend: a second identity that could now enable her to pass through enemy territory as a local, so long as she had the right papers.

When Elżbieta learnt that the Home Army had established a secret resistance cell inside Nazi Germany and needed couriers to smuggle material between Warsaw and Berlin, she immediately volunteered. With her language skills, conveniently fair colouring, and many months' experience of crossing wartime borders, she should have been a shoo-in for the role. Elżbieta, however, was also female. In the summer of 1940, Polish women were not being considered for this astonishingly dangerous work. Should permission be given, she was told, the secret confirmation phrase would be, 'the white dress is ready'.[1] Elżbieta was not a white dress kind of woman, but she had learnt the importance of orders. All she could do was prepare.

Two hundred women were now sworn into the Silesian Coal network. Handing over command to Teresa Delekta, her 'hardworking, devoted' deputy, Elżbieta returned to Warsaw, delivering her last reports on arrival.[2] The capital was bathed in August sunshine, but its streets and parks were now full of German soldiers. Elżbieta was glad to receive her new assignment just a few days later – it was not German courier work, but pioneering 'diversionary action' inside Berlin itself. First, however, she was to report for training at one of Warsaw's municipal slaughterhouses.

The light in the abattoir, near a vodka factory on the east bank of the Vistula, came from arched windows high up near the rafters. Rusty light-fittings and old pipework had leaked dark stains down the walls, and drains on the wet floor were filled with butchery tools. Elżbieta's instructor fetched a wooden crate, and a scrawny rat stuck its head out of a small hole cut in one side. Elżbieta immediately felt apprehensive. There were huge colonies of rats in the rubbish dumps of Berlin. After injecting some with bacteria, she was to release them near German barracks – but there would be no controlling the disease-ridden rodents once they had been set free. 'I didn't like it,' Elżbieta admitted.[3]

The Geneva Convention of 1925 prohibited the use of chemical and biological weapons, but in 1940 General Rowecki, now commander of the Home Army, reported that he had 'created a special unit concerned with chemical-technical-bacteriological operations'.[4] Nazi records would later reveal details of intercepted packages containing biological agents posted to German cities, but no casualty numbers. Elżbieta, however, refused to take part. From now on, she would never be uncritical of resistance policy.

As the summer slid into autumn, Elżbieta's cousin Leonard was also sworn into the Home Army. Within weeks, that October he was abruptly woken at three in the morning by the Gestapo kicking down his front door. Marched to their car with a revolver at his back, Leonard was held with nine others in the windowless basement of Warsaw's Pawiak prison. Luckier than most, his German language skills meant he could act as a translator, and eventually he was given a bunk and better rations. He would nevertheless spend five months in Pawiak, enduring repeat interrogations as his cellmates were taken away for execution.

Elżbieta finally learnt that her 'white dress' was ready as temperatures plummeted and the first snows of winter 1940 settled on the Polish capital.* Her new instructions were to report to Emilia Malessa,

---

* Maria Wittek and Henryk Kowalówka, aka 'Topol', had supported Elżbieta's candidacy. She was informed by Maria Szczurowska, Zofia Franio's partner.

the head of *Zagroda*, meaning 'Farmstead', the Home Army's overseas communications team.* Elżbieta had heard of Emilia jokingly referred to as 'the farmyard woman', conjuring up images of a stout lady in galoshes carrying a pail of swill, but she had never met her.[5]

Rendezvousing in Warsaw's Old Town, Elżbieta was surprised to see an elegant lady whose well-cut coat lent her a distinctive silhouette. Emilia had wavy chestnut hair falling to her shoulders beneath a stylish felt hat, expensive leather gloves, and fashionable shoes whose heels were now rapping on the snowy pavement. She looked more like the impatient wife of a German officer than a farmworker or resistance leader. Elżbieta hurried over, feeling unusually intimidated. Ten minutes later, with only their passwords exchanged, the two women entered an undistinguished residential building and descended a small staircase to 'somewhere in the depths'.[6] 'I've got her,' Emilia announced as she shrugged off her coat.[7] Four faces turned towards them and Elżbieta was delighted to recognise them all.† 'The joy,' she said, was that 'all of us were working in one cell, all in one department.'[8] Stepping into the room, she introduced herself . . . as 'Zo'.

Elżbieta had known she would need a new nom-de-guerre to be sworn into Farmstead. When asked why she chose Zo, she usually replied that it was in honour of Zofia Zawacka, the 'beloved wife' of her brother Ali, who had taken her own life when it was clear that he was dying.[9] Occasionally, however, Elżbieta confessed that 'the name Zofia has another meaning for me. It is the name of Grzegorzewska. The one who was actually the first victim of the war.'[10] This was her friend who had been killed in the Pruszków train disaster. Not wanting to be thought sentimental, she sometimes added that as 'Zo' was just two letters it was also perfect for telegrams. In fact, wireless operators often mistook 'Zo' for '70', causing Elżbieta to reiterate frequently, 'It was "Zo" from Zofia.'[11] Her choice of name was important to her. Not only deeply personal, it was also indicative of the value she placed on the loyalty, service and commemoration of women.

Zo, as she was now known, was lodged with a member of the

---

* *Zagroda* (Farmstead, Farm) was also known as Zenobia (a female name), *Załoga* (Crew, Team) and Łza (Tear). For consistency, it remains Farmstead in this book.
† Ewa Korczyńska and Maria Szerocka (couriers to Budapest); Eugenia Litwinow, a 'confident woman . . . a tomboy' (smuggled radio equipment); and Jadwiga Puchalska (communications across eastern Poland).

Farmstead team who wrote reports at night, muffling the sound of her typewriter beneath a pile of blankets.* It was here that Emilia introduced her to the secrets of long-distance courier work; the various border crossings into Nazi Germany, and her false papers, identities and passwords. Most of it had to be learnt by heart. At first Emilia remained quite formal, something Zo accepted as entirely appropriate. 'She always inspired respect,' Zo felt, but over time 'she became cordial, friendly.'[12]

'Try to imagine a brilliant, intelligent, elegant woman with a good figure and quiet appearance, who could easily win your sympathies', another member of Farmstead wrote. 'This was Emilia Malessa. She combined female subtlety with military courage.'[13] The same age as Zo, Emilia also came from a family with a tragic past. Her grandfathers had served in the uprisings of the 1860s, being sent to Siberia for their pains. Both of her parents had died before she turned thirteen, and she had lost two brothers in the Polish–Soviet War. Left in the care of her remaining brothers, Emilia had quickly earnt her own money, bought her own car, and married a distinguished public servant who would later leave Poland with the government. Having watched her surviving brothers sign up, she began her own military service on 1 September 1939, as a driver.

Emilia's 'inexhaustible resources of entrepreneurship' were quickly recognised during the occupation.[14] Having played a key role in establishing Farmstead, the foreign communications unit, she was appointed as its head. Farmstead was responsible for sending all 'mail' to the exiled government. This included anything too sensitive or cumbersome to be sent by encrypted radio message, including maps, film footage, original documents, microfilmed intelligence reports and, once, an anti-tank rifle requested by the French. Successful couriers had returned with orders, information, money and materials. Others were never seen again.

With the fall of France, and Romania and Hungary's alignment with Nazi Germany in November that same year, new routes to Britain were desperately needed. Towards the end of 1940, one courier travelled from London to Warsaw via Portugal and Egypt.† By the

---

* Jaga Spasowska, arrested in 1942.
† Emissaries Kazimierz Iranek-Osmecki and August Emil Fieldorf both took routes via North Africa. Fieldorf's flight route followed the Nile, hence his nom-de-guerre of 'Nil'.

time he arrived, his information was obsolete. Emilia was now looking at routes through Switzerland and Sweden, but Nazi Germany itself offered a faster potential solution. Zo was to test this new route.

Zo first set off for Germany in late December 1940. Travelling with her was a young woman called Zofia Gapińska, a member of the Berlin unit that Zo had refused to join. Zofia had chosen the pseudonym of 'Ela'. Each woman smiled to herself, unable to reveal that the other had chosen a diminutive of her real name – Elżbieta was 'Zo', and Zofia was 'Ela'. It was only years later that Zo learnt Ela's real name and noted sadly that it was 'as if we had exchanged names, and also fates'.[15]

Zo and Ela carried forged *Kennkarten*, the green-grey foldout papers that identified them as German citizens. These had been meticulously copied from real documents stolen by pickpockets. Photos were stuck or stapled on, false names and details added, and real fingerprints inked into place before the documents were appropriately weathered. Using a variation of her own first name, Zo was now travelling as Elizabeth von Braunneg, an oil company secretary. As oil was a strategic war industry, her journey was quite credible. She kept her Kennkarte in her purse, along with her forged travel permit, a couple of photos and an old bus ticket from Berlin. The secret documents she was smuggling were rather 'primitively packed', she felt, in a part-used tin of toothpaste that could be unscrewed from the back.[16]

From Warsaw the women headed across the General Government border by train. Zo had not travelled in a first-class 'Germans Only' carriage before. The windows were curtained and the space dimly lit. The harshest winter in a century was on its way but, although a blast of icy air whipped in whenever the carriage door opened, the compartment was surprisingly warm. One glance at their papers was enough at the checks and, changing trains in German-annexed territory, the women headed on to Berlin.

⚓

By now the 'Phoney War' had been bombed out of existence. After the fall of France, Hitler had turned his attention to Britain. Between July and October 1940, in what became known as the Battle of Britain, 145 Polish airmen served in the skies alongside thousands of their allies.* Polish pilots were now fêted on British streets, their courage and sacrifice strengthening the bond between the two nations. That August, RAF Bomber Command began night-time raids on Berlin. By November, the Luftwaffe was targeting London, British port cities and industrial centres. Civilian casualties were mounting on both sides. While incensed to see German airspace invaded, Hitler was still confident of victory and the Berlin that Zo and Ela descended into from their train reflected this angry but defiant, almost righteous, mood.

Careful to look casual, Zo did not stare at the swastika flags decorating the station, which in any case also hung across much of Poland. Nor did she baulk at the U-Bahn stations with names such as Adolf-Hitler-Platz. What struck her was simply how healthy people looked, without the pinch she had got used to seeing in every Polish face.

She and Ela went first to Ela's contact, a tall, taciturn man who burnt sections of Ela's report as soon as he had read them.† After a few words the women left, walking briskly down the tree-lined Siegesallee, Victory Avenue, towards the Tiergarten. Berlin's famous park was filled with women walking arm in arm under the leafless winter trees, and well-wrapped children sliding down the icy paths. Within a week, the first snow would settle in the city and hundreds more people would head to the Tiergarten to skate on the frozen ponds. Ela said that she sometimes met Gestapo officers there and had 'supposedly liquidated one of them by giving him a poisoned cigarette', Zo later wrote, unable to withhold a note of scepticism.[17] Before they parted, the women found the small confectionery shop that was to be their contact point, and Ela headed inside.

Zo's orders were to contact 'Kuba'. Captain Alfons Jakubianiec was an intelligence officer working as a translator at the Manchurian Embassy, a mansion dominated by the Japanese Embassy next door. At around thirty years old, Kuba was 'a handsome man', Zo said, using her default description for most men in the resistance, polite but light on substance.[18] Kuba took her mail without a word. Later, he would pass it to a Japanese contact who regularly flew to Sweden. From there, a Scottish aircraft left for Britain once a week. Within

---

* There were two Polish fighter squadrons, 302 and 303. Although delayed in joining the battle, 303 scored more kills than any other squadron. Their leading ace was the Czech pilot Josef František. The Poles also fielded bomber squadrons with the RAF.
† Major Franciszek Pawela, nom-de-guerre 'Lech'.

seven days, the intelligence Zo had smuggled into the heart of Nazi Germany was safely with the Polish government in London. It was an audacious operation, but now the fastest communication route between Poland and Britain.

In return, Kuba gave Zo the latest intelligence from London, along with some cash from Stockholm. When he left the arrangements for transporting the money to her, she made a mental note that Kuba was 'enterprising but not careful enough'.[19] He did at least provide her with the address of a safe house for the night. It was dark by the time Zo left the embassy. Almost immediately she had to jump out of the path of a car whose headlights were covered with blue filter paper to comply with the Berlin blackout. In Warsaw few people travelled at night. Here she quickly learnt to be alert for shadowy vehicles and the bobbing red ends of cigarettes belonging to cyclists and pedestrians. Her room was provided by a White Russian, 'a disgusting woman' in Zo's opinion, with no love for the Nazis but no great affection for the Poles either.[20] Zo left early the next morning.

Emilia Malessa was waiting in a small café on Warsaw's Iron Gate Square. Once painted by Canaletto, the plaza took its name from the gates of the beautiful Saxon Garden, one of the world's first public parks when it opened in the early eighteenth century. Now, as she hurried across the icy square, Zo sheltered from the wind in the lee of the high brick wall that formed one edge of the ghetto. Almost half a million members of Poland's Jewish community were trapped inside, and she could hear the calls of street vendors trying to raise some business within.

Perched in a corner of the café, from where she could see the door and leave through the kitchen, Emilia was warming her hands around a cup of black tea. The place was packed, and Zo had to jockey with the waitress as she pushed her way around the tables. Emilia beamed at her, impressed. Her new Berlin courier had made her first delivery and was back with cash and new orders within forty-eight hours. Although demanding, Emilia often sparkled 'with fireworks of wit, charming in words and gestures, cordial to all around her', one Home Army captain wrote.[21] Zo was now treated to this second side of Emilia, although she was not sure which side she preferred.

Emilia impressed everyone with her 'exceptional beauty, elegance [and] great manners'.[22] Zo was short, plain and could be brusque. Provided that her outfits suited her given identity, she was content.

When required to look elegant, Emilia provided her with the appropriate outfit and lipstick. Similarly, Zo's only interest in men was in their value as fellow soldiers. Her most intimate friendships were all with women. 'I was all about service,' she liked to claim.[23] In contrast, Emilia thrived on male company. Aware that she was 'super attractive', her flirtatious nature led to 'a lot of arguments and fights because everyone wanted to be special . . .', Zo noticed, 'and jealousy could drive them to become unkind.'[24] Both women put duty first, but ultimately Emilia had a weakness in her attraction to men that Zo did not.

The first difficulty Zo faced in her new role was the weather. As temperatures plummeted across Germany, railway points froze, and rail and road traffic ground to a halt. It was late February 1941 before the melting snow started slipping from the city's roofs. Throughout that year, Zo rushed between Warsaw and Berlin 'like a whirlwind' one friend wrote, or in another's words, 'like a weaver's shuttle'.[25] She always travelled under her own steam but never under her own name. She had specific clothes and hairstyles for each set of papers, and she became used to sailing through checks and not glancing back.

Zo usually returned from Germany within a few days, bringing back her observations on changing travel regulations, rationing and morale. Increasingly, she also brought some of the money, sewn inside her clothes, that was needed to buy everything from arms and medicines to documents and silence. The intelligence she took the other way was eagerly awaited not only by her own government but by the British. The War Office in London even added their own requests. After one Berlin air raid, Zo was asked to walk around the city and later discreetly mark up a map to help assess the accuracy of the campaign. 'The English know almost everything about the results of their attacks on Germany', Joseph Goebbels, the Nazi minister of propaganda, sullenly complained to his diary.[26]

⚓

In London, the Polish government had now exchanged their cramped rooms in the embassy for more spacious quarters in buildings across London. In the Rubens Hotel, the young officers of the Polish Sixth Bureau, responsible for communications with Poland, occupied the well-appointed rooms once decorated for the staff of Buckingham Palace, just a stone's throw away.

Meanwhile, in Scotland the first of the Polish troops being prepared as Cichociemni, the Silent Unseen, had already completed their parachute training. Colin Gubbins, formerly with the British Military Mission in Poland, was now head of the British SOE that took the Silent Unseen under their wing. Recognising that the Home Army was 'already well organised under the nose of the occupying German forces', Gubbins channelled significant funding their way and the first Silent Unseen officer was parachuted home in February 1941.[27]* 'The sight of that first German uniform' so shocked him, he later wrote, that 'a curse exploded within me.'[28] What shocked Gubbins was the evident 'sheer impracticability of attempting to equip an underground army in Poland by means of air sorties from the UK'.[29] There would never be enough aircraft, and within a few weeks there were not even enough hours of darkness to fly to Poland undetected. Without reliable air links, courier routes on the ground remained vital.

⚓

Zo was now travelling to Berlin at least once a month, spending the Warsaw weeks in between with Marianna. They celebrated her name-day that year with potato salad, bread and black-market beetroot marmalade, all washed down with 'carrot tea'.[30]† More often, though, Zo found her friend wrapped in a blanket because there was no fuel, or occasionally restoring the feeling to her fingers beside an electric heater so she could carry on with her coding work. 'She had beautiful hands,' Zo noticed, and when messages were urgent, 'this frail girl would sit up all night and cipher.'[31]

Marianna was the only person with whom Zo could talk freely. Their conversations, peppered with resistance gossip, helped her to make sense of their service. It was immensely important to Zo that she was not just 'the heartless executor' of orders from above.[32] She needed to know the value of her work, and 'we were never uncritical of our superiors,' she laughed. 'Quite the opposite . . . we always wanted to understand their shortcomings.'[33] Maria Wittek was brilliant but had still not secured official military status for women, limiting their

* Józef Zabielski, nom-de-guerre 'Zbik'.
† Name-days, celebrated in many Christian countries, mark the Church calendar day associated with a person's baptismal name, such as a saint's day.

potential contribution. Emilia Malessa was a remarkable organiser, but could often be 'official, despotic and authoritative, hating opposition'.[34]

It was Marianna who suggested that Zo return to education as a way to relax between missions. Zo had already been coaching a few of her former students, including her liaison officer, Irene Klasa. Soon, she was also teaching mathematics at two 'secret schools' and studying adult education herself.[*] It was work that helped to sustain her when the resistance faced painful reversals. That spring, the diversionary unit in Berlin was destroyed. Ela was arrested and would later die in Ravensbrück, the Nazi concentration camp for women sixty miles north of the German capital. Her reticent Berlin contact was executed the following summer. Deeply affected by the news of these arrests, Zo also realised that had she not objected at her slaughterhouse training, she might have been serving alongside them.

Doubts about Kuba's security measures were also growing. Having agreed that he seemed 'incautious', Emilia encouraged Zo to explore alternative routes to Berlin.[35] She already constantly changed her travel arrangements, never buying a through ticket. Sometimes she stopped over at her sister Klara's Katowice apartment, with friends in Poznań, or occasionally with her parents in Toruń. She usually used a forged Volksdeutsche identity card on the Polish side of the frontier and a Reichsdeutsche[†] card when in Germany, and she had 'all sorts of tricks' for crossing borders.[36] On trains, she could tell when checks were coming by the fidgeting of her fellow passengers, 'hiding things here and there'.[37] She also learnt a few good places to cross on foot, religiously avoiding the more formidable river frontiers, where it was harder to escape if required. There was 'always this fear that they would catch me . . . it was always dangerous', she admitted, but she hadn't been stopped for almost a year.[38]

Emilia now charged Zo with also finding new routes west. The obvious starting point was Silesia but, for security, she kept her distance from Teresa Delekta and the Coal intelligence network. Teresa already had her own security worries. In May, a passer-by had warned

* Zo's teacher was Professor Helena Radlińska, affectionately known as 'Grandma' on account of her wisdom, age and infirmity.

† 'Reichsdeutsche' referred to German citizens, as opposed to 'Volksdeutsche' which was people with German ethnicity who were citizens of other countries.

her that she was being followed. Turning into a side street, she had ripped up the report she was carrying and swallowed the pieces; 'not easy', she admitted, 'as my mouth was dry'.[39] She and Zo both knew that the risks they took would only grow by association, so, instead of looking to the PWK, Zo went to her pre-war teaching contacts. Within a few weeks she had established a new Farmstead outpost, which she christened 'Circus'.

The Circus ringmaster was a teacher and Scout leader called Eleonora Rostalska, who lived in Silesia but worked in Alsace and northern France. 'Naturally she was delighted to help,' Zo believed.[40] Routes were rapidly organised from Alsace to Paris, Bern and Zurich. The arrival of a postcard notified the team of when a courier was on their way, and a twelve-year-old lad received confirmation of their arrival while out on his milk round. Within a few months, a Farmstead courier could travel from Berlin to Bern in a couple of days. Zo also recruited her former colleagues and pupils from the Raciborz boarding school for German girls of Polish descent. In the four years since she had taught there, these women had set up their homes across the Reich. One by one, she visited them. Stefania Horst was astounded to find her adored former teacher on her Berlin doorstep one spring afternoon in 1941. Within an hour, Zo had recruited both her and her young husband, Dominik, into Farmstead. Then, choosing a busy patisserie as their contact point, they started building a new resistance cell in the German capital.

ॐ

As Zo was growing her networks, her cousin Leonard was among the Pawiak prisoners selected for Auschwitz. One evening, he was with a few hundred men being herded into a cattle car at a Warsaw railway siding. The next day, he staggered out into a yard, beaten forward by bullwhips and rifle butts, to become one of thousands of starving camp inmates. His life now depended on his ability to labour; an ability daily degraded by the appalling camp conditions. One of Leonard's first chores was to shake out the prisoners' thin bedding after the vermin in the barracks had been gassed with Zyklon B. As he worked, he could feel a thick layer of dead fleas and lice 'crackle like broken glass' beneath his feet.[41] A few weeks later, the same gas would be used to murder the first Russian prisoners to arrive at the camp.

Bulgaria signed the Tripartite Pact, initially negotiated between Germany, Italy and Japan, in March 1941. After considerable resistance, Yugoslavia joined the Axis that April, having been invaded by Germany. On 22 June, supercharged by their recent victories, Nazi German forces tore through Stalin's ill-prepared border defences during Operation Barbarossa, and started ploughing relentlessly on towards Leningrad. Hitler's betrayal came as a catastrophic shock to Stalin.* Twelve hours later, Churchill broadcast the offer of British help, leading to an Anglo–Soviet Treaty of Mutual Assistance. Heavily leant on by the British Foreign Office, Władysław Sikorski, the Polish prime minister and commander-in-chief, was now in the unenviable position of having to re-establish diplomatic relations with the Soviets, who had invaded and annexed eastern Poland in September 1939.

The Sikorski–Maisky Agreement, named after the Polish leader and the Soviet Ambassador to Britain, was signed on 30 July.† The terms included an 'amnesty' for all Poles detained and deported since the Russian invasion. Released from Moscow's Lubyanka prison, General Władysław Anders set about creating an army from the survivors. By the end of the year, he had three divisions. Thousands of the Polish women also released from the gulags joined a new 'Women's Auxiliary Service', to be trained as nurses, secretaries and drivers. Although she had no military experience, Sikorski's own daughter was appointed as their commander.‡ Yet thousands more Polish officers, including Klara's fiancé, remained unaccounted for. As the weeks passed, the whereabouts of these missing men began to weigh ever more heavily on Polish–Soviet relations.

From the fall of France to the German invasion of the Soviet Union, Britain's main ally had been Poland. Although occupied, the country had never capitulated and her armed forces, both at home and abroad, were of considerable strategic significance. The realignment of the Soviet Union, with its vast resources, radically changed this dynamic, permanently relegating Poland from the Allied top table. There were also direct repercussions for clandestine resistance. 'Floods of soldiers

---

* Having seen Polish resistance film footage of preparations, smuggled out by Krystyna Skarbek aka Christine Granville, Churchill had warned Stalin about the imminent invasion. Stalin had not believed it.
† Ivan Maisky's name, Майский, can also be transliterated as Maysky and Mayski.
‡ Zofia Leśniowska.

milled about' in the stations, one Home Army officer wrote, and soon 'there were wounded soldiers everywhere'.[42] There were also ever more Gestapo moving among the crowds. Even the right papers could not help now if a lack of confidence or split-second hesitation aroused suspicions.

Kuba was detained in Berlin that July, just two days after Zo had brought him the latest mail. Later, it was rumoured that he had been 'extracting information from officers' wives' and Zo believed he was betrayed 'by the vengeful spouse of one of his agents'.[43] In fact, the Manchurian Embassy had been under German surveillance since the summer before. Nazi security men dressed as park workers, complete with gardening tools, had arrested Kuba during a clandestine exchange in the Tiergarten. Microfilm was found inside a clothes brush and some unopened toothpaste, both hiding places regularly used by Zo. The information on them detailed the political situation across occupied territory, Nazi military data and Polish resistance plans. The German armed forces supreme command was 'amazed at the accuracy of the figures . . . which were correct even to the most precise details'.[44] When a paragraph on German policy not yet enacted was found, they realised that the information could only have come from their own loose-tongued officers and concluded that, 'Polish women must have done excellent work among them.'[45] It was rare recognition for networks such as Zo's, but none they would have wanted.

After Kuba's arrest, Stefania and Dominik Horst took over some of the Berlin liaison work. Several options to replace the now defunct Japanese diplomatic postal route were frantically discussed, but Emilia Malessa was distracted by problems at the Swedish base. When she heard that a military attaché was bringing a large amount of dollars to the American Embassy in Berlin, she promptly dispatched Zo to collect it.

It was only as she boarded her train that Zo was given a slip of paper with the American Embassy address and her new password phrase. Having learnt these, she discreetly rolled up the paper and slid it into the hem of her skirt. The address was easy to remember but the phrase was complicated. When she checked again a few hours later, the slip of paper was gone. 'To lose a written address,' Zo knew, was 'the worst crime a courier can commit.'[46] Her risks were increasing. Already anxious, on arrival Zo botched the password phrase. The attaché looked at her suspiciously, then asked her to leave. For three hours Zo circled round the U-Bahn, wracking her brains for the exact phrase. Eventually, she returned to Warsaw empty-handed.

Emilia was not pleased. Hastily arranging a new password, she sent a male courier, one of her admirers, to collect the money.* The job was done in a few days, the American attaché even finding time to report how surprised he had been before to see 'some young lady, acting very badly'.[47] 'And then there was one more ugly remark,' Zo bridled. He said that the resistance must have 'had no one to send, except a woman'.[48] One mistake in a year of courier work had been taken as proof of women's inherent fallibility.

While happy to exploit the sexism, and any other weakness, of the Germans, Zo was incensed by the double standards she encountered among the Poles and their allies. She felt they should know better, given the women's invaluable service. Yet she saw that when a colleague corrected a male intelligence officer, he clearly 'could not stand the fact that the commander of the unit was a woman, and much better informed than he was'.[49]

When Zo was promoted to serve as Emilia's deputy, some of these men had to report to her. One, known as 'Sławek', 'was very fond of women', she knew; something that 'was always a difficulty with male officers'.[50] Zo did not mind that Sławek smuggled stockings and perfume on the side. 'It was better if he . . . was caught for smuggling than for conspiracy,' she conceded. 'It could even protect him.'[51] But he was sloppy with his arrangements, drawing attention to them all. Zo tried to discipline him, only to find that 'he couldn't stand that at all'.[52] So she made her concerns official, passing them up the line. Eventually, Sławek was sent to a male officer who clapped him on the back, laughing that, 'That's women for you!'[53] 'And that was the end of it,' Zo told a friend angrily. 'That was the attitude.'[54]

Later that summer, Zo received a desperate letter from her mother. The Gestapo had arrested Zo's beloved brother, Egon. The charges against him included listening to the foreign radio news, 'strengthening the spirit of the resistance' through propaganda, maliciously studying Hitler's book *Mein Kampf,* and holding resistance meetings under the guise of giving private language lessons.[55] In another letter, kept in the Gestapo files, Marianna Zawacka begged for her son's release. Her whole family was loyal to the German Reich, she swore.

---

* Tadeusz Niedbalski, aka 'Seweryn', was a Farmstead courier on routes west.

The Gestapo themselves described Egon as 'Aryan', 'blond' and speaking fluent German.[56] 'They hunted for such people,' Zo felt, 'they needed them.'[57] But when offered the chance to register as a Volksdeutsch, Egon would not sign up. 'It appears he would rather starve to death as a Pole than become a German', the Gestapo noted.[58]

Although reportedly keeping his answers 'careful and vague', Egon's interrogation did not go well.[59] Classified as 'presumptuous and defiant' and 'a stubborn Polish nationalist', he freely gave his opinion that 'the Germans call others barbaric but are themselves the worst barbarians on the earth'.[60] Adding that Hitler had an inflammatory eye-disease that 'makes him insane', he concluded his responses with his conviction that 'the Germans will lose this war'.[61] An official request was submitted to put him on the next train to Auschwitz.

Zo had always adored Egon. Making contact with the local resistance cell, she was given the right, and responsibility, to attempt a rescue. In her head she carried the noms-de-guerre and addresses of hundreds of resisters, vital courier routes and safe houses. Not knowing whether she would be able to withstand torture, she knew she could not risk her comrades' lives, and all their work, on some ill-prepared attempt. Yet within weeks of his arrest, Egon was transported to Auschwitz. Klara was already helping arrange parcels of food, medicines and clothing for the prisoners at the camp. These were left in sheds and ditches, to be secretly collected by those sent out on work details. Some of the provisions may have reached Egon. 'Klara is good', he wrote, in the last note to reach the family.[62]

Klara was not the only one trying to help the enemies of the Third Reich. Poland's Jewish population had been persecuted from the moment the country was occupied. In early 1940, the SS began rounding up Polish Jews for forced labour. The Warsaw Ghetto was among those established that November, and Zo herself had recently seen and reported on the 'absolutely terrible' deportation of Jewish Poles from the small city of Sosnowiec in Silesia.[63] Yet Żegota, the secret 'Polish Council to Aid Jews',* would only become active in 1942, after the Nazi Wannsee Conference had produced plans for the so-called 'Final Solution'.

* The 'Polish Council to Aid Jews', known as Żegota, operated in German-occupied Poland from December 1942 to January 1945. The membership has since been honoured at Yad Vashem.

Until then, Poles who were not Jewish either felt unable to act, or denounced their Jewish neighbours, or risked their own lives to shelter them. Dr Zofia Franio, still organising female sapper units in Warsaw, was among the last group.* When she had fled Lwów in November 1939, she had been given a sweater and rucksack by a Jewish friend. Now she gave this woman shelter. Later, a teacher she knew arrived from Vilnius, where she had been denounced. Zofia gave her a bed too, securing false papers and employment for her until another safe house could be found.†

∬

As the autumn nights lengthened, the window for moonlit operations from Britain to Poland reopened, enabling a few more of the highly trained Silent Unseen paratroopers to be dropped back to their homeland. Emilia Malessa's Farmstead unit helped with the reception arrangements, selecting isolated fields, confirming dates and organising teams to meet the 'birds', as the parachutists were known. She did not often help to collect the men herself, but stories later circulated about her joining one reception committee in early November 1941.

'A young, tall, brown-haired woman' confirmed the drop 'while sipping steaming milk from a colourful mug', the story goes.[64] The leader of the committee 'would have been much more comfortable if she were a man', but could nevertheless not resist 'stealing furtive, admiring glances at her'.[65] That night, Emilia joined the men waiting under the trees to receive Jan Piwnik, a Silent Unseen paratrooper due to arrive with radio equipment, a welding set and $30,000.

Piwnik had had a tough childhood. His house had been destroyed during the First World War, when he was an infant. His parents, agricultural labourers, were the only people from their village to send their child to school. He got into fights, but he got good grades. In October 1939 he had escaped internment in Hungary and crossed the borders of Yugoslavia, Italy and France to rejoin the Polish forces. The following June, he secured passage for himself and his men on one of the last

* The sappers were combat engineers, trained to place or clear mines, build or demolish bridges, airfields, etc.
† Both of these women, M. Jędrzejewska and Andra Aszkenazy-Wirska, survived the war, as did Wirska's brother, but none of the rest of their families.

ships leaving for England, earning himself a place on the Silent Unseen training programme. Reports reveal that he excelled in shooting and sabotage, and he was deemed 'exceptionally well suited' to becoming a commander in the field.[66] A broken leg sustained during parachute training meant he was only now returning to Poland.

Shocked at finding himself met by a woman, legend has it that Piwnik swiftly pocketed his gun and held out his hand for 'a quick manly shake'.[67] He was, Emilia thought, an impressive chap. Dark hair swept back from his tanned face revealed an aquiline nose, sculpted lips and a single brow that ran like a rustic shelf above his deep-set eyes. Few in the resistance had so fitting a nom-de-guerre. Piwnik had chosen *Ponury*, which means 'gloomy' or 'grim', as in the reaper. He radiated a sullen ferocity.

That evening, sitting around a table in the dim light of a kerosene lamp, Emilia is said to have watched Ponury devouring eggs as he 'eyed her up shamelessly'.[68] Whatever the truth behind their first meeting, they were soon hungrily devouring each other. Zo knew that as well as the excitement of romance, her boss 'needed reassurance from others, someone warm around her'.[69] In this impressive young commander, Emilia had finally found the male appreciation, affirmation and authority she craved. For Ponury, she embodied the spirit of the Polish resistance: beautiful, noble and courageous.

While Emilia was finding love behind enemy lines, Zo was secretly being awarded the Cross of Valour. The honour was partly in recognition of her courageous courier journeys into Berlin, but also for helping to build vital new routes through Vienna and across southern Germany to the Swiss border, and through Flensburg towards Denmark. In place of a medal, she was handed a piece of paper stating simply that the award was made to 'Zo'. It was personally signed by 'Grot', the nom-de-guerre of General Rowecki.

Deeply impressed by female resisters, Rowecki now declared that 'women remaining in active military service at a time of underground warfare are soldiers facing the enemy'.[70] It did not give them the legal military status they needed, but it was a step in the right direction. Four months later, in February 1942, Rowecki officially redesignated the women's auxiliary as the Women's Military Service, appointing Maria Wittek as commander. Orders followed that Home Army leaders were to 'make comprehensive use' of them.[71]

Comprehensive use was already being made of Zo. America had

entered the war after the devastating Japanese bombing of their naval base in Pearl Harbor on 7 December 1941. The evacuation of the American Embassy in Berlin dramatically increased the pressure for new courier routes. By the following April, Zo had reportedly crossed wartime borders over one hundred times, after which she stopped counting. Keeping a tally was beginning to feel like tempting fate and she was not so confident that she thought her luck would hold forever. She had now seen German police handcuffing women in Berlin.

A couple of weeks later, Zo was sent to collect a final large transfer of US dollars from the German capital. Rowecki had specified that the money was to be supplied in the two- and five-dollar notes that could easily be spent without raising suspicion. As this would make the package immensely bulky, Emilia requested that the notes arrive already concealed for smuggling across the border. Unable to imagine the difficulties in the field, the London Sixth Bureau staff simply sent the cash in large blocks wrapped in brown paper, mostly in small denominations but some in $100 notes. They had 'no understanding of Farmstead's needs', Zo railed.[72] She had already had two missteps in collecting bulky dispatches of cash, once when she had had to leave money in the air vents of a train toilet, and again when she had botched the passwords in Berlin. This time she was determined there would be no mistakes. Retrieving her German identity papers, she set off on what would be her last courier mission to the capital of the Nazi Third Reich.

5

Evading the Gestapo
(May–August 1942)

Zo was exhausted. It was two in the morning and her task was only half done. Mechanically, she pasted another $10 note with a thin glue of precious flour and sugar dissolved in water. Then she stuck the note to the others now lining the inside of a cheap cardboard suitcase. She, Stefania and Dominik had been at this for hours, surrounded by bricks of American currency in the couple's small apartment in central Berlin. It was late May 1942. If anyone had arrived, their only hope would have been to throw a sheet over the scene: scant protection from the Gestapo. By dawn they had pasted in the final note and carefully replaced the marbled paper lining with its classic maker's label over the top.

'It was a primitive hiding place,' Zo admitted, making the suitcase surprisingly heavy, 'but there was no other way.'[1] She carefully put a couple of books into the now precious case to disguise its weight, then threw in her bathrobe and some underwear. Reaching for her coat and beret, she said her goodbyes and set off for the station, the case clunking against her leg. She was already a day late to deliver the much-needed cash to Warsaw.

The now familiar spans of Berlin's Schlesischer railway station echoed with activity. Wehrmacht troops filled the long platforms, leaning against their canvas packs, smoking and writing letters as they waited to be sent east. Despite their recent successes, Zo thought their morale appeared to be fairly low. As military transports took priority she settled in for a long journey, stowing her case on the overhead racks. In normal times, her poor-quality luggage would have stood out in a first-class carriage. Now, it was surrounded by similarly battered grips and old leather valises. She turned her thoughts to other things. Once she had handed over the money, she was to invigilate the first exams of the clandestine university in Warsaw, a landmark of which she was immensely proud. Her features took on a tired but not unhappy expression: once again she was Elizabeth von Braunneg, smart young oil company secretary, travelling for work.

Zo arrived at Poznań in the late afternoon. Knowing that the Gestapo kept Warsaw's main station under close observation, she changed trains for Katowice. Then she caught the tram to industrial Sosnowiec, where her sister Klara lived with Nina Kowalska. Although it was now past eleven, long after the curfew, she did not rush. Elizabeth von Braunneg was a card-carrying Reichsdeutsche, exempt from local restrictions, so she felt no anxiety on this home stretch. As usual, she picked up a pebble in her sister's front yard and threw it up to her second-floor window. Then she waited, but no light flicked on. She walked around, past the outside toilet where they sometimes hid a report on a beam, then threw up another small stone. It clattered back down to no effect. Something was wrong.

Climbing the stairs up to the first floor, Zo knocked at the downstairs neighbour's door, timidly at first, then more urgently. A face appeared, 'as pale as a wall' Zo noticed, her mind whirring, 'as white as a petal . . . as a corpse'.[2] Seeing her, the woman's eyes widened. Before she could slam the door shut, Zo had her foot over the threshold and was demanding answers. The Gestapo had arrived two days earlier. Klara and Nina had been arrested. 'Get away, by God. They are here!' the woman hissed.[3] Seeing the pleading in her eyes, Zo stepped back and the door was firmly closed. For a second, she stood there, unmoving.

If thoughts could meet, then Klara and Zo's were together in that moment. Klara was in the filthy basement of a Gestapo building in the city. She and Nina had been beaten during their initial interrogation, but neither had provided any useful information. Klara had known that Zo was due to arrive, but she had had no chance to leave a warning. Zo had always believed that her sister's quick wit would protect her from the cruelties of the world. Now Klara used all her schlagfertig to protect Zo.[4] Eventually, she told the Gestapo that Zo would be arriving in a few days, by bicycle, from a remote town in the Silesian highlands. Sending men to search for her, they had left only one to wait in the apartment.

'Klara has been arrested,' Zo was screaming inside, 'her life is at risk!'[5] It was she who had recruited her younger sister, swearing her into the resistance, bringing her from their parents' home in relatively safe Toruń and setting her up in this apartment. Yet even in her shock, guilt and grief, Zo knew that letting herself be caught would not help anyone. Blinking her thoughts away, she turned, headed smartly down the stairs and back out into the street.

Zo would always believe that she owed her life to Klara, 'to her cleverness and presence of mind, but probably also to her beauty and attitude'.[6] She had also been extraordinarily lucky. She had arrived a day late, and that evening the lone Gestapo man stationed in Klara's apartment had stepped out to get some supper. Zo may have passed him in one of the late-night cafés for 'Germans only' as she walked, more briskly now, round to the small, 'shabby' flat of another friend, Stasia.[7]* When Zo knocked on her window, Stasia immediately opened up and pulled her inside. Although an experienced conspirator, she was clearly agitated. Klara and Nina's had not been the only local arrests.

Among the former PWK instructors serving in Silesia was a 'tiny, but very brave' woman known as 'Saba'.[8]† An intelligence officer from Kraków, Saba had given courageous service both as a courier transporting explosives locally, and through her work in the offices of the occupying authorities issuing German Kennkarten – identity cards. Over the course of eighteen months, she and her friends had managed to steal dozens of these potentially life-saving documents for resistance spies and couriers. Zo had first met Saba back in their PWK days, when Saba had been director of training. So when Zo had been ordered to establish a Women's Military Service branch in Silesia, in early 1942, Saba had been an obvious choice. Giving her Klara and Nina's address, Zo had provided precise details of how she would be smuggled across the wartime border. Arriving in late March, Saba had started training new recruits in the cellar of a pre-war laundry.

A few weeks later, the Gestapo had arrested Saba's two younger brothers. One would later die in Auschwitz, the other in Gross-Rosen, in transit to Sachsenhausen. Determined to care for her parents, Saba had 'wilfully' left for Kraków, Zo noted rather coldly.[9] Once home, she had planned to break all contact with the resistance, 'but', as she later put it, 'at the insistence of Mrs E. Zawacka', aka Zo, she agreed to courier some last military training materials back over the border.[10] Zo remembered it differently. Finding Saba 'in utter despair', she felt

* 'Stasia' was Stanisława Sojka.
† 'Saba' was Jadwiga Zatorska.

that only another assignment might pull her out of her depression.[11]

Whatever the truth, Saba's last mission was to prove fatal. The smugglers who were meant to bring her across the border had got drunk the night before. In the morning, while Zo was still in Berlin, Saba had decided to set off alone. 'Such stupidity,' Zo later fumed.[12] While attempting to cross the 'green border', she was intercepted by German frontier police. Finding a military training manual in her bag, they promptly called the Gestapo.

Saba was extremely courageous. Even when beaten, stripped naked and strapped to a metal bedframe, she refused to speak. Electrodes were then fixed to her body, and a high-voltage current run between various parts of her in ways designed to maximise her pain and distress. Still she did not talk. It was only when her torturers threatened to return her to the bed that Saba could stand no more. Breaking down, she gave details of Zo and her young liaison officer, Irena Klasa, along with Klara and Nina's names and address, and details of several more contacts, including the local head of intelligence.*

It was then that the arrests had begun. The intelligence chief was raided first and 'unfortunately did not have time to remove materials' from her apartment.[13] After enduring lengthy torture, she died without betraying anyone. Klara felt her conduct was 'heroic', but her papers were already revealing their secrets.[14] When Zo later spoke about the information leak, she used the German word regengusze: a downpour.[15]

Zo and Stasia pieced together the little they knew as they sat around the small krystek cooker in Stasia's kitchen. It was clear that Saba had broken down under torture, and that the wider resistance needed to be warned. Large numbers of people had to hide, fast. Safe houses, contact points, weapons and information stashes all needed to be moved. And Zo still had to deliver her 'unfortunate suitcase', as she now regarded it, lined with the many thousands of dollars desperately needed in Warsaw.[16]

Of all the women named by Saba, only Zo now remained at liberty. She knew that the Gestapo would have her name and a detailed physical description of her, most likely with a note that she would be carrying luggage, so her first priority was to stash the case. It was not yet dawn when she left Stasia's flat. She had had very little sleep over

* Halina Konieczna.

the last forty-eight hours but walked with a spring in her step, carrying the suitcase as lightly as possible as she headed to the left-luggage store at the station.* As it was still so early, she felt she had both a duty and a realistic chance to pass on a warning before finding somewhere to hide the luggage ticket and lie low herself.

Sosnowiec station was always busy on weekday mornings when the occupying authorities brought in German-speaking women from across Silesia to clerk in the city's offices. Zo knew that several members of the Women's Military Service would be among them. Watching as first one train, then another, discharged batches of secretaries, she finally spotted a contact and managed to warn her of the arrests. By chance, she then saw another friend on the concourse, one of the sisters who used to distribute the underground press. Giving a sign to let her know that she should not be approached, Zo whispered her the news as they passed. She had managed to send out at least a ripple of warnings.

Zo had now been at the station for some time without boarding a train and, although it was hard to be sure, she had the uncomfortable sensation of being watched. Turning quickly, she saw two men staring at her. Immediately she flushed, then cursed herself. Walking briskly out of the station, she leapt onto a tram as it was pulling away. To her disappointment, one of her shadows followed behind. It was still only eight in the morning when they both disembarked in nearby Katowice – he might as well have raised his hat to her.

The pharmacy at Katowice station served as a resistance contact point. Marching in, Zo asked for headache tablets. No one would be surprised to learn that her temples were throbbing, she thought. As she paid, she slipped the pharmacist the left-luggage receipt. With an intense sense of relief, she realised that she had issued some warnings and, if not delivered it, she had not lost the resistance bankroll. So far, she had also evaded arrest.

Leaving the pharmacy, Zo turned a corner, took off her distinctive pale coat and pulled her beret from her hair. She spent the next couple of hours walking around 'these awful Katowice buildings', going in one way and out another, but she could not shake her tail.[17] By mid-morning she was flagging. Her smart shoes were pinching and her shirt

* In most accounts, Zo said she took the suitcase herself but at least twice, in 1990 and 2005, she said Stasia took the case.

was sticking to her sweaty chest. Afraid that if she could not withstand torture, she might betray the whole of Farmstead, she returned to the station and caught a train to Kraków, across the wartime demarcation line in the General Government zone. 'Now they will catch me!' she thought, but found herself being waved through.[18] Astounded, she reasoned that the Gestapo had 'presumably told the frontier control people that they were watching me'.[19] The onwards journey at least gave her a few hours rest as they passed through suburbs, then green farm fields, open countryside and eventually a few more buildings, a row of villas and city apartment blocks once more.

Zo spent another hour trying to outwit her observers in Kraków. 'I put on my coat, so light, so bright, then I took it off . . . I went upstairs in a house, then out another way . . .'[20] It was late afternoon before she felt safe enough to visit Celina Zawodzińska, Marianna's sister, whose old tenement apartment was her regular bolthole in the city. Celina ushered her in. Checking the street ten minutes later, she saw a stranger perched on a nearby wall, cigarette in hand. He must have lost her nearby, and was waiting in case she reappeared. Zo stayed for several hours, resting and eating. Mainly, she urged Celina to report everything to Warsaw, but she knew that it might take her friend a couple of days to reach the capital – and all the time more people might be arrested.

It was with 'shaking legs' that Zo set off again that evening.[21] The stranger on the wall had gone but she nevertheless took a scenic route back to the station, using all the evasive tricks she knew. Her plan was to catch the last service to Warsaw and, if possible, warn resistance HQ herself in the morning. The building was reassuringly gloomy. As a precaution against Allied air raids, 'German' stations were lit only by dim down-lights. Given her false papers, Zo chose a carriage marked 'Germans Only' and climbed on board. An army nurse was sleeping in one corner, her long uniform coat hanging temptingly on a hook behind her. Zo reached for it but, waking, the woman looked up at her reproachfully. At the same moment, a man in civilian clothes joined them in the carriage, his eyes fixed on Zo. Shaken, she walked through to the next compartment, took a seat, and turned her face to the window 'in despair'.[22]

It was then that a 'complete miracle' happened.[23] Looking out across the dark platform, Zo saw Maria Wittek striding towards her platform. Finding some paper in her purse, Zo scribbled: 'Saba is leaking.

Silesia has fallen. I am being watched. Zo.'[24] Hastily folding the note, she left her coat on her seat and stepped back out onto the platform, following Wittek towards the Polish coaches at the rear of the train. Even at this time of night there was a crowd, jostling to board. Zo elbowed in behind her commander, pushing the paper into her hand. Wittek, an experienced conspirator, accepted it without comment, then 'turned away, as though she did not know me at all', Zo noted with admiration.[25]

Back in her own carriage, Zo inhaled deeply, kicked off her shoes and hugged her knees to her chest. Her duty was done. She could have stayed with Stasia or Celina, or found another hiding place, but she had pressed on. Now Maria Wittek would be able to organise, and hundreds of lives might be saved. The compartment door opened and a few more passengers filed in. Among them was the now familiar figure who sat opposite Zo with such a sense of entitlement that the other passengers automatically shuffled up. Returning her feet to the floor, Zo turned and looked at her own face, reflected in the carriage window. 'Now it's only about my life,' she thought.[26] 'I have to finish with myself.'[27]

Zo was, above all, a practical person, determined, logical, proud. A moment later, she decided she would be better off jumping from the train while it was travelling through Silesia. She had plenty of hiding places across the region, and she might even be able to organise help for Klara and the others. But now Zo encountered a new problem: she was scared. Ever since she had been shaken awake while trying to climb out of the window of her student room in Poznań, finding herself staring at a drop of several storeys, Zo had been terrified of heights.

Leaping from a moving train required more courage still. Memories of Zofia Grzegorzewska, whose broken body she had identified after the Pruszków train crash, came flooding back. As her train accelerated out of Kraków, Zo imagined her own body smashing into one of the telegraph poles that ran parallel to the tracks. If she could, somehow, jump from the other side, she risked being hit by an oncoming train. Either way, she might fall onto the track, and under the heavy steel wheels of the coaches behind. It was only now that Zo realised how much she wanted to live: vitality was the very essence of her.

Midnight found Zo still in her seat, across from her observer. One o'clock passed, then two; 'those were terrible hours', then slowly the hour-hand of her watch reached three.[28] The relentless rhythm of the train seemed to mark every moment of indecision. She could not wilfully throw herself out, but she was tormented by the fear of betraying Emilia, Wacka, Zofia and Marianna. It did not seem long before the unwelcome light of dawn began to breach the night sky. They were now well beyond Silesia, almost approaching Warsaw. Feeling the train begin to slow as it curved towards the suburbs, Zo made her decision. If she could not jump now, she would take her own life by throwing herself under a locomotive at the terminus in the capital.

Leaving her coat and purse on her seat and nudging her shoes to one side, Zo shuffled out of the compartment and along the corridor towards the toilet. Glancing back, she saw her follower lean his head round to watch. 'Shit,' she thought, pressing on.[29] Ahead of her, a railwayman in Polish uniform, one of many employed by the Germans, was standing by the passenger door, ready to open it at the first suburban station. Zo was direct. 'I am from the Home Army,' she told him, her eyes bright. 'Get the door, I'm going to jump.'[30] For a moment, he thought she might be mad, but Zo had natural, impatient authority. Dropping his hand to the lock, he leant in and pushed the door wide. As though partners in a dance, in the same fluid gesture Zo swung herself round to face the rushing night air and threw herself from the moving train.*

'In moments of such mortal danger,' Zo later recalled, 'thoughts run like this . . . I recalled cowboy literature, of which I was very fond. The thought occurred to me that these chaps jump upwards into the air to slow down their momentum', so she sprang up.[31] Then she fell down. Hard. She landed on gravel, skinning one palm and an elbow, and gashing her knees. Blood stained her blouse and smudged across her arms and legs as she tumbled back towards the tracks, grasping at the earth as she tried to find purchase. Behind her, the train's last coaches seemed to turn and pull away on the curving line. At any moment she expected her pursuers to force the brake, stop the engine and set bloodhounds on her, but the train powered on. Stumbling to her feet, she scrambled back up the embankment.

It took Zo some time to scale the barbed wire fence that separated

---

* One romantic account has the railwayman take the time to reply, 'I always like to oblige beautiful women . . .' This unlikely exchange is in Pawel Kędzierski (dir.), *My Cichociemni Głosy Żyjących* ['My Cichociemni, Voices of the Living'] (2008).

the trainline from the surrounding fields. Two anglers, sitting patiently on the grass beside a stream, watched her. Without attempting an explanation, Zo ran on until she reached a small copse and collapsed among the trees. She could still hear the train, now in the nearby station. Then came its throaty whistle, a few doors slamming and the wafting pulse of the engine like a mechanical heart pounding away in time with her own. She had no idea whether a delegation had got off to lead a search, and once she had caught her breath she did not wait to find out.

Hurrying through the trees as best she could with bare feet, Zo came across a 'wretched woman' in a shawl, walking to her factory shift.[32] Without a moment's hesitation, the woman cleaned Zo up and handed over her slightly rancid headscarf along with her breakfast, although she kept her shoes. Zo in turn pressed her gold ring into the woman's hand. Set with an aquamarine stone, it had been a Christmas present from her mother before the war. She could imagine no better use for it than to help this generous soul in return. Fixing the scarf over her hair, peasant style, she headed to the station. There, taking a calculated risk, she went up to a reasonably well-dressed man and asked him for her fare to Warsaw. 'We were all brothers and sisters' during the occupation, she felt.[33] The man gave her the money, no questions asked.

Zo was back in the capital that evening, reporting the catastrophe to a Home Army outpost. While she was being patched up, Emilia took a train to Katowice and, with the help of a German-speaking courier and two fat cigars, retrieved the precious suitcase. She also took the time to visit Celina Zawodzińska discreetly, checking whether she was under observation. Celina had already moved apartments: it was wise to be cautious.

Zo's courageous warnings at the stations in Katowice and Kraków meant that, although the Coal network had been destroyed, several hundred women had evaded arrest. One, who had once smuggled reports on Silesian factories producing submarine parts, got across the border into the General Government and effectively disappeared.[*] The three sisters who had delivered the underground press all alerted their colleagues, before also getting away. Even Teresa Delekta evaded the Gestapo, spending thirty-six hours beneath a mound of potatoes

---

* Halina Zapolska.

in the cellar of a vegetable wholesaler. When her name appeared on wanted notices, she moved to Kraków to run a new circuit. Zo's separate Circus network, supporting long-distance couriers, was largely untouched. Eleanora Rostalska changed her address, contact points and safe houses but kept the routes working, maintaining contact with London throughout.

In recognition of the risks she had taken to warn her colleagues, Zo was nominated for the Virtuti Militari, Poland's highest award for gallantry. Devastated by Klara's arrest and the loss of so many, the honour meant little to her. The entire Women's Military Service branch in Silesia had fallen, 'the whole staff, all my friends', Zo later testified.[34] Several dozen women were arrested, and twenty-five lost their lives – mostly shot. Among these was Zo's young liaison officer, Irena Klasa, who had once claimed that her dog had savaged their smuggled bank notes, and whom Zo had been tutoring ahead of her underground university finals. Irena was executed at Auschwitz, alongside Nina Kowalska, Zo's old friend from Lwów and Klara's flatmate. 'Murdered by the Germans,' Zo told friends bitterly.[35]

Klara, considered small fry, was held in a cell for six months. Occasional interrogations were accompanied by beatings. Knowing German well, and using her legal training to give shrewd answers, she was eventually offered the opportunity to register as a Volksdeutsche. 'Remember what happened to Egon', her mother wrote, begging her to sign the list.[36] But like her brother, Klara refused. She was too proud and too angry, and she knew she would be expected to demonstrate her loyalty to the Third Reich in more ways than simply renouncing her Polish heritage. She would not consider it.

As punishment, Klara was detained with some local prostitutes, which may have saved her life. By then she was suffering from both dysentery and rheumatoid arthritis. One of her new cellmates massaged her aching limbs, while others tried to raise her spirits. Her father and elder sister, Dela, sent food parcels. Most of the contents were taken by the guards but Klara shared what was left, keeping for herself only a small bottle marked 'socus citratus' – freshly squeezed lemon juice. A few weeks later her parents and Dela were also arrested. For a while, Zo's entire surviving family were either in a prison or a concentration camp.

Zo travelled back to Silesia, heavily disguised, twice in July, hoping to organise help for Klara and the others. On her second trip, she met a woman from a scout network who informed her that her sister and a dozen others had been beheaded by guillotine. In that moment, all Zo's beliefs about the cause being greater than personal losses rang hollow. The information, however, was not entirely correct. Several women had been guillotined but, after long and fruitless interrogation, Klara had been deported to the women's concentration camp at Ravensbrück.

Zo was not the only one returning to Silesia after weeks of lying low. Several of those who had evaded arrest in May were detained in July. Among them was Stasia, the friend who had sheltered Zo on the night she had found Klara's apartment empty. After a couple of months during which she refused to talk, Stasia was sent to Auschwitz. Her brother was later informed that she had been 'executed for high treason'.[37] Two of the sisters involved in distributing the press were also arrested, and Zo later learnt that it was they who had been guillotined in Katowice. She started to keep a sombre list in her head of all the women who had given their lives to their country, and the debts that could never be repaid.

The Gestapo arrested Celina Zawodzińska, Marianna's sister, twice – she had been right in fearing she was being watched. The first time she was so shocked that she fell into a kind of catatonic state. Later, she could only remember the horror of seeing the man with whom she had shared her journey in a prison train, being dragged along a road with both his legs broken. When she was detained a second time, Celina was held in a cell with thirty other women. Like Klara before her, she now discovered the kindness of cellmates. Places by the window were reserved for those incarcerated the longest, interrogation wounds were cleaned and tended, and the women taught each other languages and crafted checkers sets for weekly games, culminating with ceremonial finals on Sundays.

A sparse line in the Auschwitz 'hospital' register records Egon's death, on the morning of 11 August 1942, as being due to hydropericardium: an excess of watery fluid in the membrane surrounding the heart – often the result of acute trauma. Egon, the ever busy child with hair as fair as wheat, who had grown into a gentle teacher with thick round glasses, strong principles and a liking for a homburg hat, had probably been beaten to death. He was thirty-seven. The Gestapo cynically informed his father that the state had 'paid for his cremation' but that the urn had to stay at the 'urn grove' in Auschwitz.[38]

By the autumn of 1942, Zo would have known both of Egon's death and that Klara had been deported. Learning of Celina's detention, she hurried to her sister Marianna, her own closest friend, to share all she knew. Marianna was once again in a sanatorium. Her lungs, already weak with disease, had been further damaged by her long nights of coding. Now she had to bear the news of her sister's arrest and the loss of so many friends.

Returning to Warsaw, Zo was not surprised to learn that she was also on the Gestapo wanted list, the *Fahndungsbuch*, at number 237. Posters printed with her real name, Elżbieta Zawacka, pasted onto station walls in Kraków, even gave her correct date of birth and Toruń address – the Gestapo were making headway. Any further visits to her home town or Silesia would have been not only pointless but also reckless. She was ordered to remain in Warsaw.

In the capital at least, Zo's personal danger seemed to have passed. The Home Army forgery team gave her a new identity, she dyed her hair a deep auburn, wore a hat and changed apartment several times. On the day that Teresa Delekta passed her on the street without a sign of recognition, Zo felt her transformation was complete. She knew she was burnt on the Silesia–Berlin route, but she desperately needed to serve.

Resourceful, determined and courageous, for many of her colleagues Zo had become 'a true legend of the Home Army' as soon as she had crossed wartime borders for the hundredth time.[39] 'She is a courier of extraordinary self-reliance,' one report recorded. 'She is decisive and steady, which is why she was capable of escaping by jumping from the train.'[40] Already decorated with the Virtuti Militari, Zo was now nominated for a further honour: an extraordinary new role.

Zo had no false modesty about her abilities, but she was astounded when her new orders arrived. It was, she admitted, 'unbelievable, stunning news'.[41] Zo, a female volunteer with no military rank, was to be the first and only woman appointed as an emissary, in her case the personal representative of General Rowecki himself, commander of the Home Army. Her improbable, perilous assignment was 'to cross the whole of Europe', several thousand kilometres, 'and reach the General Staff of the Polish Forces in London'.[42] She was to carry with her some carefully hidden microfilm and, on Rowecki's direct orders, she was to undertake two vital missions on his behalf once in Britain.

Part Two

6

Emissary to Paris
(August 1942–January 1943)

Elisabeth Kübitza, a clerk in a German oil company with branches in Paris and Warsaw, loved her chic new suit. It was stylish and well tailored. The material did not crease easily, making it perfect for travel, and the skirt did not rise up when she sat down. She had 'never felt so elegant', she admitted, but the main reason she took such pleasure in her outfit was that it had 'a lot of pockets'.[1] Stowed in one was a dainty working ladies' lighter, 'a lovely jewel of brass' whose reassuring weight was always within reach.[2]

Elisabeth did not smoke. The lighter contained five hundred pages of microfilm: the latest Home Army mail, plus a set of special reports. Elegant Emilia had chosen the suit, the smart handbag, gloves and hat, and even found a pair of the stockings that were now as rare as snowballs in summer. It was Elisabeth Kübitza, however, aka Zo, who had selected the lighter as the information cache. She knew this device had fooled the Gestapo before, and that more than her own life was about to depend on the effective concealment of the intelligence she was carrying.

Promoted by Emilia as 'a courier of outstanding independence', but burnt for regional routes, Zo would be the only woman selected to serve as an army commander's emissary between Warsaw and London.[3] She was not, however, the first Polish emissary of the war. Her predecessors had taken various circuitous routes, including a three-month journey through the Balkans, North Africa and Canada.* The last to leave had been Jan Karski, who had brought out some of the earliest accounts of the Holocaust in Nazi-occupied Poland.

Zo was to travel through France and Spain, carrying reports on the

---

* Emil Fieldorf and Kazimierz Iranek-Osmecki took the North Africa–Canada route. Others, like Józef Zabielski, aka 'Żbik', crossed through Europe over more than two months.

Nazi 'liquidation' of the first Jewish ghettos in Poland, and evidence of further plans for the mass murder of European Jews. There was also vital military information, including dossiers on the development of Hitler's so-called Vengeance weapons, the Vi missile and V2 rocket. As Rowecki's emissary, Zo had also been entrusted with two missions to undertake in London: to rectify the problems with land communications between Britain and Poland, and to present his demands for the full, legal integration of women into the Home Army.

Rowecki was deeply dissatisfied with the communications from his government. It was clear that the Sixth Bureau in London, the department responsible, had little understanding of the perils inside occupied territory. Even small delays left couriers dangerously exposed, and the supply of large blocks of cash made smuggling money, in Zo's guarded words, 'immeasurably more difficult'.[4] Emilia had tried sending detailed instructions to London, but Rowecki was now clear that change was needed. 'We are sending you, via France, our emissary Zo, to discuss questions connected with land communications', he telegrammed London. 'She has full powers regarding the organisation of land routes from Poland to you.'[5] A ripple of anxiety ran through the officers of the Sixth Bureau.

Zo's second mission was even more controversial. The Home Army still operated on the pre-war basis that female auxiliaries had duties but no right to pay, rank or promotion. Whatever their experience or ability, they were also excluded from military briefings. This not only deterred women from signing up, it also caused resentment and compromised operational efficiency and general security. Zo had seen for herself that 'the fact that' Emilia Malessa 'was a woman in a position of authority over men . . . had enormous consequences, often resulting in great difficulties'.[6] Emilia navigated such issues 'with dignity and civility' but this took time and diplomacy, resources often in short order.[7] By drafting a decree on 'women's military service', Rowecki was aiming to maximise the human resources available to him, while minimising the security risks. As an enterprising, effective and highly decorated female soldier, Zo was the perfect advocate for such a decree. A signed copy was photographed and included with her mail.

For Zo, talk of being in London at first 'sounded unbelievable', but the reality sank in as the preparations dragged on.[8] Emilia tutored her over reports, literally dug up from the secret archives beneath Warsaw, so that they could trace all the courier routes, identify problems and consider solutions. Maria Wittek drilled her on the women's military service decree, anticipating the objections that might be raised. She also ordered Zo to report on the structures of the British women's military auxiliary services, highlighting any lessons that could be learnt.

'Agaton', the Silent Unseen forgery specialist, created Zo's *ausweis* identity card, travel papers, food coupons and oil company employment documents under the name 'Elisabeth Kübitza'.* Among his team was a clever young newly-wed called Alicja, serving under the touching nom-due-guerre of *Wiewiórka*, the Polish word for 'squirrel'.† Her husband, a tall, confident courier called Jan Gralewski, had adopted the less modest pseudonym of Pankrac, meaning 'almighty'. Alicja envied her husband's travels. Compared to her previous work, smuggling messages between prisoners and their families, she found forgery tedious. She proved her mettle when her apartment was raided. Feigning innocence, Alicja insisted on practising her German with the officers. 'There are so many idiomatic expressions and the grammar is so difficult,' she fawned. 'I would love to discuss it with you.'⁹ Half an hour later, they simply told her to leave. Heart pumping, she headed to a favourite café on the far side of Warsaw with a handbag full of papers. Like Zo, Alicja had a sweet tooth and found that 'Warsaw biscuits had a truly calming effect'.¹⁰

Later, Zo would also receive a set of French papers identifying her as Madame Elise Rivière from Alsace. She had to perfect her high-school French to become Elise, and she took intensive English lessons. Last of all, she was taught how to destroy the intelligence she was carrying. The brass lighter would protect the microfilm inside, even when used. To burn the film, she would have to remove it first. Zo was never told how to destroy the knowledge in her head, but she was offered a small, round cyanide tablet. Covered in rubber to prevent it melting in the mouth, if crunched the poison would kill in seconds.

ॐ

Known in Britain as Remembrance Day, and as Veterans Day in the

---

* Having reached Britain in June 1940, Stanisław Jankowski, aka 'Agaton', parachuted back to Poland in March 1942. His wife and mother had been arrested for sheltering both escaping British soldiers and a Jewish woman. The soldiers survived, but all three women perished in Auschwitz.

† Alicja Iwańska.

USA, 11 November recalls the end of First World War hostilities. In Poland, it is marked as Independence Day and is traditionally when honours are announced. On 11 November 1942, as combined Allied forces under General Eisenhower seized the offensive in French North Africa, Zo was still in Warsaw, being awarded Poland's Cross of Valour, for the second time. Zofia Franio was also honoured, for bravery in combat. While Zofia still worked as a doctor during the day, she also secretly provided medical care to Jewish patients, and sheltered Jewish friends in her own home.* At night, meanwhile, she was moonlighting as head of the female sapper units.

By late 1942, Zofia had recruited fifty female sappers. In units of five, they learnt to assemble petrol bombs and prepare various mines with chemical, electric and clock-detonators for the destruction of railway tracks and bridges. When one grenade detonated prematurely, ripping the arm from their instructor, Zofia rushed him to hospital as the victim of a railway accident. Looking doubtfully at the scorch marks on his skin, the medics silently set about their life-saving work.[†]

Female sappers were not expected to undertake active service until the national uprising – being planned for when the Allies retook the offensive in Europe. For now, Zofia's brave teams transported their armaments, in five-kilo packets, to the partisans, the Jewish fighters in the ghetto, or to depots around the city. This required not only courage but creativity. Zofia issued them with tuberculosis certificates, hoping to protect them during round-ups, and the women hid their explosives in marmalade tins, pickle jars and, once, a stuffed toy monkey. At least five of the women were arrested and executed between 1942 and 1944. When the identity of a man who had betrayed two sisters and their maid was discovered, he was tried in absentia and executed by two of their fellow female saboteurs.[‡]

Ponury, the Silent Unseen officer who had parachuted into Emilia Malessa's embrace, was among the partisans deploying these home-made weapons. After six months of debilitating attacks on Wehrmacht forces, Ponury was arrested but, to Emilia's relief, he managed to

---

* Zofia Franio's latest guest, Anna Weinstock-Janczura, was one of only 30,000 to 60,000 Jewish Poles to survive in hiding.
† Leon Tarakowski survived the war.
‡ Sisters Jadwiga and Maria Kuberska and their maid, Irena Kalinowska. The executioners were Irena Bredel and Letycja Ostrowska.

escape. By November, as Zo and Zofia Franio were receiving their awards, Ponury was once again inflicting losses on the enemy. But not all the armed action was carried out by men.

On 16 November, Zofia was part of the team attacking the rail lines at Łuków. Three-quarters of the city's Jewish population would be deported to Treblinka through the railway station, and thousands of German soldiers passed through on their way to the Eastern Front.* Zofia arrived with a suitcase so heavily laden with explosives, three revolvers and some mines, that its handle had ripped off. She had to cradle the battered case under one arm as she went through the station checks, then drag it along by the belt she had buckled around it to join the team derailing the 11pm intercity.

At seven that evening, 'the place turned into hell' as two military transports were blown up on the far side of Łuków. 'Fire alarms started wailing . . .' one sapper reported, 'church bells tolled, ambulances raced through the streets transporting wounded soldiers from the burning train carriages, and German military policemen immediately set out in pursuit of the saboteurs.'[11] Zofia and her team were hiding nearby. As German patrols flooded the area, they worried that some heavy-footed soldier might damage their delicate wiring but, after another four hours, they blew up their rails 'with flawless precision' at exactly 11pm.[12] Sparks flew from the approaching train's wheels as the driver instinctively applied the brakes, but the engine ploughed off the blasted rails, pulling its carriages with it. By then, Zofia's team were long gone. Zo applauded their work but, as German security heightened, she was keen to be on her way.

⚓

'Transfer of Zo indispensable and urgent', Rowecki radioed London on 11 December.[13] Within a week she bade farewell to Marianna, giving her the last of her cooking oil in case she did not return. Marianna never knew if she would see her friend again, but Zo's thoughts were running in a different direction. 'How many more times', she wondered, would she have to say these goodbyes 'before freedom comes?'[14]

Because the intelligence she was carrying was so sensitive, General Rowecki had ordered Zo to follow only 'a safe route' – one that had

---

* Of the 12,000 Jewish civilians living in pre-war Łuków, only around 150 survived.

been successfully tested.[15] Orders were orders, but Zo knew from experience that 'no roads were really safe'.[16] It was only as her train approached the first border, however, and with it the first test of her new papers, that she started to worry. Her rising colour added to her discomfort. She felt certain that one day her blush would betray her, but, fanning herself as though menopausal, a heated Elisabeth Kübitza sailed through the checks. She was in the Greater German Reich before another 'most secret' telegram informed London that 'Zofia Zofkowska', aka Zo, had left Warsaw. At Strasbourg, Zo felt herself flush again as the border guards discussed telephoning to confirm her employment. As British intelligence later noted, since 'this firm was non-existent, she would of course have been finished had the authorities ever checked up'.[17] Fortunately, they decided not to bother. The journey to Paris required five controls, and all of Zo's nerve, but eventually she arrived at the Gare du Nord.

Zo's first stop in the French capital was the German *Kommandantur*, command headquarters, where all visiting national workers had to register. Inside, she found a reassuringly busy admin department – with so many people passing through, it seemed less likely that her details would be checked. 'Elisabeth Kübitza,' she told the officials, adding that she would only be staying a few days. Then she fished her documents out of her bag and passed them over with a smile. That smile that didn't falter, even when she was unexpectedly asked for the address of her Paris office. Montmartre, she said, inventing a street name. At another desk she exchanged her forged food stamps for a real ration card, declared her reichsmarks, and requested a list of the requisitioned hotels where she might stay. It was only when she headed out to eat that she discovered how much the ostmarks in her pocket could buy in France. As a self-respecting German professional, she felt it only fitting to order a glass of wine with her meal, followed by cheese and dessert – treats she had not enjoyed for years.

Paris shocked Zo. A Polish family might survive on one loaf of bread a week. Here, people were hungry but not obviously starving. French was spoken openly in the streets. Parisians still flocked to the Folies Bergère and to hear Maurice Chevalier sing, and somewhere in the city Madame Chanel was dreaming up a new spring fashion collection. In Warsaw, the occupying forces despised the Poles, kicking or beating those too slow to get out of their way. Here Zo never heard '*Raus!*' or '*Schnell!*' and, despite wearing the same uniforms, the Germans acted like tourists. 'They all visited the sites with Baedekers in their hands,' she saw in astonishment.[18] Yet it was impossible to tell who, among the locals, was a resister and who a collaborator, and there were many more of the latter in Paris.

Zo's contact was Maria Protasewicz, the French wife of Michał Protasewicz, head of the Polish Sixth Bureau in London. A true Parisienne, Maria had refused to leave her beautiful apartment for suburban London, even after the fall of France. Zo felt that she cared more for French wine than for the Polish cause. 'Her greatest misfortune,' she commented acidly, 'was that the Germans only gave ration cards for one bottle of wine per week.'[19] Yet Maria was risking her life to support the Poles, and she did something else for Zo too. With temperatures rarely above 10°C that December, Maria felt that 'Elisabeth Kübitza' should have a smart winter coat. Taking her to Mme Lesien's, a couturier, she bought her a warm one 'with a real silk lining'.[20] This blue coat was perhaps Zo's favourite ever item of clothing, the perfect partner for her stylish business suit. Perhaps some of Emilia's feeling for fashion had finally rubbed off on her, or the relative freedoms of Paris had released her from her usual restraint. For a few weeks, 'be careful with the coat' became her new mantra.[21]

Maria also arranged Zo's first meeting with Kazimierz Leski, the Home Army officer whose job it was to get her into Spain. Since their defeat in June 1940, France had been a divided nation. The north was Nazi-occupied, while southern 'Vichy France' was governed by the former Great War hero, now Nazi collaborator, Marshal Pétain. 'That traitor' were all the words that Zo could spare for him.[22] In November, however, German forces had crossed the demarcation line in response to the Allied landings in North Africa – which had been supported by the French forces in that region. From then on, all France was effectively occupied, although the demarcation would only be officially annulled the next spring. For now, there were simply more guards on both sides of the border.

'Bradl,' Leski told Zo, extending his hand. Although shocked that Rowecki was sending a woman to London, a slight Zo never forgot, the two of them would become firm friends. Bradl, as Zo knew him, had started the war as a Polish Air Force pilot, but his leg had been shattered when his aircraft was shot down by the Soviets. While he was a POW, his sister, Anna Leska, was serving as a reconnaissance pilot. After the Polish retreat, she scaled the wire fencing of a Nazi-occupied airfield, climbed into the nearest machine and took off before the enemy could start firing. Eventually, she signed up with the British Air Transport Auxiliary.* Bradl was as bold as his sister. Escaping Soviet captivity once his leg could support him, he walked back to Warsaw, developing a permanent limp. Sworn into the Home Army as an intelligence officer and courier, he initially travelled by posing as a lieutenant in the Wehrmacht. The crowded third-class carriages so tortured his damaged leg, however, that he dyed his hair grey, grew a moustache and promoted himself to *generalmajor*. Thereafter he only travelled first class, which had the added advantage of exempting him from many of the checks.

When Bradl told Zo that there were going to be delays, given the recent increase in border patrols, she returned to the Kommandantur to extend her Paris stay. This time she was asked to provide her Nazi Party membership number. As anything too high or too low would arouse suspicion, she told the clerk she was not a Party member. It was one of the many small decisions that probably saved her life. Although many women did join the NSDAP, because the regime excluded women from political life their party membership was not demanded.

Bradl now introduced Zo to several other couriers. They were a bold and brilliant bunch, each remarkable in their own distinct way. 'Aruś' was an aristocrat also heading to London, with invaluable connections in the de Gaullist resistance.† Former cavalry captain 'Wilski', distinguished by his sharp moustache, felt hat and monocle, was better known as 'Baron von Lückner'.‡ Just before Zo had arrived, Bradl had been trying to get him south on a route that required a fast dash across a heavily patrolled border road. Halfway over, Wilski had 'suddenly stopped cold'.[23] He had lost his hat, and stubbornly refused to go on without it. Dashing back, stoically ignoring Bradl's abuse, he 'then proudly wore this magnificent head covering to the end'.[24] Wilski could not let even Bradl know about the microfilm sewn inside his hat's lining. Wilski, Aruś and Zo were all supposed to cross into Spain within the month.

Zo usually met Bradl at a little café in the Latin Quarter, where

---

* In April 1941, Lee Miller famously photographed Leska in a Spitfire cockpit at White Waltham airfield.

† Andrzej Lipkowski.

‡ Aleksander Stpiczyński.

he updated her on developments over excellent boiled crabs. It was here that he introduced her to the French Colonel 'Médéric'.* 'Direct and cordial in his manner', Zo was delighted that in exchange for some Polish-forged 'German' documents, Médéric introduced them to his contacts with the French railways.²⁵ The plan was to smuggle her across the demarcation line hidden inside the water tender of the so-called 'Laval train' that shuttled between Paris and Vichy. The brilliance of the scheme lay in its audacity. This train was reserved for Pierre Laval, the head of Pétain's government, and the checks were minimal.†

As Zo had been ordered to take only tried and tested routes, Wilski agreed to attempt the journey first. After about seven hours, soaked and shaky, he emerged from the darkness of the water tank, still clutching his hat, into what seemed the dazzling light of 'Free France'. Zo simply had to wait a week until she could catch the next train.

Walking up the stairs to Maria Protasewicz's door one day, Zo nearly collided with another Polish courier bounding down. It was Pankrac, the young husband of Alicja, aka Squirrel, from the Warsaw forgery team. Pankrac was surprisingly exuberant but his long-limbed stride and the corresponding bounce of his hair made him seem too self-assured to be suspicious. Immediately warming to him, Zo described Pankrac not as 'handsome', her polite default for male officers, but more honestly as having 'an original face'.²⁶

Finding they were both briefly stuck in Paris, Zo and Pankrac went to see the sights. Together they watched the morning mist rise from the Seine, and drew solace from seeing the Champs-Élysées, Eiffel Tower and the cool white dome of the Sacré-Coeur at Montmartre, all unscathed by bomb damage. Pulling up the hood of a horse-drawn carriage, Pankrac enthused about 'Mouse', his little sister with her long fair plaits, and Squirrel, his courageous bride. His wartime wedding ring, proudly exhibited, was not cast in gold but carved from wood. It was clear that Pankrac was determined to help restore freedom to

---

* Gilbert Védy, aka Médéric, was a leading figure in the de Gaullist *Ceux de la Liber-ation* ('Those of the Liberation'), one of the eight organisations forming the French National Resistance Council.

† Pierre Laval, who oversaw the deportation of French Jews, remained as head of government until the liberation of France. In 1945 he was arrested and executed.

his homeland, where he hoped to one day raise a family.

At two in the morning, a week after Wilski had left, Zo was delighted to find Pankrac also round the back of the Gare d'Orléans-Austerlitz; they were to be fellow passengers on the Laval train. The water tender was already hitched behind the heavy locomotive and, feeling through a cloud of steam, Zo found the ladder welded to the side of the tank and climbed up. An engineer guided her along to the hatch. The aperture was narrow, and deep. Peering down, she shivered as the dank air above the water hit her face. Taking off her beautiful blue coat, she turned it inside out to save it from the worst damage, and lowered herself, feet first, through the hatch.

Above the water, wooden planks had been laid across the tank's steel baffles – the vertical dividers that limited the extent the water inside could slosh about. Crouching down on the boards, she shuffled back until she could lean against the iron side of the tank. Pankrac lowered himself down after her, his feet still unsteady on the planks when the closing hatch cut out the last light. Hardly able to move and forbidden to speak, the two of them could only listen impatiently for the footsteps, voices and first chug of the engine that would tell them they were about to depart.

After three or four hours, it was hard to tell, footsteps did echo through the tank's dank chamber; someone was coming their way at a pace. A quick tread on the ladder, then the hatch swung open and the engineer's face appeared, fearful now. Wilski had been arrested. If he talked under duress, they would all be compromised. Hauled back out of the tank, legs stiff and nerves frayed, Zo and Pankrac were hurried away.

With his false papers close to expiring, Pankrac was forced to return to Poland. Emilia Malessa quickly sent him back out with new documents, this time travelling through Switzerland to France. Then he disappeared. In Paris, Bradl was urgently seeking alternative routes for Zo. Aruś raised the possibility of their being collected by British Lysander, a light reconnaisance aircraft. Flying straight from France to Britain seemed fantastical to Zo. It was now midwinter, the best season for flying by the moon, but no such airlifts had yet been agreed, let alone organised.

In desperation, she and Bradl took a train down the heavily armed Atlantic coast towards Bordeaux. There were regular checks in this area, but they were running out of time while Zo's papers were valid.

The weather got steadily worse as they headed southwest to Saint-Jean-de-Luz, a coastal village near the Spanish border. Before the fall of France, the Basque fishermen here had ferried an entire Polish army to waiting ships anchored in the harbour. Now one offered to take Zo across the Bay of Biscay and drop her on the Spanish shore. For a moment, she imagined the heady feeling of watching the French coastline disappear. The sea was rough, however, enemy submarines patrolled the bay, and without a Spanish guide she would be lost even should she reach Spain. It was far too uncertain.

Bradl then took her to Pau where, he suggested, she could be driven in a truck full of cattle to a farm at the frontier. 'In one moonlit night,' he told her tantalisingly, she could hike across the lower, eastern part of the Pyrenees and 'already be in Spain'.[27] Later, Bradl took this route himself, enjoying being 'nudged by some cows, licked by others, constantly avoiding dangerous positions astern of any of them [and] diving below their bellies at every stop of the lorry'.[28] But while with Zo he had to admit that, 'I did not yet have the route worked out.'[29]

Zo returned to Paris in a foul mood. On Christmas Eve she ate alone in a restaurant near the Louvre, brooding on her failure. That night she imagined sharing the traditional Polish Christmas wafer with her family and resistance friends. Later, the thought of Egon dying alone came back to her in all its anguish. After a few days, she had no option but to return to Warsaw before her papers expired. 'What a strange kaleidoscope of possibilities and realities', Bradl wrote. One day a courier could be a German citizen, untouchable in occupied France, and a few hours later they would be just one more Pole, 'a baited animal that any German can shoot in the head with impunity'.[30]

When Zo angrily reported back to Emilia in early January 1943, her boss greeted her sympathetically. Zo had obeyed her orders to the letter and was determined to try again once new papers were prepared. But Emilia was soon distracted. On 18 January her partisan lover, Ponury, was to organise and lead an audacious rescue of four Silent Unseen officers imprisoned in Pinsk prison.* His chances of success were slim. Some three thousand German troops were garrisoned in the city, and the prison heavily guarded. Even the Home Army leadership judged that the operation was 'extremely bold and risky'.[31]

The Pinsk prison raid was over in fifteen minutes. All four men were

* Pinsk is now in Belarus.

rescued. No losses were incurred. Delighted by the much needed good
news, Rowecki touted it as a morale boost for the Home Army. But
although Ponury's team had carefully spoken Russian throughout the
operation, a few days later thirty Polish hostages were shot in retaliation. By then, Ponury had already become legendary. He would keep
the Pinsk prison keys as a lucky talisman for the rest of his life.

In early February 1943, Rowecki awarded Ponury the Silver Cross
of the Virtuti Militari. Seizing the opportunity, the hero of the day
successfully requested permission to lead his own forest-based partisan unit. Perhaps inspired by Ponury's bravura, Zo also petitioned
Rowecki. She had two requests: permission to start immediately for
London again, and the authority to choose her own route. Rowecki
agreed. She left four days later.

7

Escape to England
(February–May 1943)

Zo stared at the seams of the faded red material that lined the walls of her hotel room. She ran her fingers round the dusty doorframe and tested the strength of the window putty. She was searching for the best place to hide her 'mail', terrified that the Gestapo might call for her that night. It was 10 February 1943 and Zo had arrived back in Paris the night before. As well as her brass cigarette lighter, she was now carrying an additional five hundred pages of microfilmed reports hidden inside the shaft of a small door key, along with some forged reichsmarks, a few paper dollars, and two gold sovereigns sewn into her clothes. She might leave the key, she thought, on the lintel of her door. She usually kept the lighter with her, innocuous rather than concealed, but if arrested she knew that all her possessions would be thoroughly examined.

Zo had been badly spooked. Arriving late to register at the Kommandantur the night before, her documents had attracted attention for being 'too sharply printed'.[1] The late hour, at least, seemed to be in her favour. The clerk had simply confiscated her papers, telling Zo to return in the morning. Walking round to her allocated hotel, she had wondered about the competency of the forgery team in Warsaw. Not so good that she might take risks with her intelligence but, since she had not been immediately arrested, not so poor that she should abandon her mission for a second time. 'I will not return to Warsaw,' she swore, walking firmly past the Art Nouveau metalwork of a metro station.[2]

After 'a horrible night' spent pacing her room, Zo dutifully returned to the Kommandantur.[3] Pulling her confiscated papers from a drawer, the clerk showed them to a colleague. 'These are what stamps are supposed to look like,' he said, pointing at Zo's finely printed documents.[4] Her papers had been kept to compare against a set of possible forgeries. She mentally tipped her hat to her Warsaw colleagues – she was still on her way to England.

♪

'Even in optimal conditions', Bradl believed that crossing the Pyrenees required 'tremendous effort and superior mountain-climbing skills' and was therefore suitable only for 'the fittest couriers'.[5] The granite mountains run 270 miles from the Bay of Biscay to the Mediterranean Sea, rising to over 11,000 feet at their peak. Climbing them meant a trek through the exclusion zone, heavily guarded by Nazi patrols, before an uncompromising ascent into the icy clouds. Hoping to avoid such perils, Aruś once again urged Zo to wait for the next full moon and fly to London from a field he knew. Zo thought the men were deluded. No Lysander had yet arrived and there was no indication that one was likely now.[*] 'They like to fantasise, young boys,' she thought cuttingly.[6] Swearing that 'it was impossible' to delay, as there had been no repercussions from Wilski's arrest, she insisted on travelling to Vichy in the water tender of the next Laval train and then attempting the mountains herself.[7]

It was with a terrible sense of déjà vu that Zo returned to the Gare d'Orléans-Austerlitz. As well as her brass lighter and door key, money and false papers, this time she had armed herself with three kilos of chocolate for the journey, an amount 'unthinkable in Poland'.[8] A party of eight young Frenchmen were already waiting on the station platform, keen to join their 'Free Forces' overseas.[†] Zo was the last to lower herself in through the hatch, and a dozen hands reached up to guide her onto the planks. The men were curious and keen to be gallant, but Zo's demeanour made clear it would be better not to ask questions of this determined woman who smelt of chocolate and wore her coat turned inside out.

This time there was no space for Zo to shuffle along the boards. 'There we lay, just like herrings,' she felt, one tough Polish soldier and eight optimistic young Frenchmen.[9] Despite a few holes high up in the

---

[*] Zo was right not to wait. 'Such plane flights did not come for Polish couriers until four months later', the British noted. See EZ Foundation, 'Misc Particulars of Elżbieta Zawacka', 3 May 1943.

[†] In most accounts, Zo mentions eight Frenchmen, but her 1943 interrogation records that she left Paris with three, was joined by another in Vichy, and two more in Carcassonne.

tank, to let in air as the water below was channelled out to the engine, the enclosed space soon hummed with sweat and stale breath. A few hours later, Zo heard the stoker shovelling coal to feed the engine. Laval must have climbed aboard as, with some hissing and a gentle lurch, the engine started to tow its load out of the station. Zo's senses were now assaulted by a blast on the whistle that reverberated through the tender, followed by the steady pulse of the chimney drawing the fire, and the rhythmic rumble of the wheels rolling over track. The steel around her rattled. The water sloshed between the baffles, soaking the stowaways, and every now and then there was a deafening clatter as an avalanche of coal slid down the sloping floor of the coalbin above.

As Zo adjusted to these rhythms, she felt the train pick up speed and begin to climb, pulling out of the city. When they went through a tunnel, some of the gritty, ashy smoke was sucked in through the air holes, leaving the stowaways coughing and gasping until the train emerged again. Eventually the water level lowered enough for Zo and the men to dry out a little and, sitting tightly in rows, they swung their legs over the side of the planks. Inevitably it was not long before heavy footsteps presaged the opening of the hatch and a refill pipe was inserted. Zo was so delighted to be making good progress that she had to stop herself from laughing at the sudden downpour. She had always loved swimming and canoeing. 'Water was my element,' she beamed, 'as befits a Pisces.'[10]

Zo had no way of knowing when they crossed the demarcation line, but Bradl later recorded that by morning she had 'arrived without mishap in Vichy'.[11] Once the train's official passengers had disembarked, the uncoupled locomotive was moved to its own shed. It was here that the tender's occupants were finally hauled free. They emerged stiff, sodden and filthy, stumbling and blinking even in the shadowy light of the railway siding. Turning her coat back the right way round, Zo tried to make herself look respectable as she was led to a safe house. She would never forget her first breakfast in southern France, 'a *bowl* of milk with a few drops of coffee'.[12] She nearly fell asleep with her face in it.

When Zo moved on the next day, she found she still had the Frenchmen in tow. None had money, so she bought them onwards rail tickets before discreetly sitting in a different carriage. She was now Elise Rivière from Alsace, travelling alone. Changing trains at the medieval city of Carcassonne, Zo spent a few hours walking in the shadows of the citadel walls. She knew she was safer in those narrow streets than waiting on a platform near eight men of conscription age. In any case, she felt drawn to the city. Shaped by commerce and conflict, Carcassonne was not so different from her home town of Toruń. Zo returned to the station feeling as fortified as her surroundings, which was good, because the men were still sitting there, waiting for her.

The first control of their papers came when they entered the defence area, near the Spanish frontier. Zo was convinced they would all be 'done for'.[13] To her mind, these French documents were poor quality things compared to Polish forgeries. Fortunately, they were given only a cursory glance. Darkness was falling when they arrived in Foix, another ancient town of ochre-coloured houses but set in the foothills of the Pyrenees. Giving the men some money, Zo found herself a room elsewhere. The next day she made contact with Bradl's guide in the mountain village of Tarascon, ten miles further south.

Bonet Paco was a recalcitrant Catalan communist who had fled from Francisco Franco's rule. Many guides risked their lives for money. Others were motivated by honour, compassion or patriotism. Close-knit Catalan and Basque communities, struggling to preserve their languages and cultures, were generally sympathetic to other oppressed peoples. According to one Polish report, many were also 'excellent connoisseurs of the border' and 'animated by a formidable fighting spirit'.[14] Paco was a case in point. Zo hired him on the spot, paying part in advance with her dwindling funds. They agreed to meet at a mountainside inn at eight the following evening.

Although almost March, there was still snow in the foothills, both in the air and deep underfoot. Knowing the journey ahead would be bitter, Zo layered on her clothes, stowing only a few toiletries and what was left of the chocolate in her leather bag. Darkness fell quickly, the sharp contours of the peaks softening into the dusk. Soon heavy clouds were obscuring the moon.

The Frenchmen were already at the inn when Zo arrived: Paco was clearly maximising his returns. A couple of the boys were coming over to greet her when two German officers entered the lobby, the white edelweiss insignia of a mountain regiment clearly visible on their grey caps. Surprised to see so many fit young men together, the officers asked for their papers. Zo noticed how polite they were, not yet sure what they were dealing with, but the French lads panicked. When asked what business brought him to the mountains, one stuttered that he was selling shoes. A check of his backpack revealed only hiking provisions. 'Those stupid boys had no idea what they were doing,' Zo realised.[15] The officers grew less polite.

Zo quietly edged away, pulse and mind both racing. Quickly stowing her bag in a heavy wooden armoire, she then slipped off her hat, scarf and gloves, and now rather worn blue coat, and shoved them inside too. Then she looked down at her feet. Not having decent boots, she had bound her ankles in strips of cloth to protect them in the mountains. It would be impossible to unwind the tell-tale material without attracting attention. Trying to walk purposefully on legs that 'felt like cotton', she squeezed past the men and started to climb the inn's stairs.[16]

Zo was in full self-preservation mode. Striding into an upstairs dining room, when she saw no exit she took a napkin from a table, draped it over her arm, and headed back to the staircase. Before she could climb any further, someone pulled her roughly to one side. Gesturing her to be silent, Paco steered Zo into a back room. It struck her that she had no idea whether he was playing both sides, or if the guards had simply come to the inn for a glass of beer and been lucky. Before she had gathered her thoughts, Paco shoved her out of a side-door directly onto the mountainside. The land was higher at the back of the inn than at the front, and she landed safely in a bank of snow.

Sitting silently in some scrubby bushes, Zo could picture the depressing scene round the front of the inn all too well. A truck pulled up, wheels crunching on the snow, brakes complaining. The inn door banged and there were protestations and curt orders, perhaps a bit of a skirmish but no gunshots. Then the truck drove off.* Fearing that a German officer might have stayed behind, Zo remained put. It was only when her adrenaline ebbed that she began to feel cold. She had no idea how long she had been sitting there, or whether she was restored to life by the weight of the jacket laid over her shoulders or the stale odour it emitted. The owner of the jacket, a young workman at the inn, had watched the whole episode, quietly keeping his distance until the coast was clear. 'Gilbert,' he told her, stretching out his hand.

Gilbert Haerinck was younger than Zo, still in his early twenties she guessed, and 'intelligent and energetic', which was more praise

* The Frenchmen were sent to Toulouse prison.

than she gave most men.[17] He had travelled from his home near Calais in the hope of joining the Free French in North Africa, and had spent that week in Foix, working as a labourer to earn the money for a guide. He didn't say much more, but neither did he ask any questions. Like his jacket, he seemed to have seen better days, but Zo could tell that the basic fabric of the man was good. When Paco returned it became clear that he also had an arrangement with Gilbert, but there could be no mountain crossing while the guards were on high alert. Paco had brought Zo's clothes and bag. Now he led her out along 'trackless foothills' to an isolated farmhouse where she was to stay in a void below the stairs, not comfortable but safe and dry.[18] She begged him for a compass and map but had to content herself with the promise that they would leave in two nights' time.

Zo's birthday fell on 19 March. No one raised a glass to her as she turned thirty-four in the lonely mountains, but her thoughts naturally ran to her friends. She was now the same age that Zofia Grzegorzewska had been when she was killed in the Pruszków train crash.[19] Marianna, the third member of their 'spiritual co-operative', was now desperately ill in Warsaw but, when she could, still coding radio messages through the night. Their youthful pledge to serve their nation now rested largely on Zo's shoulders. She felt the weight of the honour keenly. That birthday, she later came to reflect, 'was the high point of my life, a kind of apogee'.[20] It was then that she was at her strongest, both mentally and physically, for the 'very important soldierly task' ahead.[21]

⚓

Of Zo's other friends, Wacka was now serving as a courier. She had been meant to leave Poland with Zo in February, but an accident requiring stitches had kept her in Warsaw.* Emilia Malessa now had her working the routes to the Baltic coast, from where her intelligence would be taken on via Sweden. Wacka was briefed for these journeys by 'Jarach', a new recruit to the Farmstead team.† Emilia had

---

* Wacka was lucky. The team she was to visit were soon arrested and executed, so her injury probably saved her life.

† 'Jarach' was the Czech national Rudolf Zarzdel or Zarzdil, aka Antoni Mazurkiewicz.

appointed him after the last man in the post had walked out following a quarrel. 'There were often such personnel problems,' Zo later admitted, worrying about the security implications, and 'always of a sexual nature'.[22] Tall and lean, the red-headed Jarach seemed a safe pair of hands. He had previously been a courier on the Kraków–Prague–Budapest route.[23] For Wacka's journeys, he arranged for her to stay over with Zo's parents in Toruń.

Emilia and Zofia Franio were still in Warsaw, the former overseeing Farmstead, the latter supplying more arms now to the Jewish fighting resistance. Surrounded by a high wall swathed in barbed wire, the ghetto's population was crowded into buildings with poor sanitation, and very little food or medical supplies. Children risked death every day to squeeze through the holes that connected cellars below the ghetto wall, or along the sewers beneath the streets, to beg and steal food in the city, before smuggling it back to their families. Those caught were shot.

Around 100,000 Varsovian Jews had died, mainly from starvation and disease, before the first mass deportations started. Their bodies were collected twice daily by street-cleaning teams, 'like garbage', one Home Army officer noted.[24] Yet at the end of 1942, some 400,000 people were still crammed into the ghetto. It was only in December that the secret 'Polish Council to Aid Jews' was established. From then on there was more assistance for Zofia's sappers smuggling in weapons, ammunition and explosives from the Home Army's secret depots. There would never be enough arms, nothing like, but every delivery was perilous and every weapon was put to good use.

⚓

A few days after the arrests at the Tarascon inn, Paco, the Catalan guide, sent his uncle to collect Zo for a second attempt on the Pyrenees. This time she was to travel with 'a whole caravan of smugglers', risking their lives to trade their goods in Spain.[25] There were also two Austrian Jewish men who had escaped the Viennese pogroms. One was tall but wiry, the other 'seemed very fragile', Zo noticed anxiously, and 'both were very poor and thin'.[26] Zo's own appearance was hardly reassuring. Her blue coat, its silk lining now stained and torn, was once more stretched over every other piece of clothing she possessed. She had again bound her ankles with strips of woollen cloth and, having lost her hat at the inn, her head was wrapped in her scarf. Short and shapeless, she looked more like a stout village grandmother than a mountaineer.

It was 'a clear, cold night' when they finally set off, the peaks ahead dark against the deep blue of the sky.[27] Zo was prepared for a gruelling journey, but not for the beauty of the foothills bathed in moonlight. A couple of miles out, following an ancient road, white marble columns stretched up from the snowy hillside – the bleached bones of a Roman bath house once fed by mountain springs. Zo was far from sentimental, but her imagination was captivated by the 'utterly fairy tale image'.[28] Beyond the ruins was a snow-covered meadow. As the group hurried over, Zo heard a gunshot. 'Germans!' she thought, although later she wondered whether it had been one of the smugglers firing a pistol, or simply the sound of cracking ice.[29] The 'meadow' was a frozen river that had once supplied the ancient baths. In their panic, some of the group plunged through the ice, gasping at the freezing water. Paco ran for Zo, 'that precious woman with the money' as she now saw herself through his eyes, hauling her back while the others followed.[30]

Three days later, for a further fee, they tried again. There were fewer smugglers this time, but the group included the two Austrian Jews and Gilbert. Paco now led them on a 'brisk march' up a steeper, less well-known path.[31] Zo had to jump between the steep rocks that the men took in their stride, but she was fit and had no doubt about her ability to keep up. The climb was getting tougher when a blizzard began to whip up the loose snow on the ground. As the temperature plummeted to -20°C, the wind seemed to cut straight into Zo, lashing at her cheeks and smothering her breathing. Soon she lost the feeling in her face, feet and fingers. Her chapped lips swelled and her eyes ached. Lagging behind the men, she could feel the strength that she had had so much faith in only an hour earlier, rapidly draining from her.

Zo's world was now reduced to a contourless blizzard of white. Grateful to hear curses carried on the wind, she realised she was not the only one to fall behind – the two Austrians were somewhere nearby. One shouted that he could not go on and was sheltering by some rocks. Zo had finished her chocolate, but she pressed a little sugar into his hands. Then she stumbled on. Eventually, she found the others by a shepherd's hut, now filled with drifted snow. It took half an hour to clear it, their sweat freezing on their skin as they laboured. When they collapsed inside, Zo lay huddled between Paco and Gilbert, sharing the heat of their aching bodies.

After several hours, the storm blew itself out and Paco urged them on. They found they must have circled around, disorientated in the blizzard, because before long they came across the body of one of the Austrians, entombed in snow against the rockface where he had sought shelter. One of his hands protruded from the drift. 'Alone, frail,' Zo thought piteously, with 'no warming second body'.[32] After a short prayer, they pressed on in silence.

For some hours, Zo plodded forwards like King Wenceslas's frail page, marking only the footsteps of the man in front. The monotony helped, establishing a rhythm through which her thoughts could wander, taking her back to Poland and skiing at the PWK camps years earlier, and to her bitter journeys as a courier, and Marianna's cold Warsaw kitchen. When she next raised her face, Paco and Gilbert were barely discernible and the rest of the group had either pressed ahead or been left behind. Without a word, Gilbert fell in behind her. From then on, he and Paco took turns to walk ahead and astern, shoving Zo onwards if she faltered.

They were still toiling upwards when Paco announced that they were now in Spain. It seemed a good moment to pause. Zo's lips were so swollen, 'each one like a pillow', that she could hardly open her mouth.[33] The last of her supplies was gone, and all she could do was suck at the snow to ease her thirst. As she bent down, her eye was caught by an empty packet of cigarettes, a jarring strip of colour on the white. German. They were almost certainly still in occupied France, and they were not alone on the mountain. A moment later German voices carried to them on the wind.

Charging back down the mountainside, Zo saw an icy stream ahead but felt herself grabbed under both arms as the men wordlessly lifted her across. On the far side, a bank of snowy shingle shifted beneath her feet, rushing her down into a ditch where she lay, gulping in the cold air and heaving out clouds of steam until her heart stopped thumping. Paco had at least found his bearings again. There was a German watchtower around the next escarpment: two guards, but luckily no dogs. Retracing their steps once the patrol had passed, by morning they were back in Tarascon.

Zo was too tired to be livid. She slept for twenty-four hours straight until woken by her hunger. She had only a couple of dollars left, sewn inside her clothes. Her legs ached and her face and lips were bruised and bleeding, but after eating she felt she had enough fight left for one last attempt. Paco was unimpressed when she tried to bargain with him, but his uncle agreed to lead her, Gilbert and two other Frenchmen for promises in place of payment.

They set off in the second half of March, taking a route that ascended more steeply, with no allowance for their aching limbs. At around two in the morning, when the night was at its coldest and the greatest peaks still lay ahead, Zo knew she could no longer go on. Like the Austrian before her, she had lost the will to live. Lying down on the snow, her body 'on strike', she looked up at the pale stars, too exhausted to even make peace with herself.[34] Paco's uncle kicked her. Then he kicked her harder. What 'a terrible man' she thought, throwing him a hateful glance as she staggered to her feet.[35] Dragging a goatskin sack from his bag, he fired a stream of wine into Zo's face. She spluttered and gulped down a consoling mouthful. As the deceptive warmth of the alcohol spread through her, she marvelled at the power of a bag designed 'to piss wine on to your tongue'.[36] Then she stumbled on.

The new route was hard, but magnificent. At four in the morning, the sky's darkness began to shift and soften. Zo watched in awe as the highest peaks 'were bathed in a glorious pink and then in red gold, like fire'.[37] The fleeting beauty of this 'burning of the mountains' was, she felt, the most wonderful natural phenomenon she had ever seen.[38] Soon the sun was blazing, reflecting off the snow to the extent that Zo had to unwind her scarf and, fumbling, undo her coat buttons. Chamois goats were foraging in the scrub nearby, still in their light-grey winter coats, their anxious faces striped like badgers. Further ahead, she saw mountain eagles gliding on the thermals, their shadows rippling over terrain another thousand feet below.

Towards midday, Paco's uncle stopped at the tree line and searched the distant peaks through his binoculars. He told them he could see the silhouettes of frontier guards moving high across the valley but, with a sweep of his hand, also gestured that Spain lay ahead. Then he turned and started walking back. Hearing the others discussing how they could leave 'the woman' behind, Zo curtly nodded them on.[39] She and Gilbert followed more slowly. The air, blowing up from the valleys, smelt enticingly of pine and by midday it was very warm. There were still a few peaks ahead, but none as high as those they had crossed, and there were more trees to give them shade and shelter.

Eventually, the last snow gave way to full forest, ragged grass, then fields and a stream. Sitting on a sun-warmed rock beside the water, they washed their throbbing feet. Zo's clothes were now in tatters and the sides of her shoes were flapping loose. She was, she felt, 'inhumanly tired'.⁴⁰ No one blinked when the two fraying figures entered the nearest village. This was smuggling country where questions were rarely asked. Zo was asleep in her clothes as soon as she found somewhere to lie down.

It was only the next morning that they learnt they were in Andorra. This tiny sovereign state, dwarfed by its neighbours, was struggling to maintain its neutrality. Over a plate of fried potatoes and, joy of joys, fresh oranges, Zo told the only English official they could find that she was a Polish emissary expected at the honorary consulate in Barcelona, and that he had a responsibility to get her there. 'I must have made a strange impression,' she admitted, but a couple of hours later a car drove them to Sant Julià de Lòria, the last Andorran town before the Spanish border.⁴¹ On the way, they passed the men who had deserted them in the mountains. As the driver would not stop, Zo 'only gave them a wave' and sat back in her upholstered comfort to enjoy the look of 'astonishment' on their faces.⁴²

Still dressed 'in rags and completely filthy', at Sant Julià the two itinerants were taken to eat and rest.⁴³ Zo woke to find that her old clothes had been replaced with a dress, jacket and some thick espadrilles. The British could not, however, drive them into Spain. Although officially neutral, Franco was ideologically aligned with the Axis powers.* In the Spanish Pyrenees, anyone found illegally crossing the border was either deported back to France or detained in a holding camp. Zo was, however, provided with an experienced guide, this time 'a Spanish Red'.⁴⁴

Zo eyed the last peaks with dread; despite her brief rest she felt 'quite broken'.⁴⁵ Although no longer so cold, the ground was still white with snow and it was not long before her legs started cramping up. Gilbert let her lean on him, grumbling as kindly as he could, 'You are as heavy as a dog made of lead.'⁴⁶ Three hours later, they stopped at a hut near the border. It was mid-morning when they emerged, yawning and stretching, into a drifting mountain mist. Without a

---

* Two years earlier, Franco's 'Blue Division' had served with German forces against the Russians.

word, their guide suddenly started running. Snatching his kit from the ground, Gilbert hared after him. Zo glanced back. Through a break in the cloud she saw two border guards heading her way. Both were armed with rifles. Leaving her bag, Zo pelted after the men. Gilbert had outstripped their guide and she saw him leap a ridge. A moment later the Spaniard followed, disappearing from view. Zo was not fast enough.

The first gunshot cracked through the air beside her. She flinched and half ducked, but she did not stop running. Another bullet hit some rocks. By the time she reached the ridge, she could hear them whizzing 'over my head and to either side of me'.[47] Flinging herself over, she was relieved to find a thicker mist beyond. Instead of charging on after the men, she took cover behind the peeling grey trunk of a juniper tree growing high up through the rocks. Covering her face and hands with her scarf, she focused on controlling her breathing and prayed that sun would not burn off the mist.

The laboured breathing of the frontier guards was almost as loud as their footfall when they scrambled over the ridge. As they slithered down to the rocks beside Zo's tree, she noticed that one was holding her leather bag. Glimpsing Gilbert and the guide racing ahead, the guards moved on to steadier ground, and took aim. They were still close enough for Zo to hear them talking before they fired. A small avalanche of stones tumbled down from the ridge as the sound echoed around the valley. Moments later, the guards moved off and 'I was left alone on that rock,' Zo later reported matter-of-factly.[48]

Zo sat behind her tree for a long time. She had no guide, no map and no compass, but her brass cigarette lighter and key were still in her pockets and there were a few paper dollars sewn into the lining of her new jacket. Suddenly sneezing, to her astonishment she heard Gilbert bless her. He had circled back to find her and together they climbed, slid and scrambled down into Spain.

It was spring in the foothills. That afternoon Zo and Gilbert walked through orchards of almond trees in full bloom into an almost deserted village, its inhabitants working the fields. In one empty house, they ate the cold beans left in a pot on the stove. Then they met the village teacher, heading home on a donkey with a large black umbrella as protection from the sun. A deal was struck. In exchange for translating the BBC radio news that evening, the schoolmaster gave them another modest meal and a bed for the night.

Elżbieta Zawacka with her siblings, Toruń, 1919.
Back row: Alfons (Ali), Maria holding Elżbieta, Jan
Front row: Adela (Dela) and Egon

Elżbieta's parents, Marianna
Zawacka and Władysław Zawacki

Elżbieta's Poznań University
student ID photo, 1927

Egon Zawacki, Toruń, 1930

Zofia Zawacka and Alfons Zawacki,
Toruń, 1930

Elżbieta on horseback at a PWK camp, c.1932

Maria Wittek, the PWK commander in chief

Marianna Zawodzińska in PWK uniform

Elżbieta (centre, standing) as a PWK trainee, with friends, 1932

One of Zofia Grzegorzewska's PMK sketches, c.1932

Elżbieta, photographed
by Klara, 1937

Klara on the family
sofa, Toruń, late
1930s

PWK commander Zo, centre, with friends, c.1938

Dr Zofia Franio

Wacka Zastocka

Toruń, winter 1940

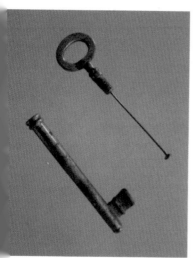

Maria Wittek's key, with secret storage space for microfilm

Zo's clothes brush with removable back, to hide documents

Emilia Malessa, head of Farmstead

Jan Piwnik, aka 'Ponury'

Ponury as commander of
the partisan group in the
Holy Cross Mountains,
December 1943

Zo in PWK uniform, left, and in civilian clothes while serving in 1942

Zo's London Sixth
Bureau papers, May
1943. She corrected
their spelling. She was
known to the British
as 'Elizabeth Watson'

Kazimierz Bilski, aka 'Rum', 1943

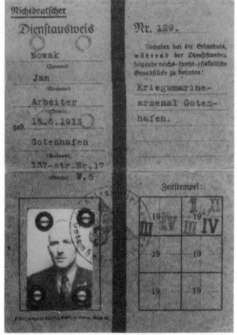

Jan 'Nowak' Jezioranski's
forged service card, 1943

The forged German identity card of Kazimierz Leski, aka 'Bradl', 1945

Silent Unseen (Cichociemni) weapons storage label, Audley End House, Essex

Silent Unseen trainees, Audley End House

Silent Unseen ropes training at Audley End House

Silent Unseen 'Polish Paratroops' booklet, 1943

Sue Ryder serving as a FANY during the war

Zo's Home Army armband, worn during the Warsaw Uprising,
1 August–2 October 1944

Home Army soldiers on Moniuszki Street barricade during the
Warsaw Uprising, 1944

Emilia Malessa, left, with her adopted son, Michał Westwalewicz, after the war

Emilia Malessa, far right, leaving prison with others pardoned by Bolesław Bierut, 7 February 1947

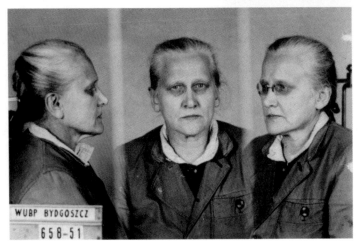

WUBP BYDGOSZCZ
658-51

Dr Zofia Franio, Bydgoszcz prison photos

Klara Zawacka and Maksymilian
Gołembscy, wedding portrait

Zo on a ski lift, 1964

Zo, 1980

Left: 2015 mural dedicated to Zo, by Andrzej Poprostu and Damian Jędrzejewski, on one side of her Gagarin Street apartment block, Toruń

Below left: Obelisk organised by Zo, to commemorate the Polish women who fought for freedom, in Wolności Park, adjacent to the Warsaw Uprising Museum

Below right: Memorial to the women flown from RAF Tempsford, Bedfordshire, to support the resistance behind enemy lines, 1941–1945. Zo's is the last name

It took Zo and Gilbert two days to reach the nearest train station, sixty miles away. Overnight, they slept in the ruins of a house destroyed during the civil war. The next morning Gilbert found them water and Zo begged some bread and salted fish from a woman they met on the road. Gilbert was 'a very brave boy', she felt. 'We liked each other very much.'[49] Once on the train, for a couple of hours they watched the countryside pass by as the dust of Spain built up on the window. Eventually the soaring lace towers of the Sagrada Família announced their approach to Barcelona and, promising to write through the poste restante and meet in Toulouse after the war, Gilbert headed off to the French Consulate.

It was 29 March when a serious young woman in dilapidated espadrilles shrugged apologetically to the woman washing the beautiful mosaic-tiled floor of the British Consulate in Barcelona, and asked to see the consul. Told that he had not yet arrived, a tired smile crept across Zo's face. As she was 'absolutely filthy', she went to wait in the garden.[50] 'I am a member of the clan Chisholm,' she told the consul when he arrived.[51] Delighted to hear her pass phrase, he ushered her upstairs and sent word to Emilia in Warsaw that 'Zo has been found'.[52] Zo objected to the wording. As far as she had been aware, the only people searching for her had been the enemy, but she let it go.

Zo was now issued with new false papers in the name of British citizen 'Elizabeth Watson'. She also received a clean set of clothes, a small amount of cash and a hotel room in which to await her transfer to London. 'Arrived . . . reception very good', she cabled the Sixth Bureau in London. 'Crossing the border very strenuous, 200km on foot in the mountains but possible without Spanish arrest . . . Further passage most likely in a couple of days . . . Zo.'[53]

Some hours later, Elizabeth Watson, aka Zo, headed out for some fresh air, but at the city's harbour she suddenly stopped in her tracks. Aruś, one of the Polish couriers she had known in Paris, was standing on the pier. Zo stared at him, watching as first recognition and then relief registered on his face. Having left Paris after Zo, Aruś had followed a similar route – only to be arrested in the Pyrenees. Although he had destroyed his microfilm, he had still been detained in the overcrowded white huts of the notorious Miranda de Ebro prison camp, the largest of the almost two hundred internment camps constructed by the Franco regime.

In 1942, the Polish authorities in London estimated that there were about four hundred Poles interned in the Miranda camp, 'the bulk of whom are of high military value', 'excellent fellows' and 'gallant fighting folk', a succession of British officers reported.⁵⁴ It was 'only in the case of men of very special qualifications', however, that the British would provide the papers and pressures needed to secure their release.⁵⁵ Aruś was among the select few. With evident pride, he told Zo that the British were now sending an aircraft from Lisbon.

Zo had always thought Aruś's talk of an airlift was fanciful. She was delighted to be proved wrong. Their ride was to be a Boeing 314 Clipper, a pre-war American flying boat built to take almost seventy passengers on long-distance luxury breaks. As London prepared her landing forms, they noted she was carrying 'confidential documents' and issued her with an 'Emergency Certificate', overprinted with a large 'E', to exempt her from British customs and interrogation.⁵⁶ A few days later, however, Aruś and Zo were told that the Clipper would now have only one spare seat.

As an emissary of the Commander of the Home Army, with two urgent missions in London, Zo had precedence, especially over a courier no longer carrying his mail. In case there was any doubt, the Home Army HQ in Warsaw radioed over the succinct instruction: 'Send emissary Zo before Aruś.'⁵⁷ Yet Aruś was allocated the seat. Dutifully, Zo handed him her brass cigarette lighter and key. The decision to send him in her place was never explained, but Zo had no doubt as to the reason. 'Naturally they take a man and not a woman,' she fumed, 'because a woman cannot be more important than a man!'⁵⁸ It was another reminder of the urgency of securing legal military status for the women in the Home Army. Without the formal recognition of rank, they would continue to be relegated by male officialdom, irrespective of their experience, abilities, duties or orders.

Stuck in Barcelona, Zo was reduced to 'begging' the consul to get her on another flight.⁵⁹ When that proved impossible she changed tack, demanding a train ticket to Gibraltar and sea passage from there to Britain. Pleased to see the back of this difficult woman, the consul arranged tickets for the following day. 'I was in such a hurry,' Zo stumbled to explain, if not as a recognised soldier then 'like a woman who wants to complete her task'.⁶⁰ A few days later, the Polish Sixth Bureau in London contacted the consulate to discuss Zo's onward travel, only to learn that she had already left. 'Each bit of news from her journey came to us too late to be of any use', their shamefaced staff admitted. 'Each of our attempts to direct her misfired, the instructions arriving after she had left . . . London headquarters had lost control of the situation.'[61]

In Madrid, Zo impatiently paced around the 'sunburnt city' while further arrangements were made, everywhere noting the recent destruction and spending her last money on a ticket for a bullfight.[62] The show was undoubtedly spectacular but she found herself looking 'not so much at the poor bull, as at the people'.[63] Half of the arena was flooded with sunlight and alive with the flutter of fans, the rest in deep, still shadow. Most of the women wore Spanish costume with high combs and veils and, when the toreadors strode in, they leant over their benches, cheering and slapping their fans on their arms. Zo felt that 'it was cruel' to make a wounded, taunted animal fight for its life.[64]* That evening she watched more women dance the flamenco, 'this beautiful Spanish dance', in the courtyard of her hotel.[65] What a country, she thought, as she watched them tilt their faces to the sky, their heels stamping the cobbles below, and, in their hands, their fans snapping open and shut as capriciously as life's opportunities.

⚓

On 19 April, the eve of Passover, German forces stormed the Warsaw Ghetto, aiming to present its 'liquidation' as 'a little gift' to Hitler for his birthday the following day.[66] The Jewish fighting resistance met them with a hail of rifle fire and hand grenades.[67] The Warsaw Ghetto Uprising was the first urban uprising of any underground movement in the Second World War.

Initially, the astounded German forces were driven back and 'German dead soon littered the street', one of the Jewish commanders noted.[68] The Luftwaffe then dropped incendiary bombs, setting the ghetto alight. The Home Army's attempt to blow a hole in one wall, providing a potential escape route, was abandoned after four of their men were killed and more wounded. The Germans then returned in tanks and armoured cars, heavily armed with grenades, flamethrowers

---

* Heinrich Himmler had been Franco's guest at a Madrid bullfight in October 1940. It was rumoured that the animal lover and architect of the Nazi's 'Final Solution' was so appalled by the cruelty of the spectacle that he almost fainted.

and machine guns. Despite being vastly out-gunned, the ghetto fighters forced their enemy to fight for every building. Instead of clearing
the ghetto in two days, the battle raged for six weeks.

⚓

The Warsaw Ghetto was still under attack when, a thousand miles
west, staff from the British Embassy in Madrid drove Zo the ten
hours to Seville, then on towards the distinctive outline of the rock
and, below it, the border with Gibraltar. While queueing to cross the
frontier, Zo was handed a telegram from Michał Protasewicz, head
of the Polish Sixth Bureau. 'Await your arrival here with impatience',
he had written. 'Place yourself for safe conduct entirely in British
hands.'[69] They were instructions she would soon be taking literally
as she endured a rigorous body search before stepping onto British
territory.

Gibraltar had been a British fortress since the early eighteenth century. In preparation for Operation Torch, the Allied landings in North
Africa, more than 100,000 troops and 400 aircraft had briefly con-
verged on the promontory. In the months since, it had served mainly
as a supply base, with depots and dry docks for the convoys coming
through. Now Gibraltar was filled with Polish servicemen, largely
those released from Soviet captivity, heading to Britain to regroup.

Zo was delighted to find herself surrounded by her military compatriots. Deflecting their curiosity, she suggested a visit to the garrison
cinema. It was the first film screening she had seen in over three years
and she watched in fascination at newsreels of Allied bombers heading
out to strike Berlin, hundreds of aircraft in the sky at once. 'The Führer
is having lots of trouble, especially with the war in the air', Goebbels
had noted in his diary.[70] Despite a few raids over London, Churchill
had meanwhile announced that restrictions on the ringing of church
bells could be lifted as the threat of invasion had passed.

There was no news yet of the Warsaw Ghetto, but the Polish government in London was flagging reports of the execution of large numbers
of prisoners at Auschwitz. Zo's beloved brother, Egon, had already
perished at the camp, but these deaths were specifically of Jewish men,
women and children. The rest of the newsreel covered the progress of
Allied troops in North Africa, America introducing rationing, and the
release of the latest film by Abbott and Costello, a comedy duo.

It was from the Polish soldiers themselves that Zo learnt what was, to her, the most shocking news. On 13 April, Berlin radio had broadcast the discovery of 'a ditch . . . twenty-eight metres long and sixteen metres wide, in which the bodies of 3,000 Polish officers were piled up in twelve layers'.[71] Several more mass graves were soon being excavated in the forests of Katyń, in western Russia. Many of the corpses had their hands bound behind their backs. All had been shot in the head. Although Zo did not yet know it, among them was Klara's fiancé, one of the 22,000 who had never returned from Soviet captivity. German analysis suggested a crime date of early 1940. This was when the area was in Russian hands, before Stalin had joined the Allies. 'We are now using the discovery of 12,000 Polish officers, killed by the GPU [Soviet secret police] for anti-Bolshevik propaganda on a grand style', Goebbels scrawled cynically in his diary. He had deliberately delayed the media announcement until the attack on the Warsaw Ghetto, to deflect international attention.

Zo boarded a troopship, the RMMV *Stirling Castle*, the following evening. Before the war, passage from Spain to England was measured in hours rather than days. Zo's ship, travelling in a convoy of nineteen, took over a week, heading first along the coast of Africa, and then in a great curve across the Atlantic. Even so, they faced aerial bombardment and, Zo noted succinctly, 'survived a submarine attack'.[72]

As Elizabeth Watson, Zo had been given a first-class cabin with three other Englishwomen, each of whom had survived the Siege of Malta and carried a bottle of whisky in her bag. Zo was tempted to take one bottle to the Polish soldiers in the sickbay, but instead brought some wine she had inveigled from 'an officer who wanted to please me'.[73] She preferred spending her time up on deck, watching the surface of the sea shift in the wind like a rippling field of wheat, now silver, now dark. On Easter Sunday she joined an open-air mass celebrated by a Scots chaplain wearing a kilt; a 'plaid skirt' she called it, not having seen one before.[74] This chaplain, the three doughty Englishwomen and the British troops 'were overjoyed', she felt sure, 'to hear the Poles singing hymns so loudly and with such fervour'.[75]

Eight days later, Zo left her cabin in the early morning chill and climbed up to the deck, still wet from overnight rain. It was nearly two months since she had left occupied Warsaw. During that time, she had been soaked to the skin in the tender of a steam train, thrown out into the snow from the first-floor window of an inn, and shot at in the freezing mountain passes of the Pyrenees, but she had evaded the enemy at every turn. As the morning clouds dispersed on May Day 1943, she could finally see the British coastline.

8

A Rather Difficult Woman
(May–June 1943)

'The interrogation of Miss Zajkowska proved to be rather difficult,' Zo's MI6 interviewing officer reported a couple of days after her arrival. 'Being on a special mission from the underground organisation to the Polish Sixth Bureau in London,' he added feebly, 'she was rather reluctant to pass . . . information on to me.'[1]

Zo was not in the mood for talking to Englishmen. Having been detained on board ship after docking at Liverpool, she had watched the Polish soldiers, Scottish clergy, British crew and even the three doughty Englishwomen, now with less weighty bags, all disembark. While they were on shore, enjoying the cups of tea provided by pinafore-wearing members of the Women's Voluntary Services, Zo was being subjected to further searches by perplexed British customs officials. Eventually a policewoman escorted her onto land.

As most place signs around the coast had been removed, Zo would always believe she had docked at Bristol.* Before she could be corrected, she was on the train to London. The English countryside seemed to be bursting with promise. Deer ran through the woods near the tracks, the hawthorn was in bloom, and the embankments frothed with cow parsley as though spring had been poured too fast. Yet a few hours later, Zo found herself going through security screening again, now at the women's offshoot of MI6's south London reception centre, in bomb-damaged Wandsworth.

Zo was unimpressed. Admittedly, the conditions in 'this English prison', as she called it, were 'very good', but it was all further delay.[2] Secret service memoranda show that Zo stuck to her 'legend', reporting only that she was Elizabeth Watson, real name 'Zofia Zajkowska', an officer expected by the Poles. She was willing to give a résumé of her journey, but would not share any intelligence that might be better

---

* Seeing advertising hoardings, some people believed they had arrived at Bovril.

reported to her compatriots first. Although allies, British and Polish national interests did not completely align, particularly with regards to the Soviet Union. Knowing intelligence was currency, Zo felt that, as another officer colourfully put it, 'we are the Polish Underground, and we do not wish the British to peek inside our underpants'.[3]

Once MI6 was satisfied that Zo was not an enemy agent and 'might well have been exempted from interrogation', she was escorted over to the Rubens Hotel on Buckingham Palace Road, now home to the Polish General Staff.[4] In the once-plush rooms upstairs, the men of the Sixth Bureau were still anxiously 'pondering over the fate' of Rowecki's remarkable female emissary.[5]

Running his fingers through his thick chestnut hair, one square-jawed officer admitted that they had always been one step behind Zo. Tall and distinctly handsome in the 1940s film-star mould, Kazimierz Bilski was Polish military chivalry incarnate. Powered by patriotism and deeply courageous, he had soaring ambition and no shortage of self-respect. In the last days before the war, he had exhorted the company he commanded to: 'Be men. Be brave. And when the war starts, do not let your country down.'[6] Less than three weeks later he had been forced to retreat across the border into Hungary. To his intense frustration, he had not set foot in Poland since.

Having served honourably in France, Kazimierz had reached Britain in June 1940 and was selected for further training. In Scotland, he learnt to lay mines and blow up bridges, speak English with a Scots accent and stay silent under duress. Despite once inadvertently laying barbed wire fencing on the lawns and fairways of the Royal and Ancient Golf Club of Saint Andrews, he returned to London commended as a 'first-class man of high intelligence' and 'a striking personality . . . [who] would inspire all with respect and confidence'.[7]

Kazimierz was sworn into the ranks of the Silent Unseen under the nom-de-guerre he had chosen, inspired by the bottle of dark Jamaican rum he saw standing 'resolutely, almost defiantly on its own against the oppression of the books' on his commanding officer's shelves.[8] It was as 'Rum' that he had been kitted out to parachute back to Poland in April 1943. Navigational error meant the flight was aborted, after which, Rum learnt, there were no longer enough hours of darkness to support further flights until the autumn.

Rum had been transferred to the Sixth Bureau while Zo was struggling across occupied Europe. Of the other couriers who had left

Poland on Rum's watch, Wilski had been arrested in France, there was still no news from Pankrac, and Aruś had only reached London with British help, carrying Zo's microfilm as he had had to destroy his own. Already honoured for her service as 'a courier of outstanding independence', the brilliant Zo was 'fast becoming a legend' and her arrival was 'an event of unusual importance' for the Sixth Bureau.[9] Registration forms had already been prepared for her, if rather haphazardly. Her name had been misspelt, and she was listed, bizarrely, as 'Wife Senior Captain'.[10] All that was needed now, was the woman herself.

Downstairs in the hotel lobby, Zo was wiping the lenses of her new glasses on the material of her skirt. Returning them to her nose, she saw Aruś staring at her. Her curt nod was all the invitation he needed. Rushing over, he kissed her three times, in the Polish custom, and dragged her up to the second floor. An awkward moment followed as Colonel Protasewicz wondered whether to salute her, or stoop to kiss her hand.[*] After a moment's hesitation he simply ushered her into the Sixth Bureau's rooms. 'Stop trying to predict Zo's whereabouts,' he told the assembled men triumphantly. 'Here she is!'[11]

'Before us stood a woman of middle height, fair, full of life and temperament, and very simply dressed,' Rum noticed. 'I looked at her as though at a person from another world.'[12] To this desk-bound soldier, Zo was 'the embodiment of courage and heroism', he continued rapturously. 'We touched her hand with great respect.'[13] Zo was not interested in reverence. 'She looked at us through her spectacles', Rum went on, 'and with great self-assurance said, "Oh, so you are the people running the liaison with us!"'[14] At first Rum was too 'struck with wonder and admiration' to take in Zo's tone.[15] It soon dawned on him, however, that her words were 'not to be taken as an expression of enthusiasm or delight' but were 'clearly more of a rebuke than anything else'.[16] Before he could intervene, one of his wide-eyed colleagues blurted out a question. How had it taken her, he asked eagerly, 'barely seven days to cross occupied Europe?'[17]

Zo sighed. The journey had taken almost two months. No one could have done it in a week. Why, she wondered, did they not know this? These were the men responsible for land communications with Poland.

---

[*] The colonel's wife, Maria Protasewicz, had recently arrived from Paris. Zo could have been forgiven for wondering how she had secured a flight.

Their tardiness in decrypting messages and disregard for instruction increased the risks faced by couriers, coders and wireless operators every day. Instead of answering, she set to work with questions of her own. Her first mission, after all, was to overhaul the courier communications system.

Military intelligence was one of Poland's 'most valuable contributions to the war', Zo knew, yet a significant part of the Home Army's 'mail' remained uncollected in Paris, Alsace and elsewhere.[18] 'Apart from the bitterness and discouragement which this state of affairs produces . . .' Rowecki had telegrammed London, 'a considerable part of our contribution to the war effort is being wasted.'[19] How did they track the mail, Zo now asked Rum. What happened when a courier disappeared from the radar, and what was the process once messages had been received? When vague responses failed to satisfy her, Zo sent the men running to pull out files and retrieve reports. From time to time someone popped their head round the door to see what was causing the unusual commotion, only hastily to withdraw again.

'With untiring energy Zo turned the office upside down, seeking out our inadequacies, mistakes and defects', Rum wrote sulkily, adding that she became 'progressively less pleased as the afternoon wore on'.[20] 'We worked quite well at first,' Zo agreed, until she discovered that the men seemed 'unconcerned about the fact that some message had not been fully deciphered in time'.[21] From then on, she reported, 'I started to point out their mistakes . . . I'm quite direct in these matters.'[22] When Protasewicz returned, Zo told him there were many things she found hard to understand, but she already doubted 'whether these gentlemen will be able to explain them to me'.[23] In one afternoon, she had unwittingly squandered the good will of the men who had held her in awe, but they had squandered the courage, hard work and bitter sacrifices of their Warsaw colleagues over many months.

Rum had booked Zo into a hotel near Piccadilly Circus, giving her some much-needed privacy along with her first insight into what she came to consider as 'the beautiful civic characteristics of English people'.[24] She loved to hear the newspaper vendors outside Piccadilly tube, freely shouting out the day's headlines. When an air-raid siren sounded, she was impressed by how calmly people went down to the shelters, and the next morning she was pleased to see a milkman back out on his rounds. Rum was right in thinking that Zo had come from 'another world'.[25] Life in Britain required a huge mental shift. There might be raids, but there were no 'Germans-only' spaces to negotiate or rules about deferentially stepping off pavements, and there were no street round-ups, beatings or public executions. In London, people still smiled at policemen. It took some getting used to. For the first time in over three years, Zo could stop looking over her shoulder and start speaking her mind.

Zo also loved the novelty of hearing so many languages spoken. Polish pilots on leave, American GIs and officers of the French Foreign Legion all brought a sense of shared endeavour to London that was hard to imagine inside occupied Poland. One evening, she heard someone shouting, 'Madame Rivière!'[26] Turning, she saw two of the young Frenchmen who had been arrested at the Tarascon inn. Having escaped their prison transport, this pair had managed to reach Spain by fishing boat, and Britain by troopship. When they told her they were off to join the French forces, Zo started to feel a new optimism seep through her.

Zo's official debrief started on 5 May. She had not examined the microfilms she had brought to Barcelona 'in case I was captured and subjected to torture', but she knew they contained a wide-ranging haul for General Sikorski, the Polish prime minister and commander-in-chief.[27] There was information on the German U-boats threatening Allied supply lines; troop movements across Europe; German industry including munitions; and Home Army sabotage, both planned and executed. Collectively, this could help protect Allied convoys and inform strategy for military ground forces, as well as RAF Bomber Command.

There were files on enemy aircraft and 'experiments with mysterious weapons'.[28] These were the prototype V1 flying bomb, an early cruise missile that the British would nickname the 'buzz bomb' or 'doodle-bug' from the sound of its pulse-jet engine, and the V2 rocket, the world's first long-range guided ballistic missile. Increasingly investing his hopes for final victory in this technology, Hitler had called them his 'Vengeance Weapons'.*

Escape, evasion and courier routes were also covered in the reports, with photographs of the many papers required, and an overview of

---

* These reports supported previous intelligence from Denmark, met with initial scepticism, and France, delivered by Marie-Madeleine Fourcade's network. On 17 to 18 August 1943, the Peenemünde testing site was partially destroyed in an Allied raid, delaying the V-weapons for some critical months.

resistance co-operation across Europe. To this, Zo added accounts of her own experience, where to register, where to stay, and how to buy train tickets, coffee and beer (she advised taking packed lunches). Every detail was crucial not only for Polish couriers, but also for other Allied agents being sent behind enemy lines. Within Germany there was not only a Polish network but also an independent domestic resistance, Zo added. She had to admit that she had not seen any resistance slogans daubed on the walls of the Nazi capital. Nevertheless, 'general morale appeared to be fairly low', she reported, and there was 'considerable despondency'.[29]

Finally, Zo had brought out the latest Polish reports on the persecution of their Jewish community, including accounts of the Warsaw Ghetto before the uprising, a dossier on Auschwitz, and broader German plans for the 'extermination of Poles and Jews' in territories annexed to the Reich.[30] This all added weight to earlier reports by men such as Jan Karski, the previous emissary to London and now the Polish government's delegate for Jewish matters.

In 1942, Jan Karski, an angular man with piercing blue eyes, had made two clandestine trips into the Warsaw Ghetto and another to a transit camp.* 'Everywhere was hunger, misery, the atrocious stench of decomposing bodies, the pitiful moans of dying children', he wrote, all 'enveloped in a haze of disease and death'.[31] As well as his own witness testimony, a meeting with leaders of the Jewish Bund had enabled him to bring out the community's own defiant demands for action. He had arrived in London in late 1942. That December, the Poles had published an official warning about Germany's 'aim, with systematic deliberation, at the total extermination of the Jewish population'.[32] One week later, eleven Allied governments had issued a statement of condemnation that made the front page of the *New York Times* and, in Britain, was read out in the House of Commons by Foreign Secretary Anthony Eden. Poland, Eden concluded, 'has been made the principal Nazi slaughterhouse'.[33] His words were followed by a minute's silence.

On Churchill's directive, the RAF then dropped a million leaflets over Germany, warning the regime of potential reprisals should they continue their persecutions. But no bombers were sent to destroy the railway tracks that led to the camps. By March 1943, a new crematorium

* Karski believed he had been smuggled into Bełzec extermination camp, but it is now thought to have been a nearby transit camp.

at Auschwitz enabled the incineration of over three thousand bodies a day, and Goebbels pledged that he would not 'rest until the capital of the Reich . . . has become free of Jews'.[34]

The Warsaw Ghetto Uprising was still raging when Zo was being debriefed in London. 'The extermination of the Jews is confirmed', one of her interviewing officers recorded bluntly.[35] Afterwards, she joined Jan Karski at a meeting with the Polish minister of information, Stanisław Kot, a quiet, grey-haired man, Karski observed, 'inclined to be pedantic'.[36] Zo's contribution was minimal, but every testimony carried weight. Karski would travel to the United States that July, where he lobbied President Roosevelt for action.[37] Yet neither Britain nor America was willing to divert resources from the main war effort, as it was perceived. 'We have repeatedly told the Poles, reprisals are ruled out', the British Foreign Office noted, while one diplomat grumbled that 'the Poles are being very irritating about this'.[38]

⚓

When Zo had been fully debriefed, Protasewicz arranged her return to MI6. At first there was some scepticism. 'She has had several pieces of luck', British officers noted, and 'narrowly escaped arrest on at least three occasions'.[39] But after initial concerns that she might have 'had her journey facilitated by the Germans without having knowledge of that fact' had been dismissed, interest grew in the 'vast amount of information' she was in a position to provide.[40] Zo now also took the opportunity to raise her concerns about the threat posed by the Soviet Union. The Poles 'believe that the Western Allies will in some way prevent the Russians from entering Poland', she told the officers earnestly. 'Confidence in Britain is 100 per cent.'[41] She was starting to fear that such faith might be 'a form of wishful thinking'.[42]

Zo's interrogation report was forwarded to, among others, the Special Operations Executive. Already sending agents behind enemy lines, SOE was always alert for good contacts. Harold Perkins, the tough head of the Polish Section, was not easily impressed but he recognised results when he saw them. 'This straightforward, intelligent, very brave woman . . . has undoubtedly contributed greatly to the common effort', he wrote to his boss, Colin Gubbins.[43] 'I do feel there should be some recognition of her services . . . some such decoration as the OBE.[44]

Gubbins had witnessed the Polish defence first-hand as a member of the British Military Mission in the autumn of 1939. Zo may even have been among the women he had seen 'building barricades with their bare hands against the brutal invader' as his convoy fled through Lwów and into Romania.[45] Like Perkins, he greatly admired the Poles, but OBEs were rarely awarded to foreign nationals. 'Thanks for letting me see this', Gubbins scrawled back in thick pencil. 'She sounds a splendid person.[46] Zo had no interest in honours, but it was perhaps good that she did not see these exchanges. The British closed their file on her with the patronising note that 'she's a grand girl'.[47]

The Poles also felt that Zo deserved a decoration, and she was ordered to report to General Sikorski. Although she had been in civilian clothes since 1939, Protasewicz now noted that she put on 'a uniform with a captain's insignia'.[48] He had provided the uniform, but Zo had added the badge. 'I didn't consider the rank of Polish army captain to be an excess of ambition!' she laughed when learning of his disdain.[49]

In his sixties, Sikorski's heavy jowls and drooping eyelids were a gift to caricaturists, but he was a shrewd politician and inspiring military leader. 'Tall and upright in bearing', Jan Karski felt that he was 'one of the rare, great men'.[50] Knowing that Sikorski was 'already a legend in Poland', Zo felt the honour of the meeting keenly, but she also considered the opportunity.[51] She had no doubt that once this 'Man of Providence' had been made aware of the problems Farmstead was facing, immediate action would follow. Yet the Polish war had changed fundamentally over the weeks it had taken Zo to reach London, and Sikorski had been engulfed by events of which she had little knowledge.

Zo was a resistance soldier, loyal, courageous, determined, a brilliant opportunist, but not a strategist. When Marianna, in Warsaw, had liked to spend an evening considering how they might help shape the political future, Zo had always brought their focus back to winning the war that day. And when she had heard, from the Polish soldiers on her troopship, about the discovery of mass graves at Katyń, Zo had been struck by the human tragedy rather than the political implications.

Goebbels' claim that the massacre had been committed by the Soviets had provoked Stalin to furious denials. As Britain and America could not afford to alienate their mighty Soviet ally, this put Sikorski in an impossible position. When he had called for an independent International Red Cross investigation, five days before Zo reached London, Stalin accused him of co-operating with the Nazis and broke off diplomatic relations.* Even moderate attempts to placate the Soviet leader were then met with Polish opposition. There were 'hostile machinations in London', one general wrote, and 'whispered propaganda discrediting everything'.[52]

It was little wonder then that, when Sikorski met Zo, he 'did not take a specific interest in the affairs of Poland', as she understood them.[53] What riled her, however, was that 'he didn't even try to understand'.[54] Instead, Sikorski seemed to be wasting their hour together, talking with 'a tinge of personal resentment' about himself and 'the many obstacles thrown at his feet'.[55] As Rum knew, 'Zo always said the truth as she saw it . . . irrespective of the rank or position of those she was addressing'.[56] Determined to take something from this meeting, she next raised the issue of regulating women's 'participation in battle'.[57] After some surprise, Sikorski told her to submit a report when he returned from his tour of the Middle East.

It was with some impatience that Zo then stood to attention while she was awarded her third Cross of Valour, 'for fruitful work fighting for the military cause in Poland'.[58] But when she saw a photographer raise his camera, she abruptly turned away. An image in the papers would have prevented her from returning to clandestine service. 'This proves that he had absolutely no idea,' Zo seethed.[59] The meeting had been an 'utter disappointment'.[60]†

Zo would report to several more Polish dignitaries over the next few weeks, but the longer she stayed in London, the more irritated she became by what she dismissed as 'émigré politics'.‡ Her colleagues were 'all very patriotic', she granted, but constantly distracted by having to position themselves in support of rival political factions.[61] Her heart

---

* This paved the way for Stalin to impose an alternative, communist government on Poland.

† Protasewicz saw the meeting differently. Zo 'replied to most questions with "I don't know"', he wrote scornfully, 'and consequently the Commander-in-Chief gave up on the conversation'. See PUMST, KOL 23/326, EZ personal file.

‡ President Raczkiewicz, Deputy PM Mikołajczyk, and Generals Marian Kukiel, Kazimierz Sosnkowski and Haller – who she had last seen leading his troops through the triumphal gateway into Toruń in 1920.

sank whenever a portrait of Piłsudski was taken down before a visit from Sikorski or his daughter. Once they had left, the picture would be rehung. 'Such petty things' struck her as 'utterly repulsive'.[62] In those first weeks in London, 'the émigré atmosphere hit me like a blow to the head,' she later admitted. 'During the whole war I never cried through so many sleepless nights . . . as I did there.'[63]

Telling everyone that she had orders to return after just six weeks, Zo now threw all her furious force into overhauling the land communication system. She has 'fantastically overblown personal ambition', Protasewicz decided, and 'untrammelled curiosity and inquisitiveness . . . She is not very intelligent, but is very cunning.'[64] Nevertheless, he allocated Zo a personal adjutant to help in the work. 'I protested but it did me no good', Rum wrote resentfully.[65]

Rum's first task was to retrieve the paperwork Zo needed to identify the problems with the courier system. 'It was,' she admitted, 'enormous, tedious work.'[66] Polish leaders were in constant communication, with thousands of documents travelling between Warsaw and London. Only the most urgent messages were sent by radio, because, as one officer explained, 'clandestine coded wireless traffic . . . is cumbrous, tedious, and highly vulnerable' to interception and 'dangerous misunderstandings'.[67] In any case, reports, maps and diagrams, photographs, film footage and original documents could not be reduced to Morse.

Because the Sixth Bureau did not appreciate the peril involved in collecting and processing this intelligence, they had not treated the mail with the respect it deserved. 'Whenever I thought of a message being sent out of occupied, fighting Poland, I would think about the mortal danger of a dozen or so soldiers', Zo wrote. So she was 'utterly dismayed' to find that days might pass before the messages were decoded, and she 'refused to believe that this tardiness couldn't be prevented'.[68] Next, she set about tracing the route of missing messages. These were not journeys that Rum was keen to join her on. 'She kept devising more and more difficult problems for me to solve,' he moaned. 'Their solution required the assistance of the Gestapo or the gift of second sight' but Zo was 'always complaining of carelessness and inefficiency'.[69]

Rum was used to praise from his bosses, admiration from his colleagues and appreciation from women. He found Zo's lack of deference, indeed her lack of any apparent interest in him at all, perplexing and deeply vexing. 'I wanted so much, even if only for an instant, to see Zo as a woman,' he confessed. 'My ambition was piqued. Out of a bachelor's long-standing habit, I did my best to draw her into some semblance of flirtation.'[70]

It was late May 1943. Most of the cherry blossom had fallen but London's parks were full of the scent of bluebells, the sound of bird-song and 'all over the lawns', Rum noticed, 'American soldiers sat tightly clasping their female companions'.[71] Hoping that 'after office hours her femininity would assert itself', he decided to launch a charm offensive.[72]

The very concept of office hours offended Zo. While working through the night with Emilia and Marianna in Warsaw, she had imagined the London team also at their desks. Now she realised 'the men were like clerks, working nine-to-five and drinking tea'.[73] 'That's the way it is with men,' she concluded. 'They are not as focused on duty as women . . . women have a different attitude to work.'[74]

Rum was now fully focused on Zo. Once he was happy that 'the lush green foliage and the atmosphere all around us were most conducive to romance', he produced some silk stockings from his pocket like an amor-ous magician, and 'tried to lead the conversation onto topics suggested by the picturesque scenes'.[75] 'Her reaction', he wrote, 'was startling.'[76]

Abruptly stopping in her tracks, Zo turned to stare at Rum. It took her a moment to process his overtures. 'He was having some trivial conversation, with flirting,' she realised, while 'I still had the tragedy of occupied Poland in my mind. Egon had died in Auschwitz, and here he is, talking to me about stockings.'[77] His natural self-assurance cracking like an eggshell beneath the impact of her scowl, Rum tried to fill the awkward silence by pointing out that all English ladies wore stockings, and that Zo's bare legs were 'not elegant'.[78]

The only women wearing silk stockings in Poland were the wives of German officers. But instead of being dragged into a debate about nylons, Zo launched into a spirited lecture on the future role of Poland in liberated Europe. This was where his thoughts should be directed, she was telling him. Perhaps seeing her personal struggles as aligned to those of her country, she then suggested that the Polish nation had such spiritual strength that it could withstand oppression for years to come and might eventually lead all wronged countries towards a better future. Such views seemed 'pretty far-fetched' to Rum but, shaking his head, he pocketed the stockings and parked the romance.[79]

Deeply patriotic, Rum was a frustrated soldier determined to serve his homeland but also keen to enjoy all that life had to offer. He simply could not understand that Zo did not want to be seduced; she wanted military results. The next morning Zo was back in the Sixth Bureau's rooms as soon as they were open. She worked furiously until three, when the desks were sealed. Then she went through her notes at her lodgings. She was so uncompromising as she fought against neglect that 'the male staff . . . had to organise defensive action against her', Rum wrote, and one of his colleagues admitted that 'she was feared by all of Section Six'.[80] The way Rum saw it, 'war was declared – Zo singlehandedly against the three of us'.[81] One of the team even composed a rallying couplet to recite in hushed tones when Zo left the room: 'You have to admit, though little and frail, the fight I shall win, as I am a male'.[82]

Zo would never be satisfied with her Sixth Bureau work. 'I could not complete the assignment', she reported, requesting a 'communications specialist' be sent from Warsaw.[83] Yet despite the 'state of war' that Rum imagined existed between them, together they did make progress. Danger points were identified, as were redundant 'post offices' where mail got stuck in Istanbul and Lisbon, and the European bases to which London staff could be sent to ease the burden on couriers. A new sense of respect, urgency and care was also instilled in the office. Slowly, the reluctant Protasewicz lent Zo more support, and even Rum came grudgingly to respect this 'captain in a skirt' with such 'drive, conscientiousness and experience'.[84] It was a drive born of the frontline service that she would not discuss, and which the men could not imagine.

The irony that tainted Zo's relationship with her colleagues was that it was she, the woman, who had lived the life of a soldier behind enemy lines, but Rum and Protasewicz, sitting behind their desks, who wore the uniform. Zo had long understood that, had she been Rum's superior officer, his attitude would have been different. The Sixth Bureau team 'could not stand criticism', she saw, 'especially from a woman who they did not consider to have authority'.[85] 'Constantly exposed to torture and death', Zo knew that women were soldiers in every meaningful way, yet legally they were still 'volunteers in auxiliary military service', without recognition and unable to pull rank.[86] It was time for Zo to turn to her second mission: securing the legal status of female soldiers in the Home Army.

9

A Militant Female Dictator
(June–July 1943)

'Women perform frontline service in occupied Poland on par with men', General Rowecki had written in the preamble to his draft decree on women's military status.[1] He knew it was true; he had seen it for years. Zo knew it was true; she was a case in point. The problem was that few of the staff officers in London could believe it.

The resistance Home Army had been designated as an official army by its exiled government, and the more than 400,000 men eventually sworn in were recognised as combatants. The 40,000 women, who took the same oath, were not. Certainly, fewer of the women bore arms but a significant number did, including Zofia Franio's teams. And among the army's most important contributions since 1940 was the constant flow of intelligence west, which was overwhelmingly collected, coded and transported by women.

Rowecki's sole focus was the operational effectiveness and overall security of the army he commanded. He was not concerned about female morale, and he did not consider himself to be progressive, a feminist, or an equal opportunities employer. But he saw that these women were 'soldiers facing the enemy' while undertaking service 'identical to ours', and he appreciated that their requests were no substitute for orders, and male chivalry was no replacement for military respect.[2] As Zo put it, Rowecki's decree would enable him to make best use of all the resources available to him simply by 'enabling us to be normal soldiers'.[3]

Honoured to have been selected as Rowecki's emissary, Zo had already started opening the right London doors to get his proposal considered, and she had rehearsed plenty of arguments to stop them slamming shut again. But it was Rowecki's own words that she relied on to carry the case. So when the devastating news of his arrest arrived from Warsaw, Zo felt the blow twice over.

Rowecki had been betrayed by three of his own: two men and a woman.* Once they had built up the trust needed to learn his address, sixty cars had brought over two hundred armed men to arrest him. 'Even the rooftops swarmed with soldiers', one eyewitness reported.[4] The following day, a Home Army unit secretly removed the seals placed across the door of Rowecki's apartment and rescued $15,000 and numerous papers, before escaping through the gardens. Rowecki, however, could not be rescued. Knowing the value of their catch, the SS took him straight to Berlin where he endured interrogations by Heinrich Himmler, among others. After he had rejected a proposal to co-operate with the Third Reich against the Soviet Union, he was incarcerated with other prominent prisoners in Sachsenhausen, the Nazi's 'model concentration camp', just twenty miles outside the German capital.

'At the end of June, I *survived* the arrest of Grot Rowecki', Zo later wrote.[5] 'Grot', meaning 'Spearhead', was his wartime nom-de-guerre, and Zo felt the blow deeply. His arrest had not only removed the greatest champion of military rights for female soldiers, it was also Rowecki who had successfully welded together the many politically diverse early resistance groups into a single national force during the first years of the war.

Sikorski heard the terrible news while on his month-long tour of the Middle East. Despite the strain put on his leadership, the tour had been a great success, helping to quell rumours of a possible coup.[6] He flew out on the first leg of his journey back to Britain, via Gibraltar, on 3 July. There had been serious concerns about him travelling by air throughout 1943. Despite believing that 'death awaits him on one of the flights', one colonel wrote, Sikorski tended to bat such worries aside.[7] His worst mishaps in the skies to date had been the discovery of an incendiary bomb on a flight over Canada, an emergency landing in the Middle East due to a problem with his aircraft's undercarriage, and the airsickness of two colleagues that had 'completely destroyed Colonel Protasewicz's new Burberry coat'.[8]

The following evening, Sikorski's aircraft, an American Liberator, crashed into the sea just sixteen seconds after take-off from Gibraltar,

---

* Eugeniusz Swierczewski, Ludwik Kalkstein and Blanka Kaczorowska were all sentenced to death by an underground court. Swierczewski was executed. Kalkstein was protected by the Gestapo. Kaczorowska had her sentence commuted because she was pregnant.

instantly killing every passenger on board.* As well as Sikorski this included four British men, several senior Polish military figures, two of Sikorski's adjutants, and his daughter, Zofia Leśniowska, who had 'firmly demanded' to accompany her father as his trusted secretary and to oversee Women's Auxiliary Service business.⁹ There was also one unidentified passenger on the high-security flight, leading to speculation that he might have been an assassin. Although a British court of enquiry later established that there was no evidence of sabotage, conspiracy theories quickly blossomed.

Churchill, among the first to be informed of Sikorski's death, was 'profoundly moved and shocked' by the news. At 10 Downing Street, in a room 'dense with smoke', he claimed to have loved Sikorski as a younger brother, and then 'started to cry'.¹⁰ Churchill felt Sikorski's loss personally, but he also knew how much it would further diminish Poland's standing. 'I shall not forget you,' he broadcast to the Polish people. 'My thoughts are with you and will always be with you.'¹¹

The British prime minister was not the only one moved to tears. The loss of Sikorski just four days after Rowecki's arrest 'shook the whole country', one Home Army officer reported.¹² In Warsaw people stood silently in the streets in shock and grief, listening as the news was announced 'triumphantly' through the loudspeakers erected by the Germans for propaganda communiqués.¹³ 'Some women had tears in their eyes,' the officer noted, while another recalled whole crowds 'weeping'.¹⁴

Zo, who had been sent to Scotland to learn how to use a new container for microfilm that would incinerate its contents if not correctly opened, heard the news shouted out by paperboys in a Glasgow street. Within hours, she had been recalled to London. To her surprise, she was needed to help solve the mystery of the unidentified body from Sikorski's flight. Meeting her at the Rubens Hotel, Protasewicz passed her a post-mortem photograph of a man of medium weight, tall – almost lanky – and with dark hair. 'Pankrac!' Zo cried out in dismay.¹⁵

Having returned to Poland after he and Zo had had to abandon their attempt to cross France inside the water tender of Pierre Laval's train, Pankrac had been given new false papers by Emilia Malessa, and sent back out almost immediately. He was arrested a couple of

---

* Only the Czech pilot, Eduard Prchal, survived, badly injured.

weeks later, disappearing into Spain's notorious Miranda del Ebro camp. There Pankrac started keeping a diary for his wife and sister, 'to whom', Zo knew, he was 'immensely attached'.[16] A few months later, Emilia traced him to the camp and leant on the British to extricate him, as they had done with Aruś. Eventually reaching Gibraltar, Pankrac was arranging his onward travel when one of Sikorski's adjutants had introduced him to the great man. Sikorski had immediately invited Pankrac to join his flight, stowing his small case on top of his own.

After the air disaster, Protasewicz had flown to Gibraltar to collect Sikorski's possessions, along with those of the other passengers that had been recovered by English divers. 'They fished Sikorski's leather suitcase out of the shallow sea,' Zo later recounted.[17] As well as the general's case, medals and suede shoes, and his daughter's five dresses, two bathing costumes, her wellingtons and seal-skin coat, but not her body (which was never recovered), Protasewicz collected Pankrac's briefcase. It had been quickly identified by the papers inside, but they had to confirm that the anonymous body was his. Zo would later read her friend's 'strange, poetic letters' to his wife, along with his last diary entry, penned just before the crash.[18] 'I could not be any happier,' Pankrac had written. 'Today I reported to the Commander-in-Chief.'[19]

Rowecki's arrest and detention, so quickly followed by the death of Sikorski, made Zo take stock. Her task had been made immeasurably more difficult by the fates of both of the crucial decision makers. Within the space of a week, Poland had lost two of its most senior wartime leaders, throwing the government into turmoil. The legal status of women in the Home Army, never a priority, was now seen as a distraction and most of the remaining leadership were sceptical about any change to the law.

Stanisław Mikołajczyk, the frontrunner to replace Sikorski as prime minister, was virtually unknown in British circles. When Churchill asked who he was, Mikołajczyk was described as 'the man who looks like a fat, slightly bald, old fox'.[20] Zo had already met this apparently uninspiring man, who had seemed unable to grasp that there was little distinction between the home front and the frontline inside occupied Poland. To Zo's dismay, he now 'declared that he was strongly opposed to women's involvement in frontline fighting'.[21]

It was clear that Zo had her work cut out if she were to convince the new leadership to adopt Rowecki's draft decree. Should she overcome the political inertia on the issue, the predominant view was that the status of women in the Home Army should simply be aligned with that of the Polish women volunteering overseas – largely based on British models. Zo would need to familiarise herself with both nations' auxiliary services to see what might be learnt.

Polish women's auxiliaries had been established long before their British equivalents, but the women in them had never been expected to see frontline service, hence the need for the PWK. In late 1939, when Polish forces had regrouped in France, many of these women had gone with them as clerks, medics and drivers. Two years later, after Stalin joined the Allies, thousands of the Polish men, women and children previously deported to Siberia by the Soviets had been granted an 'amnesty'. Female volunteers of conscription age received training to become medics, welfare and education officers, cooks, clerks, coders, wireless operators and some eight hundred military drivers. It was they who made up the core of the new Polish 'Women's Auxiliary Service', widely known as the *Pestki*, from its Polish acronym of PSK, and which translates as 'Pips' or 'Seedlings'.

Since early 1942, there had also been Pips formations in Britain. Initially they were commanded by Zofia Leśniowska, Sikorski's daughter, and later by the wife of another Polish officer. Since neither woman had been a member of the PWK or received any military training, Zo was contemptuous of both appointments. 'As men do, they made an officer's wife, who knew nothing, a commander,' she commented scornfully.[22]

The Pips' organisational structure was modelled on the British women's auxiliaries. 'The English army was made on a grand scale,' Zo commented admiringly. 'There were five million women mobilised.'[23] This was an exaggeration, although female recruitment had swelled after the National Service Act of December 1941. 'Men in the Forces generally have been emphatic that they would not allow their wives to go into the services,' one MP had claimed during the bill's lively debate, while another had called the move 'revolting'.[24] Yet others had argued that 'the vast majority of women will be behind them . . . [as] we wish to win the war at the earliest possibility'.[25] The bill passed, but women were still not permitted to serve in combat roles.

The largest British women's military organisation, the Auxiliary Territorial Service, or ATS, was 250,000 strong at its peak. Initially cooks, clerks, drivers and mechanics, ATS women eventually took hundreds of roles, including manning searchlights and anti-aircraft batteries. The Women's Royal Naval Service, affectionately known as the Wrens, and the Women's Air Force Auxiliary, or WAAF, had 74,000 and 182,000 women in their ranks respectively. British women also served in the Women's Voluntary Service, the National Fire Service and the Air Transport Auxiliary, as well as in Civil Defence and military nursing. Six thousand also signed up with First Aid Nursing Yeomanry. Lovingly known as the FANY, this historic corps was a unique formation in that they served in uniform but outside British armed forces structures. It was the FANY who had been designated to support the Polish troops, and Zo put in a request to meet their commander.

Harold Perkins, the head of SOE's Polish Section, reluctantly made the arrangements. A few weeks earlier, Perkins had put Zo forward for a British honour. Now he had his doubts about her, perhaps after talking with the bruised Sixth Bureau men. She is 'delving into political and military-organisational matters', Protasewicz wrote nervously. And she has 'established extra-military contacts, especially among women. Please consider the above when using her for further work'.[26]

Rather than risking sending Zo to the FANY's royal president, Princess Alice, Perkins directed her to their staff commander, 'an energetic, somewhat elderly lady' called Marian Gamwell.[27] 'I am sure that the things you will be able to tell her without the deterrent of the male presence will be of greater satisfaction to her!' Perkins wrote to Gamwell.[28] 'As you know, I have a good deal of experience in this type of work', he added incongruously.[29] 'I may therefore be forgiven the presumption of advising you particularly to stress the democratic angle, that is to say that it is the people of this country as a whole who should decide what part women are to play in this War, rather than the dogmatic rulings of those in power.'[30] 'Elizabeth Watson', he warned, 'is inclined to take the militant female dictator view of things!'[31]

Perkins had misjudged his missive. Marian Gamwell, in her early fifties, was a veteran of the First World War and an old-school, no fuss, get-the-job-done type, affectionately referred to by her friends as 'a queer fish' and by the younger FANY as a 'battle axe'.[32] She was not about to be lectured on the dangers of militant feminism by an overbearing young chap in uniform so far from the front.

A decorated veteran of the Great War, Gamwell had been drawn out of retirement in 1939 to prevent the FANY from being sidelined in the new conflict. 'The War Office was intent on persuading everybody that the FANYs had now given up,' she groaned. 'I had to take steps to refute this.'[33] Her key ally was Perkins's SOE boss, Colin Gubbins, who realised that, being independent from the armed forces, the FANY were the only uniformed British women entitled to bear arms. Women commissioned into the FANY, and trained in firearms and explosives among other skills, could therefore serve as special agents inside enemy-occupied territory where able-bodied men were still more likely to attract attention.

SOE training reports show the prejudice these women still had to overcome. 'Would make an excellent wife for an unimaginative man', one summary read, while another trainee was assessed for her 'sex appeal'.[34]* Even praise came with caveats. 'This student, though a woman, has definitely got leadership qualities', ran the report for another trainee who would indeed later lead a resistance army in France.[35]† Eventually SOE would send thirty-nine female agents behind enemy lines in France alone. This was service that Zo could recognise and potentially use to promote her own case.

Zo first met Marian Gamwell in her London office for a brief 'business conversation'.[36] Shaking hands, both women smiled at their convergence of khaki but 'unfortunately, my English was too poor for me to show her what Polish women are like', Zo sighed.[37] Unwilling to give up, Gamwell invited Zo for an off-record supper at her apartment where they would have more time to make themselves understood.

Sinking down into an armchair, Zo balanced her drink on a table piled high with papers, a couple of Dorothy L. Sayers novels, and a FANY calendar filled with just the kind of jolly drawings of singsongs in tents lit by hanging lamps that Zofia Grzegorzewska had drawn before the war. At first, Zo worried that she 'behaved very awkward-ly'.[38] Then she decided she did not care. Perhaps Gamwell broke the ice by telling stories from her Great War service. She was, Zo felt, 'very brave'.[39] Soon they had successfully exchanged overviews of their respective organisations, Zo deciding that 'the FANY is more or less the same as our PWK – voluntary . . . great patriots, very dedicated to the cause'.[40]

By the time Gamwell's maid served dinner, the two women rec-ognised that they shared an agenda to maximise the effective female

---

* These reports were for Yolande Beekman and Yvonne Cormeau.
† Pearl Witherington.

contribution to the Allied war effort. Zo now had one specific request. She wanted to understand the British women's auxiliaries 'as precisely as possible'.[41] That meant visiting various stations and training programmes, and interviewing the servicewomen themselves. Before the evening was over, Gamwell had offered her a tour of women's bases across England and Scotland.

'May I let you know how grateful I am for your help with regard to Elizabeth Watson', Perkins wrote politely to Gamwell.[42] He and Protasewicz were committed to supporting Zo's tour but, as she was a foreign national and apparently a feminist, Perkins assigned a FANY sergeant to accompany her at all times.[*] Zo would come to refer to the FANY collectively as her 'guardian angels'.[43]

It was early when Zo was driven over to Stanmore, in the leafy north London borough of Harrow. A few looming and luminous barrage balloons, anchored by thick steel cables, marked the grounds of RAF Bentley Priory, a former royal residence.[†] Now the estate was both Fighter Command HQ and the home of the Royal Observer Corps, a body of uniformed civilians who tracked enemy bombers once over the British coastline. A house nearby had been turned into a WAAF training centre, where the women were processed through a series of halls for lectures, dinners and exams. 'No weekends in wartime!' one later recalled cheerfully, which would have chimed with Zo.[44] The course highlight was the use of old cycle-powered Walls ice cream vans to represent Spitfires, whose blindfolded 'pilots' were directed across the lawns by radio contact from the training room.

Zo met more WAAFs at various Officer Corps Training Units. Although unimpressed by the English drill with its 'horrible turns, stiff and stomping', she felt the training in general measured up well against the pre-war PWK courses in Poland – her highest form of praise.[45] She also observed WAAF plotters on radar duty at RAF Kenley near the Surrey woods, another of the three stations that had been tasked with the defence of London during the Battle of Britain. Zo found the Kenley ops room, in the middle of which stood 'a table in the shape of the British Isles', most fascinating. This map table was divided into sectors, each manned by a blue-uniformed WAAF

---

[*] Tessica Aldus.

[†] Three years earlier these cables had brought down a Czechoslovak-crewed Wellington bomber, off course while on an Allied mission. Only the pilot survived.

wearing headphones, her tie often tucked between the buttons of her shirt. As Zo watched, the women leant over to rake tiny model aircraft over the table, like wartime croupiers, mapping both home and enemy positions in response to the radio reports coming into their headsets.

Perkins later conveyed Zo's thanks to the station commanders. 'We were received with every courtesy', he wrote, and saw 'WAAFs at work in practically all trades . . . I think Miss Watson will take away with her a very good impression of the RAF.[46] She did, but that had not been the point of her tour. The WAAF performed hugely valuable duties, but even where their roles overlapped with those in the Home Army, such as radio transmission, the context of their service was completely different. The country houses of Poland had been requisitioned not for the use of their own armed forces but forcibly by the enemy. Futhermore, every Home Army soldier was also preparing for greater mobilisation. At some point, Zo knew, they would be called upon to rise up against German forces and fight for the liberation of their country. They just did not know when the call would come. Nothing in the work of the WAAF suggested any equivalence.

Determined to play her part in Poland's national uprising, Zo was terrified that, being still in Britain, she might miss the call. In mid-July, she started lobbying to return. Protasewicz, however, was not keen to let her go. Overland routes were now too dangerous, he told her, and there were no available flights. Unbeknown to Zo, the Sixth Bureau had been monitoring her messages back to Warsaw and their log betrayed both their scorn and their concern. She has made 'complaints against Headquarters', one of these notes ran. 'Also . . . report written to [the Warsaw commander] incomprehensible to an ordinary mortal.'[47]

After considerable prompting, Warsaw finally sent orders for Zo's return within the month. The last seat on a Special Duties Squadron Lysander, navigating to France by the light of the moon, was reserved for her.* From their destination, a farmer's field in southern France, Zo was to make her own way back to Warsaw, travelling on the updated papers of the industrious fictional oil company secretary, Elisabeth

* Gilbert Védy, aka Médéric, the French resister who had arranged Zo's journey on the Laval train, was now also in London. One month later, he was returned to France by Lysander. He was arrested in March 1944 and committed suicide with poison from fear he might not be able to withstand interrogation.

Kübitza. She packed 6,000 francs and 5,000 dollars in notes, and one change of clothing, into the single small suitcase she was permitted to take with her. Then she put her new identity papers, slightly dog-eared, into the pocket of her coat, and hung it by the door. There it stayed.

'We . . . hope the loss of contact with your Lysander agent does not necessarily imply bad news', a FANY in Perkin's team wrote to SOE's French section.[48] 'As you will understand, we are extremely anxious to get Miss Watson, who is a very important courier, to Warsaw as soon as possible.'[49] The F Section agents on the ground had been arrested, however, and Zo's flight was cancelled.*

Zo was still in London when Sikorski was laid to rest. She and Aruś were among those invited to pay their last respects while his coffin, draped in the Polish flag, lay in state in Kensington Palace Gardens. It was, she said, her 'second meeting' with the great commander, and no more productive than the first.[50] The funeral was held on 15 July, Zo helping to carry the largest wreath, a six-foot tribute from the Polish underground. Churchill was among the 3,000 mourners at Westminster Cathedral. Sikorski was buried the following day, at Newark-on-Trent. As Polish bombers swept overhead, his coffin was laid at the foot of a memorial to the over two hundred Polish airmen who had already died for the Allied cause.†

With no prospect of another flight to France until at least the August moon, Zo threw herself into visiting more British bases. Her FANY escort now met her in Scotland, driving her 'through towns and forests to a hidden palace', as Zo recalled, near Falkirk in the central Lowlands.[51] Set in extensive parklands and sheltered from the road by huge rhododendrons in full bloom, Kinnaird House was an imposing grey manor with a crenellated tower, the shadow of which fell over the first of twenty corrugated-iron barracks erected for the Polish military.

'Scottish headquarters has been invaded', one FANY had written jovially to Marian Gamwell a couple of months earlier. 'They pinned a great Eagle on the front door, then laid red carpets and mats galore!'[52] The friendship that formed between the FANY and the Polish forces made a great impression on Zo. One member of the corps, found scrubbing floors, was minor royalty, prompting her to make a note

---

* Zo believed that the arrests were the work of the Abwehr's Hugo Bleicher.
† In 1993, Sikorski's coffin was reinterred in the royal crypt at Wawel Castle, Kraków.

about Britain's impressive 'obligation of war service'.[53] To her surprise, after dinner she discovered that the same FANYs had put on their evening dresses to socialise with the exhausted men who had been training all day, chatting over coffee and cards before turning up the radio for some dancing.

The courses Zo was taken to see in Scotland covered everything from weather forecasting to driving armoured vehicles.* Seizing the opportunity, she climbed in to 'take a ride' in a tank, joyfully progressing around some gravel paths.[54] On the Sunday, she attended Holy Mass. There was something deeply restorative in the swell of Polish voices, male and female together, raising the roof as they bellowed out their patriotic military hymns. 'Oh God, break this sword that slices the country,' Zo sang.[55] Feeling inspired, one evening she slipped away to visit the widow of Marshal Piłsudski.

In her youth, Aleksandra Piłsudska had stockpiled weapons and raided a Russian mail train with her future husband. She had served time in Warsaw's grim Pawiak prison as a guest of both the Russians, and later the Germans – following her service for the Polish Legions during the Great War. When Piłsudski became the first leader of newly independent Poland in 1918, she had pressed him to create the first women's unit in the Polish Armed Forces. 'The feminist movement was very popular in Europe at this time', she later wrote proudly, and 'women should have equal rights with men.'[56] This was Zo's first chance to meet Piłsudska, and she later purred at how 'eagerly' she had been received, and the 'nice, simple evening' they had shared.[57]

The more Zo had seen of the women's auxiliaries in Britain, the more convinced she had become that the Home Army needed their own distinct service model. Back in London, she discussed her ideas with some of the Pips while picnicking beside the Thames. The main problem, as she saw it, was 'how best to present the difficult matters that were so completely ignored or misunderstood by men'.[58] She decided to argue for the creation of a women's officer corps. 'Only a carefully selected cadre of officers will make it possible to release that great patriotic energy which undoubtedly lies in Polish women and which forms the silent foundation of all the country's activities', she

---

* Many Polish female drivers would later be deployed in Italy, transporting weapons under fire during the Battle of Monte Cassino. The Soviets had long been deploying female tank drivers.

typed in what was both a sincere and, she hoped, a rousing conclusion to her report.[59]

It did not take long for objections to arrive. 'No one denied the need to call up women for service in the Polish Armed Forces, to impose a number of duties on women', Zo discovered. 'But the granting of rights and privileges on account of the duties performed, met with great resistance almost everywhere and always.'[60] Yet, by emphasising that women did not need to serve 'with guns in their hands', Zo secured the support of the new Polish prime minister and, slowly, the issue of women's military service rose back up the agenda.[61]

Eventually, Zo was asked to comment on a revised draft of the new decree. As usual, her input was clear and direct. She was determined that the law should be based on Polish experience rather than the British model, and to prevent any 'unnecessary comments or doubts', she removed a reference to auxiliary service and retained a section on 'the scope of general military duty'.[62] Women would not be subject to conscription without their consent, but voluntary enlistment would now be legal for 'women between the ages of eighteen and forty-five who are capable of performing military service'.[63] Furthermore, in the event of mobilisation, or at a time of war, 'any person' who had joined a military formation would automatically 'become a soldier' with the right to rank, promotion and decoration.[64] Although it would take some time to be ratified into law, the decree's fundamental statement that 'female soldiers shall have the same rights and obligations as male soldiers' vindicated all Zo's work.[65]

Along with some professional satisfaction, Zo felt a liberating sense of relief. She, Emilia, Zofia, Marianna, and many thousands like them, would soon have the authority that went with military rank, and Poland would be serving at full capacity. Zo suddenly felt desperate to return to her homeland. For weeks she had been longing to leave the factionalist politics of London behind to play a more direct role in Poland's liberation.

Protasewicz now also seemed ready to see the back of her. One of his team's last memos had noted that she was 'disloyal and inclined to abuse trust for egoistic purposes'.[66] If there were any doubt that this opinion was coloured by her gender, the next words made it clear. She is 'an insane feminist and pioneer of the "liberation" movement and equality of women', the report continued. 'A hysterical woman'.[67]

'You *are* going back,' Protasewicz told Zo when she challenged him again.[68] He just could not work out how to make it happen. 'I'm looking for a way for you,' he said, but, 'unless there's a chance that you will jump . . .' meaning from an aircraft over Poland like the Silent Unseen paratroopers, and here his voice trailed off. 'But you will not jump,' he finally said.[69] 'Why don't I jump?' Zo leapt even at the idea. 'I'll do it immediately!'[70]

10

Female, Silent, Unseen
(August–September 1943)

'I have arranged for Miss Watson to start parachute training on Sunday', confirmed Staff Officer Audrey North, an efficient young WAAF detailed to the Special Operations Executive. 'It is necessary that she be dressed in uniform for this course and, if she has them, she should take slacks with her.'[1]

Zo had been running what one friend later called 'a brief but indefatigable campaign' to secure a place on a Silent Unseen parachute course.[2] She knew that she would have to wait for the longer nights of September before an aircraft could make the thousand-mile journey under cover of darkness, but she was anxious to be ready. This did not stop her from being terrified at the prospect of throwing herself from a plane, but she was damned if a reluctant colonel or the lack of a pair of slacks was going to stop her. 'Can I go in civilian clothes, because I don't have [uniform] shoes?' she scribbled back, followed by, 'I do not have a jacket or boots. Would it be enough to have trousers from a male battledress?'[3]

The first Silent Unseen paratroopers had been recruited from the Polish troops who had defended their nation against German invasion in September 1939, then withdrawn south through Romania to regroup. Many had served in the Battle of France the following year, and reached Britain thereafter. An enterprising Polish captain proposed the creation of an elite unit from the cream of these servicemen, and Sikorski had approved the idea over breakfast one morning in September 1940.[*] The select few were trained not only in physical fitness, map-reading and survival (tramping about in the Scottish heather, as one saw it), but also in clandestine warfare (losing a tail, picking locks), sabotage and weapons (including knives and ropes for silent killing). Specialist courses included radio communications,

---

[*] Jan Górski submitted the proposal, later supported by Maciej Kalenkiewicz.

forgery and resistance to interrogation. Those who excelled learnt to parachute, then took the oath of allegiance before being dropped back to Poland. Once home, they came under Home Army command.

Churchill had launched the British Special Operations Executive two months earlier, with the rousing injunction to 'set Europe ablaze'.[4] SOE's plan was to organise, arm and train the resistance within various occupied countries, and the Polish or P Section, under Harold Perkins, was soon supporting the Silent Unseen. Perkins understood that the Poles were 'dependent on the British authorities for the provision of arms and explosives, training facilities and, above all, long range aircraft'.[5] Yet they retained autonomy in recruitment, training and radio ciphers. The guiding principle was one of co-operation.

The Silent Unseen name seems impossibly romantic, even melodramatic, but at the time it was an insider's joke. Not only were these troops to operate clandestinely in the field, but also – despite training at historic estates in the heart of the English and Scottish countryside – few outside the Polish high command and SOE structures even knew they existed. Over the course of the war, more than 800 men selected from 2,400 candidates would discreetly disappear from their regular army units to undertake Silent Unseen training. Of these, 579 would complete the course. The first three were parachuted to Poland in 1941, demonstrating both that this was possible and also how impractical it was.[*] There were never sufficient aircraft, or enough long moonlit nights – at most forty a year, weather permitting. Eventually, 316 Silent Unseen would see action in Poland. Others were dropped into France, Greece, Italy, Yugoslavia and Albania.

The trainees were chosen for their patriotism, leadership potential and honesty as well as any specialist skills. They also had to be fit, but medicals often showed a 'history of chest troubles', 'very bad teeth' and various fractures. Some men were also, understandably, found to be 'hysterical' and of 'doubtful nervous stability'.[6] A couple of weeks earlier, Protasewicz had criticised Zo for her 'fantastically overblown personal ambition', but Silent Unseen candidates could be sent back to their units if they were found to be 'lacking in ambition and forcefulness'.[7]

SOE requisitioned so many country houses for agent training, over

---

[*] Two Silent Unseen, Józef Zabielski, Stanisław Krzyżanowski, and Czesław Raczkowski, a trained courier.

the course of the war, that wags in the know joked that their acronym stood for the 'Stately 'Omes of England'. Most of the Poles were stationed in Scotland, protecting the northeast coastline, but by 1942 the Silent Unseen were based at a fine Jacobean mansion called Audley End House, on the site of a Benedictine Abbey in Essex. Initially offered as a casualty clearing station for Dunkirk, the military had rejected Audley End as it had room for only two hundred beds, just two toilets, and no electricity.* After it *was* requisitioned, a detachment of the Royal Engineers mined its elegant Robert Adam bridge and constructed concrete pillboxes, anti-tank barriers and fortifications along the nearby River Cam. Of more practical value, as it turned out, they also installed electric wiring in the house.

Overlooked from all sides, close to a village whose residents were used to crossing the park and with retired workers still living on site, Audley End was not obviously suitable for secret operations training. Nevertheless, it became Special Training Station 43, with guards on the gates and a nominal British presence. The Poles would refer to these men as 'jam-eaters', perhaps reflecting the lack of roast beef in wartime Britain.[8] Inside the house, the tower rooms flooded with natural light were set aside for forging documents and tailoring Polish clothing. Guns and munitions were stored in the dairy, below the butler's pantry, and in the stables that had once housed royal racehorses. The great hall, its fine interior protected by panelling, was used for meals and lectures, and the attics as dormitories – soon adorned by some quite graphic graffiti. More traditional use was made of the billiards room. Secretaries, drivers, cooks and cleaners were provided by the FANY.†

'Every man wanted to kill Hitler,' believed Captain Alfons Maćkowiak, the fitness instructor at Audley End.[9]‡ Alan Mack, as he

* Lord and Lady Braybrooke had preferred the soft glow of paraffin lamps. Braybrooke died before the war. His wife and daughter lived locally, the latter 'digging for victory' in the mansion's grounds until joining the FANY.
† The commandants were Terry Roper-Caldbeck, in a kilt and usually smoking; Józef Hartman, head of training, who planted a rose bush for every man lost; and FANY chief Mrs Grierson, known as 'Aunt G'.
‡ In 1950, Alan Mack pulled two men to safety from the flames of an aircraft that had crashed in Essex. He later became the Olympics coach for Sebastian Coe and others.

became known, had escaped from both German and Soviet captivity to make his way to Britain. He started the trainees' days early with a two-mile run and a swim in the lake, followed by a rope assault course over the River Cam. Only then could shooting practice begin – legend has it that over time the hungry men cleared the estate of its geese and duck and the lake of pike and carp.*

Although Zo had to be demonstrably fit before she could take the parachuting course, she did not have to pass the tough physical training for those being prepared as partisan leaders. Nor was she required to attend weapons training, although she might have enjoyed pitting the portable British PIATs against a Valentine tank in the grounds. At some point she did gain a British driving licence and complete a technical course in the latest communications systems, but most of her time was spent training others. Zo's recent service made her an invaluable source of information on conditions behind enemy lines.

The 'Briefing Course' at Audley End aimed to transform the Silent Unseen trainees into apparently ordinary citizens of German-occupied Poland. 'It was like a finishing school,' one said, 'where we received a final polish.'[10] Zo's briefings covered how the enemy organised in occupied territory, their uniforms, equipment and expectations. She advised them on preparing cover stories that were both credible and hard to check, and how to suppress the nerves that might otherwise betray them in their eyes or tone of voice. Above all, she lectured her 'quietly ignorant students' on the basics of daily life, the limited availability in shops, the requisitioned buildings that all locals would know about and, most simply, 'the papers, the dress, the behaviour on the street'.[11] As one student put it, 'pre-war memories of cafés, shops and the faces of smiling women . . . had to be substituted by the images of German soldiers marching on Marszałkowska Street and the smell of potato soup.'[12]

The men 'literally imagined that behind every bush or house there was a Gestapo officer,' Zo later laughed. 'And that you had to be on your guard against him with a gun in your trousers.'[13] The automatic action of reaching for a gun, she knew, was probably enough to get them killed. Nevertheless, 'they were heroes,' she felt, 'going straight into the lion's mouth.'[14]

---

* Carp were sometimes kept in the Victorian fountain. Hand grenades were among the debris later found in the river.

The Silent Unseen hopefuls did not always take themselves so seriously. There were regular football and volleyball matches in front of
the stately house and, as part of their training, the students would
wobble across the Capability Brown landscaped lawns while learning
to cycle in a 'slow bike race.'* A sports day brought the construction
of a perilous-looking human catapult, energetic pillowfights sent some
students toppling from a pole into the river and FANYs, dressed in
summer skirts and plimsolls, gamely joined in piggyback races. At
least one uniformed officer was seen wading into a fountain and, one
night, a trainee returning from some local drinking 'cycled into a
recumbent cow.'[15]

There was also dressing up. Photos showing men in Japanese ki-
monos suggest an in-house production of *The Mikado*, but other
trainees also dressed as stout Englishwomen, complete with stockings,
handbags and headscarves tied below their square jaws. These clothes
were probably borrowed from the FANY, but the Silent Unseen may
have had their own supplies. Alan Mack was one of several who went
on training ops to 'raid' nearby shops or 'attack' the local railway
station dressed as a woman.† It seems the Poles realised that women
would be less likely to attract attention from the police or Home
Guard, but still preferred their agents to be male.

Not all the Silent Unseen trainees were men, however. Reports from
1942 show that one was commended for her 'very considerable feminine charm' and clever use of 'feigning a manner of innocence and
ignorant helplessness' during exercises.[16] Another was described as
'very intelligent . . . extremely hard working . . . capable, resourceful
and quick witted', with 'considerable leadership qualities'.[17] 'She has
got great strength of will and is purposeful and determined, but is not
biased by any unreasonable fanaticism', her finishing report emphasised, before concluding, 'If it were not for the possible disadvantage
of her sex, she would be a grade A.'[18]

A third woman was sent on weapons training in an isolated barn.‡
'Suddenly, right in front of me, I see Hitler in the window,' she later
recalled. 'So I shot Hitler and I killed him. He flew away somewhere.

---

* As bikes were an expensive luxury in pre-war Poland, few could already ride a
bicycle.
† Franciszek Rybka was among the men who chose to dress as women.
‡ These female trainees were 'Tarnowska', 'Lubiewa' and Zofia Jordanowska.

A little bit later, I turned around and I see Goebbels. So I shot and killed him.'[19] To add a little frisson, the shooting targets, sent swooshing along strings by a system of pulleys, were pasted with photographs of the Nazi leaders. 'It *was* satisfying,' she laughed.[20] None of these women would complete their training, however, let alone take the Silent Unseen oath and parachute back to Poland. Their files do not explain why.

ꝑ

Certainly, enemy-occupied Poland was not a place to send anyone lightly. That summer, one Home Army officer noted, prisoners were being shot in reprisals 'not in tens or fifties, but several hundred at a time.'[21] Rather than intimidating the general population, however, the officer believed that this policy backfired, creating a greater 'determination to retaliate'.[22] In July, while Zo was in London, the SS had burnt the village of Michniów to the ground. Over two hundred of its residents had been murdered in a reprisal action, ninety-eight of them locked alive into barns before they were set alight. Fifty-four women and forty-eight children had been among the victims, the youngest a baby just nine days old.

Michniów was one of hundreds of villages razed by the Germans for harbouring and supporting the partisans who harassed their forces. It had also been home to many of the men led by Emilia's lover, the furrow-browed Ponury. Although it was against protocol, he immediately set out to avenge the village deaths. As the perpetrators had already fled, he and his men ambushed a local train, killing at least twelve German men before carving 'For Michniów' into the side of their carriage.

Ponury was now serving under the command of General Tadeusz Komorowski, Rowecki's former deputy who had now been promoted to lead the Home Army. Known as 'Bór', his nom-de-guerre meaning 'Forest', the safest habitat for partisan fighters, the new commander had a natural affinity with his soldiers.* Once a striking young officer with a shock of dark hair and deep-set eyes, Bór was a veteran of the Great War who had represented his nation as an equestrian in the

---

* After the war, Komorowski added his nom-de-guerre of 'Bór' as a prefix to his surname: Bór-Komorowski.

1924 and 1936 Olympics. Now in his late forties, he was losing his hair and his strained face was as hollow as a memento mori, but his passion for his nation was undimmed.

That summer, Bór appointed another emissary to travel from Warsaw to London, the first since Zo. Young Jan Jeziorański had spent three years in the resistance, distributing black propaganda to demoralise enemy troops and serving as a courier. He had also fallen in love with a 'liaison girl'. With 'a snub nose and large, beautiful, slightly slanted eyes', Jadwiga Wolska took her nom-de-guerre of 'Greta' from her film-star looks and chic Garbo hairdo.[23] Jan had adopted the name 'Nowak' for himself, on the basis that it was both helpfully short for radio transmissions and common enough to be virtually anonymous. His choice, he had since learnt, had been 'a serious mistake' – document controls had repeatedly shown how many Jan Nowaks appeared on blacklists.[24] Nowak's messages to London had been among those waiting to be processed when Zo had been striving to speed up the Sixth Bureau's responses. Now he was assigned to reach London himself, via Stockholm, carrying with him the first documentary evidence from the liquidation of the Warsaw Ghetto.

Although he knew it was an honour to be appointed, Nowak's hackles rose when he was briefed by the tall, red-haired Czech known as 'Jarach'. 'I felt an instinctive antipathy and distrust . . . from our first encounter,' he later reported.[25] 'He never shook hands firmly, and his hand was soft and wet.'[26] When the authenticity of some of Jarach's reports was questioned and a couple of his contacts went missing, Nowak urged colleagues to report their suspicions. 'If you don't,' he warned, 'you might unwittingly bring about the arrest, and perhaps death, of not just one but many people.'[27] Few of the team, however, were willing to risk the execution of a trusted colleague on the basis of some inaccurate or even 'fictitious' reports, and a damp handshake.[28]

Jarach handed Nowak his secret mail for London at a central Warsaw bus stop. 'If you are leaving family here,' he said, smiling, 'I will willingly do what I can for them. Give me their names and addresses.'[29] Thanking him effusively, Nowak made his excuses and hurried away. Glancing back as he reached the street corner, he saw Jarach still standing at the bus stop, 'apparently deep in thought'.[30]

As Nowak set off on his long journey towards London, Zo was growing ever more impatient to return to Poland. The receipt of another
honour, this time the prestigious Virtuti Militari, did nothing to
pacify her. 'The longer she stayed in London, the worse she felt,' Rum
realised.[31] It was a relief for everyone when she was finally called to
Scotland to start her parachute training. Largo House in Fife, ten miles
from St Andrews, was another country pad of the type that one SOE
trainer felt 'tried to ramble but hadn't the vitality'.[32] Despite its forbidding red-brick exterior, the place was full of holes, including one in a
ceiling that was used for preliminary jumps. This was the base of the
First Independent Polish Parachute Brigade. 'Looking for death – come
in for a moment', read the tongue-in-cheek inscription on the gates.[33]

'Paratroopers are the spearhead of all airborne forces', one Polish
training manual from 1943 opened. 'They must possess special physical and moral qualities.'[34] Zo could again skip the so-called 'Monkey
Grove' assault course between the ancient trees in the park, and swerve
some of the long treks through what one trainee described as the 'fairly
unpleasant climate'.[35] All she had to learn was how to jump from an
aircraft, including, as the manual put it, overcoming 'the innate fear
of space', and transforming herself from 'helpless victim of the air to
navigator'.[36]

Zo's instructor, a British sergeant, told her that she was the only
Polish woman he had trained, but at least three others had taken the
course.* Two of them had completed it. Yet neither had been dispatched
to Poland, 'due to the fact', Protasewicz wrote, 'that Poland did not
report any demand for women'.[37] The third female trainee had argued
'that it wasn't fair or democratic, and that this was discrimination
against women'.[38] She had nevertheless been removed from the course.

Parachute training started with jumps from a trapeze-like swing
over a bed of sand, and progressed to leaps from the first floor of Largo
House. Her determination proving greater than her fears, Zo launched
herself repeatedly, landed well, and was sent to the more vertiginous
steel parachute-tower, which looked like a small electricity pylon, in
the grounds. Terrified, she now threw herself down awkwardly, twisting both her ankles. Fearing that she might be thrown off the course,
she blamed her 'inappropriate' footwear 'with a semi-sporty heel.'[39]

* Zofia Zaleska and Zofia Wisnicka-Kleczyńska passed the course in 1942. Zofia
Jordanowska, aka Zofia Sarnowska, did not complete training.

Seeing the fierce look on her face, the instructor bandaged her ankles until they were rigid so she could climb stiffly back up for another attempt.

Zo did not know how common such injuries were. 'The breaking of arms and legs was a frequent, almost daily occurrence', one trainee recalled, while another remembered that 'several of us ended up with our ankles in plaster'.[40] Even 'an exceptionally keen type of man had the misfortune to break his ankle on his first descent', one instructor noted, and the less fit or disciplined the students, the worse the tally tended to be.[41] One group, who 'keep too late hours unless watched', finished their training with a list of 'three sprained ankles, one hurt elbow and leg, one concussed'.[42] Eventually parachute training was given the code name 'lumbago', the medical condition of lower back pain. Reports now read 'strapped in for a lumbago exercise on the trapeze' or 'broken leg during lumbago'.[43] Protasewicz himself had failed to pass 'lumbago' training, having only made one descent before reportedly becoming 'very disappointed at being called away to London'.[44]

After these intense days, Zo was grateful for the companionable evenings at Largo House. Just a few weeks earlier, she had been surprised to see FANYs in evening dress socialising with military trainees. Now she relished the chance to unwind in female company, chatting in armchairs beside a window or simply listening together to the wind shaking the boughs of the trees in the dark grounds beyond.

Passing this preliminary training qualified Zo for the final parachute course at Ringway, near Manchester.* After a day back in London, WAAF officer Audrey North drove her to Euston station. The two women respected each other but were cut from different cloth. Audrey had trained to be a 'plotter', like the women Zo had seen tracing the routes of enemy aircraft across a huge map table. Friendly and efficient, two years later she was transferred to the Air Liaison Section of SOE. Not for the first time, Zo wondered how many virtually anonymous, hard-working women kept different parts of the war machine running.

It was raining in Manchester, and the tarmac of Ringway airfield was slick with shallow puddles. Zo stood with a group of students all speaking English in a variety of accents, beside a wretched stretch of muddy grass. They were to be taught together by 'a somewhat

---

* Now Manchester Airport.

idiosyncratic commandant, as though they were English public school-boys', one wrote.[45] For him, 'the accent was on character building'.[46] Zo was not deficient there. Telling no one of her fears, she set her focus firmly on what she was now referring to as the 'thrilling learning experience'.[47]

The trainees' first jump was from the basket of a tethered balloon. This was cheerily nicknamed 'Dumbo' because of its tailfin 'ears', although it looked more like an inflatable missile than Disney's inno-cent elephant. When this jump went well, Zo qualified for her first flight. Once again, the students were weaned in slowly, acclimatising first to the noise, smell and shudder of their low-flying Halifax. The only seating inside was the edge of the 'Joe Hole', an aperture halfway along the fuselage, about one and a half metres in diameter, through which they were to drop. Several successful jumps were needed to earn their parachute badge.

There was complete silence in the bus that took the trainees to the airfield for their first jump from a moving aircraft. 'Our faces were tense, and our mood was funereal,' one recalled.[48] A few lame jokes and some gallantry saw them into the dark interior and attached to their static lines before their voices were lost in the roar of the engines. Some issued silent prayers. Others were visibly shaking. 'Everyone knew it was a matter of life and death,' Zo realised.[49] Stories abounded about chutes failing to open, and students getting tangled in their cords and swept into the slipstream to suffocate or freeze.* Zo could not shake the feeling that every second was taking her closer to suicide.

The drop zone was about ten kilometres away, beyond a large lake over which the dispatcher gave the order 'prepare to jump'.[50] Zo watched as the first pair of students shuffled towards the Joe Hole. Staring resolutely at the dispatcher, each man in turn sat, straightened his back and slipped away. There was no active jumping involved, Zo knew, you just had to 'lower your legs and fall.'[51] She fell like a stone. But before she could form a scream, her parachute burst open and she found herself floating like thistledown. Almost too quickly, the ground rose up to meet her. She just had time to bring her bent knees together when her feet hit the surprisingly hard earth. A burst of pain flared in her ankles but she was on the ground, and she was alive. 'I had a pretty

---

* Bolesław Odrowaz-Szuszkiewicz had been killed the February before, when his parachute failed to open.

good tall,' she reported proudly.[52] Now in excellent spirits, she laughed along with the men on the bus heading back to their digs in Wilmslow. The next morning, silence reigned again.

Zo would never experience the 'indescribable bliss and euphoria' that some of the men described, but she felt intense relief every time the thin silk of her chute mushroomed open above her.[53] At the end of August she was told that her next jump would be to Poland. Back in London, she was 'in slightly better spirits', Rum noticed.[54] 'It's just a sport,' she told him dismissively when he asked how the training had gone. 'I don't see any excitement in it.'[55] For Rum, 'this again raised doubts as to the delicacy of her feminine feelings', which, when expressed out loud, led to 'another storm'.[56] Zo was still too female to be a soldier, and too capable to be considered truly feminine.

'A moment came when something snapped within her', Rum later wrote. 'As if in a frenzy she started throwing people's faults in their faces ... the courage of her convictions and her uncompromising bearing had to be seen to be believed.'[57] Zo had long felt as though she were suffocating on the stale male breath in the Rubens Hotel. But even at the government headquarters, Rum heard, her meetings quickly 'degenerated into monologues of accusations and criticisms of everything and everybody'.[58] Rum held no ill will against her; it was just that he had never been able to relate to her. Now, seeing her grow 'sadder every day', he finally could. 'She was pining for life in Poland', he realised, 'and she would not be well again until she went back.'[59]

When her flight was finally allocated, Zo realised that she was now the lucky one. She knew that Rum also longed to return, and that it was there he would give his best service. Not wanting to part on a sour note, she paid him a farewell visit. He was ill, she saw, and when he mentioned that his back ached, she massaged it for him. Secretly, she wondered whether 'he was afraid'.[60] By contrast, Rum had never seen Zo in such good spirits. 'She was entirely different as she took her leave of me; she was cordial and friendly', he wrote in astonishment.[61] He even gave her a letter for his mother in Warsaw. Should they meet again there, Zo told him warmly as she took the note, 'we are bound to find a common language and ... there will never be any cause for quarrels.'[62] That night Rum lay awake, wondering whether Zo's luck 'would hold out this time, too'.[63]

Scheduled to leave on 1 September, Zo's flight was delayed by heavy rain. Audrey North drove her out of London and down the wet country lanes to an SOE holding station in the village of Chalfont St Giles, where she was to wait until the weather improved. Although Audrey had now been driving Zo around for over a month, both women stared silently out of the car windows. It had been spring when Zo had reached England, a season of promise. Now the sky was grey, and damp leaves were everywhere paling to yellow before their inevitable fall. After pulling up at Pollards Park House, Audrey placed her hand on Zo's and wished her good luck. This rare female parachuter had brought home to her the immense dangers faced by the Poles.

Pollards Park House was another 'palace for the Silent Unseen', Zo thought, looking around at the building's whitewashed wings flanking the large courtyard.[64] At least the welcome was warm. She was met by a keen young FANY called Sue Ryder, so keen that she later told friends she had lied about her age to sign up at fifteen.* Ryder's dark hair was short, her smile was wide, and the badge of the Polish eagle was sewn onto her uniform. 'Elizabeth Watson,' Zo said, shaking her hand. Because Zo was the only female parachutist, she was allocated the spare bed in Ryder's room. The young FANY noticed that she tacked a small picture to the wall. It showed two young people holding hands on a riverbank. An inscription below read, 'A Moment Out of Time'.[65] It might have been Zo with Zofia Grzegorzewska at a pre-war PWK camp. Or perhaps the second figure was Marianna, taken when Zo had visited her at the clinic by the Vistula river. Zo was not a sentimental woman but she had loved, and she kept the memory of these women close. Mindful of her roommate's privacy, Ryder never asked.

Bad weather delayed Zo's flight for over a week. Cut off from London, she did not know that Rum had been transferred for Silent Unseen training. 'Determined', his instructor recorded.[66] For most of the paratroopers now waiting for their flight, 'as long as we were stuck at that station . . . we flirted with the FANYs'.[67] Ryder, like Zo, was not interested in romance. 'We had those platonic friendships which people say are impossible', she made clear, but 'we had enormous affection and admiration' for the Poles.[68] In the evenings they 'sang and danced' in a room decorated with a huge map of Poland and mementoes from

* FANY records show that Sue Ryder was recruited, aged eighteen, in 1942.

those who had already left – a collar, a jacket, a shirt, each bearing its owner's nom-de-guerre.[69] 'Deep friendships were made', Ryder felt, 'transient but precious'.[70]

Sue Ryder and Zo grew close not only because they were women, and each doubted they would meet again, but from mutual respect for their service, their hatred of tyranny and their passion for a free Europe. Ryder found Nazi racial laws 'just totally revolting'.[71] Once furious at Chamberlain's appeasement strategy, she was now critical of the way Churchill 'kept saying that we were alone . . . he never seemed to give credit to people like the Poles.'[72] Meanwhile, she saw that Zo was 'both gay and frightened. We admired her the more because she was courageous rather than fearless.'[73]

Five days later, on 9 September 1943, Zo's flight was finally confirmed as operation 'Neon 4'. This was to be one of six missions heading to different Polish fields that night from RAF Tempsford, the Bedfordshire home of the Special Duties Squadrons. Zo was to parachute alongside two men. To protect their families from reprisals should she be caught, she knew them only by their noms-de-guerre – 'Crystal' and 'Ladder'.* Once issued with their equipment, they were given a final briefing on their destination and had the details of their safe house and passwords reconfirmed. Then they countersigned for their money belts and mail. It was only now that they were awarded their Silent Unseen parachute badge, sadly to be left behind, and swore their oath of allegiance.

This solemn moment often entailed some awkwardness. 'Did I have the right to take this oath?' one man wondered when his flight was delayed. 'I was in London, I could go to the cinema, and I was taking the same oath as colleagues in Warsaw.'[74] Here at least Zo had the advantage. She had taken her Home Army oath in a freezing Warsaw kitchen three years earlier, and had been serving behind the frontline ever since. Now she was also the only female member of the Silent Unseen, making her, in Polish, the only Cichociemna – the final 'a' denoting her gender. Many would later dispute whether it was possible for a woman to join the Silent Unseen, and ironically Zo herself never

---

* Bolesław Jan Polończyk, aka Kryształ (Crystal), was to organise the supply and storage of explosives from the coal mines in Silesia. Fryderyk Marian Serafiński, aka 'Drabina' (Ladder), 'intelligent & hard-working', was assigned to the partisans. See PUMST, SK 142, Prelim report, STS 25, Garramor, 'Serafiński', n.d.

felt she really belonged to the unit. To her mind, she was first and foremost a Home Army soldier, 'considering this something better, of course,' she laughed.[75]

Inevitably, having a female member of the Silent Unseen caused unnecessary admin. Although not officially entitled to the 'fighting allowance' given to men, Zo was awarded equal pay as an exception, and added to the list of 'jumpers' with a small pencil caveat.[76] She would never know that it was Protasewicz who had finally stuck his neck out for her, specifying in writing that 'Ms Watson . . . should be treated the same as other soldiers from the land forces.'[77]

Saying farewell, Zo and Sue Ryder agreed to write after the war. Having seen so much of the Polish spirit, Ryder felt that the Poles 'were like corks really . . . the worse the situation, so they came up for more'.[78] But although she did not doubt Zo's spirit, she was still anxious for her friend. Zo and the men were then driven to RAF Tempsford in an army lorry, with the tarpaulins down to keep the location of their destination as secret as possible.

In an old barn near the airfield, Zo pulled her bulky jump-suit overalls over her favourite navy-blue silk dress, woollen sweater and old overcoat, hoping the layers would keep her warm on the flight.* In the coat pockets were her forged identity papers, already much folded and worn. On top of all this, she was weighed down by her kit. She feared that the money belt, filled with twenty Polish zloty, eighty-five reichsmarks, fifty dollars in paper and over forty more in gold, would make her heavier than during her training jumps and perhaps mean she would fall too fast. In a bag, she also had toiletries, a change of underwear, and another shirt and skirt, all unmarked 'items that could be dropped during a pursuit'.[79] Two pistols with ammunition, a folding clasp knife and shovel, her compass, torch, map, first aid kit and a poison tablet were all stowed in the overalls. Sue Ryder had also given her a packet of sandwiches and a flask of hot tea for the journey.

Loaded up as she was, Zo was outraged to be subjected to a final thorough body search. At first she thought she had again been singled out for special treatment, but all agents being dropped to enemy-held territory were checked for anything in their clothing that might give

---

* Gibraltar Farm Barn, still standing, now contains several memorials to those who were flown behind enemy lines from Tempsford during the war.

them away. 'Bringing in private packages and pockets of stockings . . . leather, tea, coffee, chocolate, private letters' for families and sweethearts 'is a huge problem', Rowecki himself had once made clear. 'Especially since they often lose some of their belongings in the field during a nervous jump, and then require us to search for them.'[80] Yet English cigarettes, small notes including family addresses, and even a bottle of Yardley perfume had still recently been confiscated. Zo tried not to think about the note to Rum's mother, concealed somewhere on her person.

Zo and the men then climbed into their Halifax. Space was tight, and their legs were jammed up against some of the large packages containing tins of meat, biscuits, margarine, American rations and medical equipment that would follow them out through the Joe Hole. Six heavier large metal drums, filled with guns, ammunition, grenades and plastic explosive, various fuses and detonators, were stored further up, in the bomb bay, each attached to their own parachute, waiting to be released.

It was already seven when the Halifax took off, its Rolls-Royce Merlin engines seeming to make the noise of an entire factory. Soon bitterly cold, Zo sat shivering in 'the wind' that she imagined was 'blowing through the cracks in the plane'.[81] As the monotonous thrum of the engines was too loud for conversation, she may have listened to the aircraft intercom through some headphones to help pass the time. Occasionally the navigator would speak to the pilot about something technical, and one parachuter heard a little jazz music and then the crew arranging to meet some women that weekend at the cinema in London's Leicester Square. At some point Zo dozed off.

An hour later, the sky cleared and Zo woke to see the ocean below 'glistening' in the moonlight.[82] Somewhere over Denmark, she heard the strangely fairground pinging sound of bullets hitting sheet metal. A low-flying Halifax made a mouth-watering sight for the alert German gunners below. Losses were heavy on this Danish route, which traversed the German night-fighter and anti-aircraft belt designed to protect Berlin from the raids of RAF Bomber Command. Six special duties aircraft would be shot down in two nights alone that September, losses that Sue Ryder, who knew many of the men on board, described simply as 'very horrific'.[83] While Zo was in the air, Goebbels noted in his diary that 'Goering is now somewhat more optimistic about air warfare. In fact', he added presciently, 'in my opinion somewhat too optimistic.'[84] The next month, following the successful Allied invasion of southern Italy, the Air Ministry vetoed this northern flight route to Poland and the Silent Unseen began to leave exclusively from Italy and North Africa.

A four-engine Halifax bomber 'is not an aerobatic type of aircraft', one of the Silent Unseen noted dryly, while his pilot explained, 'This wasn't a Spitfire, you know, more like a heavy old tank.'[85] Zo's pilot could not make any abrupt evasive manoeuvres, but he diverted towards Stockholm to swerve further flak. Zo knew they were making headway now, turning to cross the Baltic Sea.

In central Poland, a reception committee was preparing to head to the drop zone, a field code-named *Solnica*, meaning salt cellar, near the village of Osowiec and about twenty-five miles southwest of Warsaw. After a quiet week, at six o'clock that evening the BBC had broadcast the popular tune that confirmed the operation was on. The signal had been faint, drifting in and out before vanishing altogether in a cloud of atmospherics, but it was unmistakable. The committee never knew whether some Germans might be lying in wait, either enacting a long-planned ambush or alerted that night by the sound of engines. Nevertheless, gathering gloves, hats, torches and rifles, they headed out in silence, hoping that they, too, would be unseen.

Inside the Halifax, preparations for the jumps started fifteen minutes before they reached the drop zone. Once the Joe Hole was uncovered, a blast of Polish air whipped around the fuselage, making Zo ache for her homeland. Like a heavily pregnant woman, she felt at once physically weighed down and terrified of the labour ahead, yet also full of hope and increasingly impatient. Circling down to 500 feet, the Halifax crew struggled to see the torches that should have been laid out below, confirming the drop zone and indicating wind direction.* Fuel anxiety was making the pilot consider aborting when they saw the pinpricks, a faint but distinctive constellation on the land below.

Now the three passengers had to jump as quickly as possible. Zo was pushed forward with a gallant, 'Ladies first!' Feeling a rush of adrenaline, she swung her legs over the side of 'the black, yawning hole'.[86] A second later, the dispatch light turned green and Zo pressed

* The pilot was Stanisław Król (but not the pilot of the same name held in Stalag Luft III). From that autumn, only Polish pilots flew the Silent Unseen to Poland.

up on her hands, straightened her legs, and disappeared into the Polish night.

⚓

Two of the aircraft that left from RAF Tempsford that night would be forced to turn back, one with a fuel tank completely shot through. Attacked by two Messerschmitt fighters during its return flight, Zo's Halifax limped home on fuel fumes. There, the dispatcher reported a successful drop. An inventory was made of the few personal effects that Zo had left behind in England, which were then packed into a box to be stored until no one knew when. There was not much. One lady's dark brown leather bag containing an identity card, ration book and handkerchief, three books (titles unrecorded), two ankle bandages, some lady's pyjamas, 'underpants', one bra, a suspender belt and one pair of lady's silk stockings – at some point she had bought some after all.[87]

As the men of the Sixth Bureau and Zo's friends among the Pips, the WAAF and FANY gave their sighs of relief at the news of her successful dispatch, German reports that night were eliciting a different response. 'Four enemy aircraft penetrated our airspace', they recorded. 'Probably an equipment drop.'[88] The growing number of Allied incursions was beginning to generate attention. 'Our informant suggests that we should expect increased numbers of parachutists,' the alert went out, 'and increased amounts of weapons, ammunition and equipment.'[89]

Some years later, having not received a letter from Zo, Sue Ryder assumed the worst. 'Elizabeth seemed to lead a charmed existence', she wrote in her memoirs. 'But her luck had to run out, for she never returned.'[90]

Part Three

11

The Only Daughter of the Sky
(September 1943–February 1944)

'Błysk' broke cover from the trees, sprinting to greet the first para-trooper he saw descending from what he called 'the Cichociemni clouds'.[1] He had chosen his nom-de-guerre, meaning 'Flash' or 'Beam', to reflect his role as commander of the local reception committee, a dozen people who used their torches to guide the Special Duties Squadron pilots to their dark field, before rounding up the arrivals and containers. Not lighting his torch unnecessarily now, he simply quietly muttered the password greeting and threw his arms around the figure still struggling with their parachute straps. Only when the moon illuminated Zo's face, did Błysk realise that he was holding a woman in his arms. Disconcerted, he leapt away.

It was as though he had been 'burnt' or 'had suddenly come into contact with a bunch of nettles', Zo later laughed.[2] The way she told it, Błysk 'screamed out in terror, "A WOMAN!" "No," she replied dryly, enjoying the moment, "just an ordinary soldier."'[3] While admitting he had been 'shocked', Błysk told the story differently.[4] When Zo took off her parachute helmet, he said, 'I saw her long hair, a woman. I kissed her on the hand and cheek.'[5] Another account had him exclaim, 'Welcome, the only daughter of the sky!'[6] However gallant or other-wise Zo's reception, Błysk had soon got the measure of her. 'This girl was such a martinet,' he added, 'that we forgot she was a woman.'[7] Which, of course, was perfect.[*]

They were standing in a large clearing surrounded by woodland, their feet stirring up the low-lying mist. Gathering up her chute, which was catching on the damp grass, Zo followed Błysk towards a clump of birches. 'A mass parachute descent resembles a great flight of birds

---

[*] After the war Błysk, aka Bolesław Szmajdowicz, reportedly claimed it had been an 'unusual honour' to receive Zo, 'one of the most heroic women of the Underground'. See PUMST, Elżbieta Zawacka, 'Cichociemny "ZO"', typed ms, n.d.

swooping down upon their victims', the 1943 paratroopers manual stated.[8] A group of three looked more like jellyfish caught in the currents of the dark sky. 'Ladder' had been blown onto the roof of a nearby barn, but was unhurt. Crystal, the last to jump, had drifted further. Fortunately, there was no sign of enemy patrols. Kneeling for a moment under the cover of the trees, Zo rubbed some of the loamy soil between her fingers. 'I am in Poland again,' she smiled, 'in the underground, among my comrades.'[9]

The industry around her quickly brought Zo back to earth, again. Stripping off her overalls, she handed her money belt over to the men, receiving a few zloty in return. Then, more reluctantly, she held out her two pistols and the fifty rounds of ammunition. This was 'an unpleasant moment', she confessed.[10] She had hardly held a weapon since defending Lwów in 1939, but carrying one now would be a foolish risk. Błysk then led Zo and the others to the safe house, 'a lonely building made of raw bricks'.[11] Once inside, a few of them lit cigarettes while their young hostess, 'Ewa', ushered them to the kitchen table for a meal of bread, bacon and vodka.* Zo ate gratefully. Then, as the sky lightened, she collapsed into a dreamless sleep.

Waking at midday, Zo saw someone at the kitchen stove. Fast as a sniper, Ewa shot her a look of utter contempt. Despite the meticulous checks at Frogmore Hall, and again at the airfield, Ewa had found English-language labels sewn into the lining of Zo's blue silk dress. Had a German patrol stopped at the cottage and discovered them during a search, they might all have been shot. Ewa had unpicked the labels and was burning them in the stove. For once in her life, Zo felt deeply ashamed.

Within the hour, Zo was sitting on a crowded train to Warsaw, leaving the men behind to acclimatise to life inside enemy-occupied territory. Crystal had been impatient to press on but, looking over at Ewa, Ladder had not seemed so reluctant to stay.† Pleased to be alone again, Zo sat by the window, absorbing everything around her, the 'Warsaw suburbs, the crowded streets, the watchfulness of the passengers travelling with their groceries', and even 'the anticipation of identity checks' with something like delight.[12]

---

* 'Ewa', aka Krystyna Szmajdowicz, later served as a liaison and paramedic during the Warsaw Uprising.
† Ladder and Ewa married after the war.

Emilia Malessa met her early the next morning. It was over six months since they had last been together and their knowing smiles were the equivalent of throwing their arms around each other. Although thinner, Emilia was as elegant as ever. Removing her hat, she settled down to hear Zo explain the new communications routes, and detail the outposts now to be avoided. Zo also reported on the growing potential of flights to drop mail, and sometimes to land and collect it, but even during this brief conversation, she realised how much Emilia overestimated the capabilities of the Polish Staff in London. It was wrong to expect too much, she told her boss. The émigré Poles were 'completely dependent' on their British hosts and had no feeling for the situation behind enemy lines.[13]

Zo said the same to Maria Wittek when she reported on the progress with women's military rights. Although Wittek was impressed, Zo was still 'struck by some change in perception' towards her.[14] Protasewicz, she learnt, had sent an ugly report about her 'suspicious contacts' in Britain.[15] To Zo's astonishment, he seemed to be referring to her meeting with Aleksandra Piłsudska. Wittek scowled. Later, she reassured General Bór that all was well. 'Do not spoil the atmosphere of co-operation,' Bór curtly informed the London team.[16] A few days later, Zo's new position as Emilia's deputy and head of the western section of Farmstead was confirmed.

After a quick visit to Rum's mother, to whom she handed over some money as well as his clandestine letter, Zo met the new members of the team. Jarach was briefing couriers, his russet hair combed away from a face that one of them described as at once 'expressive and sombre'.[17] It was Jarach who had prepared Jan Nowak for his journey to London and, like the new emissary, Zo took an immediate dislike to him. The limp handshake that had so offended Nowak did not register with her, but 'he gave the impression of being a slippery man', she told friends. 'I did not like him. He had such a sharp look.'[18]

Nothing would change Zo's mind about Jarach over the next couple of months. He rarely looked her in the eye, and she noticed that most people kept their distance from him. One Farmstead courier was so struck by 'the cold gaze of his shifty, insincere eyes' that she refused to work with him.[19] She could not say what exactly had spooked her, just that 'this was how our enemies and persecutors looked at us'.[20] Even Emilia, who had famously 'good intuition', was not sure about Jarach – so she checked up on him.[21] He had been introduced by a trusted

Home Army officer, he was scrupulously efficient and punctual, and most of the couriers he had sent out, including Wacka, returned.[*] In Zo's words, he 'had all the features of a good conspirator', he just seemed shifty.[22]

Zo got on better with 'Lula', their 'brilliant communications officer'.[23][†] The short-sighted Lula, an artist before the war, had a sweet face, quick mind and more courage than it seemed possible to fit into her small frame. Once, in 1942, she had been hiding a thick roll of reports within her own sketches when some German soldiers started searching the passengers on her tram. Laughingly, she stretched out the roll, teasing them that 'this is a machine gun!'[24] Her merry look took the men by surprise. 'No stupid jokes,' one had muttered, passing on.[25] Having evaded arrest again that summer, she had chosen to work instead with a radio hidden in her apartment.

Zo moved in nearby with a young nurse called Hanka Michalska. Learning by chance that Hanka had been at school with Alicja Iwańska, she asked her to arrange a meeting. Alicja, aka 'Squirrel', was the widow of Pankrac, the courier killed when Sikorski's aircraft had plunged into the sea off Gibraltar. Emilia had broken the terrible news as soon as Pankrac's death had been confirmed. Now Zo told Alicja how, in Paris, her husband had been bubbling over with love for her, and had even proudly shown off his wooden wedding ring. 'My husband . . . liked you very much,' Alicja replied warmly.[26] But when Zo gave her a few of Pankrac's possessions, recovered from the sea, Alicja cried out that 'the walls are crashing down on me'.[27] 'That was very Alicja,' Zo later commented, as uncompromising as ever, although later she conceded that the room's walls 'were kind of crooked'.[28]

Farmstead's work was unrelenting through September and October, as the long winter nights enabled more men, money and equipment to be parachuted in. Zo felt that they were 'busy from morning to night with no rest, constantly running'.[29] They now had a core team of around fifty in Warsaw, including the new liaison officers who collected mail morning and night from various churches, bakeries and tram stops, sometimes exchanging it for the Farmstead missives going out. As identity and travel documents constantly needed updating, the

[*] Jan Rzepecki, aka 'Prezes' (Chairman), vouched for Jarach when he joined Farmstead.

[†] Róża Marczewska.

forgery team were also hard at work, and another set of liaison women delivered emergency mail and supplies. Zo proudly felt that 'it was a brilliant organisation'.[30]

Once Zo's new systems were running smoothly, Emilia gave her two weeks' leave to see Marianna Zawodzińska, her beloved PWK friend. Dr Zofia Franio braced her for the visit. Now in the advanced stages of tuberculosis, Marianna was in a small clinic ten miles west of Kraków. There she read, attempted to knit, and wrote to her anxious father. 'Don't, Papa, think about coming here to me,' she told him. 'The trains are overcrowded and unreliable . . . Don't worry Papa – everything will be well.'[31]

Zo was not to be similarly put off. Marianna's eyes lit up when her friend arrived but even smiling seemed to tire her. Her skin was now thinner than coding paper and paler than her linen. Her long, elegant fingers, so admired by Zo when she had watched her working out ciphers in her cold Warsaw attic, now scratched on her mattress as she struggled to speak. A painful coughing fit sent Zo into action. Carried by water-borne droplets, tuberculosis is astonishingly contagious but Zo sat by Marianna's side, smoothing back the dark strands of hair that stuck to her face and telling her stories of the beautiful Pyrenees.

Zo was not a natural nurse, but she spent the next ten days with Marianna, bringing her soup, books and fresh linen. Marianna's fervent soul still hankered for Polish freedom and Zo assured her that, in the words of their national anthem, their country was not yet lost. She respected Marianna too much to lie about her personal prognosis. They both knew she was dying. Zo could no longer remember the face of her eldest sister, Maria, but she recognised this moment – bringing soup and comfort to a hospital. When she had to leave, Marianna insisted that Zo take her sheepskin coat. A good pre-war one lined with fleece, it weighed heavily on Zo's shoulders, like the knowledge that she would soon be the last of the three spirited PWK cadets who had once pledged their 'whole lives' to the service of their country. Zofia Grzegorzewska had been killed, Marianna was dying, and Zo understood that she would soon have to 'take over the duty of all three of us'.[32]

⚓

Ever greater numbers of women were now rallying to the cause. To Maria Wittek's relief, on 27 October the Polish president in London issued the decree 'On Women's Voluntary Service'. Finally, all women aged between eighteen and forty-five were legally entitled to 'the same duties and rights as men' in the armed forces.[33] The full text had not yet arrived but, as Zo could brief him on its contents, General Bór, the new Home Army commander, pressed ahead with the changes. Thousands of women took the oath and extensive training was rolled out.

Two weeks later, on the evening of Polish Independence Day, 11 November 1943, Zofia Franio telephoned Zo, waiting a long time to get a connection. Marianna had died. When Zo was refused permission to attend the funeral it almost felled her, but she knew that the Gestapo liked to use such occasions to make arrests. The tributes to Marianna provided some consolation. Zofia, Emilia and Hanka had all also loved her, and other friends remembered her as 'a profoundly honest person . . . who had the courage to see the truth, even when this truth was bitter'; as 'having great sensitivity towards human injustice'; and as 'faithful to the end'.[34] Perhaps the hardest to bear was when Marianna was praised as 'sacrificial beyond her strength'.[35] Choked by her grief, Zo had no grand words to offer. Marianna was 'the person closest to me . . .', she mourned, 'and for security I could not even attend her funeral'.[36]

Zo would never be able to let Marianna go completely. Eventually, she took a candle to her grave in a Kraków cemetery, where military veterans, famous writers and renowned scientists all lay buried among the other citizens. During the hard years of the occupation, all of the fallen were heroes. In late November, Zo and Hanka again 'discussed the death of their dear friend', and that evening Zo invited Hanka to join Farmstead.[37] Seeing it as an honour, Hanka did not hesitate. She even refused the modest salary. Although she had already been sworn into the Home Army, she and Zo murmured the oath again together. There was strength to be found in repeating the words that had been on the lips of so many.

It was Lula, Farmstead's communications officer, who tried to distract Zo from her grief by mentioning that Emilia had taken a new lover. Emilia's love life had long been the subject of gossip among her friends. Zo had once believed that 'a woman's relationship to a man is always relevant', but now she was adamant that 'these are [Emilia's] personal matters, which must not be taken into account'.[38] After all, she added, 'who accuses some male officer as wrong, because his subordinates adore him, love him, value him'.[39] But despite her strong words, Zo was secretly as interested in Emilia's affairs as anyone else.

When Zo had left for Britain, her boss had been seeing several men. Now Emilia only had eyes for Ponury, whose stock had risen steadily after his raid on Pinsk prison. Having supported the reverse-engineering of British Sten machine guns, he had had further successes when repeatedly attacking German troops and facilities as part of a strategic regional campaign. He was now commanding Home Army special operations in the mountainous Kielce district, about midway between Warsaw and Kraków. Despite appalling Nazi reprisals, he was regarded as a great national hero. He and Emilia would meet whenever he came to Warsaw for orders and supplies and, occasionally, when Emilia made secret visits to his camps.

'A dark-haired girl of restless beauty', Emilia was very popular with the partisans.[40] It did not hurt that during her visits their demanding leader became 'excited, gallant and cheerful', one of his men recorded, adding that, 'It was obvious that he loved her very much.'[41] In the evenings Ponury would wrap a blanket around Emilia's shoulders, and they would sit beside the campfire, singing duets. Sometimes the men joined in, thirty deep voices close in the dark night. One evening, Ponury asked them to sing the haunting 'slave tango', a fusion of Argentine, Polish and Jewish melodies that had been popular in the Warsaw Ghetto.[42]

Emilia and Ponury were married on the cold winter morning of 27 November 1943, at the Protestant church in Warsaw's Wola district.* Built in the neo-Gothic style, with handsome cast-iron pillars supporting a soaring arched ceiling and the tallest spire in Warsaw, it was not the most inconspicuous venue. But, as Emilia had been unable to provide evidence of her divorce, the Catholic Church would not officiate.† The Protestants were the most receptive – so she had converted. The church stood next to the former ghetto walls, and several of its clerics and members of its congregation had already smuggled their Jewish neighbours to relative safety. Now they were more than happy to turn a blind eye for a fellow resister's wedding. Especially when

---

* On Leszno Street, today Solidarity Avenue. The wooden parts burnt down during the Warsaw Uprising but much of the rest, including the bullet-scarred tower, survive.

† Emilia may not officially have divorced Malessa until after the war.

the only guests were two of Ponury's courageous men, one of whom walked Emilia down the freezing aisle to the priest at the pulpit and her bridegroom waiting before him.*

Emilia had taken two weeks' leave. Ponury did not trust Warsaw's narrow streets and crowded trams, so by evening they were back in the mountains. That night, he threw a great 'elk skin' on the hard ground beneath the shelter of the snowy trees. Then he covered his bride with sheepskins and furs. Sometime in the early hours, Emilia woke to see a luminous belt of stars stretching across the heavens. But when she tried to turn her head, to better see the sky, she found she was stuck fast – her long, loose hair had frozen to the ground.

Although Zo and Emilia were 'very close', Zo had not attended her friend's wedding.[43] As the deputy head of Farmstead, she was responsible for all overseas communications in Emilia's absence. 'Of course, I knew about Ponury', she wrote irritably.[44] Visiting Emilia a few weeks later, Zo was surprised to find her ever-elegant friend still in her pyjamas. Later she met Ponury in the street. 'Tall, dark, he attracted attention', Zo thought, dubiously.[45] 'He was wearing high boots and jodhpurs, and would click his heels in greeting as though he were still in the forest.[46]

⚓

Romance was also in the London air. Protasewicz and Rum were working on the latest courier arrangements that Zo had sent through when WAAF Staff Officer Audrey North, who had often driven Zo around, joined the meeting. Rum found it difficult to concentrate with this attractive young servicewoman in the room. Audrey radiated cheerful confidence. Her blue-grey uniform accentuated the colour of her eyes, beneath her cap her chestnut hair was pinned up in fashionable waves and, when she smiled, Rum thought he saw dimples in her cheeks. As Audrey took her leave, Rum 'clicked the heels of his polished boots, bowed and kissed her outstretched hand'.[47] He wanted to ask her out on a date but, for once, he was lost for words. 'Do you eat dinner,' he finally stuttered.[48] Audrey laughed, and romance blossomed over weekend cinema matinees, English afternoon teas and dances in the Polish mess that stretched out into the night.

---

* Ponury's men were Andrzej Rudziński and Łucja Stankiewicz.

Soon Rum would also meet Jan Nowak, General Bór's first emissary. Nowak had been flown to Britain from Sweden that November.
Like Zo, he had been detained by MI6 on arrival, and when he finally
reached the Rubens Hotel, he too was greeted like a hero. 'The last
emissary from Poland reached London nearly a year ago,' the men
told him, sidelining Zo.[49] Yet Nowak would quickly become just as
frustrated as she had.

Nowak's 'mail' included reports on the Warsaw Ghetto Uprising
that were 'horrible in their eloquence' yet still received with incredu-
lity.[50] His main mission in London, however, was to secure 'most
urgent and important' instructions regarding the approach of the Red
Army. Bór needed to know how to greet Soviet soldiers on Polish soil,
especially if they arrived before diplomatic relations between their two
nations had been restored. The level of support that he might expect
from the Western Allies would also help inform whether and when he
might call the much-anticipated national uprising.[51]

In London, the new commander-in-chief of the Polish Armed
Forces greeted Nowak with a warm embrace.* Impressed by his aris-
tocratic features and military bearing, Nowak felt that had the general
been wearing a fur-lined coat he could have climbed straight out of a
nineteenth-century portrait. Unfortunately, some of his information
seemed hardly more up to date. He expected Home Army soldiers to
withdraw willingly from the fight against the Germans in order to
attack the Soviets as required. Hearing this, Nowak could not keep
silent. 'The very name Home Army may be misleading,' he explained.[52]
'This is not a regular army, living in barracks under strict military
discipline . . . the soldiers are civilians.'[53] The official German reprisal
rate was now one hundred Polish lives for every German killed, but
occasionally four times that rule was applied. Such atrocities had created 'a revolutionary groundswell against the occupying power that
will erupt at the first signs of German weakness', Nowak continued.[54]
Any orders to pull back would only be enacted if they coincided with
'the prevailing mood in the country'.[55]

It was not just the Poles in London whose strategies were misin-
formed. Over the next few weeks Nowak realised that in Warsaw
'the influence and position of the Polish government in London was
seriously overrated' and 'exaggerated trust was put in the Western

* General Kazimierz Sosnkowski.

Allies'.[56] From mid-September, drops of personnel, weapons, ammunition and other equipment from Britain to Poland were drastically curtailed. The RAF blamed technical problems but the Poles began to fear political motives. Nowak now regarded Harold Perkins and SOE's Polish Section as 'our most loyal and important ally', but as he grew more critical of the Polish operation in Britain, the brightness of his star began to wane.[57] Like Zo before him, Nowak realised that 'London and Warsaw were two distinct and completely different worlds'.[58] Lacking 'the basic charts to the political and personal constellations' in London, he now found himself 'somewhat lost'.[59]

In early 1943, the Polish Armed Forces had been a crucial Allied resource. The 30,000 troops of the Polish First Corps, based in Scotland, were trained for the cross-channel invasion of mainland Europe. In Palestine, General Anders led the 60,000 soldiers of the Polish Second Corps in daily drills under the hot desert sun, until the order came to head to Italy. The Polish Air Force, over 11,000 men, had already distinguished themselves in the Battle of Britain, and around 5,000 men were serving with the Allies in the Polish Navy and Merchant Navy. The 400,000-strong Home Army, meanwhile, was lauded in a British military staff report as 'the strongest, best organised and most determined' resistance force in occupied Europe.[60] Above all, from the pioneering work on German Enigma machines, to reports on preparations for Operation Barbarossa, the location of Nazi sub-bases and the V-weapons programme, Polish intelligence had consistently proved vital to Allied strategy and operations.

Yet in late November 1943, Poland's leaders found themselves excluded from the Tehran Conference, the first face-to-face talks between the 'Big Three' Allied leaders, Churchill, Roosevelt and Stalin. With the burden of the war now resting so significantly on the Soviet Union, it was at Tehran that Britain and America finally committed to opening a second front – the time frame for the Allied invasion of Normandy had been set. But no one was there to champion Polish interests when Stalin took out a map and marked up a new post-war Polish–Russian border along the Curzon Line. This would give him much of eastern Poland, to be compensated for by German territory in the west. 'It is, even in international politics, rather a novel procedure to partition the territory of an ally on behalf of another ally,' one Polish minister in London protested, 'and without even consulting the victim.'[61] But this was believed to be the price for keeping the Soviet Union onside.

'All London was waiting for the outcome of the conference', Jan Nowak scribbled as he dashed between meetings.[62] A few days later, he watched a grave-faced Churchill brief the House of Commons. Having stressed that 'ideological differences' must be subordinated to the effort against a common enemy, Churchill paid tribute to Polish bravery. Then he repeated Stalin's assurances that the Soviets 'desired Poland's restitution as an independent state'.[63] 'When I listened to these arguments', Nowak wrote, 'I was filled with a rage that I could hardly contain.'[64] An air of gloom permeated the Polish community in London.

⚓

Christmas 1943 caught Zo by surprise. On 24 December, Hanka devoted some of her precious time to decorating a tree with paper garlands, lace stars and angels made from straw. Zo had not been able to imagine another Christmas under occupation. Suddenly she felt a rush of nostalgia for the old traditions. That afternoon, she and Hanka held a Catholic wafer celebration for a few trusted women. It was Zo who broke the first piece from the *opłatek*, the unleavened biscuit made from wheat flour and water, before passing it on. Each woman then took a piece in turn, adding a prayer for their loved ones. Zofia Franio had organised a similar celebration one day earlier and, all across Warsaw, defiant men and women were coming together to do the same.

Emilia was spending Christmas with Ponury at his freezing camp in the mountains. He had sent a partisan, the appropriately named 'Motor', to collect her from Warsaw in his black Opel.* Motor did not know that he had his chief's wife in the back, shivering despite her layers of wool, felt and fur. The information would have been so valuable to the Gestapo that few people knew the legendary guerrilla leader was married to a lieutenant from Home Army headquarters. Emilia's breath fogged up the windows as the Opel climbed the mountain paths. It felt good to leave the conspiratorial city behind, and glorious to step out into a forest of Christmas trees, all laden with glittering snow.

In London, Rum was celebrating Christmas with Audrey at her

* Jerzy Wojnowski, aka 'Motor'.

comfortable Croydon home. Having had her 'satisfactory work and conduct' recognised, she was being promoted to the rank of flight officer.[65] Rum had now graduated as a member of the Silent Unseen, but his return to Poland had been delayed by the lack of flights. Deeply in love, he and Audrey dreaded their separation. A part of Rum yearned to serve in the Home Army, but he was beginning to reconcile himself to the fact that it might never happen. RAF Bomber Command was inflicting mass airstrikes on Berlin, the Soviets were planning their offensive to end the siege of Leningrad, the Western Allies were preparing to invade Italy and France and, increasingly, Rum felt that his place might be in England.

⚓

On the last day of 1943, Zofia Franio telephoned her friend Mei, who had been at her Christmas wafer celebration just a week earlier.[*] There was no answer. Mei oversaw the storage depot where they kept several tonnes of explosives – much of it home-made and the rest parachuted in from Britain. Zofia cautiously walked over. A Gestapo man was drawing on a cigarette outside the gated entrance to Mei's apartment block. The family had been denounced and, smashing their way in, the Gestapo had found Mei's parents reading a resistance news-sheet. All of them had been arrested.

Zofia went into emergency mode. The explosives had to be moved. The store was in a bombed-out house that could only be entered through the roof. Everything had to come out the same way and be distributed elsewhere. As they could not risk breaking the curfew, Zofia's team had to move huge numbers of packages through the city streets in the darkening afternoons. It was both perilous and tedious work, and until she knew the source of the betrayal, Zofia could trust very few to undertake it. Nevertheless, they cleared the house within a few days.

When Zofia discovered that Mei had been betrayed by a work colleague, she arranged for an underground court to try the traitor in absentia. Two of her team carried out the sentence in January, shooting the man as he walked to his barber before he could betray anyone

* 'Mei' was Jadwiga Kuberska.

else.* There were no other casualties, no recorded witnesses and, as the man was Polish, there were no reprisals.

A few days later, Emilia was returning to her apartment when her neighbour opened their door and quietly beckoned her in. The Gestapo were waiting for her, they hissed. Within minutes, Emilia was heading to a safe house on the far side of the city. From there, she arranged for her apartment to be observed. Rumours were that she had been betrayed by one of Ponury's men.† Whoever it was had no idea of Emilia's role in the resistance, but had seen her importance to the partisan leader. She was to be the bait to lure him back to Warsaw. This time German plans had been frustrated, but as much by chance and community solidarity as by Farmstead's own security systems.

With two betrayals in such quick succession, Zo became concerned that the resistance was getting too cosy. Zofia's sapper units had no contact with the Farmstead team, but their own long friendship created a link. And it had been a trap intended for Ponury that had nearly led to Emilia's arrest. Emilia had already changed her hair, requested new identity papers and found a different apartment. Now Zo did the same, officially becoming 'Elżbieta Nowak' – by chance the same common surname that Jan Nowak had chosen. While her new papers were being prepared, she stayed with Marianna's sister, Stefa.

It was Hanka who purchased a new apartment for Zo, a place chosen by Emilia and paid for by Farmstead. The flat was also to house their new secret archive. Its two dark rooms, under the eaves of a large block, faced onto a park with mature trees, and it had access down a back staircase to a courtyard connected to a warren of small streets.‡ In contrast to Emilia's stylishly furnished rooms, Zo moved in with only a small, single bed and her own old linen. A trusted carpenter then created a large hiding space beneath the floorboards. To access it, a few parquet staves could be raised using a knitting needle. Zo kept a pair for the purpose, along with some wool and a half-knitted sweater in a cloth bag. Only then did her security concerns begin to ease; prematurely as it turned out.

---

* Justyna Ostrowska, aka 'Leta', and Irena Bradel, aka 'Alina', executed the traitor Mieczysław Darmaszek.
† Home Army counter-intelligence later found incriminating papers on Motor, suggesting he was responsible for several betrayals. After interrogation, he was executed by shooting.
‡ Okólnik 11/11a, on the top floor of number 68. It was later partially destroyed.

12

Betrayed
(March–June 1944)

'Black petals of burnt paper started flying all over the apartment.'[1] For a second Zo and Hanka watched in horror. Then they started scrambling after the smouldering fragments before they could leave a tell-tale trail of smuts or, worse, any scrap of intelligence. Hanka soon had ash in her hair and Zo, her sleeves pushed up above her elbows, looked like a demonic baker with grey cinders smeared across her face and arms. It was three in the morning and both women were terrified that the smell of smoke, let alone the thuds from their darkly comic antics, might wake the neighbours. If they were to survive the coming hours and days, they had to destroy all evidence of their clandestine activity and disappear into Warsaw as soon as the morning curfew lifted.

Looking back, Zo would only say that 'a thunderbolt had hit Farmstead' the day before.[2] In the early hours of Monday, 6 March 1944, the Gestapo had raided a small studio flat in the city centre, near the west bank of the River Vistula. There they found the head of Farmstead's forgery team, his deputy and two sisters busy preparing documents for a courier known as Sławek.[*] A few hours later, two officers who had escaped from an internment camp arrived to collect their freshly forged papers. All six were arrested and driven to the imposing four-storey building, a former religious centre, that the Gestapo had requisitioned as their Warsaw headquarters. Manacles and bullwhips lay among battered issues of *Wehrmacht* magazine on the front desks. Once registered, the new prisoners were taken down to stew in the holding cells below. There they sat in silence on wooden benches facing bullet-scarred walls.[†]

---

[*] Feliks Grodziski, aka 'Gryf', headed Farmstead's forgery team. His deputy was Tadeusz Deubl. The Grodziska sisters served as housekeeper and secretary. 'Sławek' was the courier Jerzy Laskowski.

[†] These cells are preserved in what is now Poland's Ministry of Education, at Al. Szucha 25, Warsaw.

The pressure on the Nazi German occupational authorities had grown exponentially since the Red Army had crossed Poland's eastern frontier that January. For over four years, the Polish resistance had harassed German troops and depleted the Gestapo's resources. Now the Germans were determined to annihilate them before the Soviets arrived. For this, they needed more information. After a few sobering hours, their new prisoners had been interrogated while tied to metal shackles set into the cell floors. Then they were subjected to savage beatings and dog attacks. For those still tight-lipped, electrocutions followed.

Unaware of the arrests, Zo and Hanka had spent that day in Zo's draughty new attic rooms, preparing intelligence reports and telegrams for London. They were still hard at it, 'working feverishly' as the light began to fade and the evening air grew cold.[3] Hanka had to race down six flights of stairs and across the street to reach her door before the curfew. Fumbling with her key, it was a moment before she saw the scrap of paper wedged into the lock. 'Everyone at Wanda's apartment is ill', read the hurried note.[4] Wanda was the archivist for Farmstead's western section.* 'Ill' meant arrested. Despite the curfew, Hanka ditched the note down a drain and bolted back up to Zo.

Zo knew that a knock at this hour could only mean bad news, and Hanka's pale face confirmed it. Pulling her inside, they digested the warning together. Given the curfew it would be difficult to run, but Zo's new address was still hardly known. They might be safe that night, or they might only have minutes. Fetching her knitting needles, Zo started levering up the parquet staves of her bedroom floor. Moments later, Hanka watched as her friend lay on her stomach, stretched in an arm, and retrieved the first of the many rolls of the thin Japanese tissue paper that they used for clandestine reports. She had hidden them there only a day earlier, adding the last just that evening. Now the whole cache had to be destroyed.

As Zo had no kitchen stove, just a couple of electric rings, the two women had set to work unrolling the reports and ripping them to pieces. With more haste than speed, they threw great handfuls down the toilet until Hanka began to find the echoing din of every flush 'unbearable'.[5] The building's groaning plumbing was, in any case, not

* Wanda Wysznacka.

up to the strain. In the early hours the women admitted defeat and pulled great lumps of the semi-sodden paper back out.

Finding an old metal serving plate in the kitchenette, Zo lit a small fire from the least damp reports. Having curled and blackened, dripping ash onto the plate, several sheets of the smouldering tissue had twisted up into the air where they were caught in a draught. As the women scrambled after them, more pages followed. It was not the fire risk that concerned Zo, so much as the fear that any stray fragment might contain the code name of an agent or a base, just enough to betray a courier's identity or destroy a route. All the ashes had to be flushed away. 'It was,' she admitted 'a terrible night.'[6]

Zo and Hanka were barely done by dawn, and then they had to replace the planks and make the rooms and themselves shipshape with some serious scrubbing. As soon as the curfew lifted, Zo was out of the apartment and hurrying down the quiet street. Hanka left a few minutes later, heading in the opposite direction. Zo had told her to keep her head down until they could meet at a tram stop the next day.

By the time Zo joined Emilia at their safe house, her boss already knew about the first arrests and of several other raids. One handcuffed prisoner had been shot dead while making a run for freedom. The rest were being held in the basement of the Gestapo building and behind the heavy steel cell doors of Warsaw's notorious Pawiak prison. Tall, red-haired Jarach had been among the first arrested, along with Sławek, the courier whose false papers had been found on the forgers' table. Several others now shared their cell. Jarach was the most affable. Sławek was later reported to have sullenly refused to speak, even to the other prisoners. A few hours later, after the next interrogations, Gestapo teams headed out across the city and, as one Home Army officer reported, 'the blows fell suddenly and all at once'.[7]

It was clear that Farmstead was facing a co-ordinated attack, not only in Warsaw but at several of their overseas bases. Raids had taken place in Alsace, Innsbruck and Berlin. Zo's friends Stefania and Dominik Horst, with whom she had once spent a long night pasting banknotes into the lining of a suitcase, were among those detained inside Germany. Stefania, heavily pregnant, was paraded through the streets in handcuffs as a warning to others, but released after the intervention of her German friends. In Zo's old stomping grounds in Silesia, another close friend, Eleanora Rostalska, evaded arrest simply by walking straight out into the fields when she noticed more Gestapo than usual on the streets. Many others were detained.

Emilia had already alerted the Home Army leadership to the unfolding catastrophe, triggering a cascade of warnings. Her friend had many skills, Zo knew, but chief among them, 'she was characterised by a sharp presence of mind in times of danger, courage and decisiveness in taking action'.[8] Emilia had sent those she believed to be in the greatest danger, Wacka among them, to isolation in a hospital for contagious diseases – one of the most secure addresses in Warsaw. A few others had fled to a forester's lodge on the outskirts of the city. Now Emilia was arranging new documents for those still in Warsaw, and fresh rooms for them to work from.

Before going to ground, several of the remaining Farmstead team risked their lives to secure or destroy vulnerable stashes of papers, cash and arms. Lula had scouted out the forgery team's apartment. Once she saw the Gestapo leave, she quietly let herself in and retrieved a batch of false documents from behind a panel in the wardrobe. She was back on the street within minutes, the incriminating papers stuffed into a suitcase. It was only when she returned to her own apartment, having delivered the case, that Lula was apprehended. Nervously pushing her hair from her face, she apparently absent-mindedly left her hat on the hallway sill. Resistance colleagues later found that it contained the secret post of that day.

Disobeying Zo's instructions to lie low, Hanka had also risked her neck, in her case by visiting Wanda's home. Everyone there might be 'ill', but the apartment also held another Farmstead archive. Discovering that the Gestapo had failed to find the secret recess beneath the floor, Hanka quickly emptied it. When she left, she had Wanda's revolver and dozens of reports and other documents hidden beneath some vegetables in her basket. Incredibly, she made it safely to the home of a friend with no connection to the resistance.[*]

On orders from Emilia, a more recent recruit, Maja, dyed her hair and borrowed a coat before catching the train to Kraków to warn the team there. It was only Maja's fourth mission for Farmstead. She

---

[*] Hanka's friend, Danusia, was a medic living on Dantyszka Street. Her parents had been arrested in 1942.

should have been unremarkable but her nerves gave her away. Arrested at the station, she could not warn anyone.* Celina Zawodzińska was detained in Kraków later that day, along with twenty-two others. Celina had already been warned that an unknown man had been enquiring about her. When challenged, he had claimed to be 'a friend of Zo's from Warsaw'. There had also been reports of an itinerant salesman with a bag full of stockings asking more questions than wartime etiquette allowed. She had just sent a warning to her sister Stefa before she was arrested.

Getting the message, Stefa disappeared while the Gestapo were still searching her sister's rooms. In frustration, the Germans slashed open Celina's sofa, tore the covers from her books and even ripped the heels from her shoes, but they did not find anything incriminating. Celina was fortunate in that she had not had any papers in her rooms that day. She was also lucky not to have been arrested two months earlier. In January, 232 prisoners from Kraków's notorious Montelupich prison had been shot, seemingly without pretext, and in early February another hundred were killed in reprisals for an attempt on the life of the governor general of occupied Polish territory.†

Zo and Emilia were devastated when news came through of these further arrests. Zo had a special place in her heart for Marianna's sisters, and Emilia was close to most of the Kraków team. At first, they estimated that some fifty people had been detained. Many were liaison women who played a vital local communications role but had little useful knowledge for the Germans. Having been left without food for a couple of days, they were beaten 'with a stick, a cane, with rubber, kicking with a heavy boot, beating with the butt of a revolver or gun', one of their husbands later reported.[9] Then came 'searing with hot iron, suspending, pulling out fingernails, giving electric shocks'.[10] Bones were routinely broken, and mock executions were carried out. Fearing that they would not be able to withstand such torture, some chose to end their own lives rather than risk betraying their colleagues. Calling at the prison gate with a basket of provisions, the fourteen-year-old daughter of one woman was told that her mother had taken

---

* Anna Koźmińska-Kubarska, aka Maja, was held in Pawiak until July 1944. She escaped from a Ravensbrück transport in May 1945.
† Hans Frank.

poison.[11] For fifty deutschmarks, she was told, she could have her ashes.[12]*

Lula, Wanda and Celina were among those enduring the 'long and vicious' interrogations.[13] As Polish medics and clerics continued to undertake prison visits, they smuggled news and notes both ways. Lula had reportedly refused to reveal even her own name, despite having pins stuck under her fingernails. Her few messages to her sister on scraps of paper were covered in drawings and lines of verse, revealing only that the once budding artist was still alive. But on 24 March, a food parcel from her family was turned away. That morning Lula had been called out of her cell. Allowed to smoke the butt of a cigarette, she lifted her chin, took a long drag and said, 'To think, this is my last.'[14] Twenty minutes later she was shot in the ruins of the Warsaw Ghetto beside sixty other women, in a reprisal action.† She was thirty-four years old.

Hanka received a prison note signed by 'Wsza', which means 'lice'. This uncharming nickname had been given to Wanda by her PWK friends during their summer camps.‡ 'They interrogate me asking for Elżbieta Nowak', Wanda had written in shaky letters.[15] She had given up everything she knew about Marianna Zawodzińska, who was already dead, but nothing more. 'Everything fine, but please send medicine to cure the accident', her note ended.[16] She was asking for poison. Appalled at the level of suffering that must have prompted this request, Hanka was still trying to fulfil it several weeks later when Wanda was deported to Ravensbrück concentration camp, along with her mother and over fifty other women.§

Celina withstood three months of brutal interrogation in Kraków prison, where she claimed not to know 'Maria Zawacka' or anyone else she was asked about. Put on a prison train to Warsaw, she managed to pass a note to a Polish policeman who delivered it to her family. It would be late July before the Germans gave up on Celina as a potential source of intelligence and sent her, too, to Ravensbrück. Zo knew she

---

* Farmstead courier Ludwika Zawierta took her own life on 3 March 1944. Her daughter, Irena, and son, Lucjan, survived the war.

† Lula, aka Róża Marczewska, was posthumously honoured with the Gold Cross of Merit with Swords, and Virtuti Militari.

‡ Wanda's family name, Wysznacka, has a similar ring to *wsza* ('lice').

§ The 5 April 1944 Warsaw–Ravensbrück transport.

owed her life to the courage, resilience and sacrifices of her friends, yet she and Emilia were increasingly convinced that these raids could only have resulted from treachery within their own ranks.

A few days after the first arrests, Emilia was astounded to see Jarach walking down a Warsaw street.* Evidently released from custody, he looked neither injured nor anxious and, unlike most prisoners, his head had not been shaved. The next day he was reportedly back in his cell, although unshackled. Together, Emilia and Zo undertook a 'frantic analysis' of the known facts.[17] Jarach had worked with Farmstead since the start of 1943, initially as a courier to Prague. Both his manner and some of his reports had raised eyebrows, but resistance work needed all types of people, intelligence could be unreliable, and the man had good credentials. The most serious accusation against him had been made by a Polish *Góral*, a highlander, who had been arrested at a border station. Although this man swore that only Jarach could have betrayed him, since he had soon been released the matter was dropped. Might the Gestapo have deliberately thrown back this highland minnow to buy Jarach more time, the women now wondered.

Promoted to become Emilia's deputy in Zo's absence, Jarach had gained an overview of various courier routes and the details of contacts at several bases. In January, he had visited outposts in Berlin, Lorraine and Alsace, all places where there had been arrests. His German was faultless, but his lack of French had prevented him from going to Paris. There had been no arrests in the French capital, and only one courier from that route had been detained: the unfortunate Sławek whose papers had been on the forgers' table. It now seemed possible that Jarach had been put in Sławek's cell specifically to find out more about the French route.

A couple of nights later, Emilia saw Jarach out in Warsaw again. His treachery was 'increasingly obvious', Zo stormed, sending a warning to the prisoners.[18] The next morning Sławek launched himself at his cellmate, fists flying, but was pulled away before he could inflict much damage. Dragged from the cell, he was not seen again but his bloody shirt was later delivered to his widow. For Zo, he was now 'the hero, Sławek', whose silence had saved the Paris team.[19]

It did not take long for the Gestapo to add 'Elżbieta Nowak' to 'Maria Zawacka' and arrive at 'Elżbieta Zawacka' – a name on their

---

* Emilia was with Helka Czarna.

cards since Klara's arrest in 1942. Soon an arrest warrant had been issued under Zo's correct name, and with a photograph attached. In mid-March, more street round-ups took place across Warsaw. Usually used to secure quotas for labour details, these mass detentions were a crude and cruel tool, often leaving families with no news of their loved ones. This time, however, the Germans were specifically detaining women in their mid-thirties. A few hundred were taken to Pawiak and told to remove their headscarves, tie back their hair and walk around the yard. Watching from a recessed window, Jarach searched for familiar faces. Zo and Emilia were not among them, but with this kind of dragnet approach 'we both expected to die', Zo admitted.[20] It just seemed a question of when.

The Home Army leadership now decided that they could not afford to lose both the head of Farmstead and her deputy. Jarach's betrayal had created a huge breach in communications and Emilia was ordered to remain in the capital and restore emergency courier routes to London via Paris and Bern. The depressing belief was that she was 'probably doomed to be captured', meaning that Zo should be sent into hiding until needed to fill the breach.[21] Emilia 'was simply sentenced to death', Zo wrote in horror, while 'they ordered me to cut myself off completely'.[22] On their last evening together, she and Emilia managed to summon a laugh at the details on the pair of stolen German Kennkarten papers, whose identities they were about to assume. Predictably, Emilia took the documents of the younger, more handsome woman. Zo was glad to indulge her brave friend in this small vanity. She felt guilty, ashamed and, perhaps worst of all, redundant.

It was still mid-March when Zo used her new documents to travel to the Sisters of the Order of the Immaculate Conception in Szymanów, thirty miles west of Warsaw. The imposing convent was a repurposed nineteenth-century palace with a white stucco exterior, balustraded balconies and broad terraces leading down to once sweeping lawns – now largely dug for vegetables. The convent and its grounds were set behind tall walls with decorative iron gates and, unsurprisingly, the impressive site had not escaped German attention.

Before the war there had been eighty-five monastic orders in Poland. Most of those in annexed territory had been closed, but in the General Government zone many were still secretly providing sanctuary for Polish Jews, resisters and others deemed undesirable by the Nazi regime. The order at Szymanów, with its girls' boarding school on site, was no exception and, as a result, they received regular visits from the German authorities, who they greeted politely with tea and distraction.

Sister Assumpta now met Zo at the gates, ushering her in through the grand, panelled entrance hall and down a long passageway leading to the nuns' private quarters.* Within half an hour, Zo was in a postulant's uniform of dark-blue cotton with a close-fitting white cap – a dull version of the sisters' more picturesque sapphire and white robes. While at the convent, she would not only dress but also live as a postulant preparing to join the religious community. Her days started at five, with prayers in the chapel followed by silent meditation, psalms and occasionally beautiful Gregorian chants, then Holy Mass. After breakfast, she spent some hours in service, teaching the schoolgirls and helping on the farm. Angrily, she cut thistle roots out of the wheat fields, planted vegetables and turned the compost. She met the convent beekeeper, who showed her how to maintain the hives, and at night she took shifts guarding the strawberry fields.

The rest of the time, Zo was left alone – for which she was immensely grateful. She needed solitude to mourn her friends, making a mental list of seventy-eight who had been arrested. She also wanted to consider her next steps. The first news from Warsaw reached her at Easter when Hanka visited with a friend.† They brought a traditional poppy-seed cake, and the bitter confirmation that many of the team had been executed. Some had been shot in Pawiak's prison yard or, like Lula, in the streets of the former ghetto. Others were hanged in public squares. A few had been beaten to death.

When another PWK friend arrived at the convent, Zo learnt that her parents and elder sister Dela had also been arrested.‡ Władysław and Marianna Zawacka had hidden Zo's letters under the last coal in their cellar and decided to take their chances. They reasoned that they had been registered as Volksdeutsch for several years and knew no details of their daughter's work. When questioned, Władysław bravely told his interrogator that he had cut her off, 'because she married a

---

* Zo thought this was Princess Sapieżanka. The Superior was Mother Zenóna.
† Hanna Żabińska-Petrykowska, aka 'Rana', who later served in the Warsaw Uprising.
‡ This messenger was Hala Antoniewicz, from the Toruń resistance cell.

German'.[23] His impolitic answer earned him a beating, but seemed honest. He had been thinking of the false papers he had once seen, in which Zo's name was given as Elisabeth von Braunneg. Marianna simply pleaded ignorance. Asked who 'Dominik' was, as she did not know of Dominki Horst, who had run the Berlin cell, she launched into a long description of her brother, Zo's uncle Dominik. There was no news of Dela.

Zo was consumed by guilt and grief just as she was most powerless to act. She imagined her parents in their prison cells, and Klara in Ravensbrück now without even food parcels. 'I knew,' Zo confessed, 'that . . . it was all my fault because, after all, Klara had been arrested for me in Silesia, and then my whole family.'[24]

♒

'The Gestapo have dealt a heavy blow to Farmstead', Emilia tele-grammed Protasewicz in London on 24 March.[25] Informing him that twenty-one people had already been executed, she explained that she and Zo had 'escaped by a miracle'.[26] 'Please send someone from headquarters to help rebuild the cell', she urged.[27] Jan Nowak was in the Sixth Bureau offices when, as he put it, this 'shattering piece of news' arrived.[28] Keen to return to his fiancé, Greta, in Warsaw, he would have volunteered but he had injured his back during parachute training. Protasewicz selected Rum for the job.

Rum was briefed that he should be in Poland for only three weeks, before returning to London. Before the Special Duties Squadron could take him, however, they had to deliver several other men and some urgent supplies. 'The secret army in Poland was delighted' by these deliveries, British files noted. 'Commander-in-Chief, General Bór-Komorowski, sent his warm thanks for the help.'[29] But ten days later, Rum had still not departed.

That evening, Rum invited Audrey to a dinner dance at the Rubens Hotel. Both arrived in uniform; a handsome picture of wartime romance. Between courses they danced waltzes, quicksteps and fox-trots, and at the end of the evening Rum pulled his date onto the floor for the *oberek*, a romantic Polish folk dance that derives its name from *obracać sie*, meaning 'to spin'. As Audrey collapsed into his arms, flushed and breathless, he leant in and asked her to marry him.

Audrey's parents objected for fear their daughter might lose her

British citizenship.* SOE had other concerns. 'It is unfortunately necessary for me to report . . . her engagement to Capt. Bielski', Perkins
wrote, misspelling Rum's surname. 'I have no reason to question
her loyalty', he added, and 'also have high regard for the integrity
of Captain Bielski. I feel, however, that in future her loyalty to the
Section . . . may be biased in favour of her fiancé.'[30] The same dim
view was taken further up the line, where there were fears about the
pressure that might be applied to Audrey should Rum be captured. 'I
know such things are not supposed to happen outside a . . . novel, but
the Poles are closer to fiction than other people', the decision came
down. We must 'harden our hearts' and transfer her.[31]

Despite all opposition, Rum and Audrey were married in front of
250 guests in the impressively colonnaded St Peter's Church, Eaton
Square, in London's posh Belgravia. The windows had been boarded
up and the railings outside requisitioned for the war effort, but over
his uniform Rum proudly wore his new military-issue Sam Browne
belt, a wedding gift from his bride, and on his chest was the Cross of
Valour, awarded in 1941 and which he had been given 'exceptional
permission' to wear on his wedding day.[32] Audrey met him at the
ornate rood screen in a handsome gown of cream satin that pooled
onto the floor, a bouquet of white roses and lilies-of-the-valley in her
hands. Afterwards, at the Goring Hotel, a three-tier wedding cake
was cut, toasts drunk, and the happy couple left to honeymoon in
picturesque Stonor near Henley-on-Thames.

The contrast with Emilia's modest ceremony in war-torn Warsaw
and her freezing wedding night between a pair of 'elk-hides' in the
mountains could hardly have been greater. With many of her surviving
team in hiding, Emilia was now working almost alone to restore communications with London. But she would not have begrudged Rum
this moment. Both of their weddings had been expressions of love and
hope in the face of the same dehumanising conflict.

⚓

Two weeks after her wedding, Audrey was forced to leave her post
'owing to [her] marriage to an alien'.[33] Rum, however, was finally

---

* Until 1948, any British woman marrying a foreign national automatically lost their
British citizenship.

ready to serve in the field. That same afternoon, a thousand miles east, a prototype V2 rocket fell softly into the wide, sandy bank of the River Bug, eighty miles east of Warsaw. It was 'a veritable god-send', one Silent Unseen officer commented.[34] Launched as part of the V-weapons test programme, this stray missile offered the Allies their first opportunity to gather technical intelligence on the V2s. Home Army soldiers secretly pushed the rocket more deeply into the mud, excavating it only after the Germans had left. Polish scientists and engineers then prepared a report – a team of cyclists even relayed a small flask of the fuel to Warsaw, where chemical analysis revealed it to be a mix of ethanol and water. The problem, then, was how to get the report, the experts and some of the 25,000 component parts to Britain.

Almost as soon as the Allies had gained a foothold in southern Italy, SOE established airbases in Brindisi to provide shorter routes to Poland. In April 1944, a Dakota had landed in occupied Polish territory for the first time, collecting post and passengers before returning.* It had been 'exceptionally hazardous', the British reported, and Perkins doubted whether the experiment would be repeated.[35] By May 1944, Britain and America were fully focused on the long-awaited invasion of northern France and, although the Polish Air Force and Navy would take part, the Home Army, still preparing its uprising to coincide with these plans, was no longer a priority. As Anna Leska, the sister of Bradl, joined her fellow ATA pilots ferrying Spitfires, Hurricanes and Mosquitoes to the airfields of east Kent in preparation for D-Day, Rum found his flight home delayed yet again.

ℬ

A few weeks later, as the combined Allied forces battled through northern France, Emilia's husband, Ponury, was still fighting in the east. On 16 June, grenade in hand while leading an attack against German fortifications near Lida, he was hit in the stomach by a burst of automatic-pistol fire.† 'A man like that could not die', one of his men wrote desperately in his diary.[36] Ponury was more realistic. 'Listen, I won't survive,' he whispered to the field doctor, before

---

* Operation Wildhorn ['Air-Bridge'] I, 15 April 1944.
† Then in eastern Poland, Lida is now in Belarus.

continuing with great reported eloquence, 'Say goodbye to the sol-
diers, to the Holy Cross Mountains that I came to love so deeply.
Tell my wife farewell, and report to the command that I died for
Poland.'[37]

Ponury was buried two days later. Two platoons of partisans, his
horse and a crowd of villagers followed the coffin, which was draped
with the Polish flag and the Virtuti Militari ribbon of honour. More
men, armed with machine guns, lined the route and when dusk came
torches were lit. The funeral 'was a manifestation of the Polish spirit',
his men felt proudly. 'People in the villages cried like children.'[38] In
Warsaw, Emilia shed her tears alone. A few weeks later, still dressed in
deepest mourning, she visited Ponury's parents. For a while they sat in
awkward silence – Zofia Piwnik refused to accept the death of her son.
Leaning over, Emilia unfolded a small bundle of white cloth. Inside
were the keys of Pinsk prison, the talisman that Ponury had carried
with him ever since the daring raid that had made his name. 'You have
me,' Emilia urged his mother as they wept together. 'Love me, because
I have nobody now.'[39]

Emilia found some solace with her grieving in-laws but admitted
to Ponury's sister that she had 'lost more in him than a husband' and
'haven't yet learnt to cope with that'.[40] Emilia feared that she had also
lost her dreams for a family. Had she and Ponury 'had a child, I might
be able to come to terms with his death', she reportedly confessed.[41*]
As it was, she was left questioning the value of her life and, with Zo
still in military quarantine at the convent, there were few friends to
whom she could turn.

⚓

Rum was lying on his back on the rose-bordered lawn of Audrey's
parents' house in Croydon, South London. Now, three weeks after
D-Day, he doubted whether any new missions to Poland would go
ahead. A moment later the drone of a V1 flying bomb sent him running
to the nearest shelter. The sound of the engine was actually a comfort.
It was the silence after the motor cut out that meant the bomb was

---

* In 1946, Prawdzic-Szlaski, testified that in early 1943 Ponury had told him that he
was married, with a son, and that Emilia had later told him that their son was with
his grandparents. However, there is no evidence of this child.

about to drop. He soon felt the shock in the air as a neighbouring house was demolished.

The next day, Rum learnt that he was finally to return to Poland. He would be hitching a lift in the Dakota being sent to collect the V2 rocket report prepared by the Polish resistance. As well as taking $5,000 to help fund escape lines, and several suitcases of specialist equipment and armaments, Rum was to report personally to Bór. His mission was to draft a communications plan, including new courier routes designed by Zo and Emilia, for use in the event of a hostile Soviet occupation. That same afternoon, Audrey told Rum she was pregnant. The baby was due on 4 March 1945, Rum's own name-day. He had been told that he was to return to Britain within six weeks, but he secretly wondered whether he would be back in time for the birth, if at all.

On 26 June, with two photographs of Audrey concealed inside his jacket, Rum was flown from Croydon to Brindisi, on the first stage of his journey home. Several hours later, walking into the Brindisi airbase briefing room, he bumped into Jan Nowak. Like Zo before him, Jan had found his time in London 'both sad and fascinating'.[42] His weeks spent studying secret reports, while V1s fell on the city 'without respite', had led him to conclude that Poland's fate was already decided.[43] He expected the Soviets to occupy his country, and only be routed by another war. His unfortunate mission was to brief Bór on the low level of military support he could expect in the event of a national uprising.

Stuck in Brindisi by bad weather, Jan had no way to get word to his beloved Greta in Warsaw, but Rum sent mildly reassuring letters to Audrey on thin, blue airmail notepaper. 'The war can't last longer than a few weeks,' he told her. 'Don't worry about me darling.'[44]

꒰꒱

Despite her clear orders, with every day that passed Zo found it harder to remain at the convent in Szymanów. She distracted herself with hard work and empathy. Among the younger students in the school, she had noticed 'a little Jewish girl, perhaps nine years old, red-haired . . . an orphan sheltered by the sisters'.[45] Jasia was one of several girls given sanctuary at the convent when the ghettos were 'liquidated'.* Although

---

* Jasia 'Kaniewska'.

welcomed with hugs and reassurances, she missed her family and felt disloyal keeping her faith secret while learning the strict Catholic regimen. Her catechism would not fool anyone and she had what was considered a 'bad appearance', meaning that her features were those typically defined as Jewish by the Nazis.[46] When the nuns attempted to dye her curly auburn hair, it turned green, and had to be cut off. As a result, she was never allowed beyond the convent walls. Zo was not a maternal woman but she spent some time trying to cheer sad, skinny, courageous Jasia.

At first, Jasia had simply been sent to the nuns' private rooms during German 'inspections' of the convent. Then she had to hide in the gardens. By the time Zo arrived, classroom bells warned the teachers to hide their Jewish students and replace Polish schoolbooks with the few agricultural manuals that were approved for training future labourers for the Third Reich. Once, when there was no time to squirrel Jasia away, one of the sisters, 'a handsome, big woman', had pushed the child beneath her skirts.[47] 'I heard two hearts beating,' she later confessed, 'but could not tell which was thumping harder.[48]*

In mid-June, the convent received another visitor. Still serving as a courier, Wacka had stayed in Poland's north-eastern Kresy district after the news of Jarach's treachery had reached her. Anxious not to be stranded, however, she had since returned to Warsaw among hundreds of others fleeing ahead of the advancing Soviet line. Maria Wittek had sent Wacka to the convent so that she and Zo could plan the deployment of the many women now signing up for military service.

Behind Wacka, the Russians had begun 'their westward flood', as Colin Gubbins, the head of SOE, put it, 'seeping like a swift rising tide through and around' the exhausted German forces.[49] The Home Army now attacked the German rear, while continuing to disrupt road and rail communications. 'Full well they knew they could expect little gratitude,' Gubbins continued, 'no mercy, and no consideration from the advancing Russian armies.'[50] Gubbins was right. Partisans greeting the Russian forces as allies often found themselves detained, even while the Soviet leadership was accusing the Home Army of

---

* Sister Magdalena Zamojska hid Jasia under her habit. Two of the convent's sisters were executed in 1944, but nearly forty Jewish children were saved. Jasia later worked for the United Nations.

deliberately restraining the Polish people from rising up against their German oppressors.

In Warsaw, Bór now realised that if the Poles were to welcome the Russians to their capital as equals, rather than as liberators to whom they would be historically indebted, they would first have to drive the Nazis out themselves. As talk of national insurrection began to reach the convent, some of the sisters sewed white-and-red armbands for the insurgents, while others used their duplicator machine to print resistance news-sheets. Several of their former pupils were already serving with the partisans, including with Ponury's old unit in the mountains.

Late June found Zo still 'sitting in Szymanów', she wrote in frustration, while 'the knowledge that there would be conflict, an open fight, hung in the air'.[51] She admired the sisters, but knew that her own contribution was to be different. She had first pledged to protect her country when she was a military cadet, and had been sworn into the resistance in November 1939. For four long years she had organised and run an intelligence network, crossed wartime borders over a hundred times as a courier and, as an emissary, challenged and changed military policy and practice at the highest level. Along with her colleagues, she had helped grow the Home Army into an organisation that could wreck over a thousand enemy train engines in a single week, and supplied the intelligence that paved the way for many of the Allied bombing raids. She had also seen her entire family arrested, and the execution of many of her friends.

It was impossible for Zo to remain hidden in a convent when the battle ahead would determine the fate of her nation. At the end of the month, intent on lending all her force and fury to the coming uprising, she disobeyed her direct orders. Swapping her postulant's dress and cap for her old civilian clothes and false papers, she set off on foot, alone, for Warsaw.

13

Calm Before the Storm
(July 1944)

Above the muted hum of Warsaw, the soft thud of cannon could be heard from far across the Vistula river. Everyone in the city felt it; the strengthening pulse of the Soviet advance.

The first German soldiers that Zo had seen in Warsaw, back in late 1939, had been well fed, well dressed and full of the superior swagger of a self-designated 'master race'. Even after her return to Poland, in September 1943, Nazi German officers still strutted down Warsaw's streets with their field-grey chests puffed out like pigeons in winter. Zo had watched them with a visceral hatred. Germany had already been on the defensive then, but the Eastern Front had still been five hundred miles away.

When Zo reached Warsaw from the convent in Szymanów, on 16 July 1944, however, she found the Germans in disarray. Their tanks were once again rumbling in convoy down the capital's grand central avenues, but now they were retreating to be redeployed in northern France. Both bridges across the Vistula were crammed with exhausted men 'dragging themselves along' in the same direction.[1] Most were dirty and hungry, and many were also badly wounded and drunk. Those too weak to walk were riding on 'miserable carts', as Zo put it, or clinging on to them pathetically.[2] 'Their uniforms were unbuttoned, their rifles and helmets hung limply, their faces were dirty and sweaty, and they were clearly dead tired', another Home Army officer elaborated.[3] Even Warsaw's street-sellers were emboldened to mock them. 'Look at these victors,' the braver ones cried out in voices thick with irony. 'See how they walk!'[4]

The Home Army had also been transformed. Instead of regular resistance, 'all thoughts' now 'revolved around the inevitable uprising', Zo wrote, with 'feverish preparations' underway.[5] Yet to her frustration, Zo could not find Emilia. Jarach had disappeared but, as far as anyone knew, he was still free in the city – so people, premises and passwords had all been changed. Hanka, with whom Zo had burnt her archive, had been commissioned to take urgent papers to Lublin and was not expected to return until August. Wacka had also been redeployed, and Emilia was working at new premises so secret that no one could tell Zo where they were.

The next morning Zo learnt that she, too, had been reassigned. Instead of rejoining Emilia at Farmstead she was ordered to report to Maria Wittek, now commanding the official Women's Military Service.* As Zo hurried through Three Crosses Square in the bright summer sunshine, loudspeakers were ordering the entire male population of the city to report for duty digging ditches. Few Poles were willing to build defences for the Germans, and none wanted to risk being rounded up and deported before they could join the open fight, so almost everyone Zo passed was female. How many of them, she wondered, were also on resistance business.

Maria Wittek smiled as Zo once again walked through her door. These two unlikely survivors had known each other for over a decade. Since the war started, they had served together in the defence of Lwów and in the Warsaw resistance. And it was Wittek who had given Zo her second mission in London – to secure the legal status of women as soldiers of the Home Army. Now Zo was to fight alongside her commander in the final battle to liberate Warsaw.

Wittek had organised the Women's Military Service on the basis of her own experience during the Great War, the interwar PWK structures and the information Zo had gathered on the women's auxiliaries in Britain. As General Bór felt that there should be no female-only companies, the largest all-female unit was a platoon. Even with the weapons caches that had been built up, there were not enough munitions to supply all the women who were now volunteering. As a result, only those who had received significant weapons training or were already experienced in sabotage and special operations were to see armed service. Most women, including the trained reserve units, were to prepare and circulate news-sheets, deliver messages, transport weapons, food and medicines, and serve as medics.

Zo was to start by briefing the latest recruits. She was delighted to find Wacka among the dozen or so women in her team. The two of them quickly fell into step, running basic training, planning comms

* The *Wojskowa Służba Kobiet* or WSK.

and supply lines, and organising the new recruits into their units across the city. 'Everyone was on edge,' Zo saw, but she and Wacka felt deep satisfaction as each new cohort of women were readied for action.[6]

Just ten days after Zo's return, on 25 July, the Polish government in London authorised Bór to launch the national uprising at his discretion. He was now waiting only for the Red Army to push closer to the city's eastern suburbs. With the great might of the Soviet armed forces protecting his back, and Allied airlifts resupplying him from the west, he believed it would take just a few days for the Home Army to evict the Germans from their capital.

⚓

That same evening, Jan Nowak offered Rum some hot tea from his flask. They were huddled together in the bitterly cold fuselage of the Dakota taking them to Poland.* The aircraft had been battered by violent crosswinds even as Jan admired the departing Italian coastline, 'bathed in the rays of the setting sun', and the temperature had quickly plummeted.[7] It was dark by the time they passed over Yugoslavia, the lights from partisan camps in the mountains clear below. Their fighter escort had then sheared away, leaving the unarmed Dakota to press on alone. Jan knew that with its protective plating removed to lighten its load, 'any encounter in the air was bound to be fatal', but he kept the thought to himself.[8] Over Hungary they were caught first in long searchlight beams, and then in the brighter, broken lines of tracer flare, but they emerged unscathed to land at *Motyl*, the dark, wet Polish field where their reception committee was waiting for them.†

A cheer went up when the aircraft landed, and some of the partisans ran over to kiss its fuselage. The engines were still running when Rum was physically pulled out and carried over the first hundred metres of Polish soil by a pair of patriotic farmers. This was the kind of reception he liked, but he quickly dashed back to help with the heavy military supplies they had brought with them. A pair of engineers were already waiting to load up the nineteen cases of V2 rocket parts and the thick dossiers from their research. Once everything was on board,

---

* Operation Wildhorn ['Air-Bridge'] III, with New Zealand pilot George Culliford, and John Appleby as wireless operator.

† *Motyl* means 'butterfly'.

the engineers climbed into Rum and Jan's seats and the pilot prepared for take-off.

Special Duties Squadron landings in enemy-occupied territory were always turned around with military precision. The aim was to leave within six minutes of landing. At Motyl, a speedy operation was particularly crucial. The local area bristled with 4,000 German troops on their way from the Eastern Front to Normandy, and 400 Luftwaffe personnel had made camp just a mile away. That very day, despite heavy rain, three enemy Storch reconnaissance aircraft had used the field for training, and the Polish reception committee knew that, as Sue Ryder later put it, 'the sound of an aircraft passing overhead was almost certain to alert every German patrol in the vicinity'.[9]

But the Dakota's wheels had sunk deep in the mud. Everyone leapt into action, digging them out and shoving wads of straw underneath, followed by planks ripped from some nearby fencing. Half an hour passed, and the aircraft still refused to budge. The pilot now felt his only option was to destroy his machine, and Rum and Jan were considering disappearing, given the priority of their own missions. Then the pilot suggested detaching the hydraulic hoses to loosen the jammed wheel-brakes. This risked not being able to raise the plane's undercarriage once it was airborne. The resulting drag might cause them to run out of fuel before reaching Brindisi. Their best hope was to replace the brake fluid in flight, using any available liquid. If that failed, they would have to parachute.

Ninety minutes after landing, the Dakota finally took off, narrowly missing a stone wall at the far end of the field.* 'Happy landings,' Rum sighed, as he, Jan and the locals set off with their packages in an old horse-drawn cart.[10] The gentle creak of the cart's wooden wheels, the warm smell of the horse and the song of the crickets, frogs and the first birds of dawn now seemed to welcome Rum home. Audrey, their house in Croydon and the Reubens Hotel all seemed to belong to another life.

It was already light when Rum glimpsed the white washed walls of a farmhouse. Heavenly 'wholegrain bread thick with fresh butter, cream cheese with chives, hard-boiled eggs and cold sliced pork' were

---

* The Dakota made it to Brindisi. The V2 intelligence enabled accurate calculations to be made about the missile's size, weight and performance before the first hit Britain in September 1944.

washed down with 'bimber', a homebrew of fermented corn and potatoes.[11] Jan now caught Rum's joy at being back on Polish soil. It was
a gloriously sunny morning by the time they set off for the station,
trying not to smile too blatantly at 'the peasant huts, the sheaves in the
fields, even the honking of the geese and clucking of chickens'.[12] When
they passed two barefoot peasant girls in traditional colourful skirts
and white blouses, Rum nudged Jan with his elbow, saying, 'Pretty,
eh?'[13] 'Cast your eyes down!' Jan reproached him, laughing. 'Think
of Audrey!'[14]

Soon the two men were sitting, in different carriages, on the train
to Kraków. To Rum's amazement, the passengers around him were
talking openly about the approaching military front and there was a
sense of excitement in the air. Wisely, he did not join in. When they
first stopped for checks, Rum saw some passengers being led away
from the train. A moment later, 'sounds of gunfire echoed around the
trees of the hazy forest'.[15] In that sharp second, all thoughts of Polish
wheatsheaves and pretty maids vanished. Instead, Rum's mind swam
with images of his forged papers, as yet untested, and the $5,000 in
his money belt. His stomach twisting, he considered hiding the belt
beneath his seat or simply running into the woods, but he sat still,
apparently impassive.

A Gestapo officer, perhaps only eighteen years old, clicked the heels
of his knee-high boots as he entered Rum's carriage; an action Rum
had performed a thousand times himself. When the woman beside
him handed over her papers, the young officer berated her for accidentally defacing them with the vinegar leaking from her pickles. He
hardly glanced at Rum's papers. Rum was now Obersturmbannführer
Tyschen and the recipient of a smart salute. Inwardly, silently, fervently,
he thanked the forgery team, and blessed every member of the Home
Army whose ranks he felt he had now finally joined.

It was a relief for Rum to spot Jan in the crowd as they changed
trains at Kraków. Although ostensibly an express, their new train
rumbled along slowly. When they stopped in the Warsaw suburbs,
to fill the tender with water, to Rum's astonishment he recognised a
local woman hanging out her washing to dry. It was lucky that Rum's
mother did not glance at the train as she pegged out his father's shirts;
any sign of recognition might have been catastrophic. Yet, after over
four years without news of his family, by chance Rum now knew that
both of his parents were still alive.

Rum had been out of Poland for so long that, like most returning Silent Unseen officers, he was sent to acclimatise in the care of two resistance 'aunties'. A few days later, Emilia collected him. 'I have heard so much about you from Zo . . .' Rum began, as they headed off.[16] Emilia was 'a well-dressed woman', he noted. 'Short, black hair, pale thin face, although she looked about forty years old, most likely she was younger, in her mid-thirties.'[17] Emilia was indeed thirty-six. She was also a captain in the Home Army but, unlike Zo, she was used to male compliments, enjoyed them, and was happy to make small talk as she and Rum made their way across the city.

Jan, who had already spent three years in occupied territory, had travelled straight to see his fiancé. Although subjected to the usual thorough search before leaving Brindisi, the next morning Greta found some pages from an old copy of the *Daily Telegraph* lining the bottom of his suitcase, along with a small bottle of hair dye marked 'made in Britain'.[18] Horrified, they burnt the paper and buried the bottle. Jan then also contacted Emilia. It was only when he had seen for himself 'the untiring energy of that woman' that he once again 'grew calmer'.[19]

It was now late July, and there were ever more signs that Germany was losing its grip on the Polish capital. The city's news stands no longer stocked Reich newspapers, Jan noticed, and the loudspeakers in Three Crosses Square had finally fallen silent. Away from Warsaw, unknown to Home Army headquarters, other changes were also taking place.

In Toruń, Zo's parents and sister Dela were still in detention. 'A young, pretty girl', Dela had been working as an accountant for 'a so-called "Good" German', as Zo carefully phrased it.[20] This man had been making every effort to secure her release. With Volksdeutsche prisoners like the Zawackis no longer a priority, no evidence against them and a bona fide German businessman championing Dela's cause, all three were eventually released.

Celina Zawodzińska was also on the move. A few weeks earlier, she had been transferred from Warsaw's Pawiak prison to Fort VII in Poznań, where she was again brutally interrogated. Not once did she give up any useful information. On 27 July she was deported to Ravensbrück. Over 130,000 women would either pass through or end their lives in this camp. Of these, 48,000 were Polish, and several had served in Farmstead. Like the thousands before her, Celina staggered down from her railway cattle car, blinking at the daylight and cursing her stiff and scabby legs. Herded forward by female guards, she stumbled into a shower block where her head was shaved and her whole body disinfected. Several naked hours later, after a 'medical inspection', Celina collected a thin prison uniform. The red political prisoner triangle on it was printed with the letter 'P', for Polish.

Like most new arrivals, Celina spent the next two weeks in quarantine barracks, where she undertook her first hard physical labour. 'They didn't shoot the women,' one prisoner later reported. 'We were to die of misery, hunger and exhaustion.'[21] Another inmate spoke of the women's pride and dignity, even though none of them 'expected to get out alive'.[22] Survival depended on luck and the vital support of those around them. Among the sick and ill women Celina met in the main camp, she was astounded to recognise Klara Zawacka – Zo's beloved younger sister who had been deported over a year earlier.

Klara was one of over seventy Polish prisoners who had been subjected to medical experiments. Sometimes Nazi 'doctors' deliberately introduced infections into healthy muscle tissue, or broke or removed the bones in the women's legs to see what could be learnt for the treatment of battlefield wounds.[*] Other prisoners, including over a hundred Romani women, were forcibly sterilised. Those who returned to their blocks, severely damaged and sometimes deranged, were sheltered by their fellows who covertly tried to cover their work quotas and sometimes hid them in the drains during selections. The only known details about Klara's treatment are Celina's understated words that the experiments had been, 'often sad and brutal'.[23]

Despite these cruelties, the limited rations, disease, lack of warm clothing and the public executions she had been forced to witness, Klara had not only survived; she had managed to pass 'a test for agile hands'.[24] As a result, she had been among those selected to manufacture electrical components and military equipment in the Siemens plant built near the camp to exploit its labour. Siemens workers were given better rations and living conditions, and even allowed to rest between shifts, enabling far more to survive. A few days after they met, Klara got Celina's name added to the Siemens list but, before she could start, Celina's whole barracks were moved to Magdeburg, administratively under Buchenwald concentration camp.

---

[*] Such women later became known as the 'rabbits', both for their hobbling walk, and from the Polish equivalent to the English term, 'guineapigs'.

Celina later credited this move with enabling her to 'escape the chimney'.[25] At Ravensbrück, the weeping sores on her legs meant that she would almost certainly have been selected for the gas chamber but, as her part of Madgeburg did not have a crematorium, there were fewer selections there. Now Celina laboured in twelve-hour shifts, standing in the heat and leaden dust over a machine making shell cases for the Polte ammunition factory. But back in her barracks, she sometimes found a raw vegetable hidden in her bed sheet, or a clean cloth to dress her wounds. 'Mutual help was stable and certain', she later testified.[26] As far as possible, the women saved each other.

⚓

The day after Celina had been deported to Ravensbrück, Emilia took both Jan and Rum to meet Bór. The general started by updating them on the situation inside Warsaw. Up to 48,000 Home Army soldiers were now yearning for revenge after five years of brutal occupation. The city was 'like a barrel of dynamite', Jan felt. 'Strike a match in one place, and everything would blow up.'[27] He then reported to Bór, warning him about the limited Allied air support he was likely to receive. Bitter though this task was, Jan was determined that the commander should have a realistic picture of the situation – but he immediately felt that his briefing had been academic. Events within Poland had already acquired their own momentum.

Since General Sikorski's death, Jan had appreciated that 'the centre of gravity' for deciding Polish policy, 'had shifted from the Thames to the Vistula'.[28] Every day, Bór saw demoralised German forces on the retreat. Every evening, he heard Radio Moscow inciting the Poles to join the fight. 'Smash the foe before he can recover from his defeat,' the Soviets demanded. 'Every Polish homestead must become a stronghold in the struggle against the invaders . . . Not a moment is to be lost.'[29] Bór's plan now was not only to drive the Germans from his capital, but also to establish a new civic authority ready to welcome the Russians when they arrived.

Bór now appointed Jan to run radio communications with London during the coming battle. As well as coded messages to co-ordinate the deployment of the Polish parachute regiment, secure airlifts and exchange military reports and briefings, Jan was to broadcast dispatches from Polish war correspondents to let the world know what was happening in real time.

Rum, who had been sent to support Farmstead for just a few weeks, was now given a longer-term role. In the event of another Soviet annexation, he was to establish secret radio stations on the Polish coast, and ideally in Riga, to maintain ongoing communications. He was also to invest his $5,000 in the creation of escape routes through Latvia or Turkey for the Home Army leadership, leading anti-communists and any escaped Allied POWs who might desperately need to flee west. Meanwhile, as a Silent Unseen officer trained in urban warfare, he was to join a Home Army battalion in the city centre.

Zo met Rum a few days later. Emilia had sent her a note requesting a meeting in the Old Town. If Zo was surprised to find Rum sitting companionably beside her friend, she was amazed to see how defensive Emilia was. Zo quickly felt sure that the two were an item, and it was clear they 'must already have talked about' how she would 'react to Rum's presence'.[30]* But Zo did not have the appetite for any unnecessary drama. She and Rum might have 'little in common', she felt, but as a soldier in the field he had earned her respect. Rum saw Zo in a new light too. In London he had considered her almost spiritual zeal for Poland to be 'pretty far-fetched'.[31] Now, 'after witnessing the spirit of the Home Army', he was able to 'appreciate how faithfully Zo embodied the feelings of the country'.[32] To his delight, she was 'extremely cordial'.[33]

For a while, Zo and Rum warmed themselves in the glow of their new-found friendship but their conversation turned more sombre when Zo asked about their Sixth Bureau colleagues. One had been parachuted into France, only to be captured immediately. Subjected to water torture in a bathtub, he had lost his memory and with it his once angelic smile. As far as Rum knew, he had at least survived. Their other colleague had been disqualified from parachute training after being diagnosed with a heart defect. Instead, he had travelled overland through France. The last news was that the Germans had arrested him as well.†

Zo was deeply affected. She had once thought these young men fools but also, to some extent, innocents. Their loss appalled her. In

* There is no evidence of an affair between Emilia and Rum.

† Majeranek parachuted to France; Zur crossed Europe by train.

defiance of her usual principles, she now talked about herself, and Rum was able to peep, for the first time, beneath her armoured plating. She told him honestly about the fear she had experienced at parachuting, but also of her intense joy to be back on Polish soil. And she talked of Farmstead's devastating losses after Jarach's betrayal, and the great courage and quick-thinking that Emilia had shown. As she left, Rum suggested that they meet again in a few days' time.

Now Emilia told Rum about a courier they had recently recruited; a man who had started asking too many questions.* When his interest had turned to her true identity, an investigation had revealed that he was in the pay of the Gestapo – another Jarach. A Home Army court had passed the death sentence, to be carried out before the end of July – in just two days' time. As he was unknown in Warsaw, Rum had been detailed to carry out the sentence. Rum's back stiffened. In Britain he had excelled on the SOE's 'silent killing' course, but this time it would be for real. Rum was no coward, but he was still only beginning to appreciate what his colleagues had been enduring in occupied territory; not just the hunger and humiliations but the fear, betrayals, arrests and executions.

To carry out his orders, Rum was given a double-edged fighting knife, wrapped in an oily cloth, and one of the white armbands that exempted select people from the curfew. On the rainy evening of 29 July, he scouted out the bar where his target was drinking, then sheltered in a nearby doorway. As it was after the curfew, the wet streets were almost empty. When the traitor left the bar, walking fast, head down, Rum stepped across his path, swiftly thrusting his knife into the man's abdomen. There was no struggle. Ten seconds later the informer was dead. Rum took no pleasure in the work but neither did he feel any remorse. He was simply 'satisfied', he later said, that the man 'could no longer inform his masters'.[34]

On the last day of July, news reached Bór that the Polish prime minister, Mikołajczyk, had been received in Moscow by Molotov, the square-faced old Bolshevik who served as the Soviet foreign minister. The two besuited bureaucrats, allies from openly hostile governments, had seemingly been brought together by necessity. Bór also heard that the Russians had started their advance towards Warsaw. This was the moment he had been waiting for. He had been pursuing a policy of

* Known only by his code name, 'Stefan'.

national uprising since the autumn of 1943, requesting air support, armaments and the return of the Polish Armed Forces overseas. Now the gulf of understanding between Warsaw and London, which Zo and Jan had both tried to highlight, had never been more evident. The Polish Armed Forces, under Allied command, had already been redeployed, and there were very few aircraft available to deliver munitions.

Bór was in an impossible position. He knew that the Germans were now embattled on two fronts. The lack of recent reprisals seemed to confirm that their hold on the city was weakening, and threats to force-march able-bodied Poles west looked like tacit admission of their own likely retreat. But the German military still greatly outnumbered the Home Army, and they were far better equipped. Meanwhile Russian leaflets, dropped by air, were now exhorting the Poles to rise up, and Bór could not risk giving the Soviets any excuse to claim Polish cowardice, resignation or collaboration. Above all, Bór knew that the citizens of Warsaw were themselves 'longing for revenge'.[35] If he were to effectively harness the furious force of Polish defiance, boot out the Germans, and establish a civic body to welcome the Soviets, he believed he had to act fast.* He gave the order to mobilise.

Warsaw's streets were suddenly full of people wearing rucksacks, and dressed in heavier-duty shoes than were usually seen in July. 'They knew that the fight, for which we had waited so long, was coming', Zo realised.[36] 'In a day or two Warsaw will be at the front', Jan wrote. 'Perhaps the Germans will withdraw at once,' he thought optimistically, 'or maybe there will be street fighting as there was at Stalingrad.'[37] The Germans could also sense change. Positioning armed sentries on the roofs of their barracks and main administrative buildings, they started setting up machine-gun nests and closing off key streets with barbed wire. Everyone in Warsaw was on high alert.

Zo was buying supplies on 1 August 1944 when, 'with some significant movement', a colleague pointed to the number five on the chemist's clockface.[38] This was to be 'W hour' – named from the Polish *Wybuch*, meaning 'Explosion' – when the Home Army was to

---

* Opinion was divided on calling the uprising. General Antoni 'Monter' Chruściel was in favour, but intelligence head Kazimierz 'Heller' Iranek-Osmecki opposed the plan as he knew of German divisions deployed in the Warsaw vicinity. Iranek, however, was not at the decisive meeting.

attack.* Rushing back to the Women's Military Service headquarters, in the Grey Ursulines building near the university, she found everyone already busy with last-minute preparations.

By half past three, Jan and Greta were on a tram to their assembly point. They found the building's door guarded inside by two young men with rifles and hand grenades on their belts. Once within, Jan was congratulated for being a member of the Silent Unseen and swamped with questions about British and American support. 'An atmosphere of excitement pervaded the air', he wrote and, unable to admit to his fears, he 'lied like a trooper'.[39]

Rum had already reported to Fighting District 1, in the city's Old Town. Assigned to special operations, he assumed command of a battalion charged with capturing strategic positions such as the university building, the telephone exchange, the garrison at Piłsudski Square or one of the bridges over the Vistula. By dawn he was expected to be able to hold his position in the face of German counter-attack. Rum looked at his battalion. Some were experienced soldiers, men and women, all armed. Others were enthusiastic volunteers in second-hand uniform and with weapons from earlier conflicts. Boy and Girl Scouts were ready to serve as messengers. Rum thought of his vows to Audrey, of the child she was carrying, and of his oath to the Home Army. 'The final outcome of the war rests with us,' he reportedly roused his troops. 'Now is the time to end five years of German oppression, cruelty and tyranny. Now is the start of a new free Poland . . . May God be with us.'[40]

Several of Dr Zofia Franio's sapper patrols were assigned to work with combat units across the capital, including Rum's battalion. Others, including Zofia herself, were detailed to focus on the production of mines, grenades and petrol bombs. Over the last few years, Zofia's sappers had distributed several tonnes of explosives between various secret arsenals, including the space beneath the stage of the city's Grand Theatre. Now they delivered the first to what they believed would become the fighting frontline.

To their intense frustration, Zo and Emilia were both to be in the second line of defence, co-ordinating critical support. Although land

* W Hour is sometimes also attributed to Wystąpienie (event) or Warszawa (Warsaw).

communications with London would be impossible during the uprising, Emilia, with her reduced Farmstead team, was ready to field liaison personnel and couriers around the city to ensure communication when radio and the telephone networks inevitably failed. Assigned the rank of captain with the Women's Military Service General Staff, Zo was to serve as a quartermaster, managing the delivery of essential supplies to Home Army field kitchens and hospitals, providing liaison support and helping with the rotation of couriers, medics and active service personnel.

These were wise appointments by Maria Wittek. Zo had invaluable relevant experience, and she was an exceptionally efficient and inspiring leader of women. To Zo's mind, however, this was 'clerical staff work'.[41] Although it chafed her not to have been given a gun, she accepted her orders. Besieged Lwów, in late 1939, had shown her how vital reliable food and medical supply lines were, and she had also experienced the dynamic nature of urban warfare. Even if the fight were over in just 'a few days', as expected, her supply routes were likely to come under almost immediate attack, and she was determined to do many of the deliveries herself.[42]

At four that afternoon, Zo handed her team their Home Army armbands. Sewn from strips of white and red cotton, the colours of Poland, each was stamped with the letters 'WP' for *Wojsko Polskie* – Polish Armed Forces – and some bore the Polish eagle in black ink. Then she climbed the stairs to the first floor of the Ursulines building and, perching by an open window, watched the last hour of unchallenged occupation in the streets below. It was mainly quiet. A few pedestrians were hurrying into doorways, and she could hear the banging of shutters in the nearby shops. Sitting there, it felt deeply satisfying to pull her own armband over the sleeve of her shirt – it might be a frail piece of cotton, but she was back in 'uniform' at last.

14

The Warsaw Uprising
(August–October 1944)

As Zo watched from her window, a Home Army platoon hurried down the street below. A light rain was falling, and the heel of one of the soldiers skidded on a cobblestone. Although the uprising wasn't due to start for another hour, the men were already wearing their combatant armbands, and several were openly carrying pistols. A gunshot rang out as the platoon reached the corner, and one of the men crumpled. 'Dense shooting' quickly followed.[1] As if pulled forwards by the men's fall, Zo found herself on her feet and half leaning out of the window. Several bodies lay awkwardly near the turning, others further back beside some fencing. Blood was pooling on the street. 'They mowed them all down,' she murmured in horror.[2]

Racing downstairs, heart pounding, Zo almost collided with Wacka in the hall. As they were grabbing a stretcher, a team of medics came bursting through the door. Insanely, for a moment Zo struggled, refusing to let go of the stretcher's frame. It took her a second to remember that there was greater need now than her own need to serve. Four of the medics went out, a pair of nuns and two civilians, all with red crosses on their white armbands. Rushing back up to the window, Zo and Wacka watched as the stretcher team edged cautiously towards the dead and wounded. Another round of fire rang out, red brick dust burst from the opposite wall, and Zo saw 'the nurses fall to the ground'.[3]

⚓

Over a million Poles were living in Warsaw at the start of August 1944. Some 40,000 to 50,000 (estimates vary) were soldiers sworn into the Home Army. Of these, 10 per cent were women.* All soldiers

---

* In 2022, historians at the Warsaw Uprising Museum revised their estimates, and

now had the same rights but, with only 3,500 weapons, General Bór decided that the 'women were not allowed to carry arms, since there were not enough for the men'.[4] Yet thousands of women would soon see armed action alongside their male colleagues.

Convinced that the Poles had to drive the Germans back before the Soviets marched in to take credit for Warsaw's liberation, Bór's priority was to seize the capital's garrisons, transport and communication hubs, power plants and other utilities. Captured territory was then to be swiftly connected, giving the Home Army control of the city centre, the Old Town and eventually the suburbs. Combatant casualties were expected to be high, but civilians were to shelter in their basements. Bór anticipated that the action would be over within a few days but he was prepared to hold ground for up to two weeks – until the Allies relieved them, either from the west or the east.

Although significantly outmanned and outgunned, a co-ordinated series of Home Army attacks on that first wet August evening rapidly overwhelmed several German units in the city. The occupying forces had anticipated some limited armed resistance, but not defiance on this scale. While Zo was helping with the wounded, seeing to the burial of the dead, and receiving the first reports to enable her to co-ordinate provisioning, she could hear bursts of machine-gun fire and feel the impact of the shells targeted at Warsaw's power station, just a few blocks away.

Rum had spent the last hours before the attack placing lookouts on the taller buildings in his sector. At five, he had led his unit into action, rapidly seizing his first targets. The German response was to fire high-explosive mortar bombs from the upper floors of the buildings in the streets they still held. Blasting through walls, these shells sent up lethal showers of broken brick, fragments of wood and shattered glass. 'A curtain of shimmering red-golden flames enveloped the whole area', Rum wrote. 'Black smoke billowed up into the air only to be captured by the rain falling heavily onto Warsaw.'[5] Despite high casualties, he held his position.*

Jan Nowak witnessed the battle for the Hotel Victoria, earmarked

---

now believe up to 12,000 women were active in the uprising.
* Rum recorded four killed and fifteen injured. One was a sixteen-year-old Scout acting as a messenger.

for the Home Army's headquarters.* With a German armoured column being bombarded by home-made petrol bombs on the street outside, Jan could only reach the hotel, staggering under the weight of his enormous radio set, through a hole blasted in the neighbouring building's cellar wall. The irony of being forced to crawl through a subterranean passage at the very moment the Home Army came out into the open was not lost on him, but Jan would eventually rise higher than most, climbing onto the rooftops to secure his radio reception.

Later that evening, the Poles seized the city's main power plant and a German arsenal while liberating much of the inner city, including Zo's neighbourhood. Zofia Franio's sapper teams helped to take the police headquarters, securing more small arms, and, among other buildings, the baroque Holy Cross Church where Chopin's heart lay buried. The main post office, railway station, bridges over the Vistula, the locations of the five main food banks, the university stocked with hidden weapons, and Mokotów with its vital airstrip for receiving troops and supplies all remained in German hands. But that night, as the Polish flag flew proudly from the roof of the sixteen-storey Prudential building, the third tallest skyscraper in Europe, jubilation spread through the ranks.

'I was filled with a sense of exultation', Jan wrote. 'I would have given my life to witness this one moment. We felt free again . . . reconquered from the enemy, with our own forces.'6 Zo was also swept up in the 'state of euphoria'.7 'The whole town rejoiced at the sight of German troops retreating', she reported.8 It 'gave us some retaliation' for 'the nightmarish evacuation' of September 1939.9 For the first time in five years, Polish flags, many very crumpled, were hung from windows, and that evening Zo saw civilians dancing in the streets, 'full of joy', while 'tender pairs of soldiers', singing romantic ballads, strolled through the dark.10

Cold as marble with most men, and almost as hard with the women she assumed to be friends and commanded as soldiers, Zo had always had a layer of sentimental sediment when it came to displays of patriotism. Yet her delight in these early victories, and the mood of the people, was tempered by the losses she had witnessed, and the death of the first member of her own unit – a young woman killed by a sniper

* General Antoni Chruściel, aka Monter, commanded the Home Army during the uprising.

as she darted across a junction with messages. Knowing the battle was not yet won, Zo felt her joy and anger harden into resolve.

On that first night of the uprising, Rum helped to dig trenches, then shared a candle-lit meal with one of his men and his pregnant wife before getting some well-earned rest.* Jan was celebrating the capture of some German soldiers by four unarmed liaison women, among them the sister of his fiancé.† Zo, her team and a group of civilians were tearing up paving stones to extend the nearby anti-tank trenches, and strengthening street barricades with overturned trams, some huge wooden reels from the cable factory, fencing, park benches, rubble and broken furniture. These barricades would provide vital shelter for messengers and couriers delivering supplies, as well as for fighters with weapons in hand.

⚓

'The action of the Poles is a blessing. We shall finish them off', Himmler assured his Führer.[11] But Hitler, still recovering from the attempt on his life on 20 July, was incandescent at news of the 'skirmishes'.[12] When informed that it would be impossible for the Luftwaffe to bomb Warsaw without immense German casualties, he demanded that the city be 'levelled to the ground' by other means.[13] Every inhabitant was to be killed, he added, 'men, women and children'.[14] 'Warsaw will be liquidated', Himmler vowed, and the Poles 'will cease to be a problem'.[15]

It was on Himmler's direct orders that, some time between 2 and 7 August, General Stefan 'Grot' Rowecki, the Home Army's first commander and champion of women's military service, was also killed. Secretly executed, his end probably came at Sachsenhausen concentration camp, where he had been held since July 1943. The news was a terrible blow for the Poles, with Maria Wittek, Emilia Malessa and Zo all feeling the loss personally but, as ever, it only strengthened their resolve.

Initially, Zo felt 'imprisoned' in the Women's Military Service HQ

---

* Two days later this 24-year-old, Wojtek, would die in Rum's arms, having been shot through the chest.

† Aged twenty-nine, Barbara Wolska, aka 'Jula', was decorated with the Cross of Valour. She was killed by a sniper on 17 August 1944.

as she wrestled with the logistics of demand and supply across the city, while the main food depots were still out of reach.[16] Before long, however, her new 'normal life' involved collecting rations and reports, inspecting field kitchens and hospitals, and prioritising and delivering supplies.[17] The nearest streets were now relatively safe, but when one of her team, a veteran of the Polish–Bolshevik war, refused to duck behind the defences because she found it demeaning, Zo shouted furiously about her 'complete stupidity'.[18]* She did not intend to lose another life, nor risk the loss of vital supplies, for the sake of wounded pride.

More battles soon secured the post office, but only with the first casualty of Zofia's sapper teams.† Within a few days, the Home Army held two-thirds of the city and moved its headquarters into the iconic PKO bank building. This vast block would soon also house the insurgents' 'Radio Lightning' station on its upper floors, where Jan would broadcast, as well as a field hospital in its basement with beds for up to four hundred, partly staffed by a company of Girl Scouts.‡ Outside, the building's façade was adorned with white-and-red banners. Just seeing it made Zo's heart swell. She wore the same colours on her arm, once more a free citizen of Poland.

In some ways, these first days of the battle were 'the most wonderful time of my life', Zo told a friend.[19] Having absolute faith in Polish victory, she felt that the return to open fighting was washing away the shameful stain of years of occupation. She was also exhilarated by the radical social and cultural ideas now being openly debated in the streets. Discussing politics with another Silent Unseen officer, Andrzej Czaykowski, left them both almost reeling with 'the most deeply felt freedom in our lives'.[20] Printing presses were churning out the once clandestine 'Information Bulletin' every day, along with news-sheets for numerous political factions. With no censorship, walls, windows and barricades were pasted with fliers as everyone debated the possible geography and political shape of post-war Poland. It was, Zo felt, 'intoxicating'.[21]

Zo's mind was whirring when she returned to her base. Talking

---

* Mrs Stokowska had had to disguise herself as a man to serve in 1918, and resented further humiliation.
† Irena Bredel, aka 'Alina'.
‡ In Polish, Jan 'Nowak' Jeziorański's radio station was Radio Błyskawica.

with her team, she referred to the 'uprising' for the first time, rather than the 'open fight' that most of them still spoke of. It was a shock to find herself reprimanded. One of the women, whose younger sister had been killed during the attack on the post office, told her ominously that 'every uprising so far has ended in defeat'.[22]* The Home Army had taken most of central Warsaw, and British and American airdrops were yet to come, but, for the first time, Zo felt a cold stab of doubt.

On 4 August, the Home Army gained a strong foothold in Warsaw's western suburbs of Wola and Ochota. Although sustaining heavy losses, it seemed they had inflicted a humiliating defeat. It was now that German military reinforcements arrived in the form of air support, tanks, an SS brigade and an infamous anti-insurgent corps.† Within hours they launched a fierce counter-attack. Stukas flew over Wola in regular waves, nine aircraft in formations of three, diving down to drop incendiaries. In their wake came powerful Tiger tanks, the crews sometimes forcing Polish men, women and children to walk ahead as human shields. Red flames burst from their 88mm guns as they fired at short range, creating havoc. The infantry followed behind, with automatic weapons. As the Poles hit back with British PIAT anti-tank guns and Sten machine guns, casualties on both sides grew exponentially.

Behind their advancing line, the German anti-insurgent corps enacted a new terror policy in Wola. All Home Army soldiers were to be shot, irrespective of whether they had surrendered, and Himmler had specified that 'the part of the population not fighting, women and children, should likewise be killed'.[23] Moving from house to house, breaking down doors, throwing grenades into cellars and setting fire to buildings as they went, the special units herded residents into the streets where they were shot in the head with small firearms or mown down by machine guns. An estimated 40,000 people were murdered on one day alone. Some of their bodies were burnt. Others were left where they fell: soldiers in their armbands and children in summer clothes and ankle socks, their limbs akimbo, often with young women beside them, hair in the dirt. Their suddenly still faces looked strangely unconcerned.

---

* Janina 'Janka' Bredel, aka 'Marianka', from the Home Army chancellery team. In fact, the Greater Poland Uprising 1918-19 had been successful.

† The SS brigade was commanded by Obersturmbannführer Oskar Dirlewanger. SS General Erich von dem Bach-Zalewski commanded the anti-partisan corps.

𝕁

On the day that the Germans started forcing their way through Wola, Churchill informed Stalin that he had authorised RAF Special Duties Squadrons with international crews, including Poles, to drop sixty tons of munitions and supplies to the Home Army. The return journey from southern Italy, where these squadrons were now based, was a marathon 1,800 miles, mainly over enemy-held territory. The crews wanted to refuel at Russian-held airfields but, although some were less than ten miles from Warsaw, the Soviet leader refused.

Stalin had plans to annex much of eastern Poland, and to control the rest. In July, Russian radio had accused the Poles of passivity and collaboration. But once Bór had launched the uprising, the Kremlin ignored Polish attempts to make contact and ordered a halt to their own advance. They 'stopped about twelve miles short of the war zone,' one FANY with the Polish squadrons later recalled in anguish. 'And let them all be slaughtered.'[24]* It suited Stalin to have the Germans decimate the Home Army, thereby eliminating many who might later resist Soviet influence. Jan, glued to the airwaves, even heard Russians describing the uprising as 'a crime, whose instigators should be brought to justice'.[25]

The first Warsaw airlift left Italy on the night of 4 August. The weight incurred by the auxiliary fuel tanks meant fewer containers could be carried, but significant numbers were still dropped as the pilots demonstrated nerves of steel when flying low over the beleaguered city. The price they paid was catastrophic. A solitary night flight to the Polish countryside was perilous enough. Of the first seven crews to fly to the aid of Warsaw, now smothered in smoke and thickly defended by anti-aircraft artillery and German fighters, five failed to return.

Although the sorties over the next few days were not so devastating, losses remained high. Some crews were shot down over German-held territory while still en route. Any that were damaged, or had malfunctioning instruments and strayed into Soviet-controlled airspace, had to dodge flak from their own ally, and those that reached the Polish capital made easy targets. The Liberators and Halifaxes that limped

---

* June Kerr Darton, in Monopoli, serving under Mary McVean, a cousin of SOE head, Colin Gubbins.

back to Italy often did so on fuel fumes, three engines and a prayer. Deeming the cost unacceptable, Whitehall cancelled further flights, only for some Polish crews to resume them voluntarily, desperate to serve their nation in its hour of need.

℔

While the battle in Wola raged on, Home Army units elsewhere took the ruins of the Warsaw Ghetto and liberated the Gęsiówka concentration camp, releasing around 350 Jewish citizens of Holland, Greece and Hungary. Of these, 130 joined the fight.* The uprising was already a remarkably international effort. Several hundred fighters came from at least fifteen different nations, including Italian and Hungarian deserters, a Nigerian Jazz musician who had settled in Warsaw, escaped POWs from France, the Soviet Union and Australia, and John Ward, an RAF crew member shot down in 1940.† To Soviet frustration, one Slovakian platoon would even fight under their own banner.

Working with John Ward, Jan transmitted English-language news reports and appeals several times a day. Radio Lightning was the first station to broadcast from the battlefield in any occupied country, and BBC recordings were circulated to the cabinet and press. 'Warsaw did not fight in silence,' one officer recorded proudly. 'She called out with a great voice for freedom and justice. She called ceaselessly for help.'[26]

Already, 'there was no real frontline', Jan noticed, and Zo wrote bitterly about seeing exhausted insurgents circling around to face German reinforcements with 'fresh and boastful' faces.[27] Soon her base, the Grey Ursulines building, was again under fire, and running supplies down the nearby thoroughfare, Nowy Świat, became 'almost a death sentence'.[28]‡ When the women evacuated to an abandoned apartment

---

* Mainly prisoners from Auschwitz, brought in to clear the ghetto ruins.

† The Nigerian was August Agboola Brown, whose testimony has since been questioned by Dr Nicholas Boston of New York City University. The Australian was Walter Smith, whose broadcast was not only one of Radio Lightning's greatest hits, but also let his mother know he was alive after three years with no news. Having become a key liaison between the British government and Polish Home Army, John Ward also became *The Times*' official correspondent in occupied Warsaw.

‡ The Grey Ursulines building was at 6 Chmielna ['Hop'] Street. Historic Nowy Świat ['New World'] connected Three Crosses Square to the ancient Royal Palace.

block further south, they were at least delighted to find some crates of excellent wine and vodka in the cellar. Zo would have preferred potatoes, tinned meat or jars of pickled vegetables, but everything was welcome.

Throughout the years of occupation, the German authorities had requisitioned the greater part of Polish produce. Officially deemed a 'lower race', the Poles were designated to need 'less room, less clothing, less food and less culture', and their rations were not far above starvation levels.[29] Polish Jews had ultimately been denied even that. Most secret stashes of flour, fat and preserves had now been eaten, the many small vegetable plots across the city were all cleared, and there was little left in the abandoned shops and warehouses. The last fresh food Zo had seen for many days were two small tomatoes, scavenged from a wild plant growing on the embankment leading down to the Vistula. Now she admitted that we were 'beginning to get very hard pressed for food'.[30]

It was a huge relief when, on 6 August, the Home Army captured Warsaw's largest brewery, Haberbusch and Schiele. Their vast warehouses in the suburbs, filled with barley and some sugar, were enough to keep the civilian and military population fed for several weeks. But reaching the brewery meant cutting through areas of bitter fighting. Zo joined the teams going out with heavy-duty rucksacks to collect the precious haul. At first, their own sentries checked their papers every few blocks, pointing the best way ahead. Once beyond the city centre they fanned out, cautiously circling around any gunfire, until Zo was amazed to see many suburban buildings still unscathed and some streets with electric lighting.

The women first carried some 70lb sacks of grain to the nearest combat unit, then delivered more to community kitchens across the city. With no surviving milling facilities, the barley had to be ground in coffee-grinders, then boiled in water to make a thin soup.[31] Sometimes a little sugar was added, or salt or pepper from captured German rations. Even so, Rum was typical of many in loathing the result. He called it 'spit soup', because he had to spit out so many barley husks and sometimes mortar grit.[32] Later, the empty grain sacks were filled with rubble to help shore up the barricades, although desperate people knifed them open, searching for remnants of barley.

Zo was now working without rest and almost without sleep. As well as provisioning kitchens, she was supplying the field hospitals set

up in school halls, cinemas and any large cellars. Soon there were
teams of young women tasked with scavenging for any useful medical
supplies. One sixteen-year-old called Hanna was returning with ten
glass bottles of methylated spirits, to serve as antiseptic, when she
heard an aircraft engine, a whistle, a rumble, a shake and a rush of air
that made everything collapse and then start to burn.* The Luftwaffe
were dropping incendiaries. As flying debris smashed one of her bottles, Hanna felt the highly flammable meths soak through her shirt,
strangely cold as it evaporated in the hot air of the now burning street.
'At that point I realised I was going to die,' she later recalled with a
wry smile.[33] Hanna was lucky, receiving only an earful of abuse for
having broken one of the bottles.

Zo was now having to spend more time in the makeshift hospitals,
where the choking moans of the wounded brought in on blood-soaked
stretchers would come to haunt her. Convinced that she would be
happier in direct combat, she petitioned Maria Wittek; but 'everyone
wanted to go to the front, to fight', and Wittek had neither the time
nor the sympathy to consider her request.[34] She was 'qualified for other
service, command service', Wittek told her, and must do her duty.[35]

Dr Zofia Franio was also working in the field hospitals. Once, while
she was helping to carry a casualty into a basement ward, the building
above took a direct hit. Even as she was blown down the stairs, she
managed to keep the stretcher level. But Zofia was also still commanding her sapper units. Much of their work now lay in blasting holes in
buildings to create shortcuts through the streets between the Home
Army headquarters, various battle positions and the field hospitals.
The men nicknamed these women the 'Bombs'. 'These are superb
girls,' one enthused. 'When necessary, they will blow up a wall. When
you get hurt, they will dress your wound, and when they get wounded,
they are light to carry.'[36] Watching them work on undaunted during
street-battles, Bór also found a new respect for the Women's Military
Service. 'In those hard days,' he later wrote, 'I realised that, psycholog-
ically speaking, the women had far greater resistance than the men.'[37]

Such fortitude wasn't needed only on the frontline. When Zo
brought flour and a couple of eggs to Zofia at one of her bomb-making
factories, she was horrified to see that her friend's lips had turned
'dark blue'.[38] When their own stocks of explosives had run out, Zofia's

* Hanna Czarnocka.

teams had dismantled captured artillery shells to redeploy the TNT. Pulverising this into powder, then compacting it into glass jars and the small metal tins that had once held cleaning products, they produced several dozen kilograms of useable explosives every day – but it was poisonous work. Understanding the risks, Zofia organised strict shifts, but if Zo or anyone else showed too much concern, she told them curtly that 'I'm as healthy as a horse', or, 'women can always manage'.[39] Although Zo agreed with the latter, she searched desperately for the milk Zofia said might help ease the symptoms, but there was none left in Warsaw.

⚓

One week into the uprising, Rum reported, 'the bombardment practically never ceased'.[40] On their way to the Home Army headquarters that Sunday, Zo and Wacka saw a small boy standing in the open, shouting out that he had shoelaces to sell, when a shell crashed down beside him. Miraculously, it did not explode. Zo made a quick assessment. The missile was 'probably 30, may be 40 centimetres in calibre' and roasting hot.[41] As she raced towards the boy, she blessed the Czechs. She knew this type of ammunition was produced by forced labourers in Czech factories, 'and there was probably sabotage there'.[42] For whatever reason, the shell did not detonate. When she and Wacka finally reached the PKO building, they found a mass in progress in the main hall. 'We sang with our whole throats,' Zo laughed, belting out the songs of praise that for many had become patriotic anthems.[43] A few days later, a large part of the PKO building collapsed after another bomb hit its chimney.

Once it had become clear that the Home Army had not conceded defeat after retreating from Wola, the Wehrmacht set their sights on the Old Town – the beautiful warren of medieval streets and squares along the west bank of the Vistula. They attacked on 11 August, dropping over 1,500 tons of bombs over the next two weeks. Then they sent in 'Goliaths', miniature remote-controlled tanks filled with explosives, to blast through the still smouldering streets. 'For the most part, Warsaw is in flames', the Nazi governor general reported. 'Burning down houses is the most reliable means of liquidating the insurgents' hideouts,' he explained, promising Hitler that the city would be punished 'with complete destruction'.[44]

Yet beneath the streets, Zofia's sappers had been busy blasting holes through the non-load-bearing walls of connecting cellars to create secret underground corridors. By now, 8,000 Home Army soldiers were well dug into the highly fortified district and they, messengers and Zo and her delivery teams largely travelled beneath the city, sometimes clambering through empty unlit basements but as often passing huddled groups of families sheltering from the bombardments above.

More support also came from the skies. 'We do not ask for equipment', one message ran, with a reminder of the Polish contribution to the Battle of Britain. 'We demand its immediate dispatch.'[45] With better weather on 12 August, several more crews flew out despite Stalin continuing to refuse the use of Russian-held airfields. 'The Soviet government do not wish to associate themselves either directly or indirectly with the adventure in Warsaw', the US Ambassador in Moscow was informed.[46] There was at least no difficulty for the Polish, South African and British aircrews to find Warsaw now. The flames, soaring hundreds of feet into the air, were visible for thirty miles. But it was almost impossible to identify the target marker-flares and, as they approached, the crews could sometimes see German gunners crouched on the rooftops, firing tracer at them.

At midnight on 13 August, Jan and Rum heard the same anti-aircraft fire echoing in the distance and saw enemy searchlights criss-cross the sky. Jan was lying on the roof of a former nightclub, ready to scribble some radio copy and collect any stray containers. 'Against the background of the dark purple sky', he wrote, 'the bombers looked like enormous black birds'.[47] When twenty Halifax passed low overhead with a deafening roar, he watched as the 'dark oblong bundles spilled out'.[48] Rum and his team were holding flares in one of the squares below, guiding the delivery home. Like Jan, he noticed that at least one of the aircraft bore the white-and-red chequerboard insignia of the Polish Air Force on its fuselage. Both men were praying for the safety of the aircrews, many of whom they had met in Brindisi. Then there was a flash and 'for a split second we could see parts of the wings and the fuselage scattering in all directions', Jan wrote.[49] Two further Halifax were lost that night, and four could only limp into Russian-held territory where the crews were interned until the British Embassy intervened.

More deliveries followed over the next few nights, the pilots flying so low that one thought the 'flames seemed to be reaching higher than the aircraft'.[50] 'The fighting city thanks the heroic airmen and sends them her highest appreciation', Bór telegrammed London. 'We bow with deepest reverence before the fallen crews.'[51] Later, however, he bluntly admitted that 'the help they brought us was too small to be of practical value'.[52] Driven by patriotism, rage and guilt, the Polish squadrons begged to fly more. One even telegrammed the Queen for her support. But the losses had been so extreme, and the supplies delivered so minimal, that even Harold Perkins, the tough head of SOE's Polish Section, admitted the recent ops had 'proved disastrous'.[53]* 'We must put aside heroics, and the honour and glory of the Polish crews dying for their capital', he wrote to Gubbins. 'For Warsaw cannot be rationally sustained in this manner.'[54]

Although international crews continued to drop supplies to the outskirts of the city, the Home Army began to feel increasingly isolated and abandoned.† To boost morale, the first film footage of the uprising, including the airdrops, was shown in Warsaw's Palladium Cinema against a live soundtrack of gunfire from the fighting for the nearby railway station. The Germans were now bombing and shelling the city around the clock. Arms, ammunition, medicine, food and water were all running out. 'The walls of the bombed and burning houses blossomed with small bits of paper,' Jan noticed, as people searched for their loved ones, while the number of corpses now buried in shallow graves or trapped under rubble meant the threat of typhoid was growing daily.[55]

As German troops pushed further into the Old Town, Rum learnt that a sniper was preventing desperately needed ammunition from reaching his battalion. Carefully avoiding the rubble on the bomb-damaged stairs, whose scrape and clatter might betray him, he climbed to the sniper's eyrie. 'A damp smell permeated the area', one account of his action recorded, and 'sunlight bounced off the dust particles in the air'.[56] Turning at the creak of the door, the sniper reached for his Luger, but Rum was faster with his Vis Radom pistol. When the German lay motionless, 'his grey-green woollen jacket stained with blood', Rum

---

* Estimates were one bomber lost per ton of supplies delivered. The Polish Special Duties Squadron alone lost sixteen crews.
† There were 199 RAF airdrops from Italy, 4 August–21 September 1944. See Halik Kochanski, *Resistance, The Underground War in Europe, 1939–1945* (Allen Lane, 2022), p.410.

took the Luger and searched for ammunition. A front pocket revealed some letters and a photograph. 'So long as your heart is still beating, I am alive', one letter from his wife began.[57] For a moment, Rum paid his silent respects. Just that week his own wife, Audrey, had confided to her tear-stained diary, 'I've been reading your recent letters and I need you and want you so much . . .'[58]

It was now two weeks since Bór had launched the uprising, the longest the Poles had believed they might need to hold out. Every evening, civilians emerged from their cellars, pale and hungry, to see how the landscape had changed, scavenge for food, and exchange anxious news, sing songs and whisper prayers. Grief, like everything, was shared. Bodies, placed in rows, were covered with newspapers before being respectfully buried, if usually in collective graves.

Zo could already hear the buzzing of bluebottles within the ruins and smell the stench of death, heavy in the smoky summer heat. Within days, the reek became overpowering. Flies seethed in clouds and the city's water conduits became polluted. To prevent the spread of epidemics, wells were sunk across the city. Zo helped organise the relays of women carrying metal buckets of water to field hospitals and dressing points. There were now 'constant air raids . . . all the time, even at night', she noted, when the Luftwaffe flew by the light of the burning city.[59] Every whining engine would send the women racing for cover. Once, cursing herself for her clumsiness as she felt water soak her skirt, Zo noticed that her bucket had been shot through, but she was still unharmed.

Not long later, Zo saw some friends running down the street through a blizzard of red-hot embers. The Germans had brought in *Nebelwerfer*, multiple rocket launchers that emitted a blood-curdling moan as they fired successive volleys of demolition and incendiary missiles. The Poles mockingly called them 'bellowing cows', but no cheery nickname could mitigate the Nebelwerfers' impact.[60] 'Mad with pain', their skin burning, the women threw themselves into the nearest fire-water pond.[61] While medics were responding, Zo grabbed a stretcher and ran through smouldering heaps of rubble to collect a casualty lying in the street. Shot in the stomach, the woman died soon afterwards but at least not alone.* Looking up in despair, Zo saw that 'the whole sky was red'. 'It was literally hell,' she thought.[62]

* Halina Korniak, Commander of the Pomeranian District of the Polish Red Cross.

Zo yearned to see clear sky. Travelling to the brewery warehouses now meant following guides through subterranean passageways. Some were named after Polish heroes. 'Sikorski Street' even had dim lighting rigged up, keeping the women from stumbling against pipes and the knees of the people sitting against the walls. In the suburbs, they descended deeper into the service tunnels running below enemy-held territory. 'Pipe over your head,' someone would shout, or, 'Pipe under your feet', before they surfaced.[63] The remaining grain now had to be sifted from chunks of mortar and splinters of wood. 'All around, in the moonlight, were the skeletons of houses', Zo wrote.[64] Somewhere, a pianist was defiantly playing Chopin.* She stopped to listen for a moment, the music surreal, almost liquid, eddying around the ruins. It was 'probably a madman' she told herself, pressing on. 'There were so many of them, these madmen, my God how many lost their minds.'[65]

It was not just the brewery that had been cut off from the Old Town. Several Home Army units still held isolated pockets of the city. To get supplies to Mokotów, Zo and Maria Wittek headed to the entrance of a large storm sewer through which a largely female platoon, known as the *Kanalarki*,† organised deliveries.[66] Descending slowly to a metal platform, they pulled on fishermen's boots to wade through the slurry below.

Built sixty years earlier, the semi-circular tunnel floors of Warsaw's network of sewers were difficult to trudge along even at their widest. The narrowest navigable tunnels were just three feet high and two wide, meaning the women had to crawl or heave themselves along on their bellies. Dead rats, broken glass and other debris from the devastation above, often sunk in effluence, had to be cleared as the women mapped and signposted the underground labyrinth. One of the busiest tunnels ran directly beneath a Gestapo building. When the Germans realised what was happening, they threw down hand grenades and tins of gas, then blocked the sewers with bags of cement. Before Zo and Wittek could set off, news came that the route to Mokotów had been destroyed.

⚓

* Chopin's statue in Lazienki Park had been toppled in 1939, and the bronze presented to Hitler.
† Kanalarki, or 'channel markers', was the name given to the women who navigated the sewers beneath Warsaw's streets.

On 19 August, as Warsaw fought on, the battle for the liberation of Paris began. Two days later, when Stalin once again denied the RAF access to Russian-held airstrips, an enraged Churchill sent a strongly worded telegram to Roosevelt, proposing that they send aircraft anyhow. Unwilling to sour American–Soviet relations before the Yalta Conference, and worried about his election prospects, Roosevelt sent his wordy regrets. Paris was liberated after just six days of fighting, the city still largely intact. Jan broadcast a French salute. 'We are fighting for the same ideals . . .' he announced. 'Vive la France! Vive la Pologne! Vive la Liberté.'[67]

The situation between the two capitals could hardly have been more different. German forces had withdrawn from Paris as the Western Allies had closed in, while in Warsaw, the Germans were reinforcing while the Soviets held back. Indeed, Jan noted, 'five European capitals fell while Warsaw waited in vain for relief by the Red Army', whose encamped battalions he could see plainly from any rooftop.[68] Zo could barely hide her frustration. The French capital had been 'taken by the Allies in a flash', she scowled, while Warsaw had been suffering and struggling for nearly a month.[69] The people of Paris were still toasting their liberation as it became clear that the Home Army could no longer hold Warsaw's Old Town.

Churchill and Roosevelt did at least now issue separate but identically worded declarations that the Home Army constituted 'an integral part of the Polish Armed Forces'.[70] Theoretically this recognition meant that the soldiers had combatant rights and, if captured, protection under the Geneva Convention. Since the Soviet Union was not a signatory, Stalin stayed silent on the matter. Germany *had* ratified the convention, yet still systematically committed war crimes. It was clear that Home Army soldiers needed any protection they could get.

The Poles had held the Old Town against a better trained and much better equipped enemy for over a month but, at the start of September, Bór felt he had no option but to order a retreat. Rum was among those charged with creating a corridor through which to evacuate thousands of civilians and soldiers. Running between the stubble of buildings that had once stood sentry around the main square, he was amazed to see Jan heading towards him. It had been only four weeks since they had flown into Poland together, yet finding each other alive seemed miraculous. Embracing, Jan told Rum about his broadcasts and asked for his friend's assessment of their prospects. Only when Jan had promised to send a radio message to Audrey did Rum tell him that, although he had fought in France in 1940, he had 'never been in such a desperate situation'.[71]*

At one o'clock the next morning, sabotage patrols started demolishing walls to create the planned escape route. Soon an enemy machine gun, some Brens, rifles and pistols had been captured, along with six prisoners but, Rum admitted, 'the enemy did not budge'.[72] After an hour, as the attack lost its momentum, the Germans took the initiative. 'Hell broke loose', Rum wrote, as his battalion suffered heavy losses.[73] By the time darkness fell again, a single unit of soldiers had got through at the cost of nearly one hundred dead. Rum awarded one of his dying soldiers the Virtuti Militari, borrowed from another man, then called the retreat, summoning 'ambulance women' to transport the wounded to what remained of the field hospitals.

The only option left was to use the sewers. That night, one Girl Scout watched as 'people, black, bearded, in rags' started to appear from the ruins.[74]† A few children were among the first to be passed down the narrow manholes and, over the next hour, several hundred civilians made the desperate journey. 'The foetid stench', Bór wrote, when he at last took his turn, 'made me sick and brought tears to my eyes'.[75] The waste water came up to his thighs, its current so strong that he found it hard to keep his balance on the curved tunnel floor. With one hand firmly on the shoulder of the man in front, he spent five hours trudging below the city before reaching safer streets above. He was fortunate. Soldiers who got lost and emerged while still within the battle zone were often mowed down by machine gun.

Home Army messenger Marzenna Schejbal was among those led out by a Scout who assured her that she should safely surface again within three hours. Even crawling, 'the space was so tight that we were knocking our heads against the wall,' Marzenna later recalled.[76] After two hours they stopped – something was blocking the passageway ahead. In the pitch-black heat, some of the soldiers began to lose their nerve. 'The girls were much stronger than the boys,' Marzenna reported proudly, 'more disciplined, more patient . . . The boys became

* The radio message reached Audrey on 17 September. She was appalled to learn that Rum was fighting.
† Irena Zychowska.

mad and wanted to shoot themselves. It was the girls that said, "You have to be quiet as the Germans will hear us.""[77] Up above, enemy patrols were listening for movement, ready to pour down petrol and set the slurry ablaze. Eventually, each of Marzenna's group of thirty tied themselves to a rope before pushing past a bloated corpse. Only twelve hours after they had descended did they eventually climb out of the sewers, still roped together 'like herrings'.[78]

Zo was stationed at a manhole near the southern end of historic Nowy Świat, ready to heave groups of 'stinking, exhausted, often wounded' soldiers out of the sewers. Hearing the echoing thuds of people below she called softly down, lay on her belly and stretched in her hand – only to find it slip from the first soldier's filthy grasp. Within half an hour, she had her first group of seventeen men lying, exhausted, on the street. Covered in brown filth, they looked like a glistening bronze memorial to defiance in the face of defeat.

Once they had gathered their strength, Zo led the men to the Palladium Cinema, where there were now barrels of rainwater along with dry clothes, some medicine and a little food. With most of the grain gone, she and her team had been baking the yeast, mixed with a few drops of water, into thin biscuits like communion wafers. As they ate, one of the men came up to touch her face. 'Washed' was all he said, staring in amazement at her pale skin and blonde hair.[79]

Eventually, over 5,000 Poles, and 150 of their German POWs, would make their way through the sewers to the safer districts of Warsaw. Among the medical staff who refused to leave, as it would have meant abandoning the wounded in their care, was 'Rana', the children's doctor who, along with Wacka, had brought poppy-seed cake to Zo in the convent at Szymanów that Easter. As a precaution, Rana had helped to move German casualties towards the shrapnel-scarred entrance of her basement ward, hoping this might protect them all. One day later, when German troops attacked, she ran forwards, shouting for them to stop. She was killed in the blast from a hand grenade.*

ℬ

---

* Hanna Żabińska-Petrykowska, aka Rana, was posthumously decorated with the Virtuti Militari, having already received the Gold Cross of Merit. She left behind a son, and a daughter who also became a doctor.

On 7 September, the Germans proposed an honourable capitulation. There seemed no alternative. 'On every conceivable little piece of ground are graves of civilians and soldiers', the RAF's John Ward reported for *The Times*.[80] Warsaw's surviving population was demoralised and starving. 'We ate horse, then all the cats and dogs, pigeons of course,' one fighter admitted. 'And then there was nothing left.'[81] But it was not lack of food but lack of arms that would eventually bring Bór to the table.

Sensing the end coming, Jan also had a proposal. 'Let's get married now,' he urged Greta. 'While there are still some churches and priests left in the city.'[82] While he found someone to officiate, she managed to trade a precious tin of meat for a pair of copper wedding rings. With the Germans just three hundred yards away, they crunched up the altar of a windowless chapel on a carpet of broken glass. Seven minutes later, despite interruptions from machine-gun fire, they were husband and wife. Two young soldiers offered Greta a bunch of gladioli, miraculously found growing in the ruins of a garden, and John Ward gave her a reproduction of the Black Madonna of Częstochowa. That night the newlyweds shared two tins of sardines. It would be the last meat they ate in Warsaw, except for two pigeons killed a few days later by the shock wave from a bomb.

After four days, Bór suspended the capitulation talks. Sensing the imminent defeat, the Red Army had finally started its advance, quickly taking Warsaw's suburb to the east of the Vistula. When the Germans retreated across the river, destroying the last bridge behind them, a few patrols from the Polish communist forces fighting with the Russians attempted to wade over in pursuit. All but abandoned by their comrades, they suffered heavy losses.[*] As Gubbins wrote, 'the Soviet Armies, by now up to the very walls of Warsaw, withheld all aid and all succour.'[83] Only on 13 September, knowing the Polish resistance had been almost crushed, did the Russians commence their own airdrops. At first, they dispatched containers without parachutes or dropped them so low that the chutes did not open. 'Everything was broken', Zo reported furiously, at first refusing to eat the Russian black bread.[84] And still, as another Polish general wrote, the Red Army 'looked on passively at the destruction'.[85]

---

[*] Units from General Berling's Polish First Army, raised from POWs. For this action, Berling was relieved of his command.

Zo now organised her team's second retreat, to an empty apartment above a small field hospital. While the women queued for the thin trench that ran to the southern sector of the city, Zo felt the heat rise in the night air as the wind wafted clouds of choking smoke and flame towards them. Several hundred terrified civilians now started pressing towards the trench. Despite having a pass, Zo waited most of the night in a crater by the barriers, as priority was given to commanders, front-line soldiers, and individual liaison officers with urgent messages. In the early hours, a fight broke out. Another Women's Military Service team, lugging a typewriter and several heavy sewing-machines, were being waved through 'as if there weren't enough sewing-machines' in the rest of the city, Zo scowled, 'furious' at their further delay.[86] When some of their equipment was set down, several people angrily kicked the machines away. Utterly exhausted, Zo started laughing. The sky was red. Nearby buildings were collapsing, sewing-machines were tangled in the barricade, and people were fainting. Her team was finally let through in the morning.

The new apartment was near the botanical gardens, once an upmarket part of Warsaw. Much of the furniture was antique, the walls were hung with fine art, and the glasses in the armoire were crystal. Zo had forgotten life could look like this. Browsing the bookshelves, her eye was caught by a beautiful edition of *Don Quixote* bound in soft, green leather. It was one of her favourite novels, a treatise on honour, optimism and individualism. She took it, 'stole it' she later admitted, without remorse.[87] She was not the only one clinging to culture amidst chaos. The next day, she found an elderly art conservator at the door. The Polish underground's 'Ministry of Culture' had sent him to inspect the paintings. Writing an inventory, he selected several to be stored in the cellar of a nearby library. Only when the conservator had left, did the women notice he had pocketed their last jar of tomatoes. No one thought badly of him. 'We knew how it was,' Zo laughed dryly.[88]

In mid-September, Emilia broke ranks to join the almost seventy women now serving with Rum's battalion. Zo professed to be unimpressed but her tone suggests some jealousy. 'She should have waited in the second line, like me,' she told a friend. 'I, disciplined, waited.'[89] Put in charge of Rum's messengers, how much direct action Emilia saw is not known. While she was caring for a wounded friend during these days, however, she saw a distressed four-year-old wandering around the casualties.* The ward was kept as clean as possible but the air was thick with the smell of death and humming with flies. It was no place for an infant but Michał's mother had died and his father was missing. Emilia had always ached for children of her own and, while trying to trace his relatives, she came to consider Michał as her son; a kind of 'regimental child'.[90]

Monday, 18 September dawned sunny and fine. 'It was the sound of cheering and shouts of joy on all sides that told me aircraft were coming over', Bór later recalled.[91] Stalin had finally agreed to support an American airdrop and the cloudless sky soon filled with over a hundred B-17 Flying Fortresses carrying almost 1,300 supply containers. Heading in from the west, they flew into the teeth of intense anti-aircraft fire, as a result dropping their loads from a height of over 10,000 feet. Bór watched the 'long trails of white dots' emerging from the aircraft to disperse across the city. 'It took a long moment to realise those dots were parachutes', he later wrote, and then he 'could merely witness the massive exhibition of power and think what might have been'.[92]

'It was a complete miracle,' Zo cried. 'The whole sky was filled with parachutes.'[93] As she watched, people emerged to help retrieve the supplies, crying and hugging one another. If the Americans had remembered them, they believed, Warsaw was not yet lost. Later, Zo would learn that only 130 containers, just 10 per cent, had reached the Poles. The rest had been lost or fallen into German hands. From Stalin's perspective, the action was worse than futile: the Americans were effectively arming the enemy. He did not facilitate another USAAF flight until the end of September, when it was too late.

Five days later, the Germans blew up Warsaw's last remaining pumping station, leaving the hastily dug wells as the only source of water in the city. With capitulation inevitable, Bór once again entered into talks. His priority was to ensure that captured Home Army soldiers, now officially part of the Polish Armed Forces, would be treated as POWs under the Geneva Convention rather than being shot on surrender or sent to concentration camps as 'bandits'. In tacit recognition of Zo's London work, on 23 September, he also finally signed the order that women in the Home Army were regular combatants and to

---

* Emilia's friend was Alina Nowakowa, the boy was Michał Westwalewicz.

be awarded military rank. As a direct result, they would become the only female units in the war to be interned as POWs. Zo's work had provided an unprecedented level of legal protection to several thousand female fighters.

Bór then turned to ensuring that, whatever Poland's immediate future, the history of the uprising should be permanently recorded. Four officers were to set off independently to reach the Polish government in London, in the hope that at least one would make it through to bear witness. Jan was among them. He was given a bundle of documents, several rolls of film, a thorough briefing and a priority sewer pass to get to Mokotów – where he was to contact Emilia for more 'mail'. At his own ardent request, he was also given permission for Greta to travel with him.

Zo knew that capitulation was imminent when Maria Wittek ordered her to also get out of the burning city. She and Emilia had been tasked with rebuilding Farmstead from Kraków. Zo considered swimming the Vistula, but the Germans had floodlit the waters and posted snipers along its banks. Seeing that 'they shot at every head', she changed her mind.[94] A plan to crawl through the sewers to the historic Powązki cemetery was abandoned when the Germans took the graveyard. Just as escape seemed impossible, Zo was ordered to organise a 'safe route' out for Jan as well. Along with her orders, she received a slip of white silk, signed by Bór himself, demanding all help be given to the bearer. In 1940, she had been notified of her first overseas courier mission by the code phrase 'the white dress is ready'. Five years later, she was going to have to rely on this thin slip of white silk to get her through occupied territory one more time.

On the last day of September, Wittek held a final Women's Military Service briefing. Zo was relieved to see both Emilia and Zofia Franio among the surviving commanders, although Zofia's partner had been killed a few nights earlier when their building had collapsed.* Wittek summarised their options. German captivity did not appeal. 'No one knew what the Germans would do to them if they didn't shoot them or hang them,' Zo noted, succinctly voicing their fears.[95] When some of her own team nevertheless chose this path, she gave one the sheepskin coat that had been Marianna's last gift to her, and officer cards to the others, hoping these might entitle them to better conditions. The

* Maria Szczurowska.

women's only other option was to remove their armbands and either return to civilian life or secretly keep fighting. Zo already had her orders.

Rum was leaving a similar briefing when he met Zo in the street. 'She looked older,' he thought. 'Her complexion, which had been flawless the previous year in London, was sallow, and her blond hair was short and unkempt.'[96] When Rum tried to embrace her, Zo pushed him away. She had considered him to be 'a trusted member of Farmstead', yet now he was telling her that he planned to surrender, 'meekly', she reportedly added, and 'follow his troops to a POW camp'.[97] This was 'the easiest way out', she told him scornfully, reminding him of the 'aggressive attitude of her London days'.[98] 'She would never have done it, not even if ordered' she added, which he did not doubt.[99] 'Nobody,' Zo said, 'could forgive him.'[100]

If Zo was angry at Rum, she was livid with herself. It was Rum who, setting aside his happiness with Audrey and his dreams of fatherhood, had literally fought with gun in hand. He knew that he could walk into captivity with his head held high, and could hope to see his wife again. Zo had also done her duty in the battle, and in the face of death and despair, but although her service had been critical she felt it had not been enough. They had not won Poland's freedom and, to Zo's mind, accepting defeat meant losing her country and with it her honour. The fight was her life.

'The atmosphere of our parting was somewhat cool', Rum later admitted.[101] Nevertheless, he took his leave convinced that, while 'Zo was always strange', she also 'worked without respite . . . blazed the trail . . . was a pillar of strength' and was, above all, 'one of Poland's ablest women'.[102] Zo dismissed Rum from her mind. She had suffered greater losses. What mattered now was the fight ahead. She had one final mission to complete as a soldier of the Home Army. Inside her jacket, she let her fingers find the white silk orders signed by General Bór.

15

Walking in Shock
(October 1944–February 1945)

'The clash of metal piercing the strange silence of the city' reverberated through the minds of thousands of Home Army soldiers as they threw down their arms after sixty-three days of deafening battle.[1] But not every fighter heard it. Rum looked for Zo but, he reported with some admiration, she had completely 'disappeared'.[2]

General Bór had signed the capitulation order on the evening of 2 October 1944, immediately ceasing all Warsaw military operations. In August, his force of around 50,000 Home Army soldiers, including one hundred Silent Unseen, had been armed with pistols and grenades but pitifully few heavy weapons. They had attacked an enemy of half their number, but quickly reinforced by artillery, armoured vehicles and the Luftwaffe. Instead of seizing a three-day victory, their two months of courageous defiance had come at an enormous cost. Some 18,000 resisters and almost 200,000 civilians had lost their lives.

Ranks and honours had been conferred on the survivors just before the capitulation. Zo and Emilia had been among the hundred women promoted to captain, although Zo had officially held the rank since 1943. A few others were promoted to major, Zofia's rank since 1942. Bór decreed that this was the highest military position women could achieve, failing to recognise that Maria Wittek was already a colonel. As Zo once said, Bór had many strengths but 'less understanding of the importance of these matters' than his predecessor, the ill-fated General Rowecki.[3] For her 'heroic deeds in combat', Zo had also been awarded the Virtuti Militari, Poland's highest award for valour, for the second time.[4] Like everyone else, she had been handed a signed slip of paper in lieu of her medal.[5]*

---

* Each class of the Virtuti Militari could only officially be awarded once. Emilia, Zofia and Rum were also awarded the Virtuti Militari. In addition, Emilia received the Cross of Valour and Gold Cross of Merit with Swords. Zofia already had the

The next morning, the German order for a civilian evacuation provided the first route out of Warsaw. Zo and Wacka set out together,
their hands over their mouths as the October wind whipped up the
ashes of the city around them. Emilia, Zofia and Maria Wittek also
joined the miserable crowds trudging out of their blackened capital.
Emilia, still mourning Ponury, was dressed in a slate-grey coat with
a black armband. Michał, her young ward, was in her arms, a small
bear cub clinging on, his fingers twisted into her hair. Each woman
was silently searching for an opportunity to slip away, hoping to meet
again in Kraków.

'We walked in shock', Zo wrote, hardly noticing the shingle of
masonry and glass beneath her feet.[6] Behind her, German trucks
loaded up anything of value before demolition crews dynamited the
surviving tenement housing in the suburbs, and whatever remained of
the inner city. The bomb-damaged Royal Castle, the national archives
and museum, Warsaw University, palaces, churches, hospitals, housing and schools were all incinerated as the Nazis razed the city to the
ground. On Hitler's orders, they were at once punishing the Poles and
denying the Russians, when they came, any shelter or supplies.

Zo's despair was 'somewhat tempered', she admitted with typical
frankness, 'by knowing the importance of her task'.[7] Wary of possible
checks, she had burnt any papers that might identify her, including
the notifications of her rank and awards. It had been, briefly, 'a wonderful thing' to be honoured, she felt, but destroying the papers was
no great sacrifice.[8] After all, 'there was nothing left . . . the Germans
were burning everything.'[9] Wehrmacht trucks now herded the civilians
westwards. Once out of the city ruins, people were loaded onto trains
and lorries heading to a transit camp set up at a railway repair works.[*]
From there, the fittest would be deported as forced labourers, the rest
sent to concentration camps.

Zo knew she had to get away before reaching the transit camp.
Spotting a military car with a trailer pulling across the flow of people,
she and Wacka hauled themselves up and under the trailer's tarpaulin.
Cold hard metal shifted uncomfortably beneath them as they breathed
in an animal smell mixed with grease and iron. They were lying on

---

first, but now also accepted the latter.
[*] Dulag 121 at Pruszków, west of Warsaw. From there, nearly 150,000 people were
deported to the Reich.

a mountain of horseshoes being driven to Germany. Several hungry hours but just twenty miles later, the car pulled up beside some others.* Zo and Wacka could hear Ukrainian guards talking nearby, the muted noise from a café, momentarily louder whenever its door swung open, and the regular footfall of a patrol. Waiting until it was completely dark, they timed their exit and ran for their lives.

Only when the sky began to lighten did Zo risk begging some water at a cottage several miles away. Learning that they had come from the uprising, the elderly homeowner produced fresh milk, rolls, butter and an egg. 'Such a miracle!' Zo beamed.[10] She had assumed the whole country was starving, not just blockaded Warsaw. Almost as miraculous, she and Wacka learnt that the convent in Szymanów, now serving as a field hospital, was just a few hours' walk away.

Usually 'so serious, so dignified', the Mother Superior at Szymanów fell to her knees when she saw Zo at her gate, pale and thin but somehow more alive than ever. Having told her briefly about the horror in the capital, Zo pulled open her coat to show the white silk pass. Weeping, the Holy Mother stooped to kiss Bór's signature.[11] Within half an hour, Zo and Wacka had more food in their bellies, money in their pockets, and were being rushed to the railway station in a wagon pulled by 'two fiery horses'.[12]

That night, the women's train terminated at the holy city of Częstochowa. As it would be several hours before their connection, they slept among other stranded civilians on the waiting-room benches, safer than they had felt for months. At first light, Zo crept out to witness the daily unveiling of the ancient icon, the Black Madonna, at the famous monastery. Although she had often passed through the city, this was her first sight of the painting and she found it 'a profoundly emotional experience'.[13] Known as the 'Queen and Protector of Poland', the icon is a symbol both of Polish patriotism and of female defiance.† An hour later, Zo and Wacka caught the morning train to Kraków.

⚓

---

* At the small town of Błonie, on the western outskirts of Warsaw.
† Legend tells that in 1432, fifty years after the icon arrived from Jerusalem, it was stolen by Hussite plunderers. Frustrated when his horse refused to carry the painting, one had slashed it with his sword. The Madonna had bled, but the thief had died.

While Zo and Wacka were absconding, many thousands of the Home Army Warsaw Corps were marching into captivity with their heads held high. Rum noticed some German troops saluting them. Others took photographs. Passing through Wola, where the worst civilian massacres had taken place, he saw fields of white crosses pushed into sand. It took him a moment realise that it was a German, rather than a Polish, burial ground. A few hours later, Rum's eye was caught by different fields. Silvery winter rye was tossing in the wind, almost animal in its movement. Half-starved from his diet of spit soup and wafers, Rum's gut churned painfully at the sight but, once again, the fields were not for Poles. Only when he was bolted into the wagon of a cargo train, did Rum bite into the small onion he had managed to grab from the roadside. When he next saw daylight, he was at Stalag VIII-B in Lamsdorf, Upper Silesia, a POW camp surrounded by six-foot-high barbed wire and patrolled by men with machine pistols and wolfhounds.

Quickly separated from the men, the female soldiers walked into captivity with their uniform armbands, now faded and torn, still over stained cardigans and flimsy summer dresses. Only the luckiest had coats or boots, and the long plaits of the young messenger-girls, stiff with blood, sweat and six weeks of mortar dust, had hardened as rigid as painters' brushes. Zo's friend Halina saw the Germans gaping at them.* One Wehrmacht soldier was 'looking at us, weeping', she later wrote, while two SS men stared, she decided, 'not with hatred, but with curiosity'.[14] She was more struck by the countryside they passed through. 'After two months in hell we were now walking through green fields where cows were grazing . . . I just couldn't believe my eyes'.[15]

Marzenna, who had pushed past the corpse in the Warsaw sewers, was now half-carrying her wounded sister. Mistakenly sent to the men's camp at Lamsdorf, she found the Germans there were 'not expecting to take female prisoners' and 'completely unprepared'.[16] The sisters spent the next couple of weeks pushing notes through the barbed wire that separated them from the men. When they eventually reached the women's camp – Stalag VI-C, some rows of wooden barracks on the windswept peatbogs at Oberlangen – they found conditions far

---

* Halina Martin.

worse.* Yet, without their official military status, these 3,000 women would either have been summarily shot or sent to die at Ravensbrück and Stutthof concentration camps, like their sisters before them.

⚓

As thousands of Home Army soldiers marched into captivity, two hundred miles further south a pair of scrawny SS officers, wooden revolvers in their holsters, were marching four Auschwitz prisoners out of their camp. Although it was only October, the officers could occasionally be heard to whistle a Christmas carol.

Zo's cousin Leonard had been deported to Auschwitz in the spring of 1941. He had been there when Egon was sent to the camp and, although they never met, he was still there when Egon was beaten to death the following summer. Leonard's survival was due in part to his position in the carpentry workshop, which sheltered him from harsher work details, but was also down to his contacts. One of his fellow carpenters was Witold Pilecki, the only prisoner to have deliberately entered the camp on a mission to learn about conditions.† Ironically, 'we rarely talked about the resistance', Leonard admitted, but, after Pilecki had broken out of Auschwitz, in April 1943, Leonard and five friends had begun to devise their own escape.[17]‡ It would take them over a year.

Leonard stole a pair of SS trousers first. Then a cap and a belt, hiding them beneath the wood in the carpentry store. Eventually the team assembled two full sets of uniform. They bribed the camp saddler to fashion a leather holster, ostensibly as a gift for an SS officer. Then a second. Their dummy revolvers were whittled from wood, as was a counterfeit stamp to print stolen papers. A Polish woman, brought in to clean the SS barracks, organised their reception on the

---

* Female officers were held in Oflag IX-C, Molsdorf, built in 1938 by slave labourers from nearby Buchenwald.

† Pilecki hoped the Home Army would liberate Auschwitz. Lack of arms prohibited the attempt. Approximately 196 of c.1.3 million prisoners successfully escaped, including four Jewish men held in the death camp.

‡ Alfons Szuminski, Tadeusz Donimirski, Wacław Maliszewski, Tadeusz Zaboklicki and Janek Prajsnew.

outside.* As a last precaution, some tight screws of paper containing stolen cyanide powder were shared between the men, to be swallowed in case of capture.

It was late September before some glazing work for an SS building outside the camp perimeter provided the opportunity they needed. A few days later, Leonard and another 'guard', in their ill-fitting uniforms, marched four 'prisoners' carrying heavy sheets of glass, not out of the main gate but through a well-used shortcut, directly under a machine-gun tower. Jumping to attention, the German guard 'saluted us and said, "Heil Hitler",' Leonard later recalled.[18] After exchanging pleasantries about the weather, Leonard shouted at his prisoners to make haste. They didn't stop as they passed some prison labourers on the road, all of whom doffed their caps, their eyes widening but their mouths staying shut. Nor when they saw an SS company heading to the shooting range. They pressed on even when the work inspector, whose duty it was to check their papers, cycled past, turning his head but not slowing his pace. They headed to the furthest building at the construction site, gratefully laid down the glass, and then marched on.

Soon they were breathing in the almost citrus smell of autumn birches and yellowing larch. Beyond a few fields was the small wood beside a river that the cleaning woman had spoken of. Sinking to their knees, the men drank deeply before wiping away some of the dirt of Auschwitz. Then they headed south. After a few miles, a peasant lad began to follow them, nervously attempting to whistle. Abruptly spinning round, Leonard demanded what tune he was trying to get out. '"They Came to Bethlehem",' the young man stammered, his eyes fixed nervously on Leonard's uniform boots. He was their resistance contact.† Half an hour later, Leonard was in a forester's cottage, gulping down soup chased by a shot of vodka. By the time the men heard the 'blast of the camp sirens', they were in the foothills of the mountains, dressed in rough peasant clothes but armed with a pair of pistols and three grenades.[19] The next morning they were sworn in to the local partisan unit.

⚓

* Zofia Zdrowak.
† Marian Mydlarz.

On the day that Leonard broke out of Auschwitz, British MPs in London were debating Poland's post-war future. 'Territorial changes on the frontiers of Russia there will have to be,' Churchill conceded. 'Russia has the right to our support in this matter, because it is Russian armies alone that can deliver Poland from the German talons.'[20] When the Polish prime minister resigned in protest, Britain withdrew support from the émigré government 'until the political situation became clearer'.[21] Outside Warsaw, the Home Army was now fighting on unsupported.

Zo's jacket, skirt and legs were still smeared with oil and her shoes had completely fallen apart by the time she and Wacka reached their contact point: a pharmacy in the centre of Kraków. It was midday on 4 October. After sending a message to the local commander, the pharmacist brought out a pair of yellow shoes, the only ladies' footwear he could find.* Twenty minutes later, Zo tottered over to a nearby café. This scrawny, filthy, exhausted blonde in ill-fitting lemon heels was not the soldier from Warsaw that the Kraków commander had expected, but his mouth snapped shut when he saw the white silk orders. Before the day was out, Zo had a room, a cipher, a liaison officer, another pair of shoes and, most crucial of all, radio access to London. Warsaw is 'in flames' she wired the Sixth Bureau, but 'Zo is in Kraków rebuilding Farmstead'.[22] It was the first news from Warsaw to reach London since the capital's capitulation.

Within days, Zo had a team of twelve, including Wacka. She spent her first few nights with Stefa, Marianna's sister and the last of the three Zawodzińska girls still at large. With barely enough food for herself, Stefa was living on foraged mushrooms and black-market rations paid for by selling her blood to the local hospital.

It was there that Emilia turned up a few days later, with now five-year-old Michał in her arms, and 'so tired', Zo saw, that 'she couldn't fulfil her duties' for at least a few days.[23] Trapped in the mass of civilians leaving Warsaw, Emilia and Michał had been herded onto a train for the holding camp. When they stopped briefly at a rural station, Emilia had peeled the child from her and launched him into the arms of a German soldier on the platform. Then she elbowed her way off to join them. Reportedly 'so overwhelmed' by this 'elegant, noble' young mother and son, the soldier let them leave.[24] He even allowed Emilia to

---

* The Kraków Home Army, aka 'Muzeum', was commanded by Edward Godlewski.

take a small bag for her boy. Inside it, Michał's teddy bear was stuffed with resistance documents.

Zo now focused on organising Jan Nowak's route to London, praying he would soon reach Kraków, while Emilia re-established communications with Budapest and tried to contact the POW camps. Soon the two women had identified possible new routes through Denmark to Stockholm and, potentially more secure, through Switzerland to liberated France. As neither Emilia nor Wacka could speak fluent German, Zo insisted on testing this southern route herself.

Rail travel was now disrupted by nightly air raids, and the requisitioning of passenger trains for German mass evacuations. Learning that Russian troops were approaching through Czechoslovakia, Zo first headed north, to Leipzig. Dressed in deep mourning, a black veil covering her face in the German style, she now carried only the most basic of identity papers and a travel permit to visit her 'wounded brother' at the large military hospital near the Swiss border.[*] Her crowded train crawled along so slowly that it took several days to pass Breslau and Dresden, and it was dark again before she arrived.[†] Like so many medieval cities, Leipzig had been badly bombed. Grey smoke blanketed the sky, making Zo wheeze as she searched for a room. Eventually she curled up under a stairwell at the station.

The next morning, Zo rubbed some life back into her stiff limbs while crushed in the corridor of a train heading to Munich. When they stopped outside Augsburg, the familiar smell of smoke, gas and damaged brickwork permeated the carriage. Some stray bombs had just hit the station. Ordered to disembark, Zo followed the others across the tracks, lifting her hands to shield her face as the wind whipped sheets of flame around the station buildings. Then she joined a new train. 'It was so orderly,' she noted approvingly, before adding more patriotically that 'the Germans were terribly afraid'.[25] From Augsburg she headed to Strasbourg, on the far side of the Rhine, then into Alsace.

Just that spring, an efficient Farmstead cell had operated in Alsace. Now there was no trace of them. Instead of dealing with Poles she trusted, she would have to approach the less certain contacts provided by the Sixth Bureau. Every enquiry exposed her. When she finally found her first contact, a German with Polish sympathies, he took her

---

[*] At Villingen. A Silesian contact of Zo's, Ada Korczyńska supplied the forgeries.
[†] German Breslau is now Wrocław, in Poland.

down to the banks of the Rhine just as the sky was darkening and most people were locking their doors. She was, she admitted, 'scared out of my wits'.[26] In a dilapidated shed, the man showed Zo a small rubber dinghy. The suggestion was that Jan could paddle into Switzerland, avoiding the border guards under cover of night.

Far from convinced, Zo hitched her way to the mountainous German *Schwarzwald*, the Black Forest region, to seek out another contact. Near the Swiss border, she walked through snowy forests under a moonlight sky, her case strapped to her back to save her fingers from freezing. This time she was to find a certain inn and ask for 'Brunhilde'. Comforting herself that this was 'not a Nazi name', but something more old-fashioned, she was relieved to be directed to a woman in her seventies.[27] That night, Zo and Brunhilde cautiously tested how much they could trust one another. 'We knew it was a game,' Zo admitted, if a perilous one.[28] Brunhilde told her that she knew guides who could lead Jan across the frontier, but warned her that they would desert anyone they considered a risk.

More satisfied, Zo dressed again in her widow's weeds, stamped and signed her forged hospital visitor pass, then caught a train back east. She was not too worried when a military policeman asked to see her documents. She knew they were searching for partisans and deserters, and that miserable widows and grieving sisters held little interest. Then, to her horror, the woman next to her pulled out an authentic visitor permit from the same hospital. Zo's papers had a completely different stamp on them, one that she and Emilia had invented. 'Jesus Mary!' Zo thought. Quickly followed by, 'Right . . . what does a woman do in this situation?'[29] Swaying to her feet, she pretended to faint. Minutes later, she was in the care of some female passengers near an open carriage window. By the time the policeman asked again for her papers, he had forgotten what the stamp looked like.

While Zo was evaluating risky routes through Austria, Jan Nowak was beginning to worry about ever reaching London. Having slipped away from the crowds being herded out of Warsaw, he and Greta had spent the next few weeks collecting more microfilm, which they hid inside a plaster cast on his arm and within her 'voluminous handbag'.[30] Eventually Jan began to panic. He had been warned that he could only expect his guides to wait until Christmas, and already there was snow in the forests and the risk of trains being cancelled. When they finally reached Kraków, in late November, Jan was greatly relieved to find 'two women of incredible energy and courage' still focused on getting him to London.[31]

Jan had heard of 'Zo'. As 'the only woman parachutist in the Home Army', she was 'a legendary figure' within the Sixth Bureau.[32] Rum had warned him that she could be 'tough and unbending', but was also clear that she 'did not spare herself either', and 'her devotion to duty was fanatical'.[33] Now Jan came face to face with Zo for the first time, and her impatient, assessing gaze did not disappoint. Looking curiously back, he noted that 'she was of middle height, blond, blue-eyed, slightly masculine . . . serious, stern, tough and very matter of fact'.[34] But what struck him most was that Zo 'did not smile once' during their conversation. In fact, she 'did not utter a single word of a personal nature, and stuck exclusively to business'.[35] Jan was no flirt, but even he was bemused by this stark professionalism. She was some-one, he rightly concluded, who 'had no time to waste'.[36]

Zo started by reassuring Jan and Greta that 'a couple of young people . . . arouse less suspicion than a lonely young man travelling on his own'.[37] Refusing to entrust their lives to a rubber boat on the wintery Danube, they agreed instead to her preferred route: a train to Nuremberg, then on to Stuttgart, Kappel and Freiburg. There they were to confirm their guide with the phrase, 'Greetings from Brunhilde', and hike into Switzerland. Emilia had arranged false doc-uments, although Jan was worried that the forgeries would not pass even a cursory inspection. Another contact had provided authentic work papers for a Freiburg sawmill. Like their travel tickets, these would only be valid in one direction. 'If anything went wrong', Jan understood, 'there would be no return.'[38]

Over the next few days, Zo drilled every step of the route into the young couple. In a Kraków street-market they bought a shabby sheep-skin coat, worn suit and cap for Jan, and for Greta a frayed but warm jacket and a pair of laced boots. The microfilm they had collected was sewn into their collars, cuffs and linings, and concealed inside a plaster saint at the bottom of Greta's handbag. It was only on 19 December, when they made their farewells, that Jan felt Zo show any emotion. Firmly taking his hand, she whispered, 'Pray God that you get there!'[39]

Jan and Greta reached Nuremberg two days later. There they slept on the waiting-room floor, and woke to the industrial howl of air-raid sirens. The following day, their train pulled into the ruins of Stuttgart just after its heaviest bombardment. Even after the destruction of Warsaw, while wandering through the debris of a once magnificent palace, the face and feet of an ancient angel adrift among the rubble, Jan could not help but curse the 'dreadful pointlessness of this annihilation'.[40] 'Greetings from Brunhilde' eventually saw them into their Freiberg safe house and, in the early hours of Christmas morning, 1944, they set off for the Swiss border. The sky above shimmered with stars, the mercury well below zero, and snow crunched beneath their boots. 'What a world!' Jan whispered to Greta.[41]

⚓

Only in January 1945, after the last Germans had left Warsaw, did Stalin send in his forces, unchallenged yet in triumph, to 'liberate' the charred ruins. Over 80 per cent of the city had been destroyed. One Russian journalist reported that as he scrambled over mounds of rubble, buckled tramlines and ripped telephone wires, he was followed by 'a file of old and young men in crumpled hats, berets, autumn coats . . .' and everywhere 'girls and young women were walking, blowing on their frozen fingers and looking at the ruins with sorrow-filled eyes'.[42]

Zofia Franio was among the first of Warsaw's citizens to return. She headed straight to what had once been Mokotów Fields to find the remains of the woman with whom she had lived throughout the occupation. Targeted by the Luftwaffe because of its airstrip, Mokotów had been flattened even before the German retreat. With few protective barricades left, Zofia's flatmate had been shot dead by a sniper as she carried vegetables to an insurgents' hospital. Clawing through the rubble, reportedly 'with her bare hands', Zofia eventually found her friend's remains and arranged for her burial in the military cemetery.[43]

The Home Army was officially disbanded that month but, although released from their oath, many of the units continued to harry the German retreat. Some served alongside Russian troops, only to later find themselves in Soviet detention. One CIA report detailed how 'mass arrests and deportations took place in the trail of the Red Army's advance'.[44] With what Gubbins called 'a treachery rarely equalled in history', many senior officers were summarily shot in a pre-emptive strike against any anti-Soviet resistance.[45] Meanwhile, foot soldiers refusing conscription into the communist Polish People's Army risked being sent to Siberian labour camps –'the dark abyss of misery', as one put it.[46]

In Kraków, Emilia, Zo and Wacka continued their Farmstead work. Emilia 'was very energetic and efficient' in maintaining radio contact with London, but Zo couldn't help noticing that she still had 'a very difficult personal life'.[47] Zo herself was travelling almost constantly in the January freeze, trying to patch the old courier networks back together. Sometimes she took 'a completely romantic route' between partisan groups in the snowy mountains, and once she dressed as a nun to follow a pilgrim path.[48] Travelling to Flensburg, on the German border with Denmark, she hoped to reconnect with Stockholm, but it proved impossible. Instead, she worked out new routes to Switzerland, often passing close to Murnau where Rum had been transferred. As most of her old associates had disappeared and, she said, 'we kept our distance from communists', it was impossible to keep up with London's intelligence demands.[49]

On 23 January, Emilia received word that Jan had safely reported in London. He and Greta were the first participants of the Warsaw Uprising to reach the west and, in Zo's excited words, were to tell 'the world about the heroism of insurgent Warsaw'.[50] Sitting in a packed room in London's Piccadilly, Greta at his side, Jan gave his testimony to journalists from around the globe. His voice rose with passion as he detailed German crimes, the perfidy of Stalin, and the courage and resilience of the Home Army. The photographs he and Greta had smuggled out were widely circulated and the film footage, edited together as *The Last Days of Warsaw*, would be shown across Britain and America. Jan then spoke about the Home Army soldiers who had welcomed their Russian counterparts on orders from London, only to be detained and deported. Next, he demanded British and American supervision of free elections in post-war Poland. It was, he later wrote, 'the climax of my entire wartime activity'.[51]

Rum's wife, Audrey, read Jan's testimony in the London papers. Four days later, she gave birth to a baby boy. She had been informed that Rum was a POW. Further details had been delayed, however, she later wrote to him, because 'it was after 6.30pm, and everybody had left your office'.[52] Still keeping tidy hours, the Sixth Bureau team was nevertheless delighted to hear about the birth and 'awfully pleased that it's a boy'.[53] Rum, too, was thrilled when Audrey's latest airmail letter reached him. 'Oh Darling,' he replied, 'how can I express my gratitude to you that you gave me a son – not a girl, but a boy!'[54]

Baby Andrew Bilski had arrived at a tumultuous moment. The skies above his Croydon cot were filled with 'flying bombs and rockets', as Nazi Germany continued to launch V1 buzzbombs and V2 long-range guided ballistic missiles at London.[55] Desperate for uplifting stories as the enemy campaign hit home, the British papers began to give more column inches to Jan and Greta's wartime wedding than to the fate of Poland. Press stories 'are like soap bubbles', Jan wrote in despair. They 'shine in the sun but burst very quickly'.[56] Ten days later, Poland's last hope for independence was crushed at the Yalta Conference.

Britain and America had already been negotiating new Polish borders with the Soviet Union.* When it was further suggested that the Polish politicians in London be included in Stalin's 'Provisional Government of the Polish Republic', the Poles rejected the proposal. The very concept of a government imposed by a foreign power, they argued, was in violation of the principles of freedom for which the Allies had fought. They nevertheless instructed the Polish troops serving overseas to continue the battle, hoping their loyalty might yet win their nation's freedom. 'They fought with distinction, in the front of the attack, in the last battles', Harold Macmillan wrote. 'They lost their country, but they kept their honour.'[57]

As the Soviet threat on Polish soil rapidly replaced that from Nazi Germany, many former Home Army soldiers started swearing their loyalty to the secret anti-communist resistance. Emilia did not at first tell Zo that she had joined a clandestine organisation called 'Independence' and was organising its overseas communications lines.† Zo was still serving flat-out as a Farmstead courier.

In late January, the day after Rum's son had been born, Zo was

---

* The Soviet Union took much of eastern Poland. Poland gained (less) German territory, but did secure significant mining, industrial and transport hubs.

† 'Independence', in Polish Niepodległość, was abbreviated to 'NIE', the Polish word for 'No', expressing their rejection of the Soviet Union. Organised by August Fieldorf, NIE was led by Leopold Okulicki, last commander of the Home Army. After Okulicki's arrest, Jan Rzepecki launched the 'Delegation of the Armed Forces' or Delegatura. This was later superseded by the more political 'Freedom and Independence Association', Wolność i Niezawisłość, known by its Polish acronym as WiN. For brevity, I refer to the 'anti-communist resistance'.

caught in the last Allied offensive against Stuttgart, rushing to a shelter as a force of over six hundred bombers destroyed the railway yards and aircraft factory. Walking through a haze of smoke after the all-clear, she suddenly saw 'a hanged *feldgrau*' – the corpse of a German soldier hanging awkwardly from a lamppost, his face tilted down as if in bemusement at his useless, dangling feet.[58] The cardboard sign around his neck read, 'I stole'.[59] Zo loathed both the 'hyenas', as she called bombsite looters, and the Germans, but she did not wish this fate on anyone.[60] Above all, she feared being mistaken for a looter herself.

A week later, Zo and Wacka were returning from Vienna when they met Teresa Delekta on the same route, transporting reports hidden inside a toy dog. That night, the three women could hear both Russian and American guns as the Eastern and Western Fronts started to converge. The next day they watched the Russians arrive. 'There was a lot of shooting', Teresa reported bluntly.[61] For a week the women stayed put, Zo humming the patriotic anthem 'May this day of blood and glory, the day of resurrection be!' Wacka more prudently sang Russian songs in her 'lovely voice', until they managed to slip south again.[62] At Częstochowa, they passed a miserable column of Polish soldiers heading into German captivity. Having heard that the Russians were hanging Home Army soldiers, one told her, with 'tears rolling down his face', they had surrendered instead to the army they had fought bitterly for five years, hoping to be later liberated by the Western Allies.[63]

Zo and Wacka eventually reached Kraków in a Russian truck. Wacka, sitting on the petrol tank, was hugging the engine to stay warm. Zo, who had paid for their passage with a bottle of vodka, was perched on 'the knees of some Bolshevik'.[64] The city was already full of Russians and Emilia who, like Wacka, had spent her youth in Soviet Russia, was in despair. 'There will come a time when we will long for Gestapo rule,' she told Zo seriously.[65] Then Emilia handed Zo her last identity card, this one prepared in her real name, Elżbieta Zawacka, along with twenty American dollars – her demobilisation pay.

⚓

With her conspiratorial service seemingly at an end, Zo hitched home to Toruń. On the way, she saw Soviet posters that promised free education for everyone under eighteen. It reminded her of how her brother Ali had been forced to join the army while still in his teens, and how, years later, her parents had had to sell their pillows to pay for her own exams. 'How hard it was for my mother,' she realised.[66] Zo had always valued education. A teacher herself, even during the occupation she had continued secretly tutoring girls. This Soviet pledge 'was something extraordinary!' she thought, even 'wonderful'.[67] It was also the best argument she had heard for helping her country to heal. 'Full of strength, full of desire' for change, she began to feel 'enthusiastic despite all the uncertainty'.[68] At Toruń, the bridge across the Vistula had been destroyed, but local men, 'completely naked' Zo noticed, were already waist-high in the icy water, hammering in piles as Russian engineers directed the reconstruction.[69] Once again, her practical mind could not help admiring Soviet organisation and yet, as she entered the empty city streets, she could sense that something was very wrong.

Russian troops had entered Toruń on 1 February 1945. Half of the 18,000 Germans in the city had been killed. Drunk on their victory, and German schnaps, the soldiers had looted shops and houses, shot anyone who protested, and raped thousands of women. When Zo knocked on the boards nailed over the broken door of her parents' house, Dela opened up cautiously, then silently threw her arms around her sister. 'Our greeting was not joyful,' Zo later ruefully told a friend.[70] Egon was dead. There was no news of Klara, and her parents' detention by the Gestapo had left them frail and 'intimidated'.[71] The Soviet soldiers now billeted with them had stolen their food, their blankets and her father's watch. Worse followed. A few days later, a neighbour was found 'dead, raped, on some rubbish heap'.[72] Everyone had 'closed eyes and tart lips', Zo saw, afraid to raise their voice, but she had to admit that 'I was also silent'.[73]* Resolving that she 'was still a soldier', Zo gave her mother ten dollars from her demobilisation pay, and left again for Warsaw.[74]

Zo was tough, but she was not impervious to the pain around her. Returning to her capital for the first time since the uprising, she sang 'The Lady of Warsaw' to keep up her spirits.† Fat rats now ran across the rubble, streaming in and out of the cellars and sewers. Over the

* Here Zo was quoting the poet Czesław Miłosz, later winner of the 1980 Nobel Prize for Literature.
† 'La Varsovienne', a Polish protest anthem.

next few months, clearance would reveal the remains of 250,000 people. It was impossible to know how many more dead had been incinerated. Everywhere, drifting across the ruins and pasted onto fragments of walls, were handwritten notes from survivors searching for their loved ones.

The first of her resistance sisters that Zo found was Hanka Michalska, who had missed the uprising, as she had been trapped by the moving front while delivering messages. Over the next few weeks, they met Wacka, Maria Wittek and, 'joy again', Dr Zofia Franio, already working at a clinic.[75] Later, Emilia joined them with her adopted son, Michał, in tow. Their collective resolve to keep up the fight was hardened in March, when the Soviets invited several former Home Army leaders to negotiations, only to arrest and deport them. It was clear that there were to be no freedoms in liberated Poland.

⚓

In late April, the sound of gunfire heralded the arrival of the US Third Army at the Molsdorf oflag, the German POW camp holding Polish female officers. The Red Cross recorded that the site looked like a concentration camp, but most of the prisoners had survived. The Americans went on to liberate Murnau, where Rum was a POW. Seeing Sherman tanks arriving, the camp's remaining SS guards turned their machine guns first on the nearest prisoners, and then at the approaching forces. The first Sherman rotated its turret and sent a heavy volley back. From behind the perimeter wire, Rum watched the SS as 'their hats fell onto the pavement'.[76]

General Maczek's First Polish Armoured Division liberated Oberlangen a few days later. Hanna Czarnocka, who had carried the glass bottles of methylated spirits through an air raid during the Uprising, now watched proudly as 'tanks crossed the fields, cut through four layers of barbed wire' and 'very dirty' soldiers wearing Polish insignia climbed out to embrace their valiant sisters.[77]* 'We lined up pretty quickly' when the Polish flag was raised, Marzenna recalled, standing 'as upright as the strings of the violin' even while 'tears of joy, pride and hope were running down our faces'.[78]

---

* The women received British army uniforms with Polish insignia. Hanna Czarnocka and Marzenna Schejbal both came to Britain with the Free Polish Forces.

⚓

On 30 April, a frail 56-year-old man tried to stop the twitching of his hand as he raised a pistol to his temple. He breathed his last in a claustrophobic room, 'encased on all sides by concrete and earth', twenty-eight metres beneath the old Reich Chancellery gardens in Berlin.[79] Moments later, Hitler and his dreams for a thousand-year Reich were dead.

It was during the purgatory days, after Hitler's suicide but before the formal surrender, that the Swedish Red Cross rescued nearly 7,000 prisoners from Ravensbrück. Over 90,000 women had perished in the camp's gas chambers, by hanging or shooting, and from starvation, cold and disease. More were killed by experimental operations, among other 'medical' trials. By March 1945, hundreds of women were being murdered every day as the Nazis tried to destroy the evidence of their atrocities; but Zo's younger sister, Klara, was a miraculous survivor, listed as one of those 'saved from German concentration camps as a result of Count Folke Bernadotte'.[80]

Bernadotte, a Swedish diplomat, had been negotiating with Himmler since February 1944. Only when defeat was imminent did the Nazi grandee agree to a 'good-will' gesture. The first of the 'shining Swedish white buses', each painted with a large red cross, set off for the camps in brilliant spring weather, their radios tuned into arias from light operas.[81] As they passed through northern Germany they started to smell, and then to see, the swollen corpses of dead cows and horses at the roadsides. The stench got far worse as they neared the camps.

At Ravensbrück, selected prisoners were lined up in long rows. A few wore overcoats marked with white crosses over their striped camp uniforms, and some had old headscarves or rags tied over their shaved heads. 'Mainly female SS officers strutted around in their impeccable uniforms,' one later recalled, using their last moments of power to inform them they were going to be gassed.[82] 'I don't want to die,' one woman was heard to whimper. 'Please don't let me die.'[83]

'Come along now, ladies,' the first Swedish driver politely cajoled them.[84] Twenty minutes later they were driving through open country-side. 'I look around with wonder', one woman wrote. 'There is rustle of leaves and the sounds of early birdsong, and the smell of morning newness.'[85] When the buses stopped for the women to relieve them-selves in a field, they fell to their knees and, using twigs or their fingers, dug out dandelion roots and anything else they could eat. Klara, among the last to be rescued, was 'half dead from hunger'.[86] Returning to her bus, for a while she just leant her face against the cool window, then she ripped the prisoner insignia from her sleeves.

⚓

At 2.41am on 7 May 1945, Germany signed an unconditional surrender. The Second World War in the west was over. The next day, huge crowds gathered to hear Churchill speak in London's Whitehall and to watch the royal family wave from the balcony of Buckingham Palace. Jan and Greta were among the singing, dancing crowds in Piccadilly Circus. The British were 'drunk with happiness and glory', Jan felt proud of the part his country had played.[87] 'Everyone was celebrating', Sue Ryder wrote. 'People in London, in all liberated countries, streamed into the streets and there was a jubilant pealing of bells.'[88] But not everyone *was* celebrating. In Warsaw, Zo faced an anxious future. Like most of her compatriots, she felt that her country's occupation by one hostile foreign power (Nazi Germany) had now been replaced by another (Soviet Russia), and Poland was still not free.

Part Four

16

A Soldier's Internal Conflict
(May 1945–September 1951)

'Like most Home Army soldiers', Emilia wrote to the new, communist, President of the Republic of Poland in 1948, she had been 'going through a soldier's internal conflict'.* Since the end of the war, the Polish people had been 'faced with the existence of two governments': the wartime authorities – still in London, and the communist regime – installed in Warsaw. For many, Emilia continued, gaining faith in the new Polish Republic would require 'a long, complicated and difficult process'.[1] She did not mention that for others, who had witnessed the Soviet invasion in 1939 or their betrayal of the Warsaw Uprising, it would be impossible.

While western Europe celebrated peace *and* freedom in the spring of 1945, Poland was forced to choose between the two. In September 1939, the world had been brought to war by Nazi Germany's assault on Poland. Within weeks, Soviet forces had also invaded. Under the terms of their secret agreement, these twin aggressors had divided Poland between them. General Sikoski had been forced to accept Stalin as an ally in 1941, when Hitler's invasion of Russian-held territory prompted a Soviet volte-face. But now, after the unconditional surrender of Germany, few Poles could countenance that their heroism and sacrifice had led not to the restoration of their country's independence, but to the imposition of a Soviet-backed communist regime.

Poland was too weak to fight on alone, but many Poles were still hoping that the Western Allies would yet rally to drive the Russians back. There was a strong moral case for action. A report commissioned by Churchill in May 1945 revealed that almost half of Britain's wartime intelligence had come from Polish sources. Their armed

---

* President Bolesław Bierut joined the Polish Communist Party in 1912. Polish imprisonment saved him from Stalin's 1930s purges. In 1943, he left the Soviet Union for occupied Poland, maintaining contact with Moscow thereafter.

forces' contribution to the Battle of Britain and the campaigns in Italy, Libya and elsewhere, had also been substantial. The British prime minister instructed his chiefs of staff to evaluate the military potential to secure 'a square deal for Poland'.[2] The Soviets expressed outrage at such 'perfidy and betrayal', but their minds might have been set at ease had they known the code name allocated to the potential action: 'Operation Unthinkable'.[3] 'The idea is of course quite fantastic', the chair of the British chiefs of staff wrote, 'and the chances of success quite impossible'.[4]

Neither Britain nor America had the economic resources or the political will for further conflict, but, as so often, there was no easy way to tell the Poles. 'We had suffered a huge national defeat, yet we did not want to or were simply unable to believe this,' one Silent Unseen veteran admitted. 'We clutched at the illusory straws of hope.'[5] As a result, 1945 would be a year of agonising dilemmas for Zo and thousands of veterans like her, torn between continuing to resist or lending their weight to the reconstruction of their nation: freedom *or* peace.

It was resistance that came most naturally to Zo. Maria Wittek, Emilia, Wacka and Zofia had all already secretly joined the anti-communist conspiracy. Styling herself as Elżbieta Grochowska, a resident of Poznań, Zo was soon running anti-communist resistance liaison and press distribution across western Poland. Wherever she went, she tried to recruit her old contacts, but few were willing to continue the struggle. After six years of brutal occupation it was impossible to recreate the naïve optimism of the early anti-Nazi resistance. Everyone had lost loved ones, bonds of trust had broken down, the capital was destroyed and the nation's infrastructure was in ruins. Soon the notorious NKVD, the Soviet secret police, started making arrests. Surviving the war only to be detained in the peace seemed absurd and after some weeks of finding 'no spirit, no enthusiasm' for the cause, Zo decided further conspiracy was 'pointless'.[6]

Rather than being 'consumed by profound despair', Zo now felt 'an overwhelming desire' to support the reconstruction of her country.[7] As a child she had been taught about sins in thought, speech and deed. Now she added negligence to the list, the sin of omission. 'It was the gravest sin for me, to have strong hands and a fit head, and not to have immersed myself completely in the work of rebuilding Poland,' she told a friend, especially when 'work was waiting, it was lying in the street . . .'[8] The building site of Warsaw 'was depressingly lack-ing in the normal bustle and movement of a city', the new American ambassador to Poland noted that summer.[9] Many veterans were stay-ing away to avoid drawing attention to themselves. Zo was willing to labour manually but, a teacher by profession, she hoped to help fulfil the communist promises of free education to everyone under eighteen. Over the six years of occupation, a whole generation had been largely deprived of their schooling.

It was now, just as she had determined to devote her energies to reconstruction, that Zo received her last resistance mission. Her orders were two-fold. First, she and Wacka were to organise an escape route to Britain for senior Home Army officers. The concern was that, if arrested, then in Zo's pithy phrase, 'the Bolsheviks would finish them off', as they already had done so many.[10] Secondly, once back in London she was to rally her female compatriots. Rather than remain-ing in the west, 'doing nothing for Poland', as she put it, they were to return to serve their nation.[11]

꜔

The British government officially recognised the Soviet-installed pro-visional Polish Republic on 6 July 1945, at the same time withdrawing support from the Polish administration in London.* Yet Britain also offered sanctuary to over 250,000 Polish service personnel.† Polish pilots had once been lionised in London, but now there was growing hostility to this sudden influx. British nationals were facing their own hardships and largely ignorant of the Soviet persecutions. Nevertheless, most of the Poles who found themselves in Britain after the end of the war elected to remain. Among them was General Bór, who was working to secure the resettlement of his men in Britain just as Zo was setting out to bring the women home.

Bór had drawn up a list of those he was 'extremely anxious' to have back on his staff.[12] 'Major Bilski', aka Rum, who 'was with him in Warsaw', was among them.[13] Having been liberated by American

* France and Sweden had already revoked their recognition of the exiled Polish government on 29 June 1945.
† The Polish Resettlement Act of 1947 was Britain's first mass immigration legisla-tion.

troops, Rum duly reported back for duty in London. It was a shock to be told, during his British debrief, that the Western Allies were now 'working closely with our Soviet counterparts to rebuild a peaceful and stable Europe'.[14] As a result, Rum carefully considered his words when questioned about his missing colleagues. When Zo's name came up, he answered only that 'she did not discuss any future plans'.[15] Rum would always be a passionate patriot, but once he had seen the tears brimming in Audrey's eyes and felt, for the first time, the soft fingers of their young son curl around his own, he knew that his first duty was to them, and that his future lay in Britain.[*]

⚓

Zo and Wacka set off for the Czech frontier later that summer with new false documents, secret mail for London, and some foreign currency hidden in the back of a small mirror. Most of their contacts had disappeared and none they found were willing to help. 'The Russians knew how to eat into the fabric of society with their network of informers and agents,' Zo concluded.[16] Hundreds of Polish professionals had already been detained in Soviet camps, in the basements of police buildings, and even in former air-raid shelters, and 'there was talk of arrests everywhere'.[17] Safe houses had been compromised, and border roads were being patrolled. Just a few months after Zo had got Jan Nowak out, Poland's western frontier had effectively been sealed. Zo did not give up lightly, but eventually she and Wacka were forced to return to Warsaw.[18]

Zo was not the only one feeling defeated. Emilia's team was so reduced that she was making most of the local journeys herself. 'Completely exhausted' and 'utterly depressed', 'she begged me' to take over, Zo later confided.[19] Certain 'that nothing would come of it', however, she turned Emilia down, then warned Maria Wittek that further conspiracy work was futile.[20] Wittek suggested that Zo take a longer-term view. She had found work at the new State Office for Physical Education and Military Training, and was planning to relaunch the PWK. Women had learnt so much during the war, she urged Zo. It was their duty to pass this on to the next generation.

---

[*] Rum became a naturalised British citizen in 1954, settling in Croydon with his growing family.

After voicing some misgivings about who might benefit most from trained reservists, Zo agreed to organise the first post-war PWK summer camp. Sentimentally, she chose to return to Garczyn, where she had first pitched a tent in 1931, been disciplined for staying out late and losing her shoe in the lake, and pledged her life to her country. Since then, the Germans had used the site as a POW camp before blowing up all the structures when they were forced to retreat. It felt good to set six hundred new female cadets to work rebuilding the camp, and soon Zo was an official state employee, directing women's military training. Within a year she had fifty camps, with cadets helping on the land and offering healthcare, childcare and study support to local communities, as well as undertaking military training. She loved the work . . . until she was assigned a deputy.

This 'cultural and educational officer' 'followed my every step', Zo moaned, as he ensured that her training followed the approved communist ideology.[21] Renamed 'Service to Poland', the PWK now had to provide political courses in place of celebrating Polish culture and traditions. At first, Zo listened 'through clenched teeth', but when this deputy insisted that the first commander of the Home Army, General Rowecki, had been betrayed by his own people 'because they wanted to liquidate him', one of her cadets firmly set him straight.[22] 'He was not happy with the speech,' Zo said, smiling with grim satisfaction, 'but he had to listen.'[23] But Zo had to listen, too, and, although fearing that it was 'a kind of desertion', she soon felt she had no choice but to 'regretfully' resign.[24]

Zo's concerns were relatively minor. As the communist grip on Poland tightened, ever more Home Army veterans were being arrested by both the Soviet NKVD and the new Polish security service, the UB.* Drawn home for stewed cabbage and 'the scent of acacia', one sentimental returning veteran was shocked to find that instead of receiving hero's welcome he was treated like 'a reactionary piece of scum, some kind of dung' and, as a potential counter-revolutionary, he was suddenly facing a prison sentence.[25] 'These were the Polish men and women who for years had fought the German enemy,' SOE's Colin Gubbins growled. 'We are left stunned by this appalling betrayal.'[26] 'His crime can only possibly be that of serving his country', another

---

* The *Urząd Bezpieczeństwa* (UB), the Polish People's Republic's Department of Security, or secret police, was known from 1956 as the Security Service (SB).

officer raged on news of another arrest, and 'while we cannot claim him as a British subject we can, however, claim him as a British agent'.[27] But being a 'British agent' was exactly the charge now being levelled against these men. 'We should do all that we can for these particularly gallant fellows', a further British memo stated. 'We may well be glad of their services and special knowledge again' and, in any case, 'British honour is at stake'.[28] But Polish nationals inside Poland were outside British jurisdiction, and eventually 103 of the Silent Unseen whom SOE had helped to train were arrested and sentenced to imprisonment or execution.[*]

In October 1945, Emilia had told the leader of the anti-communist resistance, Jan Rzepecki, that she was finished. Her latest officer admirer had proposed and they were planning to escape to Italy with her informally adopted son.[†] Five days before they were to leave, the UB knocked at Emilia's door. A search revealed her packed bag and various suspect documents, including two photos of Zo. Arrested on suspicion of resistance activities, she was driven to Mokotów prison to be held in a tiny concrete cell. Over the next few days her officer lover and the resistance leader Jan Rzepecki were also detained during a new wave of targeted arrests.

The case against Rzepecki was led by an experienced and sadistic UB officer, Colonel Józef Różański.[‡] Later notorious for his brutal interrogations, he would personally punch and kick his prisoners, sometimes beating their feet to a pulp. Instead of using violence with Emilia, however, Różański emphasised how pointless and unpatriotic it was to resist the new authorities, given the need for common endeavour in the rebuilding of their great nation. Emilia would endure many months in prison with only Różański's visits to divert her. She missed

---

[*] Of the 316 Silent Unseen who returned to occupied Poland, nine were killed in transit, and eighty-four in action or by the Gestapo (including eighteen of the ninety-one who served in the Warsaw Uprising). Ten took poison after arrest. Nine were executed by the post-war authorities. Fryderyk Serafiński, aka 'Ladder', who had parachuted back with Zo, was arrested in May 1945 but released that October. He reached Britain in 1946.

[†] Emilia's beau was Major Michał Pobocha. The child was Michał Westwalewicz.

[‡] Józef Różański, born Josef Goldberg, joined the Polish Communist Party before the war, and the NKVD after the Soviet invasion. He would later be imprisoned for his use of torture.

her friends, her freedom, and the life-affirming pleasure she found in fashion and flirting, but most of all she desperately missed her little boy, her adopted bear cub Michał. Pouring her heart into sorrowful verses, she recalled his 'curtain-like lashes' blinking open in the mornings, 'his body full of warmth' and his 'lazy little arms'.[29] Eventually she was allowed to see the boy on a few visits used to gain her trust. 'Please wait, and miss mummy's tenderness', she scribbled on sheets of paper cockled by tears.[30]

After several months of interviews, often lasting throughout the night, Różański started to impress Emilia with his apparent patriotism and personal regard. Laying on the charm, he gave his word of honour that any testimony she gave would be to him alone, a law-abiding Polish officer, and that any resisters she revealed would be under his personal protection. Those who chose to stay hidden, he made clear, would remain vulnerable to arrest. 'So many Poles have died already for no good reason,' he reportedly told her. 'We have to stop it' or 'you will be responsible for the slaughter.'[31] Still she held her tongue.

It was Emilia's anti-communist resistance chief, Jan Rzepecki, who finally broke her resolve. A former colonel in the Polish Armed Forces, Rzepecki had headed the Home Army's Information and Propaganda Bureau during the occupation.* After serving in the Warsaw Uprising, he had been held in a German POW camp until liberated by the Red Army. Since then, he had endeavoured to replace what he saw as futile armed struggle against the communist regime with more political defiance. Only forty-six years old when arrested, he still hoped to secure a future for himself. Continued resistance was destabilising society and hindering the reconstruction, he told Emilia over several long conversations. To enable reconciliation, he had already shared the names he knew, he said, so there was no reason for her to hold back. Then he ordered her to reveal her contacts.†

As the unbearable weight of sole responsibility began to ebb from her, a typewriter and paper were brought to Emilia's cell. Drained by her months in prison, exhausted by her efforts to remain reticent, charmed by her interrogator and now ordered to change tack by

---

* It was Rzepecki who had once vouched for the traitor Jarach, resulting in so many arrests among the Farmstead team.

† Jan Rzepecki was later released, then detained 1949–1954 but released again due to lack of evidence.

her former resistance commander, she slowly began to divulge the structure of the resistance and then to give up names, Zo's among them. She saw it as 'an act of donation, an act of grace', she wrote.[32] Unknown to her, the UB immediately started making arrests. Perhaps because Emilia had specified that Zo, an insignificant courier, had left the Home Army at her own request and not tried to join the anti-communist resistance, she was not detained.

Bradl, who had organised Zo's route south from Paris, was among those arrested. Having served with distinction during the Warsaw Uprising, after the armistice Bradl had been working as an engineer on the reconstruction of Gdańsk shipyard.* He was detained by the secret police on the same day that he received the communist regime's highest civilian award for his engineering work. Bradl's prison conditions were appalling. His cold, wet cell had no bed and only a bucket for waste. Regularly beaten during night-time interrogations, he lost most of his teeth and twice attempted suicide. Among his torturers was Józef Różański. When Bradl's sister petitioned for mercy, in a moment of candour Różański told her, 'You can write to whomever you please, [Bradl] will stay in prison for as long as I like.'[33]†

Zo soon learnt of Emilia and Bradl's detention, but there was no way for her to reach them. She had been living under the shadow of arrest herself for the last six years, but it was bitter to know it was not the Gestapo or NKVD who might be hunting her now, but the security forces of her own beloved nation. Drawing comfort from the thought that they had not come for her yet, although they likely had her name, in 1946 she threw herself into studying a holistic approach to education while applying for teaching work.

⚓

In June 1946, a military parade four miles long marched through the streets of London to celebrate the Allied victory and honour those who had served. Having officially recognised the communist government in

---

* After the Warsaw Uprising, Alicja Iwańska, aka 'Squirrel', Pankrac's widow, had served as Bradl's courier.
† Bradl had two sisters. Pilot Anna Leska served in the ATA and remained in Britain after the war. Wanda Bohdanowicz had stayed in Poland and now petitioned for her brother's release.

Warsaw, the British invited them to send a delegation. Protests from Churchill and the RAF led to belated invitations also being extended to representatives of the Polish Armed Forces in Britain. When both invited parties declined, Poland was left without representation.

SOE's proposal to award Zo the British War Medal was meanwhile also declined.* The Poles in Britain nevertheless awarded her another Virtuti Militari 'for distinguished courage in the courier service overseas during wartime, in danger from the enemy'.[34] She could not, of course, accept it in person, but received notice when the possessions she had left in London, 'less books', were sent to a safe Warsaw address. Fearing for her security, Zo's 'Elizabeth Watson' name was then among those removed from British military registers.[35]

ॐ

Inside Poland, thousands more people were now being arrested ahead of the country's January 1947 elections. Zofia Franio was detained in November. Although she had returned to her Warsaw medical practice, a search of her apartment revealed over 150 underground newspapers. Like Emilia, Zofia was held in Mokotów prison while the security services gathered information on what they referred to as her 'broad criminal activity'.[36] In the new year, the communists reported a landslide victory, with themselves and their allies receiving 80 per cent of the vote. Poland was now, in effect, in the grip of a single-party dictatorship.

In the months before her trial, Emilia was moved to a larger cell. Now an enthusiastic convert to her policy of 'reconciliation', she urged whoever took the second bunk in her cell to reveal themselves. She was clearly sincere, but it was also apparent that something inside her was broken. One of these cellmates later recalled that she was 'sick' and 'haggard', and her 'large, sad eyes' filled with tears as she spoke.[37†] When Emilia finally sat in the dock that January, still unaware of the situation beyond the prison walls, a witness recorded that 'her

---

* The British War Medal was given to all British, Commonwealth and Allied soldiers serving under British operational command, including those in the Polish Armed Forces. Home Army soldiers, however, while a part of the Polish Armed Forces, were not under British operational command and were therefore excluded.
† Izabella Kwapińska.

testimony was marked by dignity and conviction'.[38] Yet despite having provided many names, she now referred to her team by their pseudonyms and, perhaps to further protect Zo and Wacka, she described their last mission not as an 'official task' but rather a 'girly matter' to encourage other women to return.[39]

Emilia did not flinch when she was given a two-year prison term. She had been 'tragically deceived', the court noted, and her belief that further conspiracy was futile demonstrated 'that she is someone who may still be of value to Polish society'.[40] The crueller sentence came when she was pardoned, just two days later, by the new president of the Republic of Poland on his first day in office.[*] It was only after her release that Emilia came to realise how terribly she had been deceived. Her former lover, with whom she had hoped to flee to Italy, had been sentenced to death.[†] Many of those whose names she had delivered were now in prison, and more were being arrested every day. Later, one recalled being kept naked in an underground dungeon, where it was impossible to stand up straight and 'you constantly stepped on the faeces of your predecessors'.[41] Another reported that when they appealed that they had fought a common enemy and had already been tortured by the Gestapo, their guards screamed back, 'They didn't torment you enough, they didn't torture you enough.'[42]

'Those who broke and incriminated their colleagues by their confessions, felt the worst,' one survivor of the cells later admitted.[43] Emilia was among them. Horrified by the role she had unwittingly played, and desperate to atone, she sent a torrent of letters to the interrogator she had come to trust, demanding he honour their agreement. Instead, he gave another worthless promise that her colleagues would soon be released. Emilia then directed her energies at the new communist cabinet, again demanding the release of those detained. If read, her pleas went unanswered. She wrote appeals to the courts and the press, none of which were published. Eventually, she went on hunger strike as a 'last act of protest'.[44] 'Having fulfilled all obligations towards my country', she wrote, 'I have the right to expect . . . a decision that will prevent my death and the further imprisonment of people loyally exposed to the state.'[45] When she received no response, she started

* President Bolesław Bierut.
† In 1947, Michał Probocha's sentence was commuted to life imprisonment. He was released in 1956.

waiting on the pavement outside the prison gates, an increasingly ema-
ciated but defiant figure drawing public attention to her cause until she
was threatened with being locked into a psychiatric hospital.

'Most worthy Mr President . . .' Emilia swallowed her last remaining
pride and fired a salvo straight to the top.[46] 'Aware of the inadmissi-
bility of further underground work', she had disclosed her colleagues'
names both to end the resistance, she wrote, and to secure their freedom to work for Poland.[47] Raising individual cases, including that of
Bradl, Emilia argued for 'the right of freedom', warning that only the
prisoners' 'immediate release' could build trust in the new government.[48] 'I submit my request to the Most Distinguished President with
the deepest faith in a favourable settlement', she ended her letter.[49]
Once again, her faith was misplaced.

Despite the honour so recently conferred on him for his work at the
Gdańsk shipyards, the state argued that Bradl 'preferred to be a spy
and serve foreigners instead of building Poland'.[50] He was sentenced
to twelve years, commuted to six after appeals. Zofia Franio was also
given a twelve-year sentence for espionage and general 'hostility to the
regime'.[51] Her prison cell, designed for twenty-five people, was quickly
crammed with 120 women – but she still stood out. Her demands for
soup for the sick led to complaints from the kitchen staff, and soon she
was being punished simply for having sewn herself some slippers and
for looking 'out of the window to the courtyard'.[52] When some of the
prisoners requested longer walks, access to books and permission to
pray, they were each rewarded with a stretch in solitary, but Zofia was
singled out for double the time, because of her 'bad attitude'.[53]

⚓

In the parallel world outside the bulging prisons, Zo started her PhD
in January 1948.* Her greatest satisfaction, however, came from
teaching the young adults whose education had been disrupted by the
war. 'These people came straight from the forest, almost with a gun
in their pocket,' she laughed. 'What a pleasure it was to work with
them.'[54] Zo knew what it was to sacrifice dreams and the courage it
took to return to school benches, and her students similarly respected

* With the support of her pre-war mathematics professor, Zdzisław Krygowski, who
had also taught the Enigma codebreakers.

her commitment to them. Knowing how little teachers earned, some would bring her small bags of dried beans, wheat flour and sticks of butter. Once she was given a goose, and on the last day of term they engulfed her with flowers.

Hurrying through the Warsaw streets one early spring morning, head down against the wind, it took Zo a moment to realise that the woman bent almost double ahead of her, 'walking with a tired step, in a coat with a greasy stain', was Emilia.[55] Quickening her pace to catch up, Zo was shocked to see a passer-by suddenly lean in and 'hit her in the face'.[56] Branded a traitor, responsible for the incarceration of dozens of Home Army officers, Emilia had become used to being spat at and abused in the street. A special misogynistic hatred was being directed at her, far exceeding the public censure of Jan Rzepecki, her former chief who had urged her to provide the list of names, and who had also been released. Zo's warmth took Emilia by surprise. 'Elu!' she smiled, using her pet-name for Zo. 'Are you greeting me?'[57] With a stab of guilt, Zo realised that although she had hurried over to say hello, she had not held out her hand, because she knew that Emilia had talked.[58]

The two women walked on together, heading to the prison gate so that Emilia could deliver some parcels. On the way, she told Zo how the security staff had lied and broken their promises, but how she believed that her letter campaigns and hunger strikes were helping to secure the release of several men. Struggling to find work because her name was tarnished, she was suffering from exhaustion, a heart condition and debilitating headaches. Worst of all, she still had no access to her little boy. As far as Zo was concerned, Emilia was another victim of the communist regime, but soon after her public show of friendship Zo was called away.

The once formidable Mariana Zawacka, Zo's mother, was failing. That March, Zo spent her birthday with her family in Toruń. She was a year shy of forty, still fit and strong, and with no dependants she felt guilty for spending so little time with her parents. Dela, her elder sister, still cared for their mother as best she could, but both she and their father were working long hours simply to make ends meet. Within weeks Zo had left her various teaching jobs to return to her home town.

It was in Toruń that Zo learnt of the trial of courageous Witold Pilecki, who had volunteered to enter Auschwitz on a Home Army reconnaissance mission. His subsequent escape had inspired Zo's cousin Leonard to meticulously plan his own breakout. The two men had met again while with the Polish forces in Italy, but while Leonard had elected to stay in London after war, Pilecki had accepted orders to return to communist Poland on an intelligence mission. Arrested in May 1947, after a torturous year in prison Pilecki was sentenced to be executed. Among the judges was Roman Kryże, a man so notorious that his name, appropriately meaning 'Crosses', was seen as shorthand for the death sentence. Zo, however, knew the name for another reason. Before the war, Kryże had married Leonard's sister. Now he was condemning Polish heroes. Ten days later, on 25 May 1948, Pilecki was led into either the subterranean boiler room or the courtyard of Mokotów prison – where Zofia was among the many still being held. Then he was executed by a single shot to the back of the head.

For Zo, the turn of 1949 brought better news: Klara had returned to Poland. Count Folke Bernadotte's white buses had delivered her safely to Sweden, where she had named her parents, two sisters and brother on her entry forms, not knowing that Egon had perished in Auschwitz. She had then spent many months recovering in a school building repurposed as a 'temporary quarantine camp', its rooms 'bathed in blue-grey Swedish summer twilight'.[59] It was only after the war that Klara managed to exchange family letters, and only now that the surviving family were reunited. It was a bitter-sweet moment. Klara and Zo loved each other unconditionally, but both were now carrying heavy burdens. Zo would never shake the guilt she felt at having brought her sister into the resistance only for her to be deported to Ravensbrück, and at not having been able to save Egon. Klara carried the unspeakable pain of her years in the concentration camp.

Like her sister, Klara found relief in throwing herself into service. As the Red Cross had judged that she was not only free of contagious diseases but also had 'no political opinion', she was permitted to return to legal work.[60] It was in a Poznań court that Klara met a historian called Milek, a tall, gentle and 'calm man', Zo noted approvingly, judging him the perfect match for her clever, determined but wounded younger sister.[61*] Their wedding was modest but deeply happy. Klara, wearing a skirt suit and an irrepressible smile, carried a bunch of pale

* Maksymilian 'Milek' Gołembski.

carnations. Milek wore a trouser suit and cheerful polka-dot tie. They settled in Poznań, away from everything except their work and each other.

It was now over four years since the Soviet 'liberation' of Poland, but the UB were still busy. In the early hours of 10 March 1949, a seven-man counter-intelligence squad was sent to arrest Wacka. Having turned down the command of a youth group for the anniversary celebrations for the new republic, she had been wondering when her turn might come. While Wacka was in detention, Maria Wittek was also arrested, along with several others. Wittek had proved useful as a figurehead to relaunch women's military training in post-war Poland, but had since been quietly removed. Nothing more was heard of either woman while the UB carried out their investigations.

That May, Emilia started visiting her few remaining friends. A cousin noticed how thin she looked as, in lighter moments, she joked distractedly about her 'old otter face', or sat more seriously, fretfully repeating 'they are not letting them out'.[62] She was clearly depressed. 'I have failed in every aspect of my life,' she told another companion.[63] 'I trusted people and they deceived me', and now that her child had been taken from her, 'I have nothing and nobody to live for.'[64] She 'had come to say goodbye', she told a former colleague a few days later.[65]

Pentecost, the seventh Sunday after Easter, is a national holiday in Poland. In 1949, it fell on 5 June, a warm, sunny day, encouraging people to celebrate with picnics after church. Waiting until her building was quiet, Emilia swallowed a handful of sleeping pills, climbed into a warm bath and, pushing her dark wet hair away from her face, neatly slit her wrists. It did not take long for her weak heart to fail as her blood darkened the bathwater. She was just forty-one years old and a hero of the resistance, yet she died ashamed and alone. Her body was found late that afternoon, as cool as the bathtub that held her.

Widely considered a traitor, Emilia was not buried among her fallen comrades in Warsaw's historic Powązki military cemetery. She was quietly laid to rest in a civilian graveyard in a rebuilt northern suburb of the capital. Perhaps, the few mourners consoled one another, she might be moved 'when better times came'.[66]

Better times did, at last, seem to be coming. Wacka and Maria Wittek were both released without trial after several months in detention, having signed agreements that if they spoke about their experiences they would each face five years in prison. Wittek was reduced to working in a newspaper kiosk and Wacka could not find any work for over a year, but they were free. Zo was now teaching at several schools in and around Toruń, undisturbed by the UB and keen to keep it that way.

In February 1950, a nurse who Zo had known during the war visited her to arrange a meeting with 'a mutual friend' at an elegant old address in Kraków.* Her curiosity piqued, Zo turned up to find Andrzej Czaykowski waiting for her, the officer she had last met when they had debated politics in the optimistic early days of the Warsaw Uprising. Andrzej's sister, a close friend of Zo's, had been killed in the fighting not long after. Having seen out the end of the war in a German POW camp, Andrzej had secretly returned to Poland in 1949, three years after Witold Pilecki and on a similar mission. 'There will soon be a war between the Soviet Union and England,' he told Zo earnestly, asking her to supply intelligence including food prices, policy changes, and the Polish population's shifting attitude towards the new regime.[67] He was sending the information back to London hidden inside crates of books.

Having heard him out, Zo was emphatic. She had had 'enough of conspiracy', she told him.[68] She was a teacher, 'a good job' of real value, and she 'did not want to become a spy'.[69] Once again, it seemed to her that the Poles in London were out of touch with the realities of life inside the country they aimed to represent. She yearned for freedom, the release of her friends, justice for Emilia, and the chance to work for Poland without fear, but she could not believe that another war was imminent. Surely such intelligence was of more value for the British than for the Poles, she said, and, 'Why should we be laying down our lives for England?'[70] Then she hurried away.

Zo's mother, Marianna, died at home that May, her husband and daughters at her side. Zo planted an elm tree to shade her grave. It was 'the tree I loved the most', she wrote, evoking memories of her childhood home on Elm Street, now the site of 'a concrete housing estate with no space for elms'.[71]† Zo was distraught that she had not been able to get the medicine her mother had needed, but it was Dela, who had never left home and hardly left her mother's side, who was

* Wanda Kryńska, nurse and close friend of Andrzej Czaykowski's sister, Halina.
† Ulica Wiąz, Toruń.

hit hardest. For Dela, Zo saw, 'the world collapsed'.[72]

To honour their mother's memory while staying close to Dela, Zo now took teaching jobs in the region where Marianna had grown up. This largely rural area had not yet recovered from the destruction of the war years and the clear social need gave Zo a renewed sense of purpose. After a few months, she moved into a staff apartment consisting of one room and a kitchenette in a converted barracks on what was now called Stalingrad Street, in a small town not far from Toruń.* As well as teaching, she organised 'Polish Service' camps to help with local reconstruction and, despite knowing that tending the graves of Home Army soldiers was considered an offence, she helped to restore the local cemeteries. She also organised outreach classes. 'It was very joyful,' she felt, travelling around, and over time some of her work evolved into one of the earliest correspondence courses in Poland.[73]

At the end of the 1951 academic year, the state brought in an exam to assess the politics of the country's teaching staff. Both outraged and nonplussed to be asked about the laws of Marxism, Zo failed decisively. Two years earlier she had been reclassified as a temporary teacher, officially due to the break in her career but in effect a political warning. Now the authorities officially requested that 'Citizen Zawacka should be evaluated as far as her political and moral attitudes are concerned', and she was put on probation.[74] If she did not pass the exam on a retake that autumn, she would lose her licence to teach.

When the new academic year started in September, Zo was kept busy invigilating the entrance exams for the next student intake. As these took place in the evenings, it was usually dark by the time she headed to her rooms in the former barrack building. On 5 September, 'I saw a shadow' cross the courtyard, she recalled but, looking around, found 'there was no one else there'.[75] Only a few teachers and their families as yet lived in the forbidding building, and none of the lights were on. Striding over to the main entrance, Zo climbed the stairs to the second floor two at a time, key in hand. As soon as she opened her door, two men pushed in behind her. 'They were already waiting for me,' she realised too late.[76]

The two security officers sat on Zo's flimsy couch. A third had been in the courtyard, the shadow she had seen, ready to block any escape. Later, she learnt that her neighbours had been detained in their own

* Olsztyn.

apartments, so they could not warn her. As Zo watched, the men undertook a thorough search. 'All the . . . bedding was torn apart, couch torn apart, floor ripped up, walls torn apart,' she reported, but nothing was discovered.[77] Still they weren't finished.

The inventory of Zo's possessions made poor reading. 'A worn red wallet', two keys, a toothbrush, face powder compact and 'one pair of socks' were duly listed.[78] Among some letters, her diary and 'a large prayer book' beside her Remington typewriter, they found 'some documents confirming the death of Egon Zawacki'.[79] They did not list the neatly organised academic material they discovered, including her draft doctoral thesis, all of which was either lost or 'completely destroyed'.[80] Eventually, they found a spool of thread with a ten-dollar note hidden inside – the demobilisation pay from Farmstead that Zo had given her mother five years earlier. Marianna had never spent the cash, and Zo had taken the reel as a keepsake. It was an imprisonable offence to have foreign currency in the Republic of Poland. She was, the security men decided, 'criminally liable'.[81]

Telling her to get dressed, one of the officers held up her ski trousers. Zo skied poorly, but having once had to cross the Pyrenees in a skirt suit and jumper she had invested in the trousers when she saw them on a market. Yet she refused to be dictated to, and could not imagine why she should need them, or why she would be arrested. 'It is autumn,' she said. 'Why would I need warm ski trousers?'[82] So they led her away in her brown cotton dress and sandals.

17

Having the Time to Achieve Something
(September 1951–February 1955)

Zo started laughing as she was walked towards her cell. The sound echoed around the gallery, combining with the sonorous slaps of her sandals on the metal walkway. Zo loved her country. She had been prepared to lose her life as a soldier during the war, and she had dedicated herself to the national reconstruction afterwards. But the absurdity of her arrest now was too much to process. Stepping through another heavy doorframe, the narrow cell in front of her made her think of 'an inverted drawer' from a filing cabinet, and the 'unpleasant slam' of the door behind only made her laugh harder.[1] It was all so clichéd, the scrape of the key in the lock, the dying footsteps, even the look of horror on her cellmate's face as she stared at the apparent madwoman who had just arrived. Well, 'it was quite a shock', was all Zo later offered.[2]

She had been escorted from her rooms the previous evening, and taken under guard over one hundred miles south by rail. With some panache, she managed to buy herself a beer on the train. Eventually she arrived at the red brick monolith of the Ministry of Public Security in Warsaw, 'a terrible place' she later told a friend, where she was photographed and fingerprinted.[3] 'She is 163cm', the officers reported assiduously. 'Blonde, blonde eyebrows, large long ears, broad mouth . . . hooked nose.'[4] She speaks German, French and a little English in a 'high pitched voice', they added, ignoring the soft Pomeranian lilt of Zo's Polish and the perfect Berlin accent of her German. She has 'no known habits'.[5]

Preliminary interrogations had started immediately. Taken to the basement, Zo was surprised to be asked whether she knew Andrzej Czaykowski. She did. He was the brother of a friend killed in the Warsaw Uprising. When asked if they had ever met overseas, she admitted that they had spoken briefly in London, in 1943, before meeting again during a lull in the Uprising the following year. She did not mention that in 1949 Andrzej had asked her to gather intelligence for the Polish government now operating in London isolation. After all, she had refused to help him and 'that', she felt, 'was the end of it'.[6] Most new prisoners were kept in the ministry building for three or four days, but the next morning Zo had been escorted back up to the entrance hall. It was only when she had been put in a car for Mokotów prison that she had started to become really concerned.

Mokotów was where the most serious enemies of the communist regime were brought. On arrival, Zo's money, her white Watex watch and her black Polux fountain pen were all confiscated. In their place, she was given a metal bowl and spoon and some cotton pants. She was lucky to get these; the place was in turmoil. There had been three hundred arrests the night before, and talk of a polio epidemic in the city meant that the guards were particularly on edge. Little wonder that Zo had been herded so quickly towards her cell. It was only once inside that she had time to collect herself. Mokotów prison was where Emilia had been held. As far as Zo knew, Zofia and Bradl might still in the cells, and Witold Pilecki had been among the many executed there.

Zofia and Bradl *were* both still serving time, but not at Mokotów. After his brutal interrogations, Bradl had been sent to a labour camp. There, it was noted, he tried to 'associate with those who were known for their most reactionary attitudes' and 'disseminated hostile propaganda'.[7] As a result, he was retained in custody after his sentence expired. In protest, he went on hunger strike but a second trial resulted in an additional ten-year sentence.

Zofia had been transferred to Fordon, the toughest women's prison in Poland, just thirty miles northwest of Toruń. Already branded a difficult prisoner, she made no effort to appease her jailers. 'Prisoner Zofia Franio . . . is a critical enemy to the regime during walks', her guards reported. 'She tries to connect with prisoners from other cells, for which she is punished.'[8] Early transgressions earnt her the humiliation of being forced to wear flannel knickers sewn from men's underwear. Soon she was being put in solitary confinement, in a basement cell, for ever-longer periods. After over a year spent with almost no company, no light, no air to breath in summer and no warmth in winter, Zofia became 'increasingly withdrawn and silent'.[9]

Andrzej Czaykowski, however, was in Mokotów. Records show that he had confessed to being an intelligence agent of a hostile overseas power, a couple of weeks before Zo's arrest. Although admitting to having tried to recruit Zo, he had made clear that she had refused to co-operate, having 'had enough of conspiracy'.[10] Nevertheless, Zo's was just one of ninety-six names connected with Andrzej, prompting the state security service to, as they put it, 'liquidate this espionage web'.[11]

At 1am on her first night in Mokotów, Zo was woken by an officer shouting 'E Zet' into her cell. Not permitted to wear clothes at night, she had to stand as she was, then quickly pull on the dress that was bundled in the corridor. Stumbling forward, she was herded into an interrogation room where, her eyes dazzled by angled lights, she walked into the three metal legs of an upturned stool. As she stooped to right it, scraping the stool across the floor, she was shoved down by a hand on her shoulder. She was to sit on the stool as it was, its sharp feet pressing into her rump and her thighs. Perching gingerly at first, she pressed her feet down on the floor to surreptitiously raise herself a little, lifting her legs in turn as she shifted position. It was only now she realised how heavy she was. Her muscles quickly aching from the effort, she felt the metal feet of the stool start to bore into her flesh.

Zo tried to focus, sweating with the effort, but the same questions were repeated time and again. When had she met Andrzej Czajkowski? Where? How did she know him? Why did she have ten dollars in her flat? Any gesticulation, any shaking or shift in her weight, brought renewed spikes of pain in her legs and flaring up her spine. Willing herself to be calm and still, Zo repeated her answers, mentally gripping on to them like a rope that would either save or hang her. She had to tell the truth. She believed in her innocence. Only an hour later, when she had signed off each page of the interrogation report, was she hauled back to her cell, her bleeding legs still trembling.

These torturous night-time interrogations were repeated until the security service had a long report, and Zo was unable to sit or even stand straight. Soon she was also experiencing chest pains and she lost several teeth, yet she told herself that she would endure. Zo believed that her treatment was 'nothing compared with what others had to suffer'.[12] Nevertheless, in November she collapsed in her cell with a raging fever. At first the prison doctors thought she might be pregnant; she had been complaining of acute pain in her lower abdomen for some time, but tests revealed a non-cancerous ovarian cyst. The tumour, the size of a 'newborn's head', was surgically removed in the prison hospital, under local anaesthetic.[13] She was then left alone to recover.

ජ

A week had passed before Zo's family were informed about her arrest. Her 82-year-old father, Władysław Zawacki, had immediately travelled to Warsaw with a parcel of warm clothing, but he was not allowed to see his daughter and the parcel did not reach her. Klara, now a judge in Poznań, focused on trying to get Zo's research papers to her so she could continue working on her doctorate, knowing this was what her sister would be craving. She also organised the collection of Zo's salary, half of which was still being paid while her court case was pending. Neither of them had yet heard anything from Zo herself.

In December 1951, the state security services decided they had assembled sufficient material to convict Zo, although there were still gaps in their reports. 'She didn't serve in the army', they noted at one point, and had 'no medals'.[14] For once, the lack of recognition of women in the armed forces had served Zo well. Nevertheless, her trial was set for the following January on the basis that she had met Andrzej 'to collect and transfer spy material', and had kept 'a ten-dollar bill in a spool of thread . . . without the permission of the Foreign Exchange Office'.[15]

As a civilian accused of a political crime, namely espionage for the benefit of a foreign intelligence service, Zo's case was heard in Warsaw's new military district court. 'I do not agree with the presentation of the indictment, so I will explain,' she boldly started her testimony, with little attempt to keep the contempt from her voice.[16] She then repeated the facts that were now drilled into her brain. She had not known who she was going to meet. When he had tried to recruit her, she had 'refused straight away'.[17] The dollars were a keepsake from her mother. She was, she pleaded, not guilty.

Brought to the witness stand, an ill-looking Andrzej largely corroborated Zo's story but mentioned that she had 'hesitated', presenting the possibility that she had considered his proposal.[18] A petition that had been raised in support of her, given the limited evidence, was now dismissed. The prosecution then argued that, as someone experienced in intelligence work, Zo should have known not to attend a secret meeting and should have, in any case, reported Andrzej to the authorities. 'There is a huge reserve of bad will in her', they concluded before emphasising the 'great social danger posed by her deed'. Given the 'characteristic efforts of the imperialist camp to develop secret intelligence', they demanded a conviction.[19]

A poorly spelt report, typed later that day, recorded that Zo received two years for meeting Andrzej, and a further year for keeping the dollars. 'In total it will be five years', the author concluded incongruously.[20] Another account gave her five years for the meeting, and a further year, to be served concurrently, for possession of the dollars. Either way, Zo was lucky. Another woman convicted of working for an American intelligence network, for which she was believed to have been paid in watches and stockings as well as dollars, had been sentenced to life imprisonment.[*] Zo had been spared the same, perhaps even the death sentence, only because in focusing so tightly on her meeting with Andrzej, the authorities had not discovered her brief stint with the anti-communist resistance in the first years after the war. Investigations were usually more thorough, with no detail overlooked. As Zo was returned to Mokotów, even her unlucky ten dollars was transferred to the treasury.

Zo's case would be reviewed several times over 1952, each investigation leading to further interrogations. In May and June, Klara requested a lawyer for her sister, and then the name of her counsel – which was denied. Despite there being no new evidence of espionage activity, in the first retrial the state determined that simply by agreeing to meet someone whose identity she did not know, 'it is quite unambiguous that her object was to start co-operation'.[21] Her sentence was increased to seven years.

It was only now, ten months after her arrest, that Zo's first message reached her father, carried on a prison postcard. After sentencing she was permitted to write once a month, and Klara was granted a first visit that August. The sisters planned a request for clemency, which Klara sent directly to the Polish president. It brought no response. In November, Zo finally received the package of warm clothes brought by her father the year before, but not a blanket he had sent since. Later that month, her case was re-examined in the Mokotów prison courtroom. Summoned without warning from her prison duties, she testified cautiously this time, saying only that she had nothing further to add. The court did, however – another three years; making ten

---

[*] Maria Śliwińska-Walczuk, pseudonym 'Krysia'. See IPN, Digital Archive, 5382–4 (140) 21 – BU 1019–1054.

altogether. Her release date was set for 5 September 1961.

Zo was now being punished not only for unwittingly meeting a spy, but also for failing to provide useful information on anyone else. Giving up on her, in December she was transferred to the now infamous Fordon prison, where Zofia Franio had been incarcerated. A former garrison, the Nazis had once stationed troops in the building while they were preparing a nearby site for executions. The first of over 6,000 female prisoners had arrived in 1940, Klara possibly among those passing through on their way to Ravensbrück. Now women once again filled the largely windowless cells, twelve in each, sharing their stories, their rations and their lice. The food was appalling, and the sentences uniformly long. Fordon was a place with a history of terror that offered depressingly little hope.

Adapting to survive, Zo told Klara not to waste the family's meagre funds on lawyers but simply to write more often, and to visit whenever possible. Her monthly letters to her family showed how much she missed them, asking for photographs, remembering birthdays, recalling the anniversary of her mother's death and fussing about her grave. She liked to imagine that on her release she would live with her father and Dela. Meanwhile, she started work in the prison kitchens, scrubbing vegetables, making bread and washing dishes to help pass the days. It was comforting to discover that several of her fellow prisoners had served their country during the war, including some alongside Zofia.* But there were also many younger women, most of whom were illiterate.

Education was prohibited in Fordon, as were pens and pencils – except to write the monthly letter home. As they sat peeling vegetables, Zo started to teach the women by carving letters into potatoes and printing starchy words on the walls, the tabletops and plates. Soap was good for writing too. Even the prison toothpowder could be mixed with water in tin mugs and used for secret lessons. Soon Zo was teaching languages, mathematics and geometry as well as literacy, and learning law and biology herself. The women tried to hide their tutoring, but when inmates who had arrived unable to read started writing letters home, an investigation was conducted. Zo was punished by having her privileges removed – fewer rations, more chores and less

* Helena, aka 'Pufka', was among the female prisoners from Zofia Franio's sapper teams. Zofia had been moved from Fordon by the time Zo arrived.

exercise on the prison walkway. This last was particularly hard, as from there she had liked to watch the River Vistula, whose waters, she knew, had recently flowed past Toruń.

⚓

On 5 March 1953, Joseph Stalin 'choked to death' on his own body fluids following a stroke some days earlier.[22] During the political 'thaw' that followed, state repression in Poland started to ease and the families of political prisoners began to petition for their release. 'My sister does not feel any hatred towards the Soviet people . . .' Zofia's brother wrote. She 'is a sick, weak, elderly woman'.[23] Although only in her fifties, after so long spent in solitary confinement Zofia looked the part. With her grey hair tied back with a thin dark ribbon, Zofia's gaunt face was now dominated by deeply bruised eyes. 'Let her come back to life', her brother entreated.[24]

Zo's father also wrote to request leniency, noting that he was 'an old man of eighty-two years'. 'I am begging, I am asking for your mercy to acquit her . . . I would like to see her again at home before I die,' he beseeched the authorities.[25] 'If my daughter made a mistake, she has already suffered for it . . .' She now 'wants to work for Poland and . . . be a useful citizen.'[26] As if to emphasise the point, Zo requested official permission to start teaching her fellow prisoners, dryly explaining that 'because of my difficult material conditions . . . I cannot go myself personally to bring this request forward'.[27]

Not all such petitions were successful. Andrzej Czaykowski, too badly beaten to attend his own trial, was executed at Mokotów prison in October 1953. Not long after, however, both Zo and Zofia were at least transferred to the less harsh conditions of Grudziądz prison. For the first time in two years, Zo had access to books and newspapers. She could also earn money by sewing linen underwear, which she largely spent on prison chocolate, relishing the now unfamiliar sweetness on her tongue. Zofia was working in the prison surgery but, before they could meet, Zo was transferred again.

Bojanów prison, on the site of a former labour camp, was being used to detain Polish, German and Ukrainian girls between the ages of eighteen and twenty-one. Most were petty criminals. Some were prostitutes. Others were schoolgirls sentenced to up to fifteen years for political agitation. All those serving time for membership of illegal

organisations were required to take classes run by 'political educa-
tors'.[28] This way, the regime hoped to release good communist citizens
back into society, but the first step often had to be classes in basic
literacy and numeracy. Zo had been brought in to teach mathematics.

Among her new students was a skinny nineteen-year-old called
Bernadeta Gołecka. After months of interrogation, Bernadeta had
been served seven years for 'spreading anti-state gossip, gathering
firearms . . . and violent attempts at changing the political system of
Poland'.[29] A healthy, dimpled teenager when she entered the prison
system, by the time Zo met her she was so weak that the prison doctor
expected her to die. Several young inmates had already passed away
from exhaustion, while others had committed suicide by cutting their
veins or swallowing the chlorine used to disinfect waste water.

'My beloved Elżbieta Zawacka immediately stood out among the
lost youth', Bernadeta wrote, 'not only for her wisdom but also for her
cheerfulness and kindness . . . which she tried to instil in others'.[30] Zo
was not only teaching mathematics, but also empathy, hope and survival. She and Bernadeta shared an 'austere' cell with over twenty other
women, all sleeping on hard metal bunk beds.[31] 'Very demanding' from
the start, Zo insisted that the girls kept things in order, made their
beds, folded their clothes, and planned for their futures.[32] She 'was a
model for us', Bernadeta said.[33] 'She could endure anything. Nothing
could break her' and 'despite the chief's contempt and constant humiliation' she showed that they had nothing to be ashamed of.[34]

Eventually Zo persuaded the prison director to let her teach the
guards as well. Within a few months she was running a correspondence course linked to the nearby high school, enabling both prisoners
and guards to obtain school diplomas.[35] Classes became a 'joy', she
felt, and serving a few years was no longer so terrible if what mattered
'was having the time to achieve something'.[36]

෴

Of the estimated 300,000 Poles arrested between 1944 and 1956, Zo
had been relatively fortunate; 6,000 had been sentenced to death, and
many more simply 'disappeared'.* With Poland's borders with the west

---

* Approximately 20,000 Poles died in communist prisons up to 1963. The veterans
among them are now known as the 'cursed soldiers'.

still virtually sealed, some of the country's British friends turned their attention to the Poles overseas. Sue Ryder, the FANY with whom Zo had once shared a room, had volunteered as a humanitarian visitor at former concentration camps, then started visiting Berlin's prisons – where many camp survivors were incarcerated for both petty and serious crimes. Most were young, with no documents, money or hope. 'In a few short hours I will be taken to a place of execution . . .' one wrote in a note for his father, entrusted to Ryder. 'We must die at the hands of our allies for shooting the SS who killed our families . . .'[37] Ryder got forty death sentences commuted and over a thousand Poles released. In 1953, while Zo was still in prison, Ryder organised the first of her refuges for victims of the war. Soon she was running eighty temporary homes in fifteen countries.*

⚓

The Polish state reviewed Zo's case for the last time in February 1955, ruling that her sole crime was her 'failure to notify the authorities' about Andrzej Czaykowski.[38] With her sentence slashed to five years, she was scheduled for immediate release. 'This will pass, and we will survive,' Zo whispered to Bernadeta, promising that they would meet again on the outside.[39] Ten days later she left prison, wearing the same cotton dress and sandals as the day she had been arrested. In her arms she carried her few possessions and 720 zlotys in payment for her years of prison work. Her father, Władysław, increasingly deaf and unsteady on his feet, Dela and Klara were waiting for her in the wind-swept February street, ready to hug, argue or drag her back to Toruń. For once, Zo went passively. She needed time and rest to work out the best way to fight for her country again.

---

* The organisation became the Sue Ryder Foundation.

18

In the Polish People's Republic
(February 1955–April 1978)

Zo was released into a new incarnation of her country. Not only had
the 'Polish People's Republic' been officially proclaimed in 1952, while
she was still behind bars, but the communist authorities had also been
at great pains to enforce the Soviet version of Second World War history. She wondered how veterans like herself, who had been there,
were expected to respond to this new reality. She soon discovered that
no response *was* required.

'The Great Patriotic War', as Stalin had designated the recent conflict, was now being presented as having started in 1941 – when the
Nazi German invasion of their territory had forced the Soviets join
the Allies. This neatly circumvented the earlier Nazi–Soviet pact, and
the Russian invasion of eastern Poland in 1939. The deportation of
over a million Poles to the gulags went unmentioned, while the massacre of the 22,000 officers at Katyń, including Klara's fiancé, had
been blamed on the Nazis.* The Poles were presented as having been
betrayed by their government, and entirely indebted to the Russians for
their liberation.† Everything from statues to schoolbooks supported
this narrative, and people contradicting it were still disappearing. Zo
could no more accept the theft of her country's history than she could
its freedom. But her immediate priority was to find paid employment.

Zo had lost her last teaching role because she had 'not shown up
for work' after her arrest in 1951.[1] Four years later, the school's board
decided that although 'her ideological attitude in the course of teaching . . . was correct', they could not reinstate her because her arrest
'was known and had been commented upon'.[2] Although Poland was

---

* Soviet Russian forces executed the 22,000 men at Katyń, Charków and Miednoje.
† The Red Army had liberated Polish territory from Nazi German armed forces, in
their own time, often fighting alongside Polish partisans, many of whom were later
arrested.

desperate for teachers, suddenly some education authorities needed a 'detailed opinion' on her 'social-political work', while others could not afford her possible health bills as an ex-convict.[3]

Eventually, Zo was offered occasional work as a nightwatchman. Maria Wittek was still manning a newspaper kiosk, and other paroled friends had also accepted whatever work they could get. Zo was having none of it. Borrowing a dress, as her own were too worn, she headed to the Ministry of Education in Warsaw. The reconstruction in the capital astounded her, but at every step she wondered whether she was walking over the bones of the dead. None of the new buildings had basements. No one was digging down. Zo parked herself inside the ministry and refused to leave until she was handed a permit to teach, typed on official letterhead. It still took several months before she found a school that would employ her.

After the death of Poland's communist president, from a sudden heart attack while in Moscow the following spring, a slightly softer line began to prevail.* Zo found teaching work, and Zofia Franio and Bradl were among the several thousand political prisoners given their freedom. Zofia had served over nine years inside but having pledged to be a good citizen, she returned to work in public health. Bradl was released later that year, officially due to 'poor health'. His hair had turned silver during his incarceration, and he was missing some teeth and several months of memories.

In 1958, Zo was at her father's bedside when he died. Now the three Zawacka sisters were alone. Klara, a municipal judge in Poznań, was happily married but the mistreatment she had endured in Ravensbrück meant she could not have children. Dela had devoted her life to her parents, and now found fulfilment in her Catholic faith. 'Of course, you sometimes regret not having your own family and own children,' was as much as Zo would say.[4] 'But that's how things turned out . . . it still seems to me that I can do something useful.'[5] That something was teaching, which was vital for Poland's socio-economic recovery, and it paid her bills. But the death of her father also prompted her to think more about her nation's history. Once again, she thought, nobody was digging down.

Farmstead's main archives had been among the many Home Army records lost during the Warsaw Uprising. Much of the surviving

* President Bolesław Bierut.

documentation had been deliberately destroyed since, for fear the secret police might use it as evidence against former resisters. Zo now wrote to Wacka, to see what she recalled of their service. 'My love', she opened, their lasting bond clear on the page, 'you were in Farmstead, so you should be involved in figuring it all out.'[6] But Wacka replied that, although willing, the need 'to forget or deny knowledge, erasing from your memory everything that could potentially harm others' had 'made my memory disappear'.[7] Reclaiming their history seemed a hopeless task.

As an entire generation's studies had been disrupted by war, while continuing to teach Zo started a new PhD dissertation on distance learning, publishing a series of articles to promote the concept. She was finally awarded her doctorate in 1965. Although she had not been able to clear her criminal record, she was now offered the position of principal of a Toruń correspondence school. There was just one condition. She would have to become a card-carrying member of the communist Polish United Workers Party. Refusing, a few months later she instead took a lesser post with the adult education college in Gdańsk.

These were turbulent years in Poland, as rising inflation and stagnant wages coincided with heavy state censorship and the persecution of Polish academics and intellectuals. The banning of a provocative play in Warsaw, in 1968, was all it took to ignite protests on the streets.[*] Although many demonstrators were singing the socialist anthem 'The Internationale', the state riot squads went on the attack, badly beating hundreds even as they tried to disperse. Within days, the protests had spread to Gdańsk. That March, Zo's students joined a 20,000-strong demonstration that clashed violently with the police late at night. In April, the regime resorted to a nationalist campaign promoted through the media, playing on antisemitism to deflect blame for the unrest. By the time order had been restored, with significant changes to both the political leadership and national policy, the seeds had been sewn for later political agitation.

Zo had never been party political, hating the squabbles between different factions that had weakened the Polish leadership during the war. But she had always, fervently, supported the principles of liberty and democracy. Now she had witnessed the vulnerability of the communist regime for the first time, she wondered whether restoring a sense of

---

[*] The play was Adam Mickiewicz, *Dziady* ['Forefather's Eve'].

pride in the Home Army might help to inspire the new generation. The National Communists, an increasingly influential political faction, were also trying to harness Polish patriotism to their cause through a campaign that was both deeply antisemitic, and also commemorated war time resistance for the first time, if in terms acceptable to the regime.* Their new histories celebrated the Polish communist forces while portraying Home Army officers as reactionaries, if not fascists. Furthermore, Zo bridled, the accounts were 'almost completely silent on the participation of women . . . half of the population'.[8] It was, she felt, another 'kind of falsification of history' and 'obviously harmful to society as a whole'.[9]

Zo started by writing to those who had served alongside her, trusted her and might be willing to share their recollections. She signed off her letters as 'Zo', at once conspiratorial and commanding, hoping this might help open doors. 'Of course, if I'm needed . . . just let me know what I need to do,' Wacka replied gamely, but others urged caution.[10] 'There are many reasons why I am against', Zo's former liaison officer Hanka Michalska wrote.[11] 'Neither the times nor the atmosphere is right', making the work both 'senseless and danger-ous'.[12] In any case, Hanka continued, 'is anyone willing to confess their personal experiences' and 'who would be willing to pass all of this on to the unknown reader'?[13] Zo was undeterred. Redoubling her efforts, she wrote to friends across Poland and overseas, and roped in her students, until she had a team of 'volunteers' helping to gather testimonies.

As the old networks started to bear new fruit, Zo spent her evenings developing a standardised questionnaire, then logging the responses onto index cards, her spidery handwriting never entirely replaced by her use of an old Remington typewriter. Celina Zawodzińska queried her approach, given how nervous people were of state surveillance, but was nevertheless happy to help. Unlike her sisters, 'Marianna and Stefa, who were head over ears in it', Celina felt her time Ravensbrück had prevented her from contributing enough during the war.[14] Focused on her self-imposed mission, Zo accepted her help almost thought-lessly. 'I have unravelled your sweater', Celina wrote prosaically at the end of one long letter. 'A lot of wool from the sleeves was lost. One

---

* The antisemitic political campaign of 1968, instigated by General Moczar, also led to the emigration of thousands of surviving Polish Jews.

should not wear [clothes] so long without mending.'[15] It was clear that both women were still living on a shoestring.

As the veteran testimonies began to intersect, Zo was able to chart decisions and corroborate actions, learning of both heroism and betrayals. 'Dear Mr Bradl,' she wrote, using her old friend's wartime nom-de-guerre, 'for under that name you remain in my memory'.[16] She wanted details of the other couriers he had helped through France, and his memories of Emilia. 'Don't be afraid of detailed descriptions: the smoother the story, the sweeter it will be', she urged him, and 'do not be discouraged if you do not cover every point in detail . . . an incomplete account is better than no account at all. Encourage others . . .'[17] Each response brought new avenues to pursue, and Zo started a list of women who deserved military honours. But not every former colleague welcomed her enquiries.

In 1942, Saba's confession, obtained through torture after her capture, had led to Klara's arrest, and to the execution of many others.* When Zo arrived to interview her, she was shocked to find that Saba 'thought I had come to execute a sentence'.[18] After reassurances, Saba bravely answered Zo's questions and Zo noted down the 'very lengthy and cruel torture' she had endured, that she had been deported to Auschwitz, and that Klara had called her conduct 'heroic'.[19] Zo could forgive, she had done long ago, but she could not forget.

By the end of the 1960s, Zo was recognised as 'as an exceptional specialist' in the field of adult remote education through radio, television and correspondence courses, and her work was winning awards.[20] She was so valued by what was now Gdańsk University that when, in 1972, the state became concerned about her growing authority and leant on them to terminate her contract, they did not bow to the pressure. After the award of her post-doctoral higher degree, she was even promoted to associate professor. Her next ambition was 'to create an Open University, like the one in England'.[21] Swallowing some pride, she signed a new government oath confirming that her 'attitude as a teacher will be consistent with socialist teaching', and swore to educate her students 'to become ideological and enlightened citizens of the Polish People's Republic'.[22] It was a bitter pill, but soon paid dividends. By the mid-1970s she was a member of the UNESCO council for correspondence education, presenting her research in Leipzig, Magdeburg

* Saba was Jadwiga Zatorska.

and Moscow – although conferences in America and Sweden, on the better-lit side of the Iron Curtain, remained out of bounds.[*]

As her reputation grew and she travelled more, Zo became increasingly concerned about the security of the secret Home Army papers in her apartment. It was still illegal to own foreign language literature or Polish works published overseas, and a collection of personal accounts testifying to an alternative version of recent Polish history would have been incendiary. Eventually, she asked a post-graduate student, a great-nephew of General Stefan Rowecki, to act as a gatekeeper.[†]

In 1975, Zo left Gdańsk to accept a post at the university in Toruń.[‡] Although established after the war, this institution had a reputation for reactionary politics and only Stalin's death had saved it from closure in the 1950s. But although a fan of defiance in the right place, Zo would not tolerate any in her lectures. She was 'demanding', her students agreed.[23] Now in her late sixties, Zo's eyesight was poor and she was losing her hearing. Typically, she started tutorials by winding up a kitchen egg-timer so as not to have to keep peering at her watch. She was too deaf to hear it herself and 'in time we got used to this ticking,' one of her students sighed.[24] Gingerly trying to butter her up, they brought her a bouquet on her name-day. 'I don't want flowers,' she barked. 'Take them and put them on the monument to the victims of the war.'[25]

Yet Zo was also widely admired. Rumours circulated about her impressive war service, her self-confidence was contagious, and she was devoted to her students, often offering extra tutorials at home. She had taken a small flat on the eighth floor of a communist tower block, on a street named after the Soviet cosmonaut Yuri Gagarin.[§] There, high above the Toruń suburbs, pairs of students would cut a swathe

---

[*] Her presence in America might have caused surprise. A 1963 article in the country's Polish-language newspaper, *Ameryka Echo*, had presumed the Warsaw Uprising 'losses ... includes the only woman Cichociemny, Zo'. See B. Marek Nadolczak, 'About Women Parachutists and Cichociemni' (1 Sep 1963).

[†] The Polish historian Bogdan Chrzanowski.

[‡] UMK – *Uniwersytet Mikołaj Kopernik* [Nicolaus Copernicus University]. Copernicus is Toruń's most famous son. His statue there survived the war because the Nazis considered him German.

[§] Yuri Gagarin, pilot, cosmonaut, Soviet hero and international celebrity, died in 1968 having become the first person to orbit the Earth in 1961.

through the piles of books and papers on the floor to perch on Zo's rather hard regulation-issue sofa. Among the academic material and her own historical research now filling her shelves were many volumes of poetry, prose and drama as well as English, French and German classics, some printed in Gothic script, and a beautiful old edition of *Don Quixote*.

To Zo's surprise, in 1976 the state approved her application to visit Britain and consult with 'academics in the field of adult education'.[26] It would be her first visit to the west since 1943. Then it had taken a perilous two months to reach London, travelling on forged papers through what had been the Nazi Third Reich. She had been half-drowned while crossing occupied France, shot at by border guards in the Pyrenees, and deserted by her own compatriots in Spain. Now her passport photograph showed a stern-looking woman in heavy, plastic-framed glasses. Yet she was dressed in a remarkably similar skirt suit and shirt, just a couple of sizes up, when she boarded the Soviet-made aircraft that would take her direct to London in just a few hours. Her seat was upholstered, there were curtains at the windows and a uniformed flight attendant offered her a drink. It was an entirely unremarkable journey but, at the same time, astounding.*

In London, Zo stayed with one of her wartime colleagues. Nick-named 'Diana' because she could swim, drive, ride horses and fly gliders, the impressive Halina Martin had transported weapons and forged documents, monitored the radio, and carried the wounded to safety while running intelligence contacts during the Warsaw Uprising. Despite a leg wound, she had reached Britain in 1946, then returned for communist surveillance before making it back in the 1950s. The two women were close. 'You are . . . so beautiful', Zo later wrote to thank her friend, so 'distinguished and witty, and yet so familiar'.[27] Nevertheless, that first night Zo excused herself early. Halina noticed that her light stayed on late into the night. Zo was checking every detail on her list of Farmstead women who deserved decorations.

The next morning, Zo did not visit her academic contacts. She took a bus straight to the Polish Verification Commission, run by her exiled government. There she submitted her list, promising to deliver any medals they could get to her. Halina, Zo's host, would refuse hers, wanting no reward for the service she saw as her duty. At least one

---

* Services to London had been re-established in 1958.

other woman would not be honoured. Zo had also delivered her account of Saba's war service, 'these sad remarks' as she described them, to the commission.[28] It gave her no pleasure, but she believed emphatically that honours should be earned not by sacrifice, but by results.

Her first mission accomplished, Zo then walked an hour across London to 11 Leopold Road, a brick house in Ealing with net curtains neatly hung inside its windows. This was the Polish Underground Movement Study Trust, an archive established by émigrés including Bór-Komorowski, the Home Army's last commander, who was determined 'to get truth restored and justice done and true facts revealed to the public'.[29] The formidable Halina Czarnocka met Zo at the door.* Herself a veteran, she was the mother of the teenager caught in a Luftwaffe air raid during the Warsaw Uprising while collecting bottles of methylated spirits to be used as antiseptic. Both women had survived the war, and Halina had been running this London archive with various generals and other volunteers for almost twenty years.

Over a cup of black tea, Zo explained that she wanted to see all the paperwork connected with Farmstead, the film footage brought out by Jan Nowak, and any other material touching on women's service with the Home Army. She was 'strong, decisive, adamant, no messing around', one of the young volunteers recalled; 'a very pronounced person' speaking 'instinctively' with no attempt to soften her tone.[30] Although he thought she was 'fantastic', several others considered Zo 'very rude'.[31] Marzenna Schejbal, who as a young woman had led soldiers through the sewers during the uprising, was among those who felt ambivalent about her. She 'looked very masculine, not feminine. She wore no make-up or jewellery', Marzenna noticed, putting a hand up to her own lips, which were painted red.[32] 'She was a very, very strong lady . . . wonderful, very hard and to the point.'[33]

Among the files given to Zo were those written by Protasewicz, Rum and their colleagues during the war. Finding a manilla envelope with her own name on it, she pulled out the papers as Marzenna hovered at her shoulder. Inside was a deeply personal but anonymous 'Opinion' on her, filed away thirty years earlier. She was 'not very intelligent

---

* Halina Czarnocka had been Secretary and Head of Communications Section to General Pełczyński, Chief of Staff GHQ Home Army until her arrest in April 1943. She survived two years in Auschwitz and Belsen.

but very cunning', one of the team had reported, making the colour in Zo's face rise until she was almost the same shade as Marzenna's lipstick.[34] She is an 'unconscious feminist of the "liberation" and women's empowerment movement', another paragraph sneered.[35] Horrified, Zo thought this might have been Rum's turn of phrase, although the handwriting was more like that of another colleague. 'The Polish government-in-exile did not treat her right,' Marzenna later reported in dismay.[36] They 'didn't realise what the circumstances were in Warsaw . . . they didn't respect her.'[37]

The archive offered to remove these papers from the files, but Zo could not accept any doctoring of the records. Instead, she added a response. 'Having reflected on the opinion,' she wrote in a firm hand, 'I think that a profound difference between two perspectives lies at its root. On one hand you have a soldier actively fighting in occupied Poland – constantly exposed to the risk of torture and death. On the other, you have an office-based bureaucrat, diligently processing paper in the comfort of safe London.'[38] Rather than damning her, the documents could now be read against the grain, as indicative of the attitude of the General Staff in the summer of 1943. Zo could not resist adding one slight rebuke. Clearly her 'honest but perhaps too harshly and emotively expressed' assessment of the bureau in 1943 'did hurt the male ego and ambition', she shot back.[39]

Zo flew back to Warsaw on 10 September 1976, thirty years to the day since secretly parachuting to a Polish field. This time, a different reception committee was waiting for her. As soon as she reached the airport terminal, a public announcement ordered her to report to the security desk. When she did so, she was waved away. She returned to the passport queue with a sigh; she had clearly been identified. At sixty-seven, and wearing a nondescript skirt suit and bamboo-coloured nylons to just below her knees, no one could look less threatening but, as Zo knew all too well, appearances could be deceptive. She was carrying 535 pages of material copied in the London archives. All of it refuted the official history of the Second World War as told by the communist regime, and possession of any of it was enough to warrant her arrest.

As soon as Zo had retrieved her suitcase, two men from the state security services appeared. One took her case. The other escorted her away for a body search. Some hours later, an outraged Zo was allowed to return home without her books or four folders of research material.

The next day, she was summoned to the police station in Toruń while both her apartment and her university office were searched. Then she was formally arrested. It is hard to know whether she or her interrogating officer was more frustrated by the process. She is 'almost deaf', her file records.[40] 'It is necessary to talk to her very loudly. She refuses to explain things because she doesn't want to grass on people . . .' and 'she said she has had enough. She refused to drink coffee or tea.'[41]

Zo was released a few hours later. Over-optimistically, she demanded the return of her papers and was lucky not to be re-arrested. Files would later reveal that she had first been placed under surveillance in 1951, before her initial arrest, then again in 1964 and 1966 – when the service had been alerted to her by the amount of post pouring into her Gagarina Street flat. It seemed they had a rough idea of what she was working on, because their operations were code-named 'Combatant' and 'Historian'. More surveillance was run on Zo throughout 1976, under the name 'Penelope' – perhaps in recognition of her fidelity to her cause, or of their own unwavering resolve to track her.

Over the next few months, Zo, her family and neighbours all received threatening phone calls and letters. In October, she and Dela were detained again, at different police stations. Dela was held 'for some trivial reason', Zo later wrote, while she was questioned for several hours in what she considered 'a senseless way'.[42] When she was eventually allowed home, neighbours told her that five plain-clothes policemen had kept guard, while more had conducted another thorough search of her apartment. Zo suspected that a wiretap had been installed. 'I admire you, and I envy your passion and energy', Wacka wrote encouragingly as the harassment continued.[43]

It was not long before Zo's project to establish a faculty of adult education at Toruń University was wound up. She was overlooked for promotions, her budgets were slashed, and her name was omitted from work reports and employee lists. When she detailed this harassment to the Ministry of Education, she was finally told that her confiscated books and papers had been delivered to Toruń University library, only to be denied access to them while one of her former colleagues headed an investigation. As her materials related only to the war, Zo declared that there could be no 'possibility that they might include information harmful to the People's Republic of Poland'.[44] Furthermore, she argued, 'as the only female Silent Unseen . . . I consider it my civic duty to elaborate' on this history, which by denying access to the papers 'you have made impossible'.[45] Nevertheless, twelve key documents were permanently confiscated lest they be 'improperly used'.[46]

The argument ran on until, the following March, Zo suddenly felt the fight come home to roost inside her, squeezing at her chest until she felt she could no longer breathe. Rushed to hospital, she was diagnosed as having suffered a heart attack and firmly advised to retire. Instead, she submitted an official request for temporary sick leave from her bed on the coronary ward. Eventually the Ministry of Education informed her that her fledgling department of adult education at the university had been closed, and her retirement officially accepted. The decision to oust her was 'to the obvious detriment' of the university, Zo commented acidly, and 'a pity for Polish academia' in general.[47] Her career was over but, ironically, the state had given Zo the one vital resource she had lacked to focus on her Second World War research: time was now on Zo's side.

19

Fighting for Freedom
(1979–1989)

Zo was not the only woman forced out of work by the communist authorities in the late 1970s. The Polish economy was shrinking for the first time since the end of the war and when salaries were frozen, while prices rose dramatically, millions were pushed into poverty. The visit of Polish-born Pope John Paul II, in 1979, further encouraged people to question the communist orthodoxies. The next summer, a female trade union activist was sacked by the state-owned Gdańsk Shipyard.* In response, the unofficial trade union she had helped to establish, Solidarity, gained such popular support that the government was forced to recognise it legally. In 1980, Solidarity became first non-communist trade union in the Eastern Bloc. Zo sensed the political mood of the country starting to shift.

Solidarity's leader was the charismatic Lech Wałęsa, a Gdańsk shipyard electrician who had been sacked for agitating three years earlier. With his trademark chevron moustache and polo-neck sweater beneath his jacket, Wałęsa cut a distinctive and reassuringly sturdy figure. Now he set about co-ordinating a broad anti-communist movement with Solidarity backed by other trade unions, cultural societies and the Catholic Church. Toruń was a regional hub, with 150,000 local members led by an astronomy lecturer from the university.†

Finally feeling the wind changing, Zo was determined to hoist a sail. Almost certainly still under surveillance, she knew she was risking arrest again – but no longer cared. She had already lost four years of her liberty and her career. She had no children and few material possessions. 'For the secret police,' friends realised, 'she was a very difficult enemy.'¹ Unemployed at seventy-one, Zo felt unassailable. All

* Anna Walentynowicz.
† Antoni Stawikowski, assoc. prof. Polish Academy of Sciences, was also the regional head of Solidarity.

she wanted to own was her own past and future. 'There is nothing they can do to me,' she smiled.[2]

Zo had thrown herself into correcting the historical record when she had been forced from her job at Toruń University. The project most dear to her had been the publication of the first volume of a biographical dictionary, which she hoped would eventually detail all the female recipients of the Virtuti Militari. Although writing many of the entries herself, such a vast undertaking had required a large team. 'Her letters to me are mostly short orders,' one volunteer had laughed, and even Wacka and Zofia Franio got used to finding 'severe reprimands' between the 'heartfelt greetings' in her letters.[3]* By the late 1970s, however, the team were beginning to flag. 'I'm happy that you still have the energy to work,' Wacka wrote to Zo, 'which I cannot say about myself.'[4] Zofia was even more exhausted.

In 1978, Zofia had been astounded to receive a gold medal from Yad Vashem, the World Holocaust Remembrance Centre in Israel. She had been awarded the honour 'Righteous Among the Nations' for helping save the lives of the Jewish women she had hidden in her apartment during the war.[†] Like most of her colleagues, Zofia had spent the last few decades trying to stay out of the limelight, but she was deeply moved by this recognition. Still working long hours as a doctor, she wouldn't admit to having never fully recovered from her own brutal prison treatment, and she would not consider retiring. 'Trees die standing tall,' she told Wacka.[5]

Zofia died that November. Crowds came to pay their respects as she was buried in Powązki military cemetery. There she was finally reunited with Maria Szczurowska, the woman with whom she had shared her apartment and her life during the war years, and whose body she had rescued from the ruins in late 1944. Their dark marble gravestone records their details beneath the Kotwica, the anchor symbol of the Polish resistance.[‡] Forty years earlier, Zofia had saved Wacka's life when she had contracted tuberculosis in Soviet-occupied Lwów. 'Her

* This volunteer was Maryla Sobocińska, awarded the Virtuti Militari in 1944, number 256 in the dictionary.
† Anna Aszkenazy-Wirska gave testimony to Yad Vashem.
‡ The Kotwica, designed by Girl Scout Anna Smoleńska in 1942, combines the letters P and W for Polska Walcząca or Fighting Poland. Smoleńska died in Auschwitz the following year, aged just 23.

kindness and generosity were extraordinary', Wacka wrote in tribute. 'Everyone who knew her would say that everything she did came from the depths of her heart.'[6] Zo was similarly affected. The human coast was eroding and, as some of her closest friends left her, she too felt that service such as Zofia's must be honoured.

Zo's urgent priority now became securing 'Home Army Crosses' for those female veterans still unrecognised.* Knowing that this decoration was neither legal nor welcome in the People's Republic, the project had to be 'top secret', her closest young cousin, Dorota Zawacka, understood.[7]† Zo prepared the service details for the Verification Commission in London, with several copies posted by friends across Poland. When the medals came back, usually hidden deep within suitcases, Zo sent Dorota travelling across the country to deliver them. 'The veterans', she saw, 'were extremely moved'.[8]

By 1980, the rise of Solidarity as a political opposition was prompting public questioning of the official history of the war after years of enforced silence, threats and discrimination. Zo was already 'legendary' within former resistance circles.[9] Now sought out by new campaigning organisations, she helped to establish a veterans' association in support of Solidarity.‡ 'We were all inspired by the Second World War heroes,' Lech Wałęsa later commented.[10]

The following January, Zo received an unexpected parcel. The books and papers seized at Warsaw airport in 1976 had finally found their way back to her, 'thus declaring their confiscation unjustified', she decided rather smugly.[11] Official suggestions were now made that she write an authorised history of Farmstead, possibly to curb her credentials as a critic of the regime. Declining, she stowed the papers in her flat where they waited, like her, to resurface at a better time.

In October 1981, a new government commission was set up to examine the unjust treatment of Polish academics. Zo's was among the first cases considered. As well as formally expressing regret for the 'moral harm' she had suffered during her career, the commission

---

* Bór-Komorowski established the Home Army Cross in 1966. It was only legally sanctioned by President Lech Wałęsa in 1992.

† Dorota Zawacka-Wakarecy is the daughter of Zo's cousin Bronisław Zawacki. Their relationship was one of close aunt and niece.

‡ The Association of Home Army Soldiers. Zo was also elected chair of the National Council of Combatants for Solidarity in Gdańsk.

allocated a budget to fund a full-time post to support her future historical work.[12] Zo again demurred. Her ongoing heart disease, caused 'by persistent distress', made it hard for her to carry out intensive research, she claimed, although she continued to pursue her own, independent, work.[13]

In a last attempt to suppress the growing political unrest, on 13 December the new leader of the Polish People's Republic imposed martial law.* 'Our homeland is at the edge of an abyss,' he announced. 'The achievements of many generations and the Polish home that has been built up from dust are about to turn into ruins . . .'[14] Zo watched the television announcement in her Gagarin Street apartment with mixed emotions. She knew that it was an act of desperation by the state, but also that the authorities would now crush many of the concessions so hard-won by the Solidarity movement. By midday, tanks were once more rumbling down Polish streets and several hundred activists, including Lech Wałęsa, had been arrested.

Solidarity was being driven underground. Media censorship meant that there was no coverage of the demonstrations across Poland, during which dozens of people were killed, or of the 15,000 demonstrators protesting in sympathy on the streets of London. No news quickly became the norm as the press was tightly controlled, civilian telephones were disconnected, public telephones were tapped, and the postal service was monitored. A strict curfew was imposed, enforced by armed street patrols. Travel permits, even for domestic journeys, were now only granted in exceptional circumstances, and the country's borders were once again sealed.

A few days later, a team of security services officers drove round to arrest Zo. They came 'in the middle of the night, banging on the door and waking the neighbours', Zo's young cousin Dorota was told when she called for Zo and found her gone.[15] With no working telephones, it took some time for Dorota to discover that Zo had evaded the security police by checking herself into a clinic. The officers did not bother to trace her. 'They didn't see her as a serious problem,' one of her former students felt.[16] 'She was an old lady, she wrote a lot of letters, there were lots of old women drinking tea, eating cake . . .'[17] Zo felt similarly blasé about the incident. 'She didn't pay much attention to it,' Dorota commented.[18]

---

* General Jaruzelski.

Among the local activists who *had* been arrested was a passionate political campaigner in his early thirties. Jan Wyrowiński had been born in 1947, the year after his uncle had been murdered while a political prisoner. Jan had already spent a decade distributing illegal newspapers when, as a computer engineer, he was sent to Italy for software training. Astonished by the 'economic miracle' in the west, he had resolved to bring change to Poland.[19] Arrested several times over the next few years, he had usually been released after forty-eight hours. This time, he was being held indefinitely under the ambiguous charge of being 'a danger to the political system in Poland'.[20]

'After the imposition of martial law, many lost hope,' one of Zo's friends felt. 'Zo did not.'[21] Wearing a black armband to protest publicly her country's renewed loss of liberty, she set to work distributing the now-illegal Solidarity press topped with the famous white-and-red logo. She was also still collecting veterans' testimonies, distributing Home Army Crosses and now occasionally coaching the next generation of activists.

When one of Zo's former students, Michał Wojtczak, started publishing a secret newspaper, he traced Zo through his grandmother in order 'to go to a professional' for advice.[22] 'Do you boys realise the game you're playing?' Zo demanded as the group stepped through her door.[23] 'The UB is smarter than you . . . they are professionals and you are amateurs.'[24] As confident as they were ignorant, the lads stood their ground. 'Sooner or later they will catch you,' Zo went on.[25] Feeling somewhat chastened, the men shuffled their feet. One coughed. 'She was like a soldier, getting to the point,' Michał felt, as he waited for the denouement.[26] 'They will torture you – you realise this?' Zo asked. 'So, do you know what you should do during interrogations and torture so as not to talk?'[27] Short instructions followed, along with lessons in basic spy-craft. Zo then fetched a bulky book; a monograph of the Home Army published in London and later smuggled back to Poland. Opening it at a chapter on 'Conspiracy Instructions', 'without a blink, she tore these from the book' as Michał watched, handing them to him.[28]*

Michał and his friends went on to print a regular protest newsletter on a mimeograph machine. Learning from Zo, they also organised

---

* Some years later, Michał Wojtczak married a professional book conservator who meticulously rebound the book. He then returned it to Zo.

a secure distribution system to achieve wide circulation. Zo never enquired how their work was going. 'A good conspiracy member would never ask these questions,' Michał appreciated, not knowing that she was already helping to distribute the resistance press.[29]

By the following spring, Toruń was a hub of defiance. Although 3 May had once been celebrated as Constitution Day in Poland, the holiday had not been recognised by the communist authorities. This year, illegal marches led to riots in Warsaw, and barricades were once more erected in the Old Town. In Toruń, students pasted posters onto the city walls and a march along the River Vistula turned into a mass rally. When the crowd of thousands refused to leave the old market square, police militia with shields and batons charged them, beating even the demonstrators who sought refuge in a church. Nearly three hundred were arrested.

Zo, now seventy-three, had been watching from the sidelines. 'Full of energy and hope', she organised support for those detained and was among those waiting to greet them on their release.[30] When Jan Wyrowiński was paroled, almost five months after his arrest, he valued her absolute conviction that Solidarity would prevail as much, if not more, than the material support he received. Martial law was finally lifted in July 1983.

Within a month Zo travelled to Czechoslovakia and Hungary, testing the limits of her liberty. Ostensibly the trips were for her health, but she used every opportunity to gather historical material, distribute medals and rally more support for an independent Poland. Sue Ryder was among those she now managed to contact. Astounded to discover that her wartime roommate was alive, Ryder petitioned the Polish authorities to allow Zo to visit her in Britain. Surprisingly, they agreed. Unbeknownst to either woman, the Polish government believed that Ryder's refuges were a cover for 'collecting spy information'. They had been keeping her under surveillance since 1961 in an operation code-named 'The Philanthropists'.[31]*

---

* The communist regime's belief in Ryder's espionage activity had not been diminished by her elevation into the British peerage in 1979. In fact, Downing Street had baulked at her request to be 'Baroness Ryder of Warsaw' as this 'raised all sorts of difficulties', requiring both the Queen and prime minister to give approval. 'Nothing if not determined', Ryder got her way. See TNA, FCO 28/3402 (ENP 395/548/1 Honours and Awards), 10 Downing Street letter (31 Aug 1978).

Arriving some weeks later at Sue Ryder's pink-washed, sixteenth-century home in the pretty Suffolk village of Cavendish, Zo found she was not the only visitor. Over thirty Poles, mostly concentration camp survivors, were sharing the bedrooms. Ryder and her young family lived in the two small rooms upstairs, 'eating our meals on a folding table on the landing', her daughter later recalled, and spending their evenings playing cricket with their guests.[32] The women's reunion was a sober moment. Neither liked a fuss. Indeed, part of what they admired in each other was the way they quietly got on with practical good work. Ryder simply put the kettle on while Zo checked through her latest list of Home Army Cross nominees. Alongside her other work, she had now delivered several hundred illegal honours, while Ryder had sponsored 8,000 visitors to her Suffolk home for rest and recuperation. The way Zo came to see it, her wartime friend had, to some extent, personally 'rescued the Poles'.[33]

Zo and Sue Ryder worked together companionably for a week, reminiscing in the evenings but both more focused on the future than the past. At the end of her stay, Zo joined a group visit to Rome to mark the silver anniversary of Ryder's wedding to Group Captain Leonard Cheshire. There were parties with dancing, discussions about their charitable work, and a mass held at St Peter's, during which the Pope blessed them all. For once, Zo gave herself up to enjoying every moment. 'The friendships . . . the privilege of meeting our Holy Father; the sights of the Eternal City . . . the beauty of the Alps', she enthused when she later thanked her friend. 'The whole atmosphere of coming together – it was a truly great and happy occasion.'[34]

The pope who had blessed Zo was the Polish-born John Paul II, the first non-Italian head of the Catholic Church since the sixteenth century.* During the war, the teenage future pope had evaded labour round-ups, studied for the priesthood, and joined a resistance network around Kraków. His election, in 1978, and papal visit to Poland the following year, had helped to galvanise the nation. Zo would draw on the personal well of inspiration he had instilled in her almost immediately on her return to Poland.

In 1984, the corpse of a political opposition leader was discovered less than twenty miles from Toruń. A few weeks later, a Solidarity chaplain was detained by the security service while travelling to the

---

* Born Karol Józef Wojtyła, in Wadowice, a small town near Kraków, in 1920.

city. His beaten, lifeless body was later found nearby.* Horrified, Zo and friends including Jan Wyrowiński established an association for the defence of human rights. Meeting in the apartment of the Solidarity-supporting astronomer, they set their sights high, agreeing to collect and publish information on state terrorism, fund legal assistance, and generally act 'in defence of human honour and dignity'.[35] Soon the fledgling association was deemed illegal, the committee was put under surveillance, the files on Zo were updated, and Jan was one of several detained – but the momentum for political change was becoming unstoppable.

Refused permission to install a plaque to honour the memory of the Pomeranian Home Army, on the old premise that 'the Home Army co-operated with the Gestapo', Zo went ahead anyhow.[36] With the support of a courageous local priest, she cemented up the plaque in his church cloister, legally outside the local authority's jurisdiction. When she persuaded a second parish church to install a memorial to the Toruń Home Army, nearly five hundred people attended the unveiling. Jan Wyrowiński drove another plaque to a neighbouring parish, the chassis of his boxy little Fiat 126 slung low by the weight. Slowly but insistently, Zo was publicly commemorating the history that had been rewritten or erased, harnessing the Home Army's historic fight to the present-day cause of freedom. For her, there was a direct connection between the past and the future, a chain of defiance leading inexorably to Poland's return to independence.

Encouraged by the interest she was generating, in 1987 Zo launched a historical club to 'preserve from oblivion' the history of the Polish resistance.[37] Roping in activists such as Jan Wyrowiński, she held their first packed meeting in the whitewashed cellar of the Toruń mountaineering club.† Although quite literally underground, Zo's sights were still set high. While she continued working on her books and biographical dictionaries, and began to plan an archive, she now also gave weekly talks to inspire the younger generation to keep up the fight.

The rooms of her flat were 'swamped with books', Zo now wrote to Halina Martin, with whom she had stayed in London in 1976.[38] It was true. 'The books on her shelves reached to the ceiling,' one friend noticed, and more were stacked all over the floor.[39] She had

---

* The opposition leader was Piotr Bartoszcze. The chaplain, Fr. Jerzy Popiełuszko.
† Founder members included the student Grzegorz Górski, who had already served time in the 1960s for acting as a messenger between Home Army veterans.

also collected over a thousand personal testimonies, and piles of correspondence were yellowing on the windowsills. A metal filing-cabinet held photographs taken during the occupation, real and forged identity documents, a few issues of wartime resistance newspapers and other memorabilia. Inside the many wardrobes, donated by friends, were boxes packed alphabetically with folders dedicated to Home Army soldiers. Some bulged with typed testimonies, photographs, obituaries, scribbled notes on index cards and other scraps of paper. Others contained only a name or pseudonym waiting to be verified or consigned to the problem file. Jan felt that, for Zo, the safety of this archive 'became as important as the fate of Solidarity activists' but 'she never seemed afraid'.[40]

That year, Zo also received some unsolicited mail. 'Please accept our words of utmost admiration and pride', her cousin Bogumiła Zawacka wrote from America.[41] Bogumiła was the sister of Leonard, who had escaped from Auschwitz in 1944. 'Praise and glory to You, Dear Miss and Cousin!' she continued, before signing off, 'Deeply bowing to you, Bogumiła . . . Kryże – a widow'.[42] Zo shuddered. Bogumiła had been married to Roman Kryże, the notorious Supreme Court judge who had condemned so many Home Army officers to death after the war. Her next letter, the following year, came to the point. 'My great dream is for my brother to be awarded the Auschwitz Cross', Bogumiła wrote, for leading five men out of the camp to join the partisans.[43] 'Dear Madam,' Zo wrote with studied politeness. 'It seems your brother was in Auschwitz when my brother, Egon, was dying there.[44] Advising Leonard to apply to the Polish Embassy in America for his honour, she requested an account of his war service.

Although Bogumiła wrote of 'tears in my eyes' when she learnt of Zo's wartime endeavours, and promised her 'a kind, sister-like welcome' should she ever visit, she and Zo would never meet.[45] Leonard, however, picked up the phone. 'You seemed so close to me straight away', Zo later wrote to him, before asking whether he had met Egon in Auschwitz.[46] Regretting that he had not, as 'we might have been able to help each other', Leonard sent her his testimony.[47]

⚓

By 1989, Mikhail Gorbachev, the eighth leader of the Soviet Union, was busy pushing through his own reforms and no longer prepared to support an ailing Soviet satellite hit by repeated waves of industrial strikes. As a result, Poland's communist president offered to negotiate but the popular demand was for democratic elections. That April, Solidarity was recognised as a political party and given permission to field a limited number of candidates for the 4 June elections. Feeling too old, at eighty, to stand herself, Zo supported Jan Wyrowiński to represent Solidarity locally. Turning her flat into a campaign office, she set about distributing thousands of posters and leaflets, each featuring photographs of Jan proudly shaking hands with Lech Wałęsa. Having rallied every vote, unlike her exhausted volunteers Zo stayed up all night to hear the results come in.

'Dorota! We won!' Zo shouted joyfully down the telephone to her cousin.[48] Jan Wyrowiński had become Toruń's first freely elected representative. They celebrated at the town hall over a 'small' cake, Zo 'very, very, very happy' to 'be present to see this moment', and contributing enthusiastically to the discussions about 'what to do with such a victory'.[49] The following May, Solidarity consolidated its democratic mandate. The communist vote had collapsed so spectacularly that at first there were fears the Kremlin might yet annul the results but, in December 1990, Lech Wałęsa took office as the democratically elected President of Poland. Recognising his government's legitimacy, the exiled state authorities in London flew to Warsaw and ceremoniously handed over the presidential insignia to Wałęsa three days before Christmas.* The following year, Poland filled both houses of the National Assembly with representatives from a wide spectrum of political parties. Fifty years since Nazi German and Soviet armed forces had invaded, Poland had regained its independence.

Zo was not, and never would be, party political. She had fought for freedom for her country, for her people and for herself. 'She knew the importance of politics', Jan saw, but 'her word was only for Poland, as a state, an idea, as a duty.'[50] And this was Poland's moment; the moment that Zo, Zofia Grzegorzewska and Marianna Zawodzińska had pledged their lives to bring about in a pioneering women's military training camp over half a century earlier. Killed in the train crash just a few years later, in Zo's mind this Zofia had become one of the first

---

* The last exiled president, Ryszard Kaczorowski, was among those killed when their aircraft crashed in Smolensk, en route to mark the seventieth anniversary of the Katyń massacre.

casualties of the war. Marianna had coughed up her life blood onto the pale sheets of a clinic, dying of the tuberculosis contracted as a resistance courier. Zo and Marianna's sisters, Klara and Celina, had both served in the Home Army, and then survived the concentration camps. Dr Zofia Franio, Maria Wittek and Zo had put their lives on the line for over six years, only to be imprisoned by their own post-war government. Emilia had given her all but, betrayed by those she trusted, she had eventually taken her own life. 'I loved her', Zo wrote.[51] In truth, she had loved them all, and she had carried the flame for all their hopes and dreams. Now she was thrilled to see Poland win its freedom. She was also deeply moved. She knew she had consistently played her part, one soldier among so many, but she was not entirely satisfied.

20

Revolution is Not Made by Angels
(1990–2009)

Zo had always been a demanding woman. She had demanded that women had the right to receive military training, a uniform and weapons, rank and legal status within the Home Army. She had demanded Poland's freedom, from both Nazi Germany and the Soviet Union during the war, and from the Soviet-backed communist regime imposed on the country afterwards. She had also always demanded a lot from herself and from those who chose to work alongside her. As infuriating as she could be inspirational, what mattered to Zo was not intentions but results, and, as one of her friends laughed while describing her, 'revolution is not made by angels'.[1]

Within months of the triumphant emergence of democratic Poland, revolution swept across Eastern Europe. Hungary, East Germany, Bulgaria, Czechoslovakia and Romania all won their independence as the Eastern Bloc disintegrated. The Warsaw Pact, the regional defence treaty between the socialist republics, was dissolved in July 1991. The Soviet Union ceased to exist that December, and the communist system that had dominated central Europe for decades was consigned to history. As Poland's new government introduced a programme of radical reform, Zo slipped seamlessly from freedom fighting to revising the Polish historical record. 'She felt that the duty of remembering was the most important duty', Jan Wyrowiński understood, and now 'all she could do for those who had been tortured or killed'.[2]

In 1990, Zo's archive was given a building and legal status as a foundation 'to promote research into Polish history, especially the history of the Home Army and . . . the wartime service of Polish women'.[3] With relief, she evacuated the heroes from her wardrobes without fear of confiscations or reprisals. Over the next few years, the foundation would publish many books, including several by Zo. She dedicated a history of the pre-war PWK to Zofia Grzegorzewska and Marianna Zawodzińska, and often inscribed books to friends with personal messages. 'In remembrance of our walking camp and war experience', she wrote to Wanda Wysznacka, one of the women who had survived Ravensbrück.[4] And 'with thoughts of Marianna'.[5]

'She knew how to tell a story well', friends knew, both on paper and in person. Zo gave many talks and, when Girl Scouts visited, she would sit in her armchair surrounded by them perching on the sofa, the floor, and even on cupboards, listening enthralled until they felt *they* were wading through deep snow in the Pyrenees, shocking a male reception committee while unclipping a parachute, watching nuns run to help the wounded, and walking through the ruins of Warsaw singing the songs they all still knew.[6] Zo would never forget the Scouts' service as messengers, couriers and sewer guides during the uprising, and she saw this as her chance to thank the movement. To her surprise, she also enjoyed their company.

It had not been 'her path' to have a family, Zo now told close friends, but had she done so she would have had 'many children'.[7] Without them, she relied on others to organise her appointments, transport, meals and even her clothes; she was too busy, and too disinterested.[8] Dorota, her young cousin, was more than happy to help wherever needed, and the archive had a team of volunteers. Klara had no wish to get involved there, rarely discussing the war, but she and Zo enjoyed Sunday lunches and competitive games of chess. My 'dear younger sister . . . constantly teases me', Zo wrote to Halina.[9] One summer, Leonard came to visit, donating his maps of Auschwitz, his Home Army badge and $100 to the foundation. Dorota noticed the number tattooed on his forearm when he wore a short-sleeved shirt, but above all she was struck by how much the family cared for one another.

Zo was delighted when Lech Wałęsa appointed Maria Wittek as Poland's first female brigadier general (retired) in 1991. Four years later, he awarded Zo the Order of the White Eagle, the country's highest order of merit.* At eighty-seven, she celebrated modestly, later that evening adding the medal to her growing collection of decorations and other memorabilia.† She still had her white-and-red armband from the

---

* Wałęsa awarded this honour on 1 December 1995, having just lost the presidential campaign but before leaving office, making it one of his last official acts.

† Zo medals included the Order of the White Eagle, Silver Cross of the Order of Virtuti Militari, Officers Cross of the Order of the Rebirth of Poland, Cross of Valour and four bars, Gold Cross of Merit with Swords, Cross of Combat Deeds of the

Warsaw Uprising, washed and pressed but permanently stained. In the same drawer was her Silent Unseen 'diving-eagle' parachute badge, a hollow key and bristly old clothes brush with a removable back, and one of Zofia Grzegorzewska's sketchbooks.

Soon there were more keepsakes; her 1993 certificate as an honorary citizen of Toruń, her recent appointment as a professor of humanities, and a fountainpen from Belweder Palace, the president's official residence, still in its moulded plastic box and with a yellow post-it note stuck on the side: 'President of the Republic of Poland Lech Wałęsa to Elżbieta Zawacka, 1995', she had proudly written. When Wałęsa appointed Zo as a member of the Chapter of the Order of the Virtuti Militari, an order she had received herself during the war, she made a point of including women among those being honoured. 'Perhaps you will take this medal away from a few gentleman', Halina Martin teased her.[10]

Zo's friends knew that 'she would never give up the issue of women'.[11] 'Why is your skirt so long?' she once asked a surprised secretary at the foundation. 'We women fought long ago to wear short skirts or trousers.'[12] 'She was a feminist in the best meaning of the word,' Jan Wyrowiński felt, but she was also 'some kind of *enfant terrible* for the men'.[13] Another friend believed that 'she was not prejudiced against men at all, but she did say that men were unable to do many things.'[14] The truth was that Zo simply valued competence. Beyond that she had simply never been much interested in men.

'I am what is called a feminist . . .' Zo would say, although Dorota felt she did not much like the word.[15] 'You have to fight for women's rights.'[16] But when she discussed it with Klara, her sister told her not to be 'stupid'.[17] 'In one hundred years women will rule the world anyway,' Klara assured her. 'Women are richer than men internally . . .' she added, perhaps thinking of the female networks that her saved so many lives in Ravensbrück. 'The era of male rule must end.'[18] But Zo was 'a realist'.[19] What was important now, she felt, was her 'moral obligation' to record the 'largely unknown' stories of servicewomen, while securing them honours and military pensions.[20]

Zo was hard-wearing but not indestructible. She had suffered two

Polish Armed Forces, Warsaw Insurgent Cross, Home Army Cross, Army Medal, Distinguished Service Badge, Cross of Defence of Lwów, and the Medal Pro Memoria.

heart attacks, and was now very deaf and slowly going blind. Yet when Dorota took her to her favourite residential health clinic, Zo would issue directions all the way, including once to drive against the flow of the traffic, to hurry them up. 'I cannot waste time because I have so much to do,' she would say, almost apologetically. 'We still have a bit of time and strength to rectify (as far as women's participation in concerned) the Second World War history published so far.'[21]

To mark Independence Day, in November 1996, Zo organised the first of what became an annual conference for over a hundred female veterans and dignitaries, including the last president of the exiled Polish government. A World Association of Home Army Soldiers developed from the event, but sparks flew when Zo invited communist veterans to join them. It was only her personal authority, and her repurposed kitchen egg-timer, that stopped the fierce debates from getting completely out of hand. 'The proof that we are in true Poland is, among other things, various unfortunate quarrels', she wrote to Halina Martin.[22]

Zo was chairing veteran meetings well into her nineties. When she opened by asking the committee, many in their seventies, for their three-year objectives, 'most of them hid', the young secretary later smiled, or they stared at Zo as if to say, 'Oh my god, how can she?'[23] Then Zo would launch into her personal five-year plans. She was 'like a commander', Jan Wyrowiński felt, presenting 'orders written on little slips of paper', her handwriting now almost as demanding as the woman herself.[24] Volunteers were sometimes shocked at the impatient way she issued instructions, 'like a general talking to his soldier'.[25] She 'did not quite finish with "at ease soldier",' another laughed, 'but I would not have been surprised if she had.'[26] 'Made of stern stuff . . . she knew what she wanted', and often 'wanted it done yesterday' was the general feeling; and even old friends began to tease her about her manners.[27] 'I have fulfilled my orders', Halina Martin would write, before signing off 'your obedient sergeant'.[28]

Yet although the team would warn each other when 'General Zawacka was wearing her commander's shoes', she also continued to inspire them.[29] 'She was an iron fist in a silk glove,' one felt, 'clever beyond words' and she certainly meant to be kind.[30] She thanked them warmly for their work, often writing personal notes of appreciation, and would share out any award money she received. Above all, 'when she talked to you', one volunteer felt, 'you'd think you were the only person in the room'.[31]

Zo exercised every morning, her balcony doors open even if it was cold.* When she found the eight flights of stairs to her apartment more difficult to climb and her chest a little tighter in the evenings, she allowed herself a short nap on her 'very austere, hard bed'.[32] Books on 'Women's Health' and 'Gymnastics with the Radio' took their place in her library and she sellotaped the emergency doctor's number discreetly inside her telephone handset. But embracing new technology, she then bought a mobile phone and replaced her old Remington typewriter with a computer. She loved the immediacy of emails and urged all her friends to keep up. 'This must be learnt!' she told them.[33]

One afternoon, a friend making tea in Zo's small kitchen heard a sudden, dreadful gasp. Rushing through, she saw Zo, now ninety-two, leaning forward in her armchair. Her face was as pale as her soft wool shawl and, behind her thick glasses, her eyes were astonishingly bright. Zo was not unwell. Still as sharp as a tack, she liked to keep up with news and current affairs, but nothing had prepared her for a television newsflash. Buildings had been reduced to rubble. Thick clouds of mortar dust and smoke rolled through Manhattan streets. Shocked people, men and women, stumbled forward, some supporting others, some alone, all choking, their clothes, hair and skin coated in a thick layer of dirt. Watching New York's Twin Towers collapse on 11 September 2001, Zo had been momentarily catapulted back to the Warsaw Uprising. She remembered seeing friends stumbling down similar city streets, half obscured by billowing clouds of smoke and dust. She had never forgotten the look of shock on their faces, unable to take in the horror, the landscape instantly changed, and the loss of friends. Although momentarily stunned, Zo soon felt the fight still burning within her. Freedom, she knew, was never to be taken for granted.

'I need to live two more years' became Zo's new mantra as she strived to finish another conference, book or lecture series, or to raise the funds for memorial benches across Toruń, or get new Warsaw streets named after distinguished servicewomen.[34] Worrying 'that I'm not going to make it – not finish what I've started', she rallied veteran support for Poland's referendum to join the European Union, and

---

* In this way she made friends with the local pigeons, who she would then feed on her balcony.

organised a statue to Maria Wittek and an obelisk to commemorate
all the Polish women who had fought for freedom.[35]* Privately, she
also arranged and paid for Emilia's ashes to be reinterred in Warsaw's
prestigious Powązki military cemetery.† Checking Emilia's entry in her
foundation's copy of the biographical dictionary, she added a slip of
paper to make clear that the cause of her death 'was her protest', and
recording that she had loved her.[36]

Zo was determined not to omit a single detail from the record, but
she also kept her eye on the bigger picture. When officials at a public
event asked what she would like for her ninety-fifth birthday, she
secured new premises for her foundation. One Saturday morning later
that year, when the archive had been moved, she and Klara walked
over, disarmed the alarm and had a good look round the new building
before heading off. A taxi was waiting for them but, before reaching it,
they were stopped by the building's security team. They had somehow
managed to trigger the alarm, but had failed to hear it. As quite often
in Zo's life, it was hard to know who was more surprised by their
encounter, she or the men working in security.

Zo was recognised again when she was awarded the title 'Custodian
of National Remembrance'.‡ Her archive had been saved for the nation,
and her work was inspiring a new generation. She was ninety-seven,
however, when she received the honour she most valued – promotion to
the rank of brigadier general (retired).§ Zo had set herself two missions
in life: to bring freedom to her country and equality of opportunity,
rank and recognition to her fellow servicewomen. She had triumphed
in both. 'I had a happy life,' she told a journalist, but, 'I think I lived
a bit too long.'[37]

It was a bitterly cold day on 10 January 2009, but Zo died peacefully

---

* Zo argued that it was 'the task of every good citizen' to vote for Polish membership
of the EU (see EZ letter to Jan Wyrowiński, 20 May 2003). Wittek's statue is in the
Polish Army Museum courtyard. The obelisk is in Wolności Park, adjacent to the
Warsaw Uprising Museum, both in Warsaw.

† Zo had already organised a group of friends, including Wacka, Hanka and Bradl,
to fund the maintenance of Emilia's previous grave.

‡ Awarded by the Institute of National Remembrance (IPN), established December
1998.

§ Zo had already been promoted to lieutenant colonel in 1996, raised to colonel in
1999.

in the warmth of her sister's apartment. It was as though death itself had waited for permission to claim her. She had been staying with Klara since Christmas, finally content that her work was done. The sisters had known it was a privilege to share these last few weeks, playing chess, eating ice cream and tinned peaches, arguing happily, listening to Chopin, and reading whatever books they chose in an independent, democratic, Poland.

POSTSCRIPT

Zo died just two months shy of her centenary; her life at the heart of a hundred years of dramatic Polish history. The committee that had been convened to prepare her birthday celebrations was hastily redeployed to organise a funeral suitable for one of Poland's most decorated women. As a brigadier general, she was buried with full military honours, although not in Warsaw's military cemetery among so many of her friends. She had preferred to be laid to rest near her family in Toruń.* 'Goodbye General, checking for your last security clearance,' one of her lieutenants paid her respects at the funeral.[1] 'Thank you as an ordinary soldier of the Home Army . . . your last command was "our service continues". I report that it does.'[2]

Over three thousand people came to pay their respects as Zo's coffin, draped with the Polish flag, was carried through the streets on a cannon carriage. An honour guard fired rifle volleys over the grave, a military band played the national anthem, and three aircraft flew overhead. When the official mourners had left, Dorota stayed at the graveside for a long time. As she finally turned to go, she picked up a spent bullet shell from the cemetery lawn, later adding it to the collection at Zo's foundation.

* One of the streets leading to the cemetery is Ul. Konstanty Ildefons Gelczynski, named after a Polish poet, some of whose work Zo had on her bookshelf.

EPILOGUE

'Female readers, especially the active witnesses and co-creators of this history, are surprised to find war literature almost completely silent on the participation of women in the underground struggle . . . They observe a kind of falsification of history.'

Elżbieta Zawacka, 1992[1]

Andrzej Drzycimski lifted a Sony cassette recorder out of his bag and put it on the table between himself and Zo. She smiled to see its white-and-red Solidarity sticker. These were ubiquitous among her friends, stuck on coats, bags and coffee cups. But Zo frowned at the bundle of cassettes that came out next – a set of Communist Party speeches and some martial music. Andrzej apologised, flashing her a nervous smile which Zo, aged eighty, ignored.

It was June 1989, six months before the presidential elections through which Poland would start to win its freedom, and it was still impossible to buy blank cassette tapes. As a journalist, Andrzej had found that state propaganda were the best tapes to record over. He intended to interview Zo, capturing her voice with its soft Pomeranian accent as she described her war. He had already recorded Lech Wałęsa in the same way. Together, he felt, they might rewrite the existing narrative of Polish history. Andrzej did not know that this was something Zo had been working on for decades.

Zo eyed the young man suspiciously. Straightening her back, she launched into a lecture on adult correspondence education. Andrzej heard her out, noting her stern look, resolute tone and fawn nylon blouse neatly tucked into her skirt. She was in full commander mode. It was only after Andrzej revealed that he had been imprisoned for six months during martial law that Zo began to wonder whether this journalist might be useful. Softening a little, she fetched some tea and cake.

'Zo was a very disciplined person . . . very precise,' Andrzej came to realise.[2] Once her mind was made up, 'she had no doubts and no hesitations'.[3] Now, she did not hesitate to co-opt him. 'The war could not have been won without women,' Zo told Andrzej, yet she had been campaigning for over thirty years to get their stories told.[4] 'You should focus more on publishing information regarding women's service during the occupation', she had written to a veterans' association in 1961.[5] 'Men keep talking about their own participation', but the women's service is being passed over 'in silence' or 'stalled with sentimental or praising cliché'.[6] Yet nothing had changed. The problem, Zo decided, was that historians were, with few exceptions, men who 'as a result of age-old cultural conditioning' were generally unaware of 'the quality of women's contribution to any public activity'.[7] As a result, 'a partisan female soldier, a female officer, may seem something extraordinary, exceptional', when really they were very commonplace.[8] 'Half of the nation,' she now told Andrzej, the female half, were still being underestimated and overlooked.[9]

Seeing that Zo 'was completely focused on emphasising the role of the women in the war', Andrzej proposed that instead of an article, he write her biography.[10] At first Zo demurred. 'I do not consider my life important,' she told him.[11] She did not mention that she had been moaning to Halina Martin, only recently, that 'male historians do not write about women'.[12] Nor did she admit that she believed female veterans tended to value their own contributions 'too modestly and, knowing men's disregard of their service, were reluctant to testify'.[13] Such thoughts must have flitted across her face, however, as, sensing her dilemma, Andrzej pressed on. All the war memoirs to date had been written by and about men, he reminded Zo.

General Bór had published his memoirs in Britain, five years after the war.[*] His aim, he told friends, was 'to get truth restored and justice done, and true facts revealed to the public'.[14] Bór had at least given credit to the 'liaison girls . . . constantly exposed to danger', but his book was still unknown in Poland.[15] Zo had been unimpressed by the later memoirs of Bradl, aka Kazimierz Leski, and Jan 'Nowak' Jeziorański. Bradl had been mistaken about certain facts and Nowak was, she felt, 'writing for children . . . fairytales'.[16][†] Even when veterans

---

[*] Tadeusz Bór-Komorowski, *The Secret Army* (1950).

[†] See Kazimierz Leski, *Życie niewslaściwie urozmaicone* ['A Chequered Life: Memoirs of a Home Army Intelligence and Counterintelligence Officer'] (1989). On p.123, Leski had written that Emilia Malessa committed suicide by jumping from

she had served alongside had interviewed her for their memoirs, Zo was shocked by how little they considered women's service. 'Please don't raise your eyebrows. You heard right. I was asked to join anti-tank teams. We wanted to fight,' she reportedly told one.[17] So now she agreed to Andrzej's proposal. Then she set her terms.

Zo's first stipulation was that her PWK friendships were crucial to the story, especially with Zofia Grzegorzewska, who had inspired her choice of nom-de-guerre, and Marianna Zawodzińska, her 'closest friend'.[18] Secondly, 'there is nowhere "the love plot",' she told Andrzej, simply 'because there was none'.[19] Instead, she looked for 'excellent people' while pursuing education and, 'above all, service . . . was the meaning of my life'.[20] Over the following months, Andrzej recorded interviews on his Solidarity-stickered tape deck as Zo 'spoke with passion' about her service.[21] But if he asked about her faith, emotions or love life, 'she simply changed the subject' and when he shared a few draft paragraphs, she was so horrified at seeing herself centre-stage that she made him promise to shelve the project.[22] 'She fought in the name of women', he realised, and it was the collective female effort she wanted remembered.[23] Honourably stowing away his twenty-five cassettes of interviews, Andrzej became Lech Wałęsa's chief press secretary, and Zo's story remained untold.

⚓

During the Second World War, American combat aircraft would often return to their bases with their wings and fuselage riddled with bullet holes. Assessing the damage, ground crew would note down the places most commonly hit – information then used to determine where to concentrate the heavy protective armour. Mathematicians in New York worked on finding the optimum amount of armour for machines that needed to be as light as possible. It was an Austro-Hungarian Jewish mathematician who first asked, 'Where are the missing holes?'[24]* The reason why fewer were found in the engines was that, if hit there, most aircraft did not make it back.

This insight reportedly informed America's approach to aircraft armouring for several decades. It can now be pressed into new service,

the fifth floor of a building. See also Jan Nowak, *Courier to Warsaw* (1978).
* Abraham Wald.

as a metaphor for military history. Arguably, we have tended to add weight to the stories we know, those perhaps first told by returning servicemen and later reviewed, contextualised and presented as the great set pieces. We have been less good at asking, 'Where are the missing stories?' Focusing more attention on the absent data, such as the experience of women and other minorities in combat, supplements rather than supplants the existing history. And extending the dimensions of our knowledge can transform a seemingly familiar story into a richer understanding of the diverse human resources that ultimately, collectively, it took to bring victory.

Gendered beliefs about conflict are so profound that, despite a long history of active female engagement, the Western Allies still chose to exclude women from military service during the Second World War. Disempowered under the guise of male protection and chivalry, women were told they did not qualify for military careers. They did not have the required strength or the male *esprit de corps*. They would be a liability, distract men, weaken their resolve, and they would incur extra expenses for their sanitary requirements. Yet the demands of war prevailed, and eventually most nations mobilised all available resources to some degree.

Until recently, accounts of British women's experiences tended to focus on the home front. Bletchley Park debutantes, Women's Land Army labourers, parachute packers and aircraft rivetters, pilots with the ATA, and the servicewomen of the WAAF, WREN and ATS all played important roles. Many endured enemy attack while delivering aircraft, operating searchlights or plotting Luftwaffe positions during the Blitz. In the 1950s a different story, if a romantic version, started to be told of those who served with the Special Operations Executive. Other women worked on or behind the frontlines as accredited war correspondents and medics. Over a thousand British servicewomen lost their lives. Few received the recognition they deserved. Ineligible for military honours, when one special agent, who had led around 2,000 French maquis fighters into battle, was given civil awards she pointed out that 'there was nothing civil' about her service behind enemy lines.[25]

Nearly 350,000 American women served in uniform during the war, mostly in non-combat roles although there were at least two American-born female special agents. True to societal norms, the women's service branches emphasised femininity within the ranks, with uniforms specifying skirts and encouraging make-up and fashionable hairstyles. 'Until my experience in London I had been opposed to the use of women in uniform', General Eisenhower admitted in his 1948 memoirs.[26] But after seeing women 'performing so magnificently in various positions, including service with anti-aircraft batteries . . . I had been converted.'[27] In all, 432 American servicewomen were killed. As in Britain, after the war most of the rest were forced to relinquish their jobs, and many struggled to obtain veteran status or benefits.

Soviet women became eligible for the draft in 1942. An estimated 800,000 served in various roles. The most famous, branded the *Nacht Hexen* or 'Night Witches' by their enemy, were female night-fighter squadrons. There were also other fighter and bomber crew, snipers, machine-gunners, tank crew and infantry, as well as medical teams, although few equipped to the same standard as their male comrades. Even if draped in medals, the survivors were often ostracised and relegated to the back of victory parades.

Within occupied Europe, the best-known women are those who served with the French resistance. By October 1944, approximately 50,000 were active, mostly serving in intelligence and communications but also as armed partisans, joining the men in the hills. Yet while Frenchwomen won the vote in 1944, partly in recognition of their wartime service, only six of the 1,038 'Companions of the Liberation' recognised by de Gaulle between 1940–1946 were women. Later, more were honoured with the Médaille de la Résistance, Croix de guerre and Légion d'honneur.

Even within the Nazi Third Reich, where women's place was overtly designated as spiritual, domestic and reproductive, exceptions were made for brilliant female pilots and engineers to serve in what was considered the male sphere of the skies above Berlin. A significant number of both Jewish and non-Jewish civilian women also resisted, comprising about 15 per cent of the total *Widerstand*.

Although Polish women were among the first to take up arms in the war, they have received far less attention. The women of Poland have a proud tradition of military service, partly because their nation has such a long history of invasion, annexation and occupation, defiance, resistance and restoration. The January Uprising of 1863 is sometimes known as the 'Women's War' because of the record number of women who fought. Military service is traditionally equated with representation and in November 1918, after the Great War, Polish women were among the first in Europe to be given the vote. Many, like Zo, who served in the Second World War, had been raised in the euphoria that came with restored national independence and unprecedented female freedom. 'Patriotism was in us,' one female Warsaw Uprising veteran explained. 'It was sucked in with mother's milk.'*

The Polish Armed Forces had had women's auxiliaries long before their equivalents in Britain, but these had been disbanded. During the Second World War, a new auxiliary service, the PSK, was launched, and later reorganised into air, land and sea units. By then 7,000 Polish women were serving overseas. Many had reached Britain with the men, serving in Romania and France before establishing camp in Scotland. In 1942, female volunteers started replacing men 'in those positions where women's work is desirable'.[28] The Polish WAAF, for example, constituted over 10 per cent of the Polish ground crew in Britain, and three female pilots, including Anna Leska, the sister of Kazimierz Leski, aka Bradl, and Jadwiga Piłsudska, the daughter of Marshal Piłsudski, served in the British ATA.

After the Soviets joined the Allies in 1941, around 4,000 Polish women, released from Soviet labour camps, joined the Polish Army in the Middle East, serving as military drivers, medics, cooks and clerks in Italy, Egypt, Libya and elsewhere. Women were even represented among the missing officers murdered by the Russians at Katyń. Janina Lewandowska, a Polish pilot, was the only servicewoman among the 22,000 executed there on the orders of Stalin.

By far the greatest number of Polish women to serve, however – an estimated 40,000 – comprised 10 per cent of the Home Army, the largest organised resistance force in occupied Europe. In Poland, unlike in Britain, the 'home front' became the 'front line' as soon as Nazi Germany invaded in September 1939, prompting thousands of women to rush to the defence of their country, their homes and families. 'As of now, we are all soldiers,' Polish radio broadcast, causing Zo a wry smile as she had been working for years to get trained women equal military, rather than auxiliary, status.[29] By the time the Russians invaded from the east, Zo was making petrol bombs and was on duty with the anti-aircraft and anti-tank defences in Lwów.

Zo swore her oath of allegiance to the resistance in an icy Warsaw kitchen in November 1939, quickly organising a regional intelligence

* Halina Żelaska, aka 'Halichen'.

network. Recognising the Home Army's dependence on women in this area, as well as in communications, press and propaganda, in March 1940 General Rowecki, the Home Army's first commander, ordered that these women be treated as soldiers. A year later, he petitioned the exiled Polish government to grant equal rights for equal service. It was not until Zo's mission to London in 1943, however, that the military service of women in the Home Army was legally recognised. Almost 5,000 of these soldiers, documented by name, lost their lives.

Zo dedicated *her* life to fighting for the freedom of her country, and to securing fitting recognition for women's military service. 'In the social consciousness . . . a soldier of the Polish Underground State, a soldier of the Home Army, or any other military organisation, is a male soldier', she wrote in 1992.[30] 'Women's participation . . . [is] perceived as simple, ordinary, properly unnoticed.'[31] Servicewomen still did not feature in military encyclopaedias, she noted, nor in the research plans of academic institutions. Women still needed 'to break the silence', but Zo did not want to be singled out for praise.[32] 'I do not like the word hero,' she made clear. 'Because a hero's action is about a single effort.'[33] She had always served alongside her sisters-in-arms, women such as Emilia Malessa, Dr Zofia Franio and Marianna Zawodzińska. Even her nom-de-guerre, 'Zo', had been chosen in tribute to women she admired: Zofia Zawacka, her brother's wife, and her PWK friend, Zofia Grzegorzewska. But Zo *was* exceptional.

Having led an intelligence network, and reportedly crossed wartime borders over a hundred times as a resistance courier, Zo became the only female emissary of a Polish Army commander, reaching London in 1943. After the fall of France, up to 24,000 Polish servicemen had managed to reach Britain. Only the top 2,000 were selected for SOE training in British country houses. A shortage of aircraft and clear moonlit nights meant that just 316 of these would be sworn in as the elite special force paratroopers, the Silent Unseen. Zo was the only woman among them, and the only woman again to parachute from Britain to Poland during the war, subsequently to take part in the Warsaw Uprising.

Yet Zo's greatest wartime achievement was perhaps the most overlooked: securing legal military status for women in the Home Army. As a direct result, after the Warsaw Uprising the Germans officially recognised women as soldiers for the first time, and therefore detained them in prisoner-of-war camps. Thousands of lives were saved and, in a sense, Zo saved those lives again, when she worked for decades to preserve the historical record of the women in the Home Army.

The foundation that Zo created, which now bears her name, houses many thousands of personal files, as well as hundreds of artefacts at its premises in Toruń. There is 'this idea of a neutral voice . . . even more strong in non-fiction, the idea of the expert', the British author Kate Mosse said in 2023. 'But actually, the expert, the default voice, is male.'[34] Ubiquitous as it might be, Zo would not let this voice go unchallenged. She had provided the ammunition, and her own story provides the vehicle to use it.

ૐ

A white-haired Andrzej Drzycimski carried a bulky plastic carrier bag into the café of the Museum of the Second World War in Gdańsk. It was 2021, and the museum's press team had joined me to greet him. Having served as Lech Wałęsa's press secretary and spokesman before and after the elections that brought a close to over forty years of Soviet-backed communist rule in Poland, Andrzej was now a well-known name. I knew I was lucky to secure a meeting with him, but not yet how important it would be for my research. Setting down his bag, Andrzej fixed me with a direct yet rather quizzical gaze, shook my hand, and sat to accept the first of a seemingly never-ending supply of hot black tea and fresh pear cake.

'Would you like to hear her?' Andrzej asked me several hours later.[35] Pulling out his 1970s cassette player, still with its rather worn Solidarity sticker on the front, he chose the last tape from several bound together with elastic bands, and put it in the machine. There was a clunky whirr as the wheels started winding before Zo's voice echoed around the museum café. He quickly turned the volume down. Mostly she sounded earnest, but several times Zo let out a cheerful laugh and once she seemed to choke with emotion. When the interview ended, Andrzej reached over to turn off the deck, but not before we heard a few rousing lines from a speech by a male official of the Polish People's Republic. Andrzej had literally recorded Zo's testimony over the propaganda of the communist regime, neatly erasing it in the process. He had honoured his promise to her, never writing the biography, but, smiling encouragingly, he now pushed the tapes across the table to me.

NOTE ON SOURCES

'The Poles are closer to fiction than other people.'
D/CE, SOE Polish Section[1]

'Don't be afraid of detailed descriptions: the smoother the story, the sweeter it will be.'
Elżbieta Zawacka, 'Zo'[2]

'Why did no one in Britain know,' Hanna Czarnocka asked me, taking my hand at an event in the Polish Embassy in London, 'about the greatest Polish female resistance fighter, Elżbieta Zawacka, known as Zo?'[3] Hanna was herself a remarkable woman. Having served as a teenager in the Warsaw Uprising, she had reached London after the war, and later volunteered in the Polish archives run by her mother. I spent most of the evening transfixed by her memories of scavenging for glass bottles of methylated spirits during Luftwaffe bombing raids. Hanna then introduced me to her fellow veteran, Marzenna Schejbal, who had helped guide exhausted soldiers out through the city's sewers. She too had met Zo in London after the war. 'She was a very strong lady,' Marzenna recalled. 'For her, nothing was impossible.'[4] If these incredible women rated 'Zo' so highly, I knew I would have to find out more.

Without Hanna and Marzenna I might never have started this book. It would take the help of many more generous women and men to bring it to fruition. Because Zo spent time in Britain during the war, there are several files pertaining to her and to her colleagues in the National Archives and Imperial War Museum. The Polish Institute and Sikorski Museum (PISM) and the Polish Underground Movement Study Trust, which she visited in 1976, also hold a wealth of material, saved from the censorship of the communist authorities in post-war Poland. There are also traces of the Cichociemni (the Silent Unseen), graffiti, weapons storage labels and a few books at Audley End House in Essex.

English Heritage, who manage Audley End, kindly put me in touch with the families of several of those who had trained at the house during the war. Andrew Bilski, the son of Kazimierz Bilski, aka 'Rum', and WAAF officer Audrey North, shared his findings from an extraordinary green box packed with wartime documents and wonderful letters between his parents, found in their attic. The two daughters of Stanisław Jankowski, aka 'Agaton', the Silent Unseen forgery specialist, shared their family's moving story over soup and cake in their kitchen, and several others kindly sent photographs of medals and papers along with family recollections. Later, I had the privilege of paying my respects to all the Silent Unseen at the Audley End memorial, alongside Janusz Zabielski, the son of Józef Zabielski, the first among them to parachute home.

Most of the material I needed, however, was in Poland. When the Polish Embassy generously supplied a translator, the wonderful Paulina Chołda, she and I spent a couple of packed weeks between Covid lockdowns in Warsaw, Gdańsk and of course Toruń, Paulina dishing out restorative herbal tea as required. My first meeting was with the very kind Bogdan Rowiński, of the Silent Unseen Foundation, who drove me to an unassuming field twenty-five miles southwest of Warsaw. It was a clear, bright morning and the low sun backlit silver birches and tall clumps of pampas grass. A small brick and stained-glass memorial records the names of the fifteen Silent Unseen who had parachuted to this field during the war, including Zo on 10 September 1943. I tried to imagine her hitting the earth, pain shooting up her legs but adrenaline racing on that cold, moonlight night. Then we laid a wreath for those who did not survive.

On the way back to Warsaw, Bogdan and I stopped at the gate of the stunning former palace in Szymanów that had been converted into the convent in 1907. A young nun carrying a thermos of tea in one hand and a hot water bottle in the other invited us in. Hearing about our interest, she fetched Sister Janina, the convent's archivist and their oldest, and probably shortest, resident. Wearing a pale, hand-knitted body-warmer over her white robes, Sister Janina regaled us with stories of the sisterhood hiding Jewish girls during the war. Her pride in both this history and the convent's association with Zo and another SOE agent – Krystyna Skarbek, aka Christine Granville – was clear. When Bogdan told Sister Janina that I had written Skarbek's biography, she insisted on showing us through the great entrance hall with its dark wooden panelling and heavy chequerboard floor tiles, and along the cool corridors beyond to the schoolrooms with their historical displays.

A fruitful day was spent in the Warsaw Uprising Museum, which holds an audio interview with Zo among their incredible collection of film footage and artefacts. Later, a staff-member, Aleksandra Duda, and several female volunteers generously offered to translate documents and investigate queries. It was clear that getting Zo's story told would be a collective effort. Afterwards, I paid my respects at the monument outside the museum to all the women who served, a dark marble obelisk which had been organised and paid for by Zo towards the end of her life.

With such limited time in Warsaw, it was frustrating to be evacuated from a research room in the Central Archives of Modern Records (AAN), for 'Covid cleaning', just half an hour after we arrived. Fortunately, a chance corridor meeting with the director, Mariusz Olczak, helped produce the material needed: correspondence between Zo and Kazimierz Leski and Halina Martin, prison papers, and coded wartime telegrams. More were found in the Institute of National Remembrance (IPN), also in Warsaw.

Paulina kindly continued to translate on the move, as we caught the train to Gdańsk. It was here, in the Second World War Museum, that I met Andrzej Drzycimski with his stacks of recorded interviews with Zo, and a mass of correspondence between them. He also shared a sketched portrait of himself, heavily bearded, drawn by a fellow inmate during their imprisonment under martial law, and some old transcripts from tapes typed on the back of Lech Wałęsa's speeches. 'Accidentally, I connected them,' he laughed.[5] The next time Zo 'met' the first democratically elected president of Poland was when he honoured her with the nation's highest award for merit, the Order of the White Eagle. Later, I was privileged to interview President Wałęsa myself. I began to believe there might be enough material for a biography.

Nothing, however, had prepared me for the Elżbieta Zawacka Foundation in Toruń. Zo's cousin, Dorota Zawacka-Wakarecy, now the foundation's director, met me at the door. Even with her help, it took over a week to select what I needed translated from the thousands of personal files on individual Home Army soldiers, wartime publications, and post-war documentation, during which time I was daily supplied with hot tea and home-made cakes. This was the archive started by Zo after her release from prison in 1955, and it was still bursting with her handwritten notes. Despite funding issues, the archive continues to expand to this day, as well as hosting events, publishing books and running an outreach programme. After Zo's death, her entire front room was imported into the building, a microcosm of the woman herself, her bookcases still weighed down with books and papers, a straw sunhat and some ferns. Her armchair still has her woollen shawl draped over the back, and her collection of medals and personal mementoes are displayed in cabinets nearby.

Dorota also kindly arranged a series of interviews for me. The wonderful women still running the archive each took their turn to sit and share their memories of Zo, who was uniformly recalled as inspirational if, at times, abrupt. Jan Wyrowiński, Toruń's first democratically elected representative, talked about Zo's support for Solidarity, and some of her former students recalled seeking her advice on clandestine resistance during the communist years. Over the phone from the foundation, I even interviewed Bernadeta Gołecka Schmidt, Zo's prison cellmate in 1954. 'She could endure everything,' Bernadeta told me. 'Nothing could break her'.[6]

It was wonderful to walk through the streets of Toruń before catching the tram to Zo's Gagarin Street towerblock – one face of it now painted with a magnificent mural in her honour. Outside her foundation she is also remembered with a life-size bronze statue. There she sits, glasses in one hand, the other resting on a book, her medals and her Silent Unseen badge on her chest. It was good to see schoolchildren waving to her as they walked past.

Yet the most moving moment during my research was my last night in Toruń, which happened to be 31 October. In Poland people traditionally pay their respects at family graves on the eve of All Souls Day. That evening, St George's cemetery in Toruń was lit by hundreds of thousands of candles, illuminating the pathways, the yellowing leaves on the trees and the last resting places of the departed. A single, flickering candle was placed on Zo's grave, but beside it the grass was covered in fresh wreaths of white and red blooms, and dozens more candles glowing in glass lamps. There she rests, a beacon of remembrance in the darkness.

ENDNOTES

Preface

1   Colin Gubbins, Special Forces Club annual dinner (14 Jun 1963).
2   EZ to Assocn of Fighters for Freedom and Democracy (15 Jun 1961).
3   AD/EZ interview, tape 2 (28 Jun 1989).
4   EZ, *Sketches from the History of Women's Military Service* (EZF, 1992), p.vii.
5   AD/EZ interview, tape 2 (28 Jun 1989).
6   Kazimierz Bilski (aka 'Rum'), 'Zo', in Anon, *The Unseen and Silent* (Sheed & Ward, 1954), p.66.
7   AAN, II-Z-13F, Piotr Schick, 'A Jump in a Navy Blue Dress' (23 Nov 2000); Marek Widarski (dir.), *EZ, I Had a Happy Life* (Film Polski, 2005).

1. Born to Fight

1   'Terrible train crash at Pruszków', *Warsaw National Journal* (9 Jun 1939).
2   Ibid.
3   Ibid.
4   Widarski (dir.), *EZ, I Had a Happy Life*.
5   EZ, account of childhood (n.d.), AD files, Folder Biuro PPRP 1.
6   Ibid.
7   Ibid.
8   Ibid.
9   Ibid.
10 AD/EZ interview, tape 1 (1989).
11 EZ, account of childhood (n.d.).
12 AD/EZ, tape 1.
13 EZ, account of childhood; and AD/EZ tape 2.
14 EZ, account of childhood.
15 AD/EZ, tape 1.
16 Ibid.
17 Warsaw Uprising Museum, Spoken History Archive, EZ interview (2007).
18 EZ, *Sketches*, p.7.
19 EZ, account of childhood.
20 AD/EZ, tape 2.
21 EZF, 103/WSK, Zofia Grzegorzewska (n.d.).

22 Ibid.
23 Ibid.
24 Ibid.
25 Ibid.
26 AD/EZ interview, tape 3 (1989).
27 Ibid.
28 Warsaw Uprising Museum, EZ.
29 Anna Muller, *Oral History: The Challenges of Dialogue*, ed. Marta Kurkowska-Budzan and Krysztof Zamorski (John Betjeman, 2009), pp.118–19.
30 AD/EZ, tape 3.
31 Warsaw Uprising Museum, EZ.
32 AD/EZ, tape 3.
33 Ibid.
34 EZ, *Waiting for Orders* (University of Lublin, 1992), p.417.
35 Wanda Wysznacka quoted in *Waiting for Orders*, p.417.
36 AD/EZ, tape 18 (15 Jul 1990).
37 Ibid.
38 EZF, 'Misc particulars of EZ' (n.d.).
39 AD/EZ, tape 1.
40 AD/EZ interview, tape 16 (9 Apr 1990).
41 Ibid.
42 AD/EZ, tape 3.
43 Ibid.
44 AD papers, Biuro PP RP 1.
45 AD/EZ, tape 3.
46 Ibid.
47 Ibid.
48 Ibid.
49 AD/EZ interview, tape 13 (6 Jan 1990).
50 EZ, *Waiting for Orders*, p.296.
51 Warsaw Uprising Museum, EZ.
52 AD/EZ, tape 3.

2. On the Frontline

1 *Doliniacy*, film by Jaktorow town council (n.d.).
2 Eugenia Maresch, 'EZ (1909–2009), alias E. Kubitza, Mme E Riviere, Z Zajkowska, E Watson' (n.d.).
3 EZ, *Sketches*, p.81.
4 Warsaw Uprising Museum, EZ.
5 Ibid.
6 Peter Wilkinson and Joan Bright Astley, *Gubbins and SOE* (Pen & Sword, 1997) p.39.
7 M.R.D. Foot, *SOE: An Outline History of the Special Operations Executive, 1940–1946* (1999), p.8.

8   Roger Moorhouse, *First to Fight* (Bodley Head, 2019), p.3.

9   Ibid., p.55.

10   Ibid., p.57.

11   Ibid., p.4.

12   AD/EZ interview, tape 14 (9 Apr 1990).

13   Katarzyna Wysoczyńska, *Zofia Franio: W służbie ojczyźnie, w służbie człowiekowi* ['In the Service of the Motherland, in the Service of Man'] (Wydanie, 2018), p.65.

14   EZ, *Sketches*, p.75.

15   Ibid., p.21.

16   Ibid., p.83.

17   PUMST BI/1338: EZ, 'Own Account of Home Army Captain EZ, aka "Zelma", "Zo", "Sulica" about her military service in 1939–1945' (n.d., probably 1976).

18   EZ, 'Own Account . . .'

19   EZ, *Sketches*, p.83.

20   Józef Żbik, *First to Return* (Militaria, 2017), p.10.

21   EZ, 'Own Account . . .'

22   EZ, *Sketches*, p.87.

23   PUMST TP1: Zofia Franio personal file, Wacława Zastocka, 'Dr Zofia Franio', *Medical Review, Auschwitz* (1980).

24   AD/EZ, tape 16.

25   IWM, 4/1/11-26, Colin Gubbins, 'Talk to the Anglo Polish Society in Connection with Gen Bor Komorowski's Memorial Evening' (23 Nov 1966).

26   Wilkinson and Bright Astley, *Gubbins and SOE*, p.44.

27   Moorhouse, *First to Fight*, p.206.

28   CM/Danusia Nosek interview (Cichociemni Antoni Nosek's daughter) (11 Aug 21).

29   EZ, 'Own Account . . .'

30   Moorhouse, *First to Fight*, p.162.

31   Władysław Langner, Diary (unpublished, 17 Sep 1939).

32   Langner (18 Sep 1939).

33   Ibid. (19 Sep 1939).

34   Ibid. (20 Sep 1939).

35   EZ, *Sketches*, p.88.

36   Moorhouse, *First to Fight*, p.218.

37   Colin Gubbins, 'Preface', in *The Unseen and Silent*, p.x.

38   AD/EZ, tape 14; and Anna Muller, *Oral History*, p.119.

39   AD/EZ, tape 14.

40   Warsaw Uprising Museum, EZ.

41   Ibid.

42   EZ, *Sketches*, p.88.

43   Helena Dunicz Niwińska, *One of the Girls in the Band* (Auschwitz Museum, 2021), p.24.

44 EZ, 'Own Account ...'

3. Resistance

1   Sikorski to General Hayes Kroner of the US General Staff on a 1942 visit to the USA. Quoted in Marian Utnik, 'Liaison Branch of the Commander in Chief of the AK at the Supreme Command in Exile', Part 1, *Military Historical Review* (1981), p.133.
2   AD/EZ, tape 14.
3   AD/EZ, tape 16.
4   EZ, 'Own Account ...'
5   AD/EZ interview, tape 15 (1989).
6   EZ, *Sketches*, p.417.
7   Ibid.
8   Jerzy Chociłowki, 'The only woman among the Cichociemni: She carried microfilm in the handle of a spanner', *Weekend Gazeta* (15 Sep 2017).
9   Widarski (dir.), *EZ: I Had a Happy Life*.
10 EZ, *Sketches*, p.97.
11 Widarski (dir.), *EZ: I Had a Happy Life*.
12 EZF, 57/WSK – Teresa Delekta, 'Report regarding the participation of PWK members in the resistance movement, 1939–1945 (1969).
13 Jan Karski, *Story of a Secret State* (Georgetown UP, 2013) p.268.
14 Jan Nowak, *Courier from Warsaw* (Collins/Harvill, 1982), p.103.
15 Karski, *Story of a Secret State*, pp.265–6.
16 AD/EZ, tape 3.
17 IPN, EZ file, Władysław Bartoszewski, *Warsaw Ring of Death 1939–1944*, p.20.
18 AD/EZ, tape 15.
19 Institute of Polish Military History, Roger Moorhouse lecture, 'Poland in World War Two' (26 Mar 2022).
20 EZF, 15-K Zagr, Wacława Zastocka, 'Autobiographical Note' (11 Dec 80).
21 Ibid.
22 EZF, 74/WSK: Dr Zofia Franio.
23 Wacława Zastocka, 'Dr Zofia Franio', *Auschwitz Medical Review* (1980).
24 Ibid.
25 Ibid.
26 Ibid.
27 Ibid.
28 Wysoczyńska, *Zofia Franio*, p.65.
29 AD/EZ, tape 18.
30 AD/EZ, tape 17 (9 Apr 1990).
31 Ibid.
32 Ibid.
33 Karski, *Story of a Secret State*, p.266.

34 USA NARA, Records of the CIA, T.H. Chylinski, 'Poland Under Nazi Rule' (13 Nov 1941); Marek Stella-Sawicki, et al. (eds.), *First to Fight, Poland's Contribution to the Allied Victory in WW2* (2009); Teresa 'Grazyna' Kleniewska-Karska, 'War Memories', p.223.

35 Nowak, *Courier*, p.84.

36 AD/EZ, tape 15.

37 AD papers, Hanna Michalska, 'A few comments concerning EZ's recorded memories' (n.d.).

38 Nowak, *Courier*, p.105.

39 AD papers, Hanna Michalska, 'A few comments concerning EZ's recorded memories' (n.d.).

40 AD/EZ, tape 17.

41 AD/EZ, tape 15.

42 Ibid.

43 Ibid.

44 Ibid.

45 Ibid.

46 AD/EZ, tape 2.

47 Warsaw Uprising Museum, EZ.

48 Ibid.

49 AD/EZ, tape 17.

50 Anon, 'Liaison', in *The Unseen and Silent*, p.59.

51 Józef Garliński, *Poland, SOE and the Allies* (George Allen & Unwin, 1969), p.32.

4. Navigating Nazi Germany

1   AD/EZ, tape 13.

2   EZ Foundation, 57/WSK, Teresa Delekta, Józef Słaboszewski, quoted in 'Résumé' (anon, n.d.).

3

4   Robert Petersen, '"When a Nation is Being Murdered", The Secret Biological and Chemical Warfare Against the Third Reich' in *Scientific Journals of AON*, nr 2 (103) (2016).

5   EZ Foundation, 12K/Zagr: Emilia Malessa and Witold Sowiński, 'AK Captain Emilia, Maria Malessa-Piwnik' (20 Jun 1984).

6   AD/EZ, tape 13.

7   Ibid.

8   Ibid.

9   Ibid.

10 Ibid.

11 Warsaw Uprising Museum, EZ.

12 AD/EZ interview, tape 23 (17 Feb 1992).

13 EZF, 12K/Zagr: Emilia Malessa, 'Account of Malessa by Karolina Karpus, Sylvia Krzyncincki and Joanna Pieńkoska' (n.d.).

14 Malessa and Sowiński, 'AK Captain Emilia, Maria Malessa-Piwnik'.
15 EZ, 'Own Account . . .'; and Józef Żbik, *First to Return* (Militaria.pl, 2017), p.15.
16 AD/EZ, tape 13.
17 EZ Foundation, 'Misc Particulars of EZ', EZ, 'Reports on Berlin Contacts, Zo' (Nov 1969).
18 AD/EZ, tape 13.
19 Jan Szatsznajder, *Cichociemni, Z Polski Do Polski* ['Silent Unseen, From Poland to Poland'] (1990), p.229.
20 AD/EZ, tape 13.
21 Malessa and Sowiński, 'AK Captain Emilia, Maria Malessa-Piwnik'.
22 Ibid.
23 EZF, 12K/Zagr: Emilia Malessa, EZ, 'Emilia Malessa' (10 Oct 1991).
24 Ibid.
25 Kazimierz Bilski, 'Zo', *The Unseen and Silent*, p.61.
26 *The Goebbels Diaries, 1939–1941*, ed. and trans. Fred Taylor (Sphere, 1983), p.227.
27 IWM, Gubbins papers, 4/1/4, Colin Gubbins, 'SOE' (n.d.).
28 Żbik, *First to Return*.
29 IWM, Gubbins papers, 4/1/50, Peter Wilkinson, 'Gubbins: A Resistance Leader' (28 Apr 1990).
30 AD/EZ, tape 16.
31 Ibid.
32 AD/EZ, tape 18.
33 Ibid.
34 Malessa and Sowiński, 'AK Captain Emilia, Maria Malessa-Piwnik'.
35 AD/EZ, tape 13.
36 Widarski (dir.), *EZ, I Had a Happy Life*.
37 AD/EZ, tape 17.
38 Ibid.
39 EZF, 57/WSK Teresa Delekta 'Janka', Teresa Delekta 'Report on avoiding arrest, 1941' (12 Feb 1974).
40 AD/EZ, tape 18.
41 USC Shoah Foundation Institute, Political Prisoner Leonard T. Zawacki Testimony (10 Dec 1997).
42 Zbik, *First to Return*, p.181.
43 AD/EZ, tape 17.
44 Walter Schellenberg, *Hitler's Secret Service* (Pyramid, 1971), p.140.
45 Ibid.
46 AD/EZ, tape 23.
47 AD/EZ, tape 18.
48 Ibid.
49 AD/EZ, tape 15.
50 AD/EZ interview, tape 20 (9 Oct 1991).
51 Ibid.

52 Ibid.
53 Ibid.
54 Ibid.
55 IPN, GK 629/7433 Egon Zawacki, Gestapo report (23 Aug 1941).
56 IPN, GK 629/7433 Egon Zawacki, Gestapo report (n.d.).
57 AD/EZ, tape 23.
58 IPN, GK 629/7433 Egon Zawacki, Gestapo report (16 Aug 1941).
59 IPN, GK 629/7433 Egon Zawacki, Gestapo report (15 Sep 1941).
60 Ibid.
61 Ibid.
62 EZ, *Sketches*, p.122; and AAN, II-Z-13F, EZ, 'My Trip to London, to the HQ of the Chief Commander'.
63 AD/EZ, tape 18.
64 Cezary Chlebowski, *Pozdrówcie Góry Świętokrzyskie* ['Greet the Holy Cross Mountains'] (Epoka, 1988), p.16.
65 Ibid.
66 PUMST, Jan Piwnik personal file, 'Qualification Sheet' (n.d.).
67 Chlebowski, 'Greet the Holy Cross Mountains', p.31.
68 Ibid.
69 EZ, 'Emilia Malessa' (10 Oct 1991).
70 Marek Ney-Krwawicz, 'Female Soldiers of the Polish Home Army', www.polishresistance-ak.org. (Accessed Dec 2021).
71 Ibid.
72 AD/EZ, tape 23.

5. Evading the Gestapo

1   AD/EZ, tape 18.
2   Widarski (dir.), *EZ, I Had a Happy Life*; AD/EZ interview, tape 19 (16 Jul 1990); Jerzy Chociłowki, 'The only woman among the Cichociemni, she carried microfilms in the handle of a spanner', *WeekendGazeta.pl* (15 Sep 2017).
3   Warsaw Uprising Museum, EZ.
4   AD/EZ, tape 1.
5   Warsaw Uprising Museum, EZ.
6   AD/EZ, tape 2.
7   AD/EZ, tape 19.
8   Warsaw Uprising Museum, EZ.
9   EZF, 392/WSK: Jadwiga Zatorska 'Saba', EZ, 'About Jadwiga Zatorska' (Mar 1974).
10 EZF, 392/WSK: Jadwiga Zatorska 'Saba', Jadwiga Zatorska, 'History of Participation of PWKs in the resistance movement, 1939–1945' (1 Jun 1969).
11 AD/EZ, tape 19.
12 Ibid.
13 EZF, 392/WSK: Jadwiga Zatorska 'Saba', EZ, 'About Jadwiga Zatorska'

(Mar 1974).

14 Ibid.
15 AD/EZ, tape 19.
16 Warsaw Uprising Museum, EZ.
17 AD/EZ, tape 19.
18 Warsaw Uprising Museum, EZ.
19 Sue Ryder, *Child of My Love* (Harvill Press, 1997), p.90.
20 Warsaw Uprising Museum, EZ.
21 AD/EZ, tape 19.
22 Ibid.
23 Ibid.
24 Ibid.
25 Ryder, *Child of My Love*, pp.90–91.
26 AD/EZ, tape 19.
27 Ibid.
28 Ibid.
29 Warsaw Uprising Museum, EZ.
30 Ibid.
31 AD/EZ, tape 19.
32 Ibid.
33 Ryder, *Child of My Love*, p.91.
34 AD/EZ, tape 19.
35 EZF, 'Miscellaneous particulars of EZ', EZ to Józef Bieniek (29 Oct 1972).
36 AD/EZ, tape 1.
37 EZF, 317/WKA: Stanisława Sojka, 'Staszka' (n.d.).
38 IPN, GK 629/7433, Egon Zawacki, Gestapo note (15 Aug 1942).
39 Eugenia Maresch archive, Maryla Sobocińska (Ryśka), 'Funeral Oration for Zo' (22 Mar 2009).
40 AAN, Warsaw, II-2-13F, typed slip (28 Sep 1942).
41 EZ, 'Own Account . . .'
42 Ryder, *Child of My Love*, p.92.

6. Emissary to Paris

1   AD, Biuro Prezydenta RP2.
2   AD/EZ, tape 4.
3   Sobocińska, 'Funeral Oration for Zo'.
4   EZ, *Sketches*, p.327.
5   Kazimierz Bilski, 'Zo', *The Unseen and Silent*, p.60.
6   AD/EZ, tape 23.
7   Ibid.
8   Warsaw Uprising Museum, EZ.
9   EZF, 123-K/Zagr: Alicja Iwańska 'Wiewiórka', Alicja Iwańska, 'In Tears-24' (2 Sep 1993).
10 Ibid.

11 Major Zbigniew 'Szyna' Lewandowski, quoted in Wacława 'Wacka' Zastocka, 'Dr Zofia Franion', *Przeglad Lekarski-Oświęcim* ['Auschwitz Medical Journal'] (1980).
12 Ibid.
13 PUMST, A 374/230, radiogram Rowecki to 'Wanda' (11 Dec 1942).
14 AD, Biuro Prezydenta RP2.
15 EZ, *Sketches*, p.328.
16 AD, Biuro Prezydenta RP2.
17 TNA, HS9/1635/3, Interrogation of Elizabeth Watson (20 May 1943).
18 AD/EZ, tape 4.
19 Ibid.
20 Ibid.
21 AD files, Biuro Prezydenta RP2 (n.d.).
22 Warsaw Uprising Museum, EZ.
23 Kazimierz Leski, *Życie niewslaściwie urozmaicone* ['A Chequered Life'] (2009), p.237.
24 Ibid.
25 AD, Biuro Prezydenta RP2.
26 AD/EZ interview, tape 12 (6 Jan 1990).
27 EZF, Misc Particulars of EZ, 'Recording with Mrs EZ' (17 Jan 1984).
28 Leski, 'A Chequered Life', p.238.
29 Ibid.
30 Ibid., p.240.
31 Tadeusz Bór-Komorowski, *The Secret Army* (Victor Gollancz, 1950), p.111.

7. Escape to England

1 TNA, HS9/1635/3, Interrogation of Elizabeth Watson (20 Apr 1943).
2 AD/EZ, tape 5.
3 EZF, Misc Particulars of EZ, 'Recording with Mrs EZ' (17 Jan 1984).
4 AD/EZ, tape 5.
5 Leski, 'A Chequered Life', p.237.
6 EZF, Misc Particulars of EZ, 'Recording with Mrs EZ' (17 Jan 1984).
7 AD/EZ, tape 12.
8 AD/EZ, tape 5.
9 AD/EZ, tape 12.
10 AD, Biuro Prezydenta RP1.
11 Leski, 'A Chequered Life', p.240.
12 AD/EZ, tape 5.
13 TNA, HS9/1635/3, Interrogation of Elizabeth Watson (20 Apr 1943).
14 PISM, A XII 4/160 (n.d.).
15 AD/EZ, tape 5.
16 Szatsznajder, 'Silent Unseen, From Poland to Poland', p.234.
17 Ryder, *Child of My Love*, p.98.
18 Leski, 'A Chequered Life', p.239.

19   AD/EZ interview, tape 6 (28 Jun 1989).
20   Ibid.
21   Ibid.
22   AD/EZ, tape 20.
23   Nowak, *Courier*, p.192.
24   Ibid., p.106.
25   AD/EZ, tape 5.
26   AD/EZ, tape 5; Ryder, *Child of My Love*, p.96.
27   Warsaw Uprising Museum, EZ.
28   AD/EZ, tape 5.
29   Ibid.
30   Ibid.
31   Ibid.
32   Ibid.
33   Ibid.
34   Warsaw Uprising Museum, EZ.
35   AD/EZ, tape 5.
36   Ibid.
37   Ryder, *Child of My Love*, p.97.
38   AD/EZ, tape 5.
39   Warsaw Uprising Museum, EZ.
40   AD/EZ, tape 5.
41   Ibid.
42   Warsaw Uprising Museum, EZ.
43   Ryder, *Child of My Love*, p.98.
44   TNA, HS9/1635/3, Interrogation of Elizabeth Watson (20 Apr 1943).
45   AD/EZ, tape 5.
46   Ibid.
47   Ryder, *Child of My Love*, p.99.
48   AD/EZ, tape 5.
49   Warsaw Uprising Museum, EZ.
50   Ryder, *Child of My Love*, p.100.
51   Warsaw Uprising Museum, EZ.
52   AD files, Biuro Prezydenta RP 2.
53   PUMST, A93/189, Major Truszkowski, 'Zo's report from Barcelona' (13 Apr 1942).
54   PISM, A XII.4/155 cz II, Filenote (13.1.1942); PISM, A.XII.4/155 cz.II, Ernest R. Howlett, letter to 'Polish Leaders in GB . . .' (25 Mar 1942).
55   PISM, A.XII.4/155 cz.II, Foreign Office letter (29 Jan 1942).
56   TNA, HS4/278, SOE Poland 1943, Vol T-Z, 'Landing Form A'.
57   PUMST, KOL 23/326, EZ personal file, 1984/43.
58   Warsaw Uprising Museum, EZ.
59   Ryder, *Child of My Love*, p.100.
60   EZF, Misc Particulars of EZ, 'Recording with Mrs EZ' (17 Jan 1984).
61   Kazimierz Bilski, 'Zo', *The Unseen and Silent*, p.61.

62 AD/EZ, tape 6.
63 Ibid.
64 Ibid.
65 Warsaw Uprising Museum, EZ.
66 Judy Batalion, *The Light of Days: Women Fighters of the Jewish Resistance* (Virago, 2021), p.195.
67 Halik Kochanski, *The Eagle Unbowed: Poland and the Poles in the Second World War* (Penguin, 2013), p.310.
68 Marek Edelman, *The Ghetto Fights* (Booksmarks, 1990), p.76.
69 TNA, HS4/278, SOE Poland 1943, Vol T–Z.
70 *The Goebbels Diaries*, p.211.
71 David Engel, *Facing a Holocaust: The Polish Government-in-exile and the Jews, 1943–1945* (UNC Press Books, 1993), p.71.
72 EZ, 'Own account . . .'
73 Warsaw Uprising Museum, EZ.
74 Ibid.
75 Ryder, *Child of My Love*, p.101.

8. A Rather Difficult Woman

1 TNA, HS9/1635/3, EZ Nightingale Lane interrogation (4 May 1943).
2 Warsaw Uprising Museum, EZ.
3 Wladimir Ledóchowski, 'Christine Skarbek-Granville' (unpublished ms, n.d.), p.119.
4 TNA, HS9/1935/3, Mjr H.J. Baxter to Capt N.G. Mott (10 May 1943).
5 Kazimierz Bilski, 'Zo', *The Unseen and Silent*, p.61.
6 Andrew Bilski, 'Secrets of the Green Box' (unpublished ms, n.d.), p.2.
7 PUMST, KOL 23/17, Kazimierz Bilski personal file, 6-7940, 'Finishing report' (15 May 1942).
8 Andrew Bilski, 'Secrets', p.46.
9 PUMST, 'Honorable Mornings of Valour' (28.9.1942); Andrew Bilski, 'Secrets', p.53; and Kazimierz Bilski, 'Zo', *The Unseen and Silent*, p.60.
10 PUMST, KOL 23/326, EZ personal file, Sixth Bureau registration form.
11 Kazimierz Bilski, 'Zo', *The Unseen and Silent*, p.61.
12 Ibid.
13 Ibid.
14 Ibid.
15 Ibid.
16 Ibid.
17 Ibid.
18 EZ, *Sketches*, p.342.
19 Ibid.
20 Kazimierz Bilski, 'Zo', *The Unseen and Silent*, p.61.
21 AD/EZ interviews, tape 8 (28 Jun 1989) and tape 24 (18 Feb 1992).
22 AD/EZ, tape 8.
23 Kazimierz Bilski, 'Zo', *The Unseen and Silent*, p.61.

24 AD/EZ interview, tape 7 (28 Jun 1989).
25 Kazimierz Bilski, 'Zo', *The Unseen and Silent*, p.61.
26 AD/EZ, tape 12.
27 Ryder, *Child of My Love*, p.102.
28 Bór-Komorowski, *The Secret Army*, p.151.
29 TNA, HS9/1635/3 'Interview with Elizabeth Watson & Jan Jankowski' (10 May 1943).
30 Ryder, *Child of My Love*, p.101.
31 Karski, *Story of a Secret State*, pp.311–12.
32 Republic of Poland, Ministry of Foreign Affairs, *The Mass Extermination of the Jews in German Occupied Poland* (10 Dec 1942, reprint 2019).
33 Karski, *Story of a Secret State*, Foreword.
34 *The Goebbels Diaries, 1939–1941*, p.196.
35 TNA, HS4/278, 'Interview with Elizabeth Watson & Jan Jankowski' (10 May 1943).
36 Karski, *Story of a Secret State*, p.111.
37 Ibid., Foreword.
38 Jack Fairweather, *The Volunteer* (Penguin, 2019), p.301.
39 TNA, HS9/1635/3, 'Interrogation of Elizabeth Watson' (20 May 1943).
40 Ibid.; and Mjr H.J. Baxter to Capt. N.G. Nott (10 May 1943).
41 TNA, HS4/278, 'Interview with Elizabeth Watson & Jan Jankowski' (10 May 1943).
42 Ibid.
43 TNA, HS4/278, MP to M/CD (13 May 1943).
44 Ibid.
45 Gubbins, 'Talk to the Anglo Polish Society'.
46 TNA, HS4/278, MP to M/CD (13 May 1943).
47 TNA, HS4/278, M/CD to CD (14 May 1943).
48 PUMST, KOL 23/326, EZ personal file.
49 Ibid., EZ statement (18 Oct 1976).
50 Karski, *Story of a Secret State*, p.112.
51 AD/EZ, tape 7.
52 Marian Kukiel, *General Sikorski, Soldier and Statesman of Fighting Poland* (PISM, 1995), p.235.
53 AD/EZ, tape 7.
54 Widarski (dir.), *EZ, I Had a Happy Life*.
55 EZF, 'Misc particulars of EZ', EZ to Andrzeja Mareckiego (31 Dec 1982).
56 Kazimierz Bilski, 'Zo', *The Unseen and Silent*, p.64.
57 EZ, *Sketches*, p.334.
58 PUMST, KOL 23/326, EZ personal file, 'Request for Military Cross' (1943).
59 AD/EZ, tape 7.
60 Ibid.

61 Ibid.
62 Ibid.
63 AD/EZ, tape 24.
64 PUMST, KOL 23/326, EZ personal file.
65 Kazimierz Bilski, 'Zo', *The Unseen and Silent*, p.62.
66 AD/EZ, tape 8.
67 Zbik, *First to Return*, p.1.
68 PUMST, KOL 23/326, EZ personal file, EZ statement (18 Oct 1976).
69 Kazimierz Bilski, 'Zo', *The Unseen and Silent*, p.62.
70 Ibid., p.63.
71 Ibid.
72 Ibid.
73 CM/AD interview, Gdańsk (27 Oct 2021).
74 AD/EZ, tape 8.
75 Kazimierz Bilski, 'Zo', *The Unseen and Silent*, p.63.
76 Ibid.
77 AD/EZ, tape 7.
78 Ibid.
79 Kazimierz Bilski, 'Zo', *The Unseen and Silent*, p.64.
80 Ibid., p.62; and Nowak, *Courier*, p.405.
81 Kazimierz Bilski, 'Zo', *The Unseen and Silent*, p.62.
82 Ibid.
83 AAN, 'A report from the emissary Zo from her stay in HQ, 4 May–29 June 1943'.
84 EZ, *Sketches*, p.333; Kazimierz Bilski, 'Zo', *The Unseen and Silent*, p.63.
85 AD/EZ, tape 24.
86 PUMST, 23/326, 'Elżbieta Zawacka statement' (18 Oct 1976).

9. A Militant Female Dictator

1   EZ, 'Own Account . . .'
2   EZ, *Sketches*, p.342 and p.330.
3   Warsaw Uprising Museum, EZ.
4   Bór-Komorowski, *The Secret Army*, p.139.
5   EZ, 'Own Account . . .'
6   EZ Foundation, 718/WSK Zofia Leśniowska, née Sikorska; Kukiel, *General Sikorski*, p.235.
7   Col. Mitkiewicz quoted in Olgierd Terlecki, *General Sikorski* (Wydawnictwo, 1981), p.541.
8   Ibid.
9   Olgierd Terlecki, *General Sikorski* (Wydawnictwo, 1981), p.215.
10 Kochanski, *The Eagle Unbowed*, p.346.
11 TNA, FO/371, 'Death of Sikorski', PM's draft broadcast.
12 Nowak, *Courier*, p.163.
13 Bór-Komorowski, *The Secret Army*, p.142.
14 Nowak, *Courier*, p.163; and Bór-Komorowski, *The Secret Army*, p.142.

15   EZF, Misc Particulars of EZ, 'EZ letter to the press re death of "Pank-rac"' (14 Aug 1970).
16   AD/EZ, tape 7.
17   AD/EZ, tape 12.
18   CM correspondence with Julia Rooke, BBC journalist who interviewed Zo in 2001 (28 Jan 2024).
19   AD/EZ, tape 7.
20   Kochanski, *The Eagle Unbowed*, p.348.
21   AD, loose papers, 'EZ's meeting with the Minister for the Interior, London 1943'
22   AD/EZ interview, tape 9 (28 Jun 1989).
23   Ibid.
24   Agnes Hardie MP and Campbell Stephen MP, National Service Bill, HC Deb 10 December 1941, vol 376 cc1565-629, Hansard. Available at: https://api.parliament.uk/historic-hansard/commons/1941/dec/10/national-service-bill-1 (Accessed Mar 2022).
25   Irene Ward MP, ibid.
26   PUMST, KOL 23/326, EZ personal file.
27   EZ, *Sketches*, p.336.
28   TNA, HS4/278, Harold Perkins to Marian Gamwell (12 Jul 1943).
29   Ibid.
30   TNA, HS4/278, Couriers: Polish Personnel, Harold Perkins to Marian Gamwell (12 Jul 1943).
31   Ibid.
32   IWM, Audio archive, 10057, Sue Ryder, Reel 1.
33   IWM, Audio archive, 502, Antonia Marian Gamwell (5 Nov 1974).
34   TNA, HS9/114/2, Yolande Beekman PF; and Yvonne Cormeau PF.
35   TNA, HS9/355/2, Pearl Witherington PF.
36   AD/EZ, tape 9.
37   Ibid.
38   Ibid.
39   Ibid.
40   AD/EZ, tape 8.
41   AD/EZ, tape 9.
42   TNA, HS4/278, Harold Perkins letter to Marian Gamwell (12 Jul 1943).
43   EZ, 'Own Account . . .'
44   Joyce Anne Deane, née Morley, Article A2121148, *WW2 People's War*, BBC (20 Nov 2003), www.bbc.co.uk/history/ww2peopleswar/about/siteinformation.shtml
45   AD/EZ, tape 9.
46   TNA, HS4/278, Couriers, Polish Personnel, MP to D/AIR (7 Aug 1943).
47   PUMST, KOL 23/326, EZ personal file.
48   TNA, NS4/278, Couriers, Polish Personnel, MPK to F (16 Jul 43).
49   Ibid.
50   AD/EZ, tape 7.

51 EZ, *Sketches*, p.337.
52 IWM, Box 86/46/1 Miss A.M. Gamwell, poem: 'FANY HQ, Scotland' (May 1943).
53 EZ, *Sketches*, p.337.
54 AD/EZ, tape 9.
55 Ibid.
56 Marta Sikorska-Kowalska, 'Aims and forms of Polish feminist activity in *Ster* and *Nowe Słowo* during the First World War', *Studia z Historii Społeczno-Gospodarczej XIX i XX wieku* ['Studies in Social and Economic History of the 19th and 20th Centuries'] (2014), 13, pp.59–68.
57 AD/EZ, tape 9.
58 EZ, 'Own Account ...'
59 PUMST A 309/51, EZ to Minister for Defence, London (6 Sep 1943).
60 EZ, *Sketches*, p.334.
61 AD, loose papers, 'EZ's meeting with Minister for Interior, London 1943'.
62 EZ, *Sketches*, p.345.
63 Ibid., p.347.
64 Ibid.
65 Ibid.
66 PUMST, KOL 23/326, EZ personal file.
67 Ibid.
68 Warsaw Uprising Museum, EZ.
69 Ibid.
70 Ibid.

10. Female, Silent, Unseen

1 PUMST, SK 107/114, 'M.A. North to Capt Krzyżanowski' (23 Aug 1943).
2 Przemysław Bystrzycki, *Znak Cichociemnych* ['The Sign of the Silent Unseen'] (1991), p.198.
3 PUMST, SK 107/131 'EZ, memo' (n.d.).
4 David Stafford, *Secret Agent: The True Story of the SOE* (BBC Books, 2000), p.236.
5 Wilson and Bright Astley, *Gubbins and SOE*, p.80.
6 PUMST, SK 155, Medical Reports (18 May 1942).
7 PUMST, KOL 23/326, EZ personal file; and PUMST, SK 155, Czubac (17 Oct 1943).
8 Tomasz Kostuch in Widarski (dir.) *Cichociemni*.
9 Alan Mack, interview available at: www.english-heritage.org.uk/visit/places/audley-end-house-and-gardens/history-and-stories/silent-unseen/ (2011).
10 Antoni Nosek, Speech, SOE-Polish Section Reunion, Audley End House (24 May 1998).
11 EZ, 'Own account ...' p.38; AD/EZ, tape 8.
12 Widarski (dir.), *Cichociemni*.

13 AD/EZ, tape 8.

14 Ibid.

15 Peter Howe, 'Recollections of Cpl. P Howe, Audley End 1942–44' (ms, 29 Sep 1986), English Heritage, East of England Regional Office, Cambridge Archive.

16 PUMST, SK 167, STS 31 Finishing Report for Tarnowska (2 Nov 1942).

17 PUMST, SK 167, STS 31 Finishing Report for Lubiewa (2 Nov 1942).

18 Ibid.

19 Zofia Jordanowska interview with Tomasz Magierski, Andrezej Adamczak and Rafał Mierzejewski (1993).

20 Ibid.

21 Nowak, *Courier*, p.171.

22 Ibid.

23 Ibid., p.167.

24 Ibid., p.196.

25 Ibid., p.192.

26 Ibid.

27 Ibid., p.193.

28 Oswald Guziur, 'Tragiczna próba wspólpracy' ['A Tragic Attempt at Co-operation'] in *Zwrot* ['Return'] (March 1992).

29 Nowak, *Courier*, p.197.

30 Ibid.

31 Kazimierz Bilski, 'Zo', *The Unseen and Silent*, p.64.

32 Leo Marks, *Between Silk and Cyanide* (Harper Collins, 2000), p.2.

33 See: http://elitadywersji.org/cichociemni-szkolenie/ (Accessed 7 Nov 2022).

34 Anon, *Spadochroniarze Polscy* ['Polish Paratroopers'] (23 Sep 1942–23 Sep 1943), p.2.

35 Ludwik Witkowski in Widarski, *Cichociemni*.

36 Anon, *Spadochroniarze Polscy* ['Polish Paratroopers'] (23 Sep 1942–23 Sep 1943), p.4 and p.3.

37 Waldemar Grabowski, 'Female Paratroopers' in EZF *Bulletin* 1–2, 60–61 (2011), p.8.

38 Zofia Jordanowska interviews with Tomasz Magierski, Andrezej Adamczak and Rafał Mierzejewski (1993).

39 AD/EZ, tape 8.

40 Nowak, *Courier*, p.283; and Adolf Pilch, *Partyzanci Trzech Puszcz* ['Partisans of Three Forests'] (Spotkania, 1992), ch.4.

41 PUMST, SK 167.

42 Ibid.

43 TNA, HS9/409/7; and HS9/451/1.

44 PUMST, SK 167.

45 Wilson and Bright Astley, *Gubbins and SOE*, p.82.

46 Ibid.

47 AD/EZ, tape 8.

48 Nowak, *Courier*, p.284.
49 AD/EZ, tape 8.
50 AD/EZ, tape 9.
51 AD/EZ, tape 8.
52 Ibid.
53 Nowak, *Courier*, p.283.
54 Kazimierz Bilski, 'Zo', *The Unseen and Silent*, p.64.
55 Ibid.
56 Ibid.
57 Ibid.
58 Ibid.
59 Ibid.
60 AD/EZ interview, tape 22 (17 Feb 1992).
61 Kazimierz Bilski, 'Zo', *The Unseen and Silent*, p.65.
62 Ibid.
63 Ibid.
64 AD/EZ, tape 9.
65 Sue Ryder, *And the Morrow is Theirs* (Burleigh Press, 1975), p.40.
66 PUMST, SK 142, Prelim report, STS G25 Garramor (6 Sep 1943).
67 Ludwik Witkowski in Widarski (dir.), *Cichociemni*.
68 Ryder, *And the Morrow*, p.41; and IWM Audio archive, 10057, Sue Ryder, Reel 1.
69 Ryder, *And the Morrow*, p.33.
70 Ibid., p.38.
71 IWM, Audio archive, 10057, Sue Ryder, Reel 1.
72 Ibid.
73 Ryder, *And the Morrow*, p.40.
74 Stanisław Jankowski in Widarski (dir.), *Cichociemni*.
75 AD/EZ, tape 8.
76 PUMST, SK 169/150, list of Silent Unseen parachuters (24 Apr 1944).
77 PUMST, SK 169/109, Protasewicz filenote (1943).
78 IWM, Audio archive, 10057, Sue Ryder, Reel 2.
79 Col. Protasewicz, 'Instructions for soldiers smuggled by air to the country' (1 Jun 1943). Available at: www.warrelics.eu/forum/polish-armed-forces-est-polskie-si-y-zbrojne-na-zachodzie-1939-1947/cichociemni-polish-soe-12905
80 Ibid.
81 EZF, Misc particulars of EZ, EZ to J. Brochocki (1972).
82 Warsaw Uprising Museum, EZ.
83 IWM, Audio archive, 10057, Sue Ryder, Reel 2.
84 *The Goebbels Diaries*, p.352.
85 Stanisław Jankowski, *Agaton, With a False Ausweis in Real Warsaw* (1980), p.1; and Michael Goszczynski in Widarski (dir.), *Cichociemni*.
86 EZF, Misc particulars of EZ, EZ to J. Brochocki (1972).
87 PUMST, SK 203/194, 'Receipt' (15 Feb 1945).

88   Jędrzej Tucholski, *Cichociemni* (Instytut Wydawniczy, 1985).
89   Ibid.
90   Ryder, *And the Morrow*, p.40.

11. The Only Daughter of the Sky

1   PUMST, EZ, 'Cichociemny "ZO"' (typed ms, n.d.).
2   Schick, 'A Jump in a Navy Blue Dress'; and PUMST, EZ, 'Cichociemny
     "ZO"' (typed ms, n.d.).
3   Sobocińska, 'Funeral Oration for Zo'.
4   Bogusław Szmajdowicz, Letter to Editor, *Przekroju* ['Cross Section'] (3
     Feb 1974).
5   *Salon 24* website, 'Bridge in Toruń: One Bridge too far in Distorting our
     History?' (24 May 2016).
6   Józef Bieniek, 'Kurierka' [Courier] in *Przekroju* ['Cross Section'], no
     1486 (30 Sep 1973).
7   *Salon 24* website, 'Bridge in Toruń'.
8   Anon, *Spadochroniarze Polsky* ['Polish Paratroopers'] (23 Sep 1942–23
     Sep 1943).
9   PUMST, EZ, 'Cichociemny "ZO"' (typed ms, n.d.).
10   Ibid.
11   Ibid.
12   AD/EZ, tape 20.
13   Widarski (dir.), *EZ, I Had a Happy Life*.
14   AD/EZ interview, tape 20 (9 Oct 1991).
15   Ibid.
16   IPN, leaflet, 'General Brigadier Elżbieta Zawacka "Zo"' (1909–2009)
     (n.d.).
17   EZF, 27-M/Zagr 'Jarach', Rena Laskowska, 'Jarach' (21 Apr 1974).
18   AD/EZ interview, tape 10 (28 Jun 1989).
19   EZF, 27-M/Zagr, 'Jarach', Rena Laskowska, 'Jarach' (21 Apr 1974).
20   Ibid.
21   EZF, 12-K/Zagr, 'Emilia Malessa', EZ, 'Emilia Malessa' (10 Oct 1991).
22   AD/EZ, tape 20.
23   EZF, 19-K/Zagr, 'Róża Marczewska "Lula" (1910–1944)', EZ and
     Dorota Kromp, 'Róża Marczewska Biographical Note' (24 Aug 2005).
24   EZF, 19-K/Zagr, 'Róża Marczewska "Lula" (1910–1944)', EZ and
     Dorota Kromp, 'Róża Marczewska Biographical Note'.
25   Ibid.
26   EZF, 123-K/Zagr 'Alicja Iwańska', Alicja Iwańska to EZ (1 Aug 2003).
27   AD/EZ, tape 12.
28   Ibid; and tape 20.
29   AD/EZ, tape 20.
30   Ibid.
31   Łukasz Badnarski family archive, Marianna Zawodzińska to step-father
     Kazimierz Popiel (10 Oct 1943).

32 AD/EZ, tape 18.

33 AD/EZ, tape 20.

34 EZF, 105-K/Zagr, 'Marianna Zawodzińska', W. Wysznacka, 'Memories of Maria Zawodzińska' (n.d.).

35 EZ, 'Own account . . .'

36 Ibid.

37 EZF, 18-K/Zagr, 'Hanna Michalska'.

38 AD/EZ, tape 23.

39 Ibid.

40 Barbara Szczepuła, '"Marcysia", a soldier of the Home Army and WiN and her husband, the legendary commandant "Ponury"', *Dziennik Bałtycki* ['The Baltic Journal'] (12 Mar 2015).

41 Kacper Śledziński, *Cichociemni Elita Polskiej Dywersji* ['Silent Unseen, Elite of the Polish Diversion'] (Wydewnictwo Znak, 2012) p.266.

42 Dr Józefa Stafenowska-Rybus, quoted in Maria Weber, *Emilia Malessa 'Marcysia' 1909–1949* (Oficyna Wydawnicza RYTM, 2013), p.87.

43 EZF, 12-K/Zagr, 'Emilia Malessa', EZ, 'Emilia Malessa' (10 Oct 91).

44 Ibid.

45 Ibid.

46 Ibid.

47 Andrew Bilski, 'Secrets', p.67.

48 Ibid.

49 Nowak, *Courier*, p.211.

50 Ibid., p.174.

51 Ibid., p.188.

52 Ibid., p.213.

53 Ibid.

54 Ibid.

55 Ibid.

56 Ibid., p.176.

57 Ibid., p.236.

58 Ibid., p.216.

59 Ibid., p.215.

60 Lynne Olson and Stanley Cloud, *For Your Freedom and Ours* (William Heineman, 2003), p.277.

61 Jonathan Walker, *Poland Alone* (History Press, 2010), p.266.

62 Nowak, *Courier*, p.211.

63 Ibid., p.268.

64 Ibid.

65 TNA, P/F HS 9/1112/2, Margaret Audrey NORTH, filenote (4 Aug 1943).

12. Betrayed

1   EZF, 18-K Zagr: Hanna Michalska.

2   EZ, 'Own account . . .'

3   AD/EZ interview, tape 21 (9 Oct 1991).

4   EZF, 18-K Zagr: Hanna Michalska.

5   Ibid.

6   AD/EZ, tape 21.

7   Nowak, *Courier*, p.285.

8   AD/EZ, tape 23.

9   Zbik, *First to Return*, p.127.

10   Ibid.

11   EZF, 65-K Zagr: Ludwiuka Zawierta.

12   Ibid.

13   EZF, 27-M Zagr, Elżbieta Zawacka, 'Jarach's betrayal' (n.d.)

14   EZF, 19-K Zagr, Róża Marczewska 'Lula', EZ and Dorota Kromp, 'Róża Marczewska Biographical Note' (24 Sep 2005).

15   EZF, 18-K Zagr: Hanna Michalska.

16   Ibid.

17   AD/EZ, tape 21.

18   EZF, 27-M Zagr, Tadeusz Borowy, 'Who was Jarach?' in *Tygodnik Katolicki* ['Catholic Weekly'] (11 Oct 1987).

19   AD/EZ, tape 21.

20   Ibid.

21   EZF, 27-M Zagr, EZ, 'Jarach's betrayal' (n.d.).

22   AD/EZ, tape 21.

23   AD/EZ, tape 2.

24   AD/EZ, tape 21.

25   Andrew Bilski, 'Secrets', p.74.

26   Kazimierz Bilski, 'Zo', *The Unseen and Silent*, p.65.

27   Ibid.

28   Nowak, *Courier*, p.285.

29   TNA, HS4,184: Filenote M3/238, Lt. Col. H. M. Threlfall, 'Special Operations to Poland from the Mediterranean Theatre of Operations' (30 May 1945).

30   TNA, HS 9/1112/2, Margaret Audrey North, personal file, Harold Perkins, 'Memo MP to D/CE' (25 Apr 44).

31   TNA, HS 9/1112/2, Margaret Audrey North, personal file, 'Memo D/CE to ACD' (25 Apr 44).

32   PUMST, Kasimierz Bilski personal file, Bilski to Staff of the Supreme Commander (28 Apr 1944).

33   TNA, HS 9/1112/2, Margaret Audrey North, personal file, 'Margaret Audrey North' (n.d.).

34   'Makary' (Pasta), 'The Capture of V-Weapons', in *The Unseen and Silent*, p.167.

35   TNA, HS4, 184: Filenote M3/238, Lt. Col. H. M. Threlfall, 'Special Operations to Poland from the Mediterranean Theatre of Operations' (30 May 1945).

36   PUMST, Jan Piwnik personal file, Janusz Prawdzic-Szlaski (13 Jul 1946), wartime diary (15 Jun 1944).

37   Ibid.
38   Ibid.
39   Weber, *Emilia Malessa*, p.90.
40   Ibid.
41   Dariusz Baliszewski, 'Kapitan Marcysia' in *Wprost Historia* ['Straight History'] (1 Nov 2009).
42   Nowak, *Courier*, p.305.
43   Ibid., p.295.
44   Andrew Bilski, 'Secrets', p.116.
45   EZF, Misc Particulars of EZ, 'A Memoir of My Stay at the Convent of the Immaculate Conception Sisters in Szymanów' (n.d.)
46   Karolina Dzięciolowska, '"She took my hand tightly in hers and thus we went on". The story of sister Wanda Garczyńska', *Polish Righteous* (July 2018). Available at: https://sprawiedliwi.org.pl/en/stories-of-rescue/she-took-my-hand-tightly-hers-and-thus-we-went-story-sister-wanda-garczynska
47   CM interview, Sister Janina, archivist, Szymanów convent (24 Oct 2021).
48   US Holocaust Memorial Museum, interview, Stanisława Paciorek, Sister Maria Ena, Monastery of the Congregation of the Sisters of the Immaculate Conception, Polish Witness to the Holocaust Project, RG-50,488*0099. Available at: http://collections.ushmm.org
49   IWM, Gubbins papers, 2/11, 4/1/4, Gubbins lecture, 'SOE' (June 1959).
50   Ibid.
51   AD/EZ, tape 12.

13. Calm Before the Storm

1   EZ, *Sketches*, p.353.
2   AD/EZ, tape 22.
3   Nowak, *Courier*, p.326.
4   CM/Hanna Koscia interview, London (28 Apr 2014).
5   EZ, 'Own Account . . .'
6   AD/EZ, tape 22.
7   Nowak, *Courier*, p.317.
8   Ibid.
9   Ryder, *And the Morrow*, p.51.
10   Nowak, *Courier*, p.320.
11   Ibid., p.322.
12   Ibid.
13   Ibid.
14   Ibid.
15   Andrew Bilski, 'Secrets', p.131.
16   Ibid., p.139.
17   Ibid.
18   Nowak, *Courier*, p.316.
19   Ibid., p.329.

20 AD/EZ, tape 21.
21 Joe Shute, 'The Secrets of the Second World War Comet Line are revealed', *Telegraph* (12 Oct 2019).
22 Karolina Lanckorońska quoted in Bór-Komorowski, *The Secret Army*, p.160.
23 EZF, 21-K/Zagr: Celina Zawodzińska, 'Cela', 'Some Reflections from the Years of Imprisonment' in *Przeglad Lekrski* ['Medical Review'], No. 31/1 (1974).
24 Ibid.
25 Ibid.
26 Ibid.
27 Nowak, *Courier*, p.337.
28 Ibid., p.336.
29 The Duchess of Atholl, *The Tragedy of Warsaw and Its Documentation* (John Murray, 1945).
30 AD/EZ, tape 22.
31 Kazimierz Bilski, 'Zo', *The Unseen and Silent*, p.64.
32 Ibid.
33 Ibid., p.66.
34 Andrew Bilski, 'Secrets', p.151.
35 Nowak, *Courier*, pp.339–40.
36 AD/EZ, tape 22.
37 Nowak, *Courier*, p.339.
38 AD/EZ, tape 22.
39 Nowak, *Courier*, pp.340, 341.
40 Andrew Bilski, 'Secrets', p.156.
41 EZ, *Sketches*, p.352.
42 Ibid., p.353.

14. The Warsaw Uprising

1 EZ, *Sketches*, p.353.
2 Pawel Kędzierski (dir.), *My Cichociemni Głosy Żyjących* ['My Silent Unseen, Voices of the Living'] (2008).
3 Ibid.
4 Bór-Komorowski, *The Secret Army*, p.252.
5 Andrew Bilski, 'Secrets', p.158.
6 Nowak, *Courier*, p.348.
7 Warsaw Uprising Museum, EZ.
8 EZ, *Sketches*, p.353.
9 Ibid.
10 Ibid., pp.353, 355.
11 Norman Davies, *Rising '44* (Pan Macmillan, 2004), p.249.
12 Ibid.
13 Ibid.
14 Ibid.

15 Ibid.
16 EZ, *Sketches*, p.353.
17 AD/EZ, tape 22.
18 Ibid.
19 Ibid.
20 EZ, *Sketches*, p.356.
21 Ibid., p.354.
22 Ibid.
23 See: www.nationalww2museum.org/war/articles/german-response-war saw-uprising
24 IWM Sound Archive, 26813, June Kerr Darton, reel 1: British officers and Polish agents.
25 Nowak, *Courier*, p.359.
26 Marek Celt, *By Parachute to Warsaw* (Dorothy Crisp, 1945), p.75.
27 Nowak, *Courier*, p.346; EZ, *Sketches*, p.353.
28 EZ, *Sketches*, p.355.
29 Carmelo Lisciotto, 'How the Germans are Starving Poland', Polish Ministry of Information No 58, Holocaust Education & Archive Research Team (2009). Available at: www.holocaustresearchproject.org/nazioccupation/ polandstarved.html
30 AD/EZ, tape 22.
31 EZ, *Sketches*, p.356.
32 Andrew Bilski, 'Secrets', p.200.
33 CM/Hanna Czarnocka interview, London (28 Apr 2014).
34 AD/EZ, tape 22.
35 EZ, *Sketches*, p.353.
36 EZF, 74/WSK, Dr Zofia Franio, '"Bombs". My Mother's Recollections' in *Tygodnik Katolicki* ['Catholic Weekly'], no 20 (16 May 1965).
37 Bór-Komorowski, *The Secret Army*, p.252.
38 EZ, *Sketches*, p.354.
39 EZF, 74/WSK, Dr Zofia Franio, Zofia Franio, 'Report' (15 Sep 1971); AAN, Women's History Commission archive, syg.619_1068-171. Krystyna Reutt, Maria Stopien, Katarzyna Olszewska, 'Recollections of Dr Franio' (12 Dec 1978).
40 Kazimierz Bilski, 'The Warsaw Rising, Link-up with the Old Town', in *The Unseen and Silent*, p.242.
41 AD/EZ, tape 22.
42 Ibid.
43 Ibid.
44 Davies, *Rising '44: The Battle for Warsaw*, p.251.
45 Walker, *Poland Alone*, p.215.
46 The National WWII Museum, New Orleans, Jennifer Popowycz, 'The Allied Responses to the Warsaw Uprising of 1944' (18 Jan 2022). Available at: www.nationalww2museum.org/war/articles/ allied-responses-warsaw-uprising-1944

47 Nowak, *Courier*, p.358.
48 Ibid.
49 Ibid., p.359.
50 George Graves, quoted in Mel Rolfe, *Looking into Hell* (Cassell, 1995), p.119.
51 TNA, HS4/177, M3/238, Lt Col H.M. Threlfall, 'Special Operations to Poland from the Mediterranean Theatre of Operations' (30 May 1945).
52 Bór-Komorowski, *The Secret Army*, p.279.
53 Walker, *Poland Alone*, p.230.
54 Ibid.
55 Nowak, *Courier*, p.409.
56 Andrew Bilski, 'Secrets', p.174.
57 Ibid., p.176.
58 Ibid., p.167.
59 AD/EZ, tape 22.
60 Ibid.
61 Ibid.
62 Ibid.
63 EZ, *Sketches*, p.357.
64 Ibid.
65 AD/EZ, tape 22.
66 Marek Ney-Krwawicz, 'Female Soldiers of the Polish Home Army'. Available at: www.polishresistance-ak.org (Accessed Dec 2021).
67 Nowak, *Courier*, p.369.
68 Ibid., p.381.
69 AD/EZ, tape 12.
70 Kochanski, *The Eagle Unbowed*, p.413.
71 Nowak, *Courier*, p.371.
72 Kazimierz Bilski, 'The Warsaw Rising, Link Up With the Old Town', *The Unseen and Silent*, p.246.
73 Ibid.
74 Janie Hampton, *How the Girl Guides Won the War* (Harper Press, 2011), p.202.
75 Bór-Komorowski, *The Secret Army*, p.306.
76 CM/Marzenna Schejbal interview, Chiswick (28 Jun 2018).
77 CM/Marzenna Schejbal interview, National Army Museum (26 Jul 21).
78 CM/Marzenna Schejbal interview, Chiswick.
79 AD/EZ, tape 22.
80 Kochanski, *The Eagle Unbowed*, p.414.
81 EZF, T.439/WSK Halina Martin, p.II/16 Re Warsaw Uprising.
82 Nowak, *Courier*, p.378.
83 Gubbins, 'Preface', *The Unseen and Silent*, p.x.
84 AD/EZ, tape 22.
85 Władysław Anders quoted in *The Unseen and Silent*, p.v.
86 Warsaw Uprising Museum, EZ; AD/EZ, tape 22.

87   AD/EZ, tape 22.
88   Ibid.
89   AD/EZ, tape 23.
90   Weber, *Emilia Malessa*, p.66.
91   Bór-Komorowski, *The Secret Army*, p.349.
92   Ibid., p.350.
93   AD/EZ, tape 22.
94   Ibid.
95   Ibid.
96   Andrew Bilski, 'Secrets', p.210.
97   Ibid; Kazimierz Bilski, 'Zo', *The Unseen and Silent*, p.211 and p.66.
98   AD/EZ, tape 22.
99   Kazimierz Bilski, 'Zo', *The Unseen and Silent*, p.66.
100 Ibid; and AD/EZ, tape 22.
101 Kazimierz Bilski, 'Zo', *The Unseen and Silent*, p.66.
102 Ibid.

15. Walking in Shock

1   Wanda Gutowska quoted in Bernadeta Tendrya, 'The Warsaw Women Who Took on Hitler', *Telegraph* (27 Jul 2004).
2   Kazimierz Bilski, 'Zo', *The Unseen and Silent*, p.66.
3   AD/EZ, tape 9.
4   Katarzyna Minczykowska, *Elżbieta Zawacka alias 'Zelma', 'Sulica', 'Zo'* (EZF, 2016).
5   Ibid.
6   EZ, 'Own Account . . .'
7   Ibid; and EZ, *Sketches,* p.360.
8   AD/EZ, tape 22.
9   Ibid.
10   Warsaw Uprising Museum, EZ.
11   AD/EZ, tape 24.
12   Ibid.
13   Warsaw Uprising Museum, EZ.
14   EZF, T.439/WSK Halina Martin.
15   Ibid.
16   Olga Topol/Marzenna Schejbal interview (March 2020), Piłsudski Institute, London; and CM/Marzenna Schejbal interview, Chiswick.
17   EZF, M221/830 Pom: Leonard Teodor Zawacki, Leonard Zawacki, *Memories of the War, 1939–1945* (Rotary International, n.d.).
18   University of Southern California Shoah Foundation, Leonard T. Zawacki Testimony (10 Dec 1997), tape 6.
19   EZF, M-221/830 Pom: Leonard Zawacki, *Wspomnienia wojenne (1939–1945)* ['War Memories 1939-1945'] (28 Sep 1990).
20   Walker, *Poland Alone*, p.251.
21   TNA, M3/238 Lt Col H.M. Threlfall, 'Special Operations to Poland

　　　　from the Mediterranean Theatre of Operations' (30 May 1945).

22　Warsaw Uprising Museum, EZ; and AD/EZ, tape 24.

23　Weber, *Emilia Malessa*, pp.98–99.

24　Ibid., p.83 and p.68.

25　AD/EZ, tape 24.

26　Ibid.

27　Ibid.

28　Ibid.

29　Ibid.

30　Nowak, *Courier*, p.388.

31　Ibid., p.390.

32　Ibid., p.404.

33　Ibid., p.405.

34　Ibid.

35　Ibid.

36　Ibid.

37　AD/EZ, tape 24.

38　Nowak, *Courier*, p.405.

39　Ibid.

40　Ibid., p.410.

41　Ibid., p.414.

42　Ben Wilson, *Metropolis: A History of Humankind's Greatest Invention* (Penguin Random House, 2020), pp.309–10.

43　AAN, Women's History Commission archive, syg.619_0168-171, Dr Zofia Franio, M. Jędrzejewska, 'Remembrance of Dr Franio' (n.d.).

44　CIA, 'Poland. Study of the Origins and Activity of the Underground Movement WiN' (10 Nov 1948).

45　Colin Gubbins, 'Preface', *The Unseen and Silent*.

46　Józej Zbik, *First to Return* (Militaria.pl, 2017), p.164.

47　AD/EZ, tape 24.

48　Ibid.

49　Ibid.

50　Archives of Congregation of the Sisters of the Immaculate Conception of the Blessed Virgin Mary, Szymanów, 'Zo', unnamed manuscript (n.d.).

51　Nowak, *Courier*, p.437.

52　Andrew Bilski, 'Secrets', p.244.

53　Ibid., p.254.

54　Ibid., p.290.

55　Ibid., p.254.

56　Nowak, *Courier*, p.437.

57　Olson and Cloud, *For Your Freedom and Ours*, p.374.

58　AD/EZ, tape 24.

59　EZ, *Sketches*, p.361

60　AD/EZ, tape 24.

61　EZF, 57/WSK, Teresa Delekta 'Janka' (n.d.).

62 AD/EZ, tape 24.
63 Ibid.
64 Ibid.
65 EZ, *Sketches*, p.362.
66 AD/EZ interview, tape 25 (18 Feb 1992).
67 AD/EZ, tape 25 and tape 23.
68 AD/EZ interview, tape 26a (20 Feb 1992).
69 AD/EZ, tape 25.
70 Ibid.
71 Ibid.
72 Ibid.
73 Ibid.
74 AD/EZ, tape 26a.
75 AD/EZ, tape 25.
76 Andrew Bilski, 'Secrets', p.271.
77 CM/Hanna Czarnocka interview.
78 'Marzenna Schejbal, resistance activist who performed heroics during the Warsaw Uprising – obituary', *Telegraph* (2 Mar 2022).
79 Albert Speer, *Inside the Third Reich* (Sphere, 1971), p.631.
80 IPN, GK 165/371, Notebook, 'List of Polish citizens saved from German concentration camps as a result of Count Folke Bernadotte' (n.d.).
81 Sune Persson, *Escape from the Third Reich* (Pen & Sword, 2019), p.210.
82 Ibid., p.182.
83 Natalie Hess, *Remembering Ravensbrück* (Amsterdam Publishers, n.d.), p.37.
84 Persson, *Escape from the Third Reich*, p.210.
85 Hess, *Remembering Ravensbrück*, p.39.
86 AD/EZ, tape 25.
87 Nowak, *Courier*, p.452.
88 Ryder, *And the Morrow*, p.79.

16. A Soldier's Internal Conflict

1   EZF archive, 12K/Zagr: Emilia Malessa file, '*Do Prezydenta Bierute*' ['To President Bierut'] (4 Dec 1948), *Clues* [magazine], no 31 (2000).
2   Hastings, 'Taking Crimea from Putin has Become Unthinkable'.
3   Marshal Georgy Zhukov, quoted in ibid.
4   Alan Brooke, quoted in ibid.
5   Stefan Bałuk, quoted in Kochanski, *The Eagle Unbowed*, p.531.
6   AD/EZ, tape 23.
7   AD/EZ, tape 25.
8   AD/EZ, tape 23.
9   Arthur Bliss quoted in Kochanski, *The Eagle Unbowed*, p.532.
10 AD/EZ, tape 25.
11 AD/EZ interview, tape 26 (20 Feb 1992).
12 TNA, M3/238, Lt Col H.M. Threlfall, 'Special Operations to Poland

from the Mediterranean Theatre of Operations' (30 May 1945).

13 Ibid.

14 Andrew Bilski, *Secrets* , p.313.

15 Ibid.

16 Widarski (dir.), *EZ, I Had a Happy Life*.

17 AD/EZ, tape 26.

18 EZF, 15-K Zagr, Wacława Zastocka 'Wacka', 'Autobiographical Note' (11 Dec 1980).

19 AD/EZ, tape 26.

20 Ibid.

21 Katarzyna Minczykowska, *Cichociemna, General EZ 'Zo'* (EZF, 2014), p.168; AD/EZ, tape 23.

22 EZ, *Sketches*, p.371; AD/EZ, tape 23.

23 AD/EZ, tape 23.

24 EZ, *Sketches*, p.372.

25 Stefan Bałuk, quoted in Widarski (dir.), *Cichociemni*.

26 M.R.D. Foot, *SOE*, p.278.

27 TNA, HS4/278, SOE Poland 194, Vol T-Z, letter MP/PD/6A (ii) Alfred Whitehead (12 Sep 1945).

28 Stefan Ignaszak, quoted in Widarski (dir.), *Cichociemni*.

29 EZF, 12K/Zagr: Emilia Malessa file, Emilia Malessa, 'Mummy's Dreams in the Prison' (24 Mar 1946).

30 Ibid.

31 EZF, 12K/Zagr: Emilia Malessa file, 'Handwritten note by ZM, a student of EZ's brother' (n.d.).

32 EZF, 12K/Zagr: Emilia Malessa file, '*Do Prezydenta Bierute*' ['To President Bierut'].

33 Leski, 'A Chequered Life' (2009), p.123.

34 PUMST, KOL 23/326, EZ personal file; PUMST, KOL 23/326, 'Verification Document' (24 Apr 1970).

35 PUMST, SK148/78-79, 'Military Register of those Promoted' (23 Oct 1946).

36 IPN, Warsaw, BU 0259/148 v.4 – Zofia Franio, untitled form (26 Feb 1947).

37 AAN, Archive of the Women's Commission in the Fight for Polish independence, 1697-0080: Emilia Malessa, Izabella Kwapińska, 'Statement regarding Emilia Malessa' (n.d.).

38 Ibid.

39 IPN, Warsaw, BU 944/124, 'Emilia Malessa Court Interrogation' (16 Jan 1947).

40 IPN, BU 944/112 'Sentence on Behalf of the Polish Republic' (3 Feb 1947).

41 Henryk Żuk, *Na szachownicy życia, Wspomnienia kapitana Armii Krajowej 'Onufrego'* [*On the Chessboard of Life, memoirs of Home Army Captain 'Onufry'*] (Żuk, 199?), p.201.

42 Stefan Ignaszak, quoted in Widarski (dir.), *Cichociemni*.
43 Bronisław Gorecki, quoted Widarski (dir.), *Cichociemni*.
44 Emilia Malessa to Józef Różański (April 1949) quoted in Waldemar Kowalski, 'Life with the Stigma of a Traitor: The Tragic Story of Captain Emilia Malessa' on *Sie.pl* [Polish Police Website] available at: https://dzieje.pl/artykulyhistoryczne/zycie-z-pietnem-zdrajczyni-tragiczna-historia-kpt-ak-emilii-malessy (17 Jun 2021).
45 Ibid.
46 EZF, 12K/Zagr: Emilia Malessa file, '*Do Prezydenta Bierute*' ['To President Bierut']'.
47 Ibid.
48 Ibid.
49 Ibid.
50 IPN, BU 944/112 'Sentence on Behalf of the Polish Republic' (3 Feb 1947).
51 IPN, Warsaw, BU 0259/148 v.4 – Zofia Franio, untitled form (31 Jul 1947).
52 IPN, Warsaw, BU 0259/148 v.4 – Zofia Franio, 'Report' (2 Mar 1952).
53 Wysoczyńska, *Zofia Franio*, pp.159–60.
54 AD/EZ, tape 26.
55 AD/EZ, tape 23.
56 Ibid.
57 Weber, *Emilia Malessa*, p.191.
58 CM/Dorota Zawacka-Wakarecy interview, Toruń (3 Nov 2021).
59 Malmö Police Records, 'Criminal Police Affairs Concerning Refugees, 1945–1946', SE MSA 00453 F7 10, Vol 1., p.94; Hess, *Remembering Ravensbrück*, p.39.
60 National Archives of Sweden, Archive of the State Aliens Supervisory Commission (SUK, Kanslibyrån, F1 AC: 23118), Klara Zawacka.
61 AD/EZ, tape 2.
62 Weber, *Emilia Malessa*, p.79; AAN, Archive of the Women's Commission in the Fight for Polish independence, 1697-0018: Emilia Malessa, Ewa Korczyńska, handwritten memo (n.d.).
63 Weber, *Emilia Malessa*, p.197.
64 Ibid.
65 AAN, Archive of the Women's Commission in the Fight for Polish independence, 1697-0080: Emilia Malessa, Izabella Kwapińska, 'Statement regarding Emilia Malessa' (n.d.).
66 Ibid.
67 IPN BU 0295/604, EZ Interrogation (10 Sep 1951).
68 IPN, BU 0295/604, filenote (28 Aug 1951).
69 IPN BU 0295/604, EZ Interrogation (10 Sep 1951).
70 Warsaw Uprising Museum, EZ (2007).
71 AD collection, Biuro PP RP1.
72 AD/EZ, tape 26.

73   Ibid.
74   UMK, K-23/217, Note from Educational Authority, Toruń (31 Mar 1950).
75   AD/EZ, tape 26.
76   Ibid.
77   Ibid.
78   IPN, BU 0295/604, Filenote (6 Sep 1951).
79   Ibid.
80   UMK, K-23/217, EZ typed resumé (26 Jul 1980).
81   IPN Warsaw, IPN BU 0259/604.
82   AD/EZ, tape 26.

17. Having the Time to Achieve Something

1   AD/EZ, tape 26.
2   Ibid.
3   Ibid.
4   IPN Warsaw, IPN BU 0259/604, 'Résumé of activity' (20 Dec 1951).
5   Ibid.
6   AD/EZ, tape 26.
7   IPN BU 0259/106 vols.1–3, 'Kazimierz Leski' untitled document (18 Aug 1971).
8   IPN BU 0259/148 v.4. 'Zofia Franio' untitled document (23 Jan 1952).
9   Wysoczyńska, Zofia Franio, p.168.
10   IPN BU 0259/604, untitled document (28 Aug 1951).
11   IPN BU 0330/181 vol.11: EZ, untitled document (October 1951).
12   CM/Dorota Zawacka-Wakarecy interview, Toruń (30 Oct 21).
13   Minczykowska, Cichociemna, p.186.
14   IPN BU 0259/604, untitled document (20 Aug 1952), and 'Decision about the appeal to criminal liability' (20 Dec 1951), Eugenia Maresch archive.
15   Ibid.
16   IPN BU 1068/267 – (1951–1957) 'Files regarding Criminal Case' (21 Jan 1952).
17   Ibid.
18   IPN BU 0259/604, untitled document (28 Nov 1952).
19   Ibid.
20   IPN BU 0259/604, 'The Sentence on behalf of the People's Republic' (23 Jan 1952).
21   IPN BU 1068/267 – (1951–1957) Files regarding Criminal Case, 'Revision of the Sentence' (22 May 1952).
22   Simon Sebag Montefiore, Stalin, The Court of the Red Tsar (Phoenix, 2004), p.663.
23   AAN, Women's History Commission archive, syg.619_0168-171 'Zofia Franio', Michael Franio, 'Petition to the Polish Council of State' (Oct 1953).

24 Ibid.
25 IPN BU 1068/267 – (1951–1957) Files regarding Criminal Case, Władysław Zawacki, 'Note to the Education Department' (20 Apr 53).
26 Ibid.
27 UMK, K-23/217, EZ to Education Dept, Olsztyn (24 Mar 1953).
28 EZF, K:607/607 Pom: Bernadeta Gołecka-Schmidt, 'Bojanowo' (n.d.).
29 EZF, K:607/607 Pom: Bernadeta Gołecka-Schmidt, Sentence passed by the Military District Court of Bydgoszcz (11 Jun 1953).
30 EZF, K:607/607 Pom: Bernadeta Gołecka-Schmidt, 'Bojanowo' (n.d.).
31 CM/Bernadeta Gołecka-Schmidt telephone interview (29 Oct 2021).
32 EZF, K:607/607 Pom: Bernadeta Gołecka-Schmidt, 'Bojanowo' (n.d.)
33 CM/ Bernadeta Gołecka-Schmidt telephone interview.
34 Ibid.
35 Warsaw Uprising Museum, EZ.
36 Widarski (dir.), *EZ, I Had a Happy Life*.
37 Ryder, *And the Morrow*, p.85.
38 Minczykowska, *Cichociemna*, p.208.
39 Paulina Chołda/Bernadeta Gołecka-Schmidt telephone interview (16 Dec 2021).

18. In the Polish People's Republic

1 UMK, K-23/217, Olsztyn high school letter to education dept (20 Sep 1951).
2 Małgosia Strzelecka, 'EZ: Teacher and Educator. Work in secondary schools and the Military training of women' in Katarzyna Minczykowska (ed.), *Gen. Brig. Prof. Dr EZ (1909–2009), Biography Materials* (EZF, 2010); and UMK archive, K-23/217, Olsztyn high school to Education Ministry (25 Jun 1955).
3 UMK, K-23/217, untitled document (27 Apr 1955).
4 Widarski (dir.), *EZ, I Had a Happy Life*.
5 Ibid.
6 AD collection, EZ to Wacława Zastocka (1 Dec 1973).
7 AD collection, Wacława Zastocka to EZ (20 Feb 1975 and 17 Mar 1975).
8 EZ, *Sketches*, p.373.
9 Ibid.
10 AD collection, Wacława Zastocka to EZ (17 Mar 1975).
11 EZF, 18-K/Zagr, 'Hanna Michalska', Hanna Michalska to EZ (17/18 Nov 1968).
12 Ibid.
13 Ibid.
14 EZF, 21-K/Zagroda, Celina Zawodzińska to EZ (16 May, no year).
15 EZF, 21-K/Zagroda, Celina Zawodzińska to EZ (30 Sep 1970).
16 AAN, Warsaw, 2/2187/o/-/37, EZ to Kazimierz Leski (31 Jan 1975).
17 AAN, Warsaw, 2/2187/o/-/37, EZ, 'A scheme of relations – participants in Farmstead' (n.d.).

18 EZF, 392/WSK Jadwiga Zatorska 'Saba', EZ, 'About Jadwiga Zatorska' (March 1974).
19 Ibid.
20 UMK, K-23/217, Gdańsk teaching faulty evaluation of EZ (14 Feb 1968).
21 Widarski (dir.), *EZ, I Had a Happy Life*.
22 UMK, K-23/217, 'Oath' (10 Dec 1973).
23 Józef Zdunk quoted in Minczykowska, *Cichociemna*, p.241.
24 CM/Michał Wojtczak interview, Toruń (29 Oct 2021).
25 Ibid.
26 Minczykowska, *Cichociemna*, p.232.
27 AAN, 253, Halina Martin file, EZ to Halina Martin (3 Apr 1977).
28 EZF, 392/WSK Jadwiga Zatorska 'Saba', EZ, 'About Jadwiga Zatorska' (Mar 1974).
29 IWM, Gubbins papers, 2/11/7, Contribution of the Home Army to the Allied cause, Bór-Komorowski letter to Lord Selbourne (27 Jan 1948).
30 CM/Krzysztof Bożejewicz interview, Toruń (30 Oct 2021).
31 Ibid.
32 CM/Marzenna Schejbal interview at the National Army Museum, London (26 Jun 2021).
33 Ibid.
34 PUMST 23/326, 'EZ personal file', 'Opinion' (n.d.).
35 Ibid.
36 CM/Marzenna Schejbal interview at the National Army Museum, London (26 Jun 2021).
37 Ibid.
38 PUMST 23/326, 'EZ personal file', EZ 'Statement' (18 Oct 1976).
39 Ibid.
40 IPN BU 0330/181 vol.11: EZ, Captain Henryk Bialek, 'Note regarding EZ' (17 Sep 1976).
41 Ibid.
42 UMK, K-23/217, EZ to Solidarity committee (10 May 1981).
43 AD collection, Wacka to EZ (30 Oct 1976).
44 UMK, K-23/217, EZ to People's Republic of Poland Customs (29 Dec 1976).
45 Ibid.
46 UMK, K-23/217, EZ, 'Protocol by head of Chief Library, UMK' (11 Nov 1976).
47 UMK, K-23/217, EZ to Solidarity committee (10 May 1981).

19. Fighting for Freedom

1 CM/Jan Wyrowiński interview, Toruń (30 Oct 2021).
2 CM/Grzegorz Górski interview, Toruń (30 Oct 2021).
3 Sobocińska, 'Funeral Oration for Zo'; and AD collection, Wacława Zastocka to EZ (17 Mar 1975).

4   AD collection, Wacława Zastocka to EZ (10 Apr 1978).

5   Wacława Zastocka, 'Dr Zofia Franio', *Medical Review: Auschwitz* (1980).

6   Ibid.

7   CM/Dorota Zawacka-Wakarecy interview (30 Oct 2021).

8   Ibid.

9   Stanisław Salmonowicz, 'Professor EZ, years 1980–2008. Remembrance from a colleague' in Katarzyna Minczykowska (ed.), *General Brigadier Professor Dr EZ (1909–2009): Biographical Materials* (EZF, 2010), p.29.

10 CM/Lech Wałęsa interview (17 Mar 2024).

11 UMK, K-23/217, EZ to Solidarity committee (10 May 1981).

12 Katarzyna Minczykowska, *Cichociemna*, p.244.

13 UMK, K-23/217, EZ to Solidarity committee.

14 General Wojciech Witold Jaruzelski (13 Dec 1981). Available at: www.konflikty.pl/a,395,Czasy_najnowsze,Przemowienie_gen._Jaruzelskiego.html

15 CM/Dorota Zawacka-Wakarecy interview (30 Oct 2021).

16 CM/Grzegorz Górski interview.

17 Ibid.

18 CM/Dorota Zawacka-Wakarecy interview (30 Oct 2021).

19 CM/Jan Wyrowiński interview.

20 Jan Wyrowiński to CM (13 Jun 2023).

21 CM/Krzysztof Bożejewicz interview.

22 CM/Michał Wojtczak interview.

23 Ibid.

24 Ibid.

25 Ibid.

26 Ibid.

27 Ibid.

28 Ibid.

29 Ibid.

30 Jan Wyrowiński to CM (13 Jun 2023).

31 IPN, BU 0224/628 t.1 'Sue Ryder'.

32 Elizabeth Cheshire, 'Foreword' in Joanna Bogle, *Sue Ryder, A Life Lived for Others* (Gracewing, 2022), p.x.

33 AD/EZ, tape 9.

34 Ryder, *Child of My Love*, p.481.

35 IPN BU 1585/21425, k.4-5; also Minczykowska, *Cichociemna*, p.251.

36 Minczykowska, *Cichociemna*, p.249.

37 Ibid., p.254.

38 AAN, Halina Martin file, EZ to HM (18 Aug 1987).

39 Bogdan Chrzanowski to CM (23 Nov 2021).

40 EZF, Dorota Zawacka-Wakarecy/Bogdan Chrzanowski interview (n.d.); and CM/Jan Wyrowiński interview.

41 EZF, M221/830 Pom, Leonard Teodor Zawacki, Bogumiła Kryże to EZ (19 Mar 1987).
42 Ibid.
43 EZF, M221/830 Pom, Leonard Teodor Zawacki, Bogumiła Kryże to EZ (15 Dec 1988).
44 EZF, M221/830 Pom, Leonard Teodor Zawacki, EZ to Bogumiła Kryże (n.d.).
45 EZF, M221/830 Pom, Leonard Teodor Zawacki, Bogumiła Kryże to EZ (15 Jan 1989).
46 EZF, M221/830 Pom, Leonard Teodor Zawacki, EZ to Leonard Zawacki (n.d.).
47 Catholic University of Lublin archive, Leonard Zawacki papers, LZ to EZ (29 Oct 1989).
48 CM/Dorota Wakarecy-Zawacka interview, Toruń (30 Oct 2021).
49 CM/Jan Wyrowiński interview; Jan Wyrowiński to CM (13 Jun 2023).
50 CM/Jan Wyrowiński interview.
51 EZF, 12K Zagr, Emilia Malessa file, EZ handwritten note (n.d.).

20. Revolution is Not Made by Angels

1 CM/AD interview.
2 CM/Jan Wyrowiński interview.
3 Dorota Zawacka-Wakarecy, 'Twenty-five years of General EZ Foundation's activity' in Janusz Marszalec and Katarzyna Minczykowska (eds.), *25 Years of Independent Research on the Polish Resistance 1939–1945. People, Institutions, Events.* (EZF, 2018), p.382.
4 EZ, personal inscription (Feb 1994), CM's copy of *Sketches from the History of the Military Service of Women.*
5 Ibid.
6 CM/Dorota Komp interview, Toruń (29 Oct 2021).
7 CM/Anna Mikułska interview, Toruń (29 Oct 2021).
8 Łukasz Bednarski to CM (13 Jan 2023).
9 AAN, 253, Halina Martin file, EZ to HM (26 Sep 2000).
10 AAN, 253, Halina Martin file, HM to EZ (6 Apr 1994).
11 CM/AD interview.
12 CM/Dorota Komp interview.
13 CM/Jan Wyrowiński interview, Toruń (23 Oct 2021).
14 CM/AD interview.
15 AD/EZ interview (28 Jun 1989).
16 Ibid.
17 Ibid.
18 Ibid.
19 CM/Dorota Komp interview.
20 CM/Grzegorz Górski interview.
21 AAN, 253, Halina Martin file, EZ to HM (26 Sep 2000); and CM/Elżbieta Skerska interview, Toruń (29 Oct 2021).

22 AAN, 253, Halina Martin file, EZ to HM (19 Feb 1990).
23 CM/Grzegorz Górski interview.
24 CM/Jan Wyrowiński interview.
25 CM/Elżbieta Skerska interview.
26 Krzysztof Bożejewicz, 'My Short Story' (14 Oct 2021).
27 CM/Sofie Marta Kozłowska interview, Warsaw (26 Oct 2021).
28 AAN, 253, Halina Martin file, HM to EZ (27 Nov 1987 and 28 Apr 2006).
29 CM/Elżbieta Skerska interview.
30 CM/Sofie Marta Kozłowska interview.
31 Ibid.
32 CM/Elżbieta Skerska interview.
33 CM/Anna Rejewska interview, Toruń (29 Oct 2021).
34 CM/Dorota Komp interview.
35 Widarski (dir.), *EZ, I Had a Happy Life.*
36 EZF, 12K Zagr, Emilia Malessa file, EZ handwritten note (n.d.).
37 Widarski (dir.), *EZ, I Had a Happy Life.*

Postscript

1 Sobocińska, 'Funeral Oration for Zo'.
2 Ibid.

Epilogue

1 EZ, *Sketches*, p.373.
2 CM/AD interview.
3 Ibid.
4 Ibid.
5 AAN, II-Z-13F, EZ to Assocn of Fighters for Freedom & Democracy (15 Jun 1961).
6 Ibid.
7 EZ, *Sketches*, p.373.
8 Ibid, p.vii.
9 CM/AD interview.
10 Ibid.
11 AD/EZ, tape 14.
12 EZF, T.439/WSK Halina Martin, EZ to HM (15 Dec 1997).
13 EZ, *Sketches*, p.374.
14 IWM, Gubbins papers, 2/11/7, Contribution of the Home Army to the Allied Cause, Bór-Komorowski letter to Lord Selbourne (27 Jan 1948).
15 Bór-Komorowski, *The Secret Army*, p.60.
16 CM/Grzegorz Górski interview, Toruń (30 Oct 2021).
17 Szatsznajder, 'Silent Unseen, From Poland to Poland', p.227.
18 CM/Dorota Zawacka-Wakarecy interview (30 Oct 2021).
19 AD/EZ interview, tape 14.
20 Ibid.

21 CM/AD interview.
22 Ibid.
23 Ibid.
24 Jordan Ellenberg, *How Not to be Wrong* (Penguin, 2015), p.6.
25 *BBC News* online, 'War heroine "not classed leader"' (1 Apr 2008).
26 Dwight D. Eisenhower, *Crusade in Europe* (Doubleday, 1948).
27 Ibid.
28 General Marian Kukiel, quoted in IPN, 'Polish Women in World War II' (8 Mar 2023). Available at: https://ipn.gov.pl/en/news/10365,Polish-women-in-World-War-II.html
29 *Doliniacy*, a film by Jaktorow town council (n.d.).
30 EZ, *Sketches*, p.vii.
31 Ibid.
32 Ibid.
33 Widarski (dir.), *EZ: I Had a Happy Life*.
34 Sara Shaffi, 'Women's Prize launch award for non-fiction', *Guardian* (9 Feb 2023).
35 CM/AD interview.

Note on Sources

1 TNA, HS 9/1112/2, Margaret Audrey North, personal file, Memo D/CE to ACD (25 Apr 1944).
2 AAN, 2/2187/0/-/37, Kazimierz Leski, EZ to KL (n.d.).
3 CM/Hanna Czarnocka interview, London (10 Mar 2014).
4 CM/Marzenna Schejbal interview, London (26 Jun 2021).
5 CM/AD interview.
6 CM/Bernadeta Schmidt telephone interview, Toruń (29 Oct 2021).

SELECT BIBLIOGRAPHY

INTERVIEWS AND CORRESPONDENCE

Łukasz Bednarski, great-nephew of Marianna, Celina and Stefa Zawodzińska (13 Jan 2023)

Krysztof Bożejewicz, PUMST (30 Oct 2021)

Bogdan Chrzanowski, Vice-Dean, University of Gdańsk, Trustee, World War Two Museum, Gdańsk (23 Nov 2021)

Hanna Czarnocka, Warsaw Uprising veteran (10 Mar 2014 and 28 Mar 2014), and her daughter Wanda Koscia (7 Oct 2021)

Andrzej Drzycimski, opposition activist 1990–1994, spokesman for President Lech Wałęsa (27 Oct 2021)

Matt Ellis, Porthmadog–Blaenau Ffestiniog steam railway (22 Aug 2021)

Halina Fitzclarence, Countess of Munster (22 Jul 2021)

Bernadeta Gołecka-Schmidt, Elżbieta Zawacka's cellmate 1953–1955 (29 Oct 2021)

Hanna Gorksa and Magdalena Stajewska, daughters of Stanislaw Jankowski, 'Agaton' (4 Nov 2021)

Grzegorz Górski, Judge, politician, Elżbieta Zawacka Historical Club and Elżbieta Zawacka Foundation (30 Oct 2021)

Sofie Kozłowska, granddaughter of Warsaw Uprising veteran Zofia Kozłowska (27 Sep 2021)

Dorota Kromp, Elżbjeta Zawacka's secretary (29 Oct 2021)

Ludwik Maćkowiak, nephew of Alfons 'Alan Mack' Maćkowiak (25 Sep 2021)

Eugenia Maresch, PUMST, author, friend of Elżbieta Zawacka (17 Jul 2021)

Anna Marples, daughter of Silent Unseen Adolf Pilch (30 Sep 2021)

Anna Mikułska, Elżbieta Zawacka Foundation (29 Oct 2021)

Danuta Nosek, daughter of Silent Unseen Antoni Nosek (11 Aug 2021)

Anna Rejewska, Elżbieta Zawacka Foundation (29 Oct 2021)

Julia Rooke, former BBC journalist, interviewed Elżbieta Zawacka in 2001 (28 Jan 2024)

Bogdan Rowiński, President, Cichociemni Foundation (24 Oct 2021)

Marzenna Schejbal, Warsaw Uprising veteran (28 Jun 2018 and 26 Jun 2021)

Elżbieta Skerska, Elżbieta Zawacka Foundation (29 Oct 2021)

Remigiusz Stefani, Warsaw Uprising Museum (13 Apr 2023)

Dorota Zawacka-Wakarecy, Zo's cousin; Director, Elżbieta Zawacka Foundation (30 Oct 2021)

Lech Wałęsa, first democratically elected president of Poland.

Michał Wojtczak, political opposition activist, Elżbieta Zawacka's student (29 Oct 2021)

Jan Wyrowiński, political opposition activist, politician, Elżbieta Zawacka Foundation (30 Oct 2021)

Harry Young, British Army (30 Jun 2021)

⚓

PUBLIC ARCHIVES IN BRITAIN

English Heritage, Audley End House Collection
Audley End house, posters and graffiti
Józef Hartman photo album, gifted to Lady Braybrooke (1 Jan 1943)
P. Howe, 'Recollection of Cpl. P. Howe, Audley End 1942–44' (1986)
Antoni Nosek, *SOE Polish Section in Audley End House, 1942–1944* (1998)
Antoni Nosek letter to Mrs Dalton, English Heritage, to accompany his book (28 May 1998)

House of Commons, Hansard Archive
House of Commons Debate, National Service Bill (10 Dec 1941)
Baroness Golding, Enquiry into the publication of the study into the employment of women in the Armed Forces (22 May 2002)

Imperial War Museum
Documents
14851: Lt Col P Solly-Flood OBE
2768: AM Gamwell OBE
25021: Gubbins Papers:
  2/11/1, Sikorski to Gubbins (30 Apr 1940)
  2/11/7, Contribution of the Home Army to the Allied cause
  4/1/50, Peter Wilkinson, 'Gubbins: A Resistance Leader' (28 Apr
    1990)
LBY 17/673: Polish Heritage Society, International Military History
  Conference, 2016, Polish Embassy, London (2017)
  The Polish Section of SOE and Poland's 'Silent Unseen' 1940–
    1945 (11 Jun 2016)
Sound archive
502, Antonia Marian Gamwell (11 May 1974)
10057, Sue Ryder, Oral History (15 Nov 1987)

Piłsudski Institute
Olga Topol, Marzenna Schejbal interview (March 2020)

Polish Institute and Sikorski Museum (PISM)
KOL 177 Col Protasewicz memoirs (1943)
A XII 62/66 'Z'
A XII Spain/Gibraltar

Polish Underground Movement Study Trust (PUMST)
A 93
  89 Truskowski note on Elżbieta Zawacka's (EZ) arrival (13 Apr
    1942)
  424 EZ re Land Communications (19 Jul 1943)
  512 EZ re Land Communications (30 Jul 1943)
A 94
  113 EZ re Land Communications (June 1943)
  114 Note re EZ's mission (20 Feb 1943)
A 98
  260 EZ re Land Communications (9 Jun 1943)
  286, accounts of Home Army couriers

A 225, Zabielski to Sixth Bureau (9 Nov 1943)
A 309
  51, EZ letter to Minister for Defence (6 Sep 1943)
  53, Comments on Draft Decree on Women's Voluntary Service
    (20 Jul 1943)
  54–55, Excerpt from the President's Decree
  56, Filenote re Decree sent to Poland (17 Apr 1944)
  57–58, Official Notice of the Decree on Women's Voluntary
    Service
  59, Decree on Women's Voluntary Service (27 Oct 1943)
A 316/53, Official confirmation of EZ's Cross of Valour (x2)
A 326/51, EZ re security concerns (28 Jun 1943)
A 374/230, EZ's journey to London
A 654/178, List of encrypted messages
B 418: Zofia Jordanowska personal file
  4–5 Zofia Jordanowska/Halina Czarnocka correspondence
    (1963)
  6–10 Ameryka Echo articles (1963)
B I/1338: EZ, 'Own Account of Home Army Captain Elżbieta
  Zawacka, aka "Zelma", "Zo", "Sulica" about her military service
  in 1939–1945' (typed ms, n.d.)
KOL 23/326: EZ, personal file
  Sixth Bureau form, 'Zo' (9 Sep 1943)
  Telegram (13 Apr 1943)
  Polish Army officers, 'Opinions' on EZ.
  EZ/Staff of CinC correspondence (19 Jun 1943, 31 Jul 1943)
  'Personal items of Ms Elizabeth Watson' (14 Dec 1943)
  Form, 'Request for Military Cross' (1943)
  EZ note on the handwriting of the 'Opinions'.
  Form, 'Request to give Army Medal' (18 May 1946)
  'Deposit 179a WATSON Elisabeth' (1 Mar 1948)
  Postal Receipt (14 May 1959)
  Note re EZ's report (17 Jan 1961)
  Letter confirming award of EZ's Virtuti Militari (24 Apr 1970)
  EZ, 'Statement 'Zo', EZ' [response to 'Opinions'] (18 Oct 1976)
  'Declaration of Financial Holdings' (n.d.)
  Rawa/Lawina telegrams (1943)
KOL 23/17: Kaziemierz Bilski personal file
KOL 23/215: Jan Piwnik personal file

SK 105 / 552 Telegram to EZ
SK 106
    99 Truszkowski to Krzyżnowski (13 May 1943)
    102-3 EZ Questionnaire (21 May 1943)
    169 Protasewicz to Perkins (31 May 1943)
SK 107
    114, North to Krzyżanowski (23 Aug 1943)
    130, Perkins to Sixth Bureau (27 Aug 1943)
    131, EZ note re parachute clothing (n.d.)
    132, North to Sixth Bureau (26 Jun 1943)
SK 139
    10, Sixth Bureau filenote re Silent Unseen training
    11, List of Silent Unseen course trainees
SK 142, Instructors' Reports
SK 148/78-79, Military Register of those promoted (23 Oct 1946)
SK 154, Candidates, including 154/382 Aleksandra Dobrowolska
    155, Medical Examinations
    159, Teams of parachutists sent to Poland, and opinions on them.
    167, Parachuting training
SK 169/109 EZ's finances, filenote
SK 203/194, List of EZ's possessions
SK 850/9 EZ's finances, filenote
SK 853, 859 and 862, Finance, receipts
SK 1019 and SK 1046/104-5, EZ finances
SK/TP2: Sixth Bureau and Civilian Workers files
TP1 Zofia Franio
Zofia Franio obituaries, including *Tydzien Polkski* (16 Dec 1997)
Medical Review, Auschwitz, Wacława Zastocka, 'Dr Zofia Franio' (1980)
'CV of Zofia Franio' (typed ms, n.d.)
'Confirmation of Honours' (24 Feb 1966)
Halina Czarnocka, 'Dr. Zofia Franio' (15 Sep 1971)
Capital City, 'Female Sapper Teams: postal mail for Municipal Captain Leista' (2 Sep 1956), pp.6–7
Universal Word, 'She devoted her life to Poland and to social service: Memory of Dr Zofia Franio' (12 Jul 1978)
Handwritten note, 'Contents of package' (2 Mar 1943)

'Biography of Dr. med. Zofia Franio' (typed ms, 15 Jun 1979)
Other files
Halina Zapolska, 'Attachment to the account of EŻ, "Żelma" (n.d.)
Cardfile, Maria Wittek receiving AK Cross (7284)
Cardfile, Emilia Malessa receiving AK Cross (9782)
Leather notebook, alphabetical list of trainee Silent Unseen
Books, articles and publications
Captain Stronczak, *STS 43 (Audley End)*, photograph album (15 Feb 1945)
Krzysztof Tochman, 'Gen. prof. EZ Cichociemna' in T. Ujazdowska, K. Bożejewicz, *Biuletyn Informacyjny SPP w Londynie* (Jul 2013) pp.41–46

St Peter's Eaton Square
The Review, Kazimierz Bilski and Audrey North marriage notice (June 1944)
David Hilary, Michael Melrose, *St Peter's Eaton Square (1827–1998)* (n.d.)
Joseph A. Grogan, *St Peter's Eaton Square, A Brief History with Pictures* (2020)

National Archives
FCO 28/3402, Poland: honours and awards
FO 954/19B, Sikorski
HO 334/384/34602 Kazimierz Bilski Naturalisation Certificate (22 Sep 1954)
HS4, SOE Eastern Europe:
   177, M3/238, Lt Col H.M. Threlfall, 'Special Operations to Poland from the Mediterranean Theatre of Operations' (30 May 1945)
   184, Henry Threlfall's report on Mediterranean airdrops 1944–1945
   278, Couriers; Polish personnel
HS8, Poland, personnel:
   1007, Polish Sixth bureau
HS9, Personnel Files (PF)
   559/4 Antonia Marian GAMWELL
   1112/2 Margaret Audrey NORTH

1113/5 Jan NOWAK
1635/3, SOE, Zofia ZAJKOWSKA (Elizabeth WATSON)
PREM, Prime Minister's Office:
3/351/3 Resistance in Poland, 1940

⚓

PUBLIC ARCHIVES IN POLAND

Archiwum Akt Nowych (Archive of New Records)
VI/9: Armia Krajowa Komenda Główna
 189: Jankowski 'Agaton': Materials and Remarks
 230: Akta Kazimierz Leski
 253: Halina Martin papers
 3306: Women's History Commission in the Fight for Polish
  Independence
 II-Z-13F: EZ
  619: Zofia Franio
  1697: Emilia Malessa
 2/2187/o/-/37, Kazimierz Leski/EZ correspondence
 2/2439/o/-/953, Halina Martin
 2/2521/o/2/13108: EZ 1946-1979

**Szymanów Convent of the Sisters of Immaculate Conception of the
Blessed Virgin Mary**
EZ, 'Zo' (EZF, 1999)
Oleńka Celińska (Gdańsk, 17 Mar 2011)

Elżbieta Zawacka Foundation (EZF)
WSK files
 57, Teresa Delekta, 'Janka'
 74, Dr Zofia Franio, 'Doktor'
 103, Zofia Grzegorzewska
 1515, Janina Karaś, 'Bronka'
 144, Helena Kobernicka, 'Jana'

718, Zofia Leśniowska née Sikorska

T.439, Halina Martin

1059, Maria Mikołajczak

271, Halina Piwonska, 'Henryka'

647, Irena Semadeni

3919, Wanda Wasilewska, 'Wacek'

379, Maria Wittek, 'Mira'

1754-412/07, Hanna Żabińska-Petrynowska

392, Jadwiga Zatorska, 'Saba'

Pomeranian files

K607/607, Bernadeta Gołecka Schmidt

K69/69, Jadwiga Kowalska

M221/830, Leonard Zawacki, *War Memories, 1939–1945* (28 Sep 1990)

PWK files

PWK/K139, Elżbieta Zahorska

PWK/388, Halina Zapolska

Zagroda files

123-K, Alicja Iwańska, 'Wiewiórka' [Squirrel]

58-K, Halina Jabłońska, 'Zielonka'

25-M, Kaziemierz Leski, 'Bradl'

12K, Emilia Malessa, 'Marcysia'

19-K, Róża Marczewska, 'Lula'

18-K, Hanna Michalska, 'Hanka'

7-K, Stefania (née Horst) Ochendal, 'Stenia'

22-K, Wanda Wysznacka-Aleksandrow

15-K, Wacława Zastocka, 'Wacka'

65-K, Ludwiga Zawierta

21-K, Celina Zawodzińska

105-K, Maria Zawodzińska, 'Sabina'

27-M, Rudolf Zazdel/Zazdek, 'Jarach'

Other

Andrzej Drzycimski/EZ interview transcripts (28 Jun 1989–18 Feb 1992)

Bogdan Chrzanowski, interview to mark archive's thirtieth anniversary

EZ personal artefacts: medals, mementoes, books, furniture, etc.

Institute of National Remembrance (IPN)
BU 0259/148: Zofia Franio, personal file, arrest, imprisonment, release
BU 1043/2956/D, BU 1224/207 and B-8: Stanisław Jankowski, 'Agaton'
BU 2174/8145: Roman Kryże
BU 0259/106, 0330/221, 944/112, 944/124, Emilia Malessa
BU 01583/33: Jan Nowak-Jeziorański
BU 0224/628: Sue Ryder
BU 1019/1054 and BU 3066/86: Maria Śliwińska-Walczuk
BU 0330/181: EZ
BU 0259/106, Kaziemierz Leski
GK 105/93 and GK 105/274: Jan Piwnik
GK 629/7433, Egon Zawacki
GK 165/371 and GK 135/81: Klara Zawacka
Ki 212/392, Jan Piwnik
Further papers on Kazimierz Bilski, Bogumiła Kryże, Alfons Maćkowiak (Alan Mack), Frederyk Serafiński, Elżbieta Zahorska, Egon Zawacka, Leonard Zawacka.

University Adam Mickiewicz (UAM)
EZ's documents as a student at the university (1927–1935)

The John Paul II Catholic University of Lublin (KUL)
Leonard Zawacki papers
Leonard Zawacki, *War Memories 1938–1945* (Rotary International, 1990)
Leonard Zawacki, 'Declaration' of donation (28 Sep 1990)
Leonard Zawacki, handwritten list of 50 SS commanders in Auschwitz (n.d.)
EZ/Bogumiła Kryże correspondence (1987–1989)
EZ/Leonard Zawacki correspondence (1989–2004)

University Nicolaus Copernicus (UMK)
EZ personal files
H-74a/16: UMK application form
K-23/217: EZ at the Pedagogical Faculty, UMK
WNH-16/42: EZ, dissertation
H-30/60: EZ, academic work

Władysława Szulakiewicz, Ryszard Borowicz, Hanna Kostło, *Elżbieta Zawacka 'Zo', Academic Portrait* (UMK, 2009)

Warsaw Uprising Museum
Documents
World Association of Home Army Soldiers, *Inspectorate of the Home Army in Sosnowiec* (2001)
Office for Veterans of Repressed Persons, *Questionnaire for a person applying for a veteran's entitlement* (1975)
Andrzej Zagórski (ed.), 'Freedom Independence' Association, *Four Main Boards before the Courts of the Polish People's Republic* (Library of Historical Journals, 2000), Vol VI.3, pp.805–7
Barbara Otwinowska and Teresa Drzal, *Zawołać po imieniu, Call by Name, The Book of Female Political Prisoners 1944–1958*, Vol 1
Anon, *Poles in the Second World War*
Anon, *1938–1989, It All Started in Poland*, pp.63–5
Silent Unseen Biographical Dictionary (Civic Association 'Ostoja' Zwierzyniec – Rzeszow 2002) pp.123-31
EZ obituaries, including *Wprost* 24 (15 Jan 2009); *Gazeta Wyborcza* (n.d.)
Oral History Archive
EZ interview

⚓

OTHER PUBLIC ARCHIVES

Musée de la Résistance, Paris, France
GR 16P283257, Gilbert Haerinck

US Holocaust Memorial Museum, USA
Oral history interview with Leonard Zawacki (20 Jan 1916; 26 Jun 1996)
RG-50.488*0099, Polish Witness to the Holocaust Project,

Stanisława Paciorek, 'Sister Maria Ena – Monastery of the
Congregation of the Sisters of Immaculate Conception' (1999)

National Archives and Records Administration (NARA), USA
Records of the CIA, T.H. Chylinski, 'Poland Under Nazi Rule'
(13 Nov 1941)

Oregon Jewish Museum and Centre for Holocaust Education, USA
Leonard Zawacki, 1916–2001 (interview 17 Jul 1992)

Malmö Stadsarkiv, Sweden
SE MSA 00453 F7 10, Malmö Criminal Police Affairs Concerning
Refugees, 1945–1946

⚓

PRIVATE ARCHIVES

Łukasz Bednarski
Zawodzińska family correspondence (1943)
Jabłońska and Zawodzińska family photograph albums

Andrew Bilski
Andrew Bilski, 'Secrets of the Green Box' (unpublished ms, n.d.)

Jeff Bines
Major Antoni Nosek, SOE-Polish Section reunion speech, Audley
End (24 May 1998)

Andrzej Drzycimski
Transcripts of recorded interviews with EZ (1989–1992)
Press Office of the President of the Republic of Poland file
EZ, Account of her youth (n.d.)
EZ, Journey to GB (n.d.)
Wacława Zastocka, 'Account' (1975)

Hanna Michalska, 'Account of the Defence of Warsaw 1939' (n.d.)
Halina Zapolska, 'Appendix to the relation of EZ, 'Zelmy' (n.d.)
Wacława Zastocka 'Basia', Account
Various articles, handwritten papers and sketches.

Tomasz Magierski
Tomasz Magierski, Andrzej Adamczak and Rafeł Mierzejewski
   interview with Zofia Jordanowska (unpublished, 1993)
Tomasz Magierski, film footage of Zofia Jordanowska (not broadcast, 1993)

Eugenia Maresch
EZ/Eugenia Maresch correspondence (2006–2007)
Eugenia Maresch:
   '"Zo" – General Elżbieta Zawacka' (3 May 2006)
   'Female Soldier' (4 Nov 2009)
   'Ladies and Gentlemen' (n.d.)
   'Personal memories of Zo' (4 Nov 2009)
Bulet, 'Elżbieta Zawacka "Zo"' (EZF, 1995)
Maryla Sobocińska (Ryśka), 'Funeral oration for Zo' (22 Mar 2009)
EZ, death certificate
Various photographs

Anna Marples
Anna Herbich, 'Girls in the Warsaw Uprising' (ms, n.d.)

Alina Nowobilska
Władysław Langner, Diary (unpublished ms, 1939)

Zbigniew Semadeni
EZ correspondence (2 Dec 1997)

PRESS AND JOURNALS

English language

Guardian
Sara Shaffi, 'Women's Prize launch award for non-fiction' (9 Feb 2023)

History Today
Clare Mulley, 'Warsaw's Child of Freedom' (12 Jun 2014)

Independent
Felix Corley, 'Obituary: Jadwiga Nowak' (14 May 1999)

Northern Rhodesia Journal
Ian Singer, 'Marian & Hope Gamwell, Two Extraordinary Lives' (2 Oct 2017)

Scotsman
Alison Shaw, 'Obituary: Michael Czeredrecki, paratrooper and tailor' (9 Dec 2013)

Telegraph
'Marzenna Schejbal, resistance activist who performed heroics during the Warsaw Uprising, obituary' (2 Mar 2022)
Bernadeta Tendrya, 'The Warsaw women who took on Hitler' (27 Jul 2004)

The Times
Kamil Tchorek, 'Escaped British Airman was Hero of Warsaw Uprising' (1 Aug 2004)

Polish language

Baltic Journal
Barbara Szczepuła, '"Marcysia", a soldier of the Home Army and

WiN and her husband, the legendary commandant of "Ponury"' (12 Mar 2015)

Cross-Section
Bogusław Szmajdowicz, Letter to the editor (3 Feb 1974)

Historical Folio
Anna Marcinkiewicz-Kaczmarczyk, 'EZ (1909–2009) – distinguished soldier and active "feminist"' (105), pp.159–173 (30 Dec 2019)

Hermaion
Tomasz Krok, Zbigniew Łagosz, 'Major Andrzej Czaykowski and the "Spy Network of Theosophists" in *Security Office* documentation, No. V (2019)

Polish Weekly
Eugenia Maresch, 'General Elżbieta Zawacka – "Zo"' (3 Oct 2016)
Magdalena Grzymkowska, 'The Key to Freedom' (13 Oct 2016)

The Republic
'Women in War 1939–1945' (31 Jul 2006)

Straight History
Dariusz Baliszewski, 'Kapitan Marcysia' (1 Nov 2009)

FILM AND TV

IPNtv Bydgoszcz, 'Zo': *Elżbieta Zawacka*

Pawel Kędzierski (dir.), *My Cichociemni, Voices of the Living* (2008)

TVP2, *They Left Their Mark* (2009)

Marek Widarski (dir.)
  Elżbieta Zawacka, I Had a Happy Life (FilmPolski.pl, 2005)
  Cichociemni (FilmPolski.pl, 1989)

Urszula Zbyszyńska, Mateusz Witek (dirs.), *'Zo', The Life of Gen
  Elżbieta Zawacka* (Trwam Television / Lux Veritatis Foundation,
  2017)

ༀ

ONLINE

Bloomberg
Max Hastings, 'Taking Crimea from Putin has Become
  Unthinkable' (9 Apr 2023). Available at: www.
  bloomberg.com/opinion/articles/2023-04-09/
  taking-crimea-from-putin-has-become-unthinkable-max-hastings

BBC, WW2 People's War
Joyce Anne Deane née Morley, 'War Memories: Plotting the Battle
  of Britain' (20 Nov 2003). Available at: www.bbc.co.uk/history/
  ww2peopleswar/stories/48/a2121148.shtml

Commonwealth War Graves Foundation
Jenny Grant, 'The Polish General Buried in a Nottinghamshire War
  Cemetery' (18 Jun 2021). Available at: www.cwgc.org/our-work/
  blog/the-polish-general-buried-in-a-nottinghamshire-war-cemetery

Adam Mickiewicz Institute
Darek Makowski, 'The Polish Sound of Music' (11 Jan 2022).
  Available at: https://culture.pl/en/article/the-polish-sound-of-music

Ministry of Defence
Anon, 'Women in Ground Close Combat, Findings Paper' (17
  May 2016). Available at: https://assets.publishing.service.gov.uk/

media/5a7f10d440f0b6230268d397/20160615-WGCC-COSIfind-
ings-Public_FINAL.pdf

National World War II Museum New Orleans
Jennifer Popowycz, 'Warsaw Burning, The German Response to the
    Warsaw Uprising' (22 Dec 2021). Available at: www.national
    ww2museum.org/war/articles/german-response-warsaw-uprising

POLIN Museum of the History of Polish Jews
Katarzyna Wysoczyńska, 'Stories of Rescue – Franio Zofia', Polish
    Righteous (Jul 2012). Available at: https://sprawiedliwi.org.pl/pl/
    historie-pomocy/historia-pomocy-franio-zofia

Salon 24 (Polish public blogging platform)
'Marcysia Sleeps at the Security Gate' (24 May 2016)
'Bridge in Toruń: One Bridge too far in Distorting our History?' (24
    May 2016).
Both available at: www.salon24.pl/u/albatros/714189,most-w-toruniu-
    o-jeden-most-za-daleko-w-przeklamywaniu-naszej-historii,4

Swooping Eagle
The 1st Independent Polish Parachute Brigade. Available at: www.
    swoopingeagle.com

⚓

PRIMARY SOURCE PUBLICATIONS

English language

Anon, *The Unseen and Silent, Adventures from the underground
movement narrated by Paratroops of the Polish Home Army*
(Sheed & Ward, 1954)

Tadeusz Bór-Komorowski, *The Secret Army* (Victor Gollancz, 1950)

Winston Churchill, *The Second World War* (The Reprint Society, 1956)

Piotr Długołęcki (ed.), *Confronting the Holocaust, Documents on the Polish Government-in-Exile's Policy Concerning Jews 1939–1945* (Polish Institute of International Affairs, 2022)

Helena Dunicz Niwińska, *One of the Girls in the Band: The Memoirs of a Violinist from Birkenau* (Auschwitz Museum, 2021)

Marek Edelman, *The Ghetto Fights* (Bookmarks, 1990)

Dwight D. Eisenhower, *Crusade in Europe, A Personal Account of World War II* (Doubleday, 1948)

Józef Garliński, *Poland, SOE and the Allies* (George, Allen & Unwin, 1969)

The Goebbels Diaries, 1939–1941: the historic journal of a Nazi war leader, ed. and trans. Fred Taylor (Sphere, 1983)

Natalie Hess, *Remembering Ravensbrück: Holocaust to Healing* (Amsterdam Publishers, n.d.)

Jan Jankowski and Antoni Serafiński, *Poland in Numbers* (Nakł, 1941)

Peter Jordan, *First to Fight (Poland)* (1943)

Jan Karski, *Story of a Secret State: My Report to the World* (Georgetown UP, 2013)

Leo Marks, *Between Silk and Cyanide: A Codemakers War, 1941–1945* (The Free Press, 1999)

Jan Nowak, *Courier from Warsaw* (Collins/Harvill, 1982)

Sune Persson, *Escape from the Third Reich: Folke Bernadotte and the White Buses* (Pen & Sword, 2019)

Alexandra Piłsudska, *The Memoirs of Madame Piłsudska* (Hurst & Blackett, 1940)

Sue Ryder, *And the Morrow is Theirs* (Burleigh Press, 1975)
————, *Child of My Love: An Autobiography* (Harvill Press, 1997)

Walter Schellenberg, *Hitler's Secret Service: Memoirs of Walter Schellenberg* (Pyramid, 1971)

Andrzej Suchcitz, *The Story of Poland's Diplomatic Envoys to Britain and their Residences* (Embassy of the Polish Republic in London, n.d.)

Peter Wilkinson and Joan Bright Astley, *Gubbins and SOE* (Lee Cooper, 1997)

Józef Zbik [Zabielski], *First to Return* (Garby, 2017)

Polish Language

Anon, *Polish Paratroopers, 23.9.1942–23.9.1943* (1943)

Stefan Starba Bałuk, *Commando Cichociemni* (Wydawnictwo Askon, 2008)

Przemysław Bystrzycki, *The Sign of the Cichociemni* (Krajowa Agencja Wydawnicza, 1991)

F.B. Czaromski (ed.), *They Fight for Poland: The War in the First Person* (George, Allen & Unwin, 1941)

Stanisław Jankowski, *With Fake ID in Warsaw: Memoirs 1939–1946* (PIW, 1980)

Helena Latkowska-Rudzińska, *Foreign Communication of the Home Army Headquarters South Section, 1939–44* (KUL, 1985)

Kazimierz Leski, *A Chequered Life: Memoirs of a Home Army Intelligence and Counter-Intelligence Officer* (2009)

Jozef Lewandowski, *Stockholm Knot: Swedish Connections of the Polish Underground, September 1939 – July 1942* (Uppsala, 1999)

Katarzyna Minczykowska (ed.), *General Brigadier Professor Dr Elżbieta Zawacka (1909–2009): Biographical Materials* (EZF, 2010)
———, *Cichociemna, Generał Elżbieta Zawacka 'Zo'* (EZF, 2014)
———, *Elżbieta Zawacka alias 'Zelma', 'Sulica', 'Zo'* (EZF, 2016)

Alfred Paczkowski, *Cichociemni Survey* (1981)

Kacper Śledziński, *Silent Unseen, Elite of the Polish Diversion* (Wydewnictwo Znak, 2012)

Alexander Stpiczyński, *Against the Judgement of Fate* (Pax, 1981)

Jan Szatsznajder, *Cichociemni, From Poland to Poland* (1990)

Jędrzej Tucholski, *Cichociemni* (Instytut Wydawniczy Pax, 3rd edition, 1988; Aquila Polonica, English edition in preparation, 2022)

Elżbieta Zawacka, *Waiting for Orders: Women's Military Organisation Emergency Social Services on the Eve of the Second World War* (KUL, 1992)
———, *Information on Women in the Home Army, WW2* (EZF, 2000)
———, *Sketches from the History of Women's Military Service* (EZF, 2001)
———, *Biographical Dictionary of Women Decorated with the Virtuti Military War Order* (EZF, 2004)

Józef Zbik [Zabielski], *First to Return* (Militaria.pl, 2017)

Henryk Żuk, *On the Chessboard of Life. Memoirs of Home Army Captain 'Onufry'* (Warsaw, 1999)

⚓

SECONDARY SOURCES

English Language

Władysław Bartoszewski and Zofia Lewin, eds, *Righteous Among the Nations: How Poles Helped the Jews 1939–1945* (London, 1969)

Judy Batalion, *The Light of Days: Women Fighters of the Jewish Resistance, Their Untold Story* (Virago, 2021)

Joanna Bogle, *Sue Ryder, A Life Lived for Others* (Gracewing, 2022)

Katarzyna Brakowska and Łukasz Karolewska, *Colonel Józef Hartman* (National Digital Archives & Cichociemni Foundation, 2018)

Norman Davies, *Rising '44, The Battle for Warsaw* (Pan Macmillan, 2004)

Jordan Ellenberg, *How Not to be Wrong: The Hidden Maths of Everyday Life* (Penguin, 2015)

David Engel, *Facing a Holocaust: The Polish Government-in-exile and the Jews, 1943–1945* (UNC Press Books, 1993)

Jack Fairweather, *The Volunteer: The True Story of the Resistance Hero Who Infiltrated Auschwitz* (Penguin, 2019)

Peter Flint, *RAF Kenley: The Story of the Royal Air Force Station 1917–1974* (1985)

M.R.D. Foot, *SOE: An Outline History of the Special Operations Executive, 1940–1946* (Pimlico, 1999)

Monty Halls, *Escaping Hitler: Stories of Courage and Endurance on the Freedom Trails* (Sidgwick & Jackson, 2017)

Janie Hampton, *How the Girl Guides Won the War* (Harper Press, 2011)

David Hendy, *The BBC: A People's History* (Profile, 2022)

Halik Kochanski, *The Eagle Unbowed: Poland and the Poles in the Second World War* (Penguin, 2013)
————, *Resistance: The Underground War in Europe 1939–1945* (Allen Lane, 2022)

Jack G. Morrison, *Ravensbrück: Everyday Life in a Women's Concentration Camp 1939–45* (Markus Wiener, 2000)

Roger Moorhouse, *Berlin at War, Life and Death in Hitler's Capital* (Bodley Head, 2010)
————, *First to Fight, The Polish War 1939* (Bodley Head, 2019)

Ron Nowicki, *Warsaw: The Cabaret Years* (Mercury House, 1992)

Pearl M. Oliner, Samuel P. Oliner, Lawrence Baron, Lawrence A. Blum, Dennis L. Krebs and M. Zuzanna Smolenska (eds.) *Embracing the Other, Philosophical Psychological and Historical Perspective on Altruism* (NYUP, 1992)

Alexandra Richie, *Warsaw 1944, Hitler, Himmler and the Crushing of a City* (William Collins, 2014)

Mel Rolfe, *To Hell and Back: True Life Experiences of Bomber Command at War* (Grub Street, 1999)
————, *Looking Into Hell: Experiences of the Bomber Command War* (Cassell, 1995)

Wojciech Roszkowski, *Communist Crimes: A Legal and Historical Study* (IPN, 2016)

Simon Sebag Montefiore, *Stalin, The Court of the Red Tsar* (Phoenix, 2004)

Marek Stella-Sawicki, Jarek Garliński, Stefan Mucha (eds.) *First to*

368 SELECT BIBLIOGRAPHY

Fight, Poland's Contribution to the Allied Victory in WW2 (Polish Ex-Combatants Association of GB, 2009)

Julie Summers, *Our Uninvited Guests: Ordinary Lives in Extraordinary Times in the Country Houses of Wartime Britain* (Simon & Schuster, 2018)

Ian Valentine, *Station 43, Audley End House and SOE's Polish Section* (Sutton, 2006)

Ben Wilson, *Metropolis: A History of Humankind's Greatest Invention* (Penguin Random House, 2020)

Polish Language

Anon, *Pracownicy Nauki I Dydaktyki Uniwersytetu Mikołaya Kopernika 1945-1994: Materiały do Biografii* ['Academic Staff of Nicolaus Copernicus University 1945–1994, Biographical Materials'] (n.d.)

Cezary Chlebowski, *Pozdrówcie Góry Świętokrzyskie* ['Greet the Holy Cross Mountains'] (Epoka, 1988)

Regina Domanska, *Pawiak, Wiezienie Gestapo Kronika 1939-1944* ['Pawiak, Gestapo Prison Chronicle 1939–1944']

Janusz Marszalec and Katarzyna Minczykowska (eds.), *25 Lat Niezależnych Badań Naukowych Nad Konspiracją Niepodległościową 1939-1945: Ludzie, Instytucje, Wydarzenia* ['25 Years of Independent Research on the Polish Resistance 1939–1945: People, Institutions, Events'] (EZ Fn, 2018)

Maria Weber, *Emilia Malessa 'Marcysia' 1909-1949* (Oficyna Wydawnicza RYTM, 2013)

Katarzyna Wysoczyńska, *Zofia Franio: W służbie ojczyźnie, w służbie człowiekowi* ['In the Service of the Motherland, in the Service of Man'] (Wydanie, 2018)

PICTURE CREDITS

All photos are from the collections of the General Elżbieta Zawacka Foundation (zawacka.pl) in Toruń, Poland, with the exception of the below.

Plate:
7: (*top*) Photograph by Kurt Grimm, February 21, 1940, courtesy of District Museum in Toruń; (*below right*) Author's photograph taken at General Elżbieta Zawacka Foundation in Toruń

8: (*top left*) Archive of the Commission for the History of Women in the Struggle for Polish Independence (reference number 1697), Archiwum Akt Nowych (AAN); (*top right & below*) From the collection of the Polish Underground Movement (1939–1945) Study Trust, London

9: (*below left & right*) From the collection of the Polish Underground Movement (1939–1945) Study Trust, London

10: (*top left*) From the collection of the Polish Underground Movement (1939–1945) Study Trust, London; (*top right*) From *Courier From Warsaw* by Jan Novak, Collins/Harvill,1982 (originally published as *Kurier z Warsawy by Odnova*, London, 1978); (*below*) As published in "Perspektywy", 3rd February, 1989

11: (*top right*) Author's photograph, with kind permission of English Heritage; (*top left & below*) From the collection of the Polish Underground Movement (1939–1945) Study Trust, London

12: (*top*) Private collection; (*below*) Courtesy Biuro Fundacji Sue Ryder, Warsaw

13: (*top*) Author's photograph taken at General Elżbieta Zawacka Foundation in Toruń; (*below*) Photograph by Joachim Joachimczyk, collections of the Warsaw Rising Museum

14: (*top*) Archiwum Mieczysława Sokołowskiego; (*middle*) PAP/Stanisław Dąbrowiecki; (*below*) Collection of Institute of National Remembrance (IPN) Commission for the Prosecution of Crimes against the Polish Nation Branch Archive in Warsaw (IPN BU 0259/148 t.1 (page 125))

16: All author's collection

ACKNOWLEDGEMENTS

That the resistance in Poland was an immense collective effort, both inspired and reassured me as I researched this book. Any mistakes on these pages are, of course, my own, and the rest of it was possible only thanks to the generous support of so many.

Zo's cousin, Dorota Zawacka-Wakarecy, kindly opened her arms and her institution to me. This book would not have been possible without the wealth of information in the Elżbieta Zawacka Foundation that she and her team run. Likewise, especial thanks are due to Andrzej Drzycimski, who generously shared his many hours of recorded interviews with Zo, and both Hanna Czarnocka and Marzenna Schejbal, who first helped ignite my interest. I had been worried that there would not be enough primary source material but these kind friends and family members of Zo and other veterans ensured that I had plenty: Krysia Bancroft, Łukasz Bednarski, Andrew Bilski, Krzysztof Bożejewicz, Bogdan Chrzanowski, Halina Fitzclarence, Bernadeta Gołecka-Schmidt, Hanna Gorska and Magdalena Stajewska, Grzegorz Górski, Sylvia Harvey, Wanda Koscia, Sofie Kozłowska, Dorota Kromp, Darren Little, Leszek Luszowicz, Ludwik Mackoviak, Eugenia Maresch, Anna Marples, Anna Mikułska, Danuta Nosek, Alina Nowobilska, Anna Rejewska, Zbigniew Semadeni, Richard Serafiński, Elżbieta Skerska, Michał Wojtczak and Jan Wyrowiński.

In Poland, my very sincere thanks are also due to President Lech Wałęsa, Mariusz Olczak and all at the AAN in Warsaw; the IPN in Warsaw, including Władysław Bułhak, Małgorzata Ptasińska and Justyna Szewczak; and the Warsaw Uprising Museum, including Aleksandra Duda, Dorota Bakowska, Sylwia Biczyk, Wojciech Bobrowski, Paulina Bogusz, Stanisława Bukowicka, Dawid Cieśliński, Aleksandra Czajka, Monika Gurak, Anna Głowacka, Ryszard Mączewski, Renata Smolarczyk and Remigiusz Stefani. Also Sister Janina of the Sisters of the Immaculate Conception in Szymanów; Toruń tour guide Beata Bertholdt; Marcin Czyżniewski and Anna Supruniuk from the Nicolaus Copernicus University in Toruń; film directors Tomasz Magierski, Andrzej Adamczak, Rafał Mierzejewski and David Szurmiej; Natalia Łata and Piotr Mucha from the Elżbieta Zawacka Foundation in Toruń; Bogdan Rowiński of the Cichociemni Foundation; Wojciech Samól at the Second World War Museum of Gdańsk; and Piotr Jozefiak and Dominik Pawlik from University Adam Mickiewicz.

In Britain I am also hugely indebted to the very knowledgeable and generous teams at the Embassy of the Republic of Poland, including Clarinda Calma, Robert Gawłowski, Katarzyna Szaran and Michalina Seliga; English Heritage, including Daniel Hann, Peter Moore and Denise Hall; Lynette Beardwood from the FANY archives; Artur Bildziuk of the Polish Air Force Association; Krzysztof Bożejewicz and all at the Polish Underground Movement Studies Trust; Matt Ellis of the Blaenau Ffestiniog steam railway; Dr Dobroslawa Platt at POSK; Nathan Smith of the British Army Intelligence Corps; Valerie Smith of St Peter's Eaton Square; Andrzej Suchcitz and Krystyna Zatylna at the Polish Institute and Sikorski Museum; the Pilsudski Institute's Olga Topol; historians Jeff Bines, Jenny Grant and her veteran grandmother Teresa Carpenter, Nick Fox, Steven Kippax, Jan Ledóchowski, Paul McCue, Marek Mrozek and Mark Seaman; authors Jack Fairweather, Peter Hore and Lucy Ward; journalist Julia Rooke; and the British Army's Harry Young.

A battalion of brilliant translators, with Paulina Chołda in the vanguard, included Moni Evans, Christopher Kasparek, Janka Lloyd, Ewa Olszewski and Mike Digby, Monika Plitcha, Katarzyna Ross-Greetham, Monika Srubkowska and Terry Tegnazian. I am also very grateful to my agents Georgina Capel and Simon Shaps, and the wonderful team at Weidendeld & Nicolson, Elizabeth Allen, Georgia Goodall and my commissioning editor, Maddy Price, whose early enthusiasm helped forge this book.

Finally, my home team, Ian Wolter, Gillian Mulley, Kate Mulley, Rowan Wolter, Florence Wolter and Hester Wolter – you are all completely fantastic. Thank you.

I am profoundly grateful to every one of you, and many more, for helping me shine a wider light on the history of Elżbieta Zawacka and her many courageous colleagues in the resistance during the Second World War.

ABOUT THE AUTHOR

Clare Mulley is an award-winning author and historian, mainly focused on female experience during the Second World War. As well as her own books, she has contributed to many others (memoirs of Xan Fielding, Lili Stern-Pohlmann and Christabel Bielenberg), reviews widely (*Spectator, TLS, BBC History, Literary Review, History Today, Telegraph*), and has judged several book prizes. A regular contributor to TV (BBC's *Rise of the Nazis* and *Newsnight*, Channel 5's *Secret History of WW2* and *Adolf & Eva*), radio (Radio 4 Today, Woman's Hour, Great Lives, PM) and many podcasts. She is a recipient of the Polish cultural honour, the Bene Merito, and the Daily Mail Biographers Club Prize. She lives in Essex with the sculptor Ian Wolter, too many books, and a dog who needs more baths. www.claremulley.com.

INDEX

44